DUNCAN PHILLIPS

WRITINGS ON ART

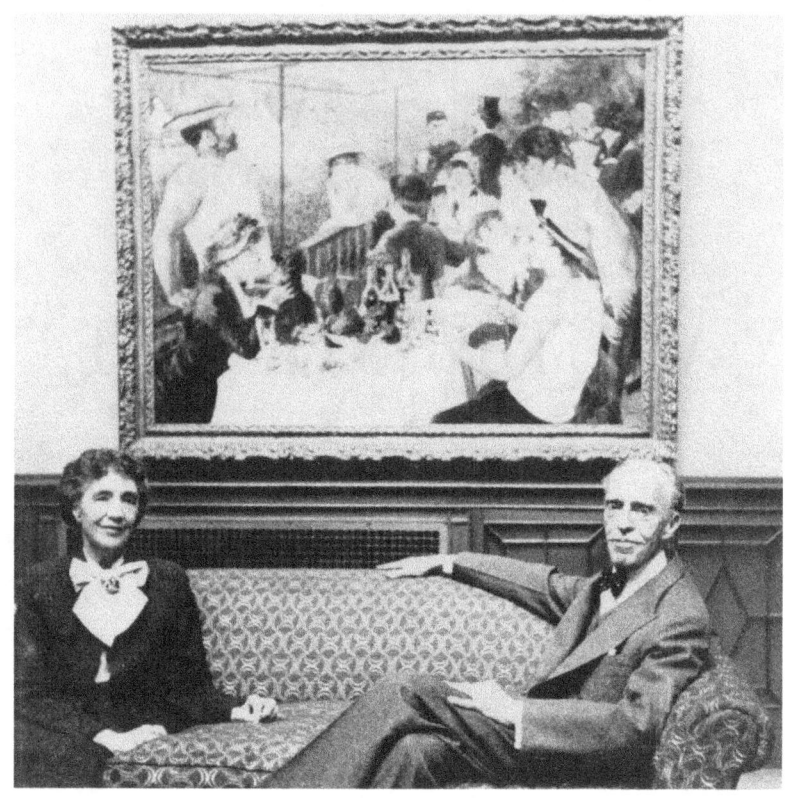

Marjorie and Duncan Phillips in front of Renoir's *Luncheon of the Boating Party*, c. 1954. Photo by Naomi Savage

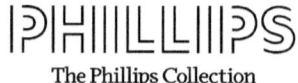
The Phillips Collection

DUNCAN PHILLIPS

WRITINGS ON ART

EDITED AND ANNOTATED
BY KLAUS OTTMANN

INTRODUCTION
BY SUSAN BEHRENDS FRANK

THE PHILLIPS COLLECTION
WASHINGTON, D.C.

IN ASSOCIATION WITH

SPRING PUBLICATIONS
THOMPSON, CONN.

Published by

The Phillips Collection
Washington, D.C.

in association with

Spring Publications
Thompson, Conn.

www.springpublications.com

First Edition 2023 (1.3)

Cover image:
Honoré Daumier
The Uprising (L'Émeute), 1848 or later
Oil on canvas
The Phillips Collection, Washington, D.C. Acquired in 1925

Library of Congress Control Number: 2023937216

ISBN: 978-0-88214-136-7

CONTENTS

EDITOR'S NOTE

DUNCAN PHILLIPS's extensive and significant body of writings covers scores of books, articles, and addresses. Phillips's thoughts on art continued to evolve over years and sometimes decades, and the texts assembled in this volume are therefore arranged in chronological order. This book is primarily meant as a reader, and thus all images are reproduced in black and white for reference only.

In order to aid the reader, Phillips's texts have been annotated with bracketed footnotes to identify the many works of art mentioned by him. Phillips quoted liberally from writers he admired and often befriended, occasionally even conflating several sources into one single quote. Thus, sources have been added for Phillips's many quotations wherever possible, and the text of the quotations has been emended when deemed necessary. As Phillips has written in the introductory essay for a new periodical he founded in 1929, *Art and Understanding*: "I have had to take some liberties with the text, paraphrasing instead of quoting exactly."

I would like to thank Alice Phillips Swistel and the entire Phillips family; Jonathan P. Binstock, The Phillips Collection's Vradenburg Director & CEO; and my former colleagues at The Phillips Collection, especially Susan Behrends Frank, Curator, for her knowledgeable advice and her insightful and well-researched introduction; Karen Schneider, former Head Librarian, for her assistance in finding many important texts; Michele De Shazo, Senior Registrar for the Collection, for providing images and permissions for this book; and Dorothy Kosinski, Director Emerita, for her early enthusiasm for this publication.

KLAUS OTTMANN
Chief Curator Emeritus
The Phillips Collection

SUSAN BEHRENDS FRANK

THE AESTHETIC EVOLUTION
OF DUNCAN PHILLIPS

THIS selection of the art writings of Duncan Phillips (1886–1966), the early twentieth-century art critic, collector, and patron, is the first gathering of these texts into a publication devoted exclusively to this essential side of the man who founded The Phillips Collection in Washington, D.C. In late 1918, Phillips took a leap of faith when he conceived a unique private art museum in the nation's capital at the end of World War I as a setting for a dialogue between the art of the past and the present with an emphasis on defining what is modern from a distinctively personal perspective. Phillips's extensive writings were the primary instruments through which he expressed and shared his views alongside the artworks he regularly acquired and exhibited in curated installations that were regularly renewed in fresh rearrangements.

This book is not a comprehensive assembly of Phillips's art writings but a representative compendium of his views over the course of his lifetime. The selection includes examples from his early efforts while a student at Yale University (class of 1908) to his thoughts in 1964, two years before his death, on the artist Mark Rothko (1903–70), whose work is inextricably linked to the Phillips Collection through the Rothko Room, the first such dedicated space (est. 1960) for the artist's work in a museum.

Raised in the 1890s in a conservative family of significant wealth, Phillips's education and growing intellectual maturity in the first decades of the twentieth century coincided with America's Progressive Era.[1] He was an idealist who he believed that both the

---

1. Duncan Phillips was born in Pittsburgh in 1886, the grandson of James Laughlin, a banker and cofounder of the Jones and Laughlin Steel Company. Laughlin's daughter Eliza married Major Duncan Clinch Phillips, a Pittsburgh businessman who manufactured window glass. They had two sons, James, born 1884, and Duncan, born 1886. In 1896, following the retirement of Major Phillips

individual and the art experience had the power to improve society. His writings reveal his journey from a young man's youthful point of view that art is representational, realistic, and inherently romantic to a mature belief that the visual arts are a universal language that can speak across time and geographic boundaries through shared formal elements that engage an audience open to the new or the unfamiliar.

THE EVOLUTION OF A YOUNG CRITIC THROUGH THE 1910S

Phillips's earliest articles on art were written in 1906 and 1908 while a student at Yale, where there were no art appreciation or art history courses. The writings of critics such as Walter Pater (1839–1894), a renowned Oxford art and literary critic known for championing the slogan "art for art's sake" in the English Aesthetic Movement, became important to Phillips's early aesthetic judgments. In particular, as noted by art historian Grayson Harris Lane, Pater's belief that painting and literature are related and could be combined into a universal creative language struck a chord with the young Phillips, as did Pater's discussions of artworks as reflections of ideal beauty and the artist's vision.[2]

Following graduation from Yale in 1908, Phillips set out to educate himself through travel and firsthand exposure to artworks. A trip to Japan in 1910 with his parents and brother, which included travel in Korea and China, gave rise to a lifelong appreciation of non-Western art. Annual trips to Europe in 1911, 1912, and 1913

---

and the 1895 death of his mother-in-law (Mrs. James Laughlin), the Phillips family of four moved to Washington, D.C. See Laughlin Phillips, "Preface," in *The Eye of Duncan Phillips: A Collection in the Making,* edited by Erika D. Passantino (The Phillips Collection and Yale University Press, Washington, D.C. and New Haven, Conn., 1999), ix; see also Erika Passantino and Sarah Martin, "Chronology," in *Duncan Phillips: Centennial Exhibition,* exh. cat. (Washington, D.C.: The Phillips Collection, 1986), 26.

2. Grayson Harris Lane, "Duncan Phillips and the Phillips Memorial Gallery: A Patron and Museum in Formation, 1918–1940" (PhD diss., Boston University, 2002), 14 n.15; 17.

furthered his self-education about the history of Western art. Throughout his European travels Phillips kept a journal to record his observations and responses to the artwork he was seeing.

When launching his career as an art critic in 1912, Phillips's aesthetic views were quite conservative. This can be attributed in some part to his lack of personal contact with progressive American artists while still living in Washington, D.C., where he relied on the Corcoran Gallery of Art's biennials for his American art enrichment. Moving to New York in 1914 opened up opportunities to visit New York galleries and artist's studios. Through 1917, Phillips advocated for an art of realism with stylistic affinities to Old Master works. In addition to Pater's writings, other important influences on Phillips during these early years include Frank Jewett Mather, the Italian Renaissance art historian at Princeton University, who became a close friend in the mid-1910s. Mather had a significant influence on the young Phillips in his belief that art grows out of tradition and is a reflection of the artist's emotional responses to nature.[3] Mather's perspective proved seminal for Phillips throughout his career as a collector and a critic.

The 1913 Armory Show in New York (officially "The International Exhibition of Modern Art") shocked Phillips. Organized by the Association of American Painters and Sculptors under the leadership of the artists Arthur B. Davies (1862–1928) and Walt Kuhn (1877–1949), the Armory Show introduced American audiences to the avant-garde work of the European moderns.[4] The young Washingtonian's belief that recognizable subject matter was key to understanding the artist's intent was challenged directly by the newest European trends on view at the Armory Show that included

---

3. Ibid., 177.

4. Walt Kuhn's letter to the critic Walter Pach, December 12, 1912, stated that the organizers' intent was "to mark the starting point of the new spirit in art, at least as far as America is concerned." *1913 Armory Show 50th Anniversary Exhibition 1963*, exh. cat. (New York: Munson-Williams-Proctor Institute and the Henry Street Settlement, 1963), 159–60.

not only works by Henri Matisse (1869–1954) and Marcel Duchamp (1887–1968), which were singled out for derision by the critics, but also the work of the cubists Georges Braque (1882–1963), Robert Delaunay (1885–1941), Francis Picabia (1879–1953), and Pablo Picasso (1881–1973), the post-impressionists Paul Cézanne (1839–1906), Paul Gauguin (1848–1903), Vincent van Gogh (1853–1890), and Georges Seurat (1859–1891), the German expressionist sculptor Wilhelm Lehmbruck (1881–1919), and the Russian-born painter and theorist Wassily Kandinsky (1866–1944). Bewildered by these European modernists who seemed to emphasize style over subject, Phillips struggled to understand the contemporary direction of European art, calling the exhibition "stupefying in its vulgarity" in his review for *The International Studio.*[5]

The year after the Armory Show, Phillips published a book of essays that he had begun to formulate in 1910–13 on "idealized visions of reality." Fittingly titled *The Enchantment of Art as Part of the Enchantment of Experience,*[6] the seventeen essays in his 1914 book are Phillips's response to the challenges presented by the Armory Show. He reissued the book in a revised and expanded edition in 1927 (*The Enchantment of Art: Fifteen Years Later*)[7] with a new preface that pronounced the earlier essays "the premature judgments of my youth." Although Phillips described Claude Monet (1840–1926) as "supreme in his own audacious way" when he encountered his work in Paris in 1911,[8] he, nonetheless, had reservations about calling him an impressionist artist. By 1919 Phillips had a more nuanced understanding of Monet's work when he acquired two of the artist's landscapes for his new museum, but in 1912 he launched himself as a professional art critic with

---

5. "Revolutions and Reactions in Painting," *The International Studio* 51, no. 202 (December 1913): cxxiii.

6. New York: John Lane Company, 1914.

7. Washington, D.C.: The Phillips Publications, 1927.

8. Marjorie Phillips, *Duncan Phillips and His Collection,* rev. ed. (New York and Washington, D.C.: W. W. Norton & Company and The Phillips Collection, 1982), 41–42.

two essays on Impressionism that reveal his initial difficulty with "Monet, Degas, and the rest of the group." "The Impressionist Point of View" and "What is Impressionism," included in this volume, were published in March and September 1912 in *Art and Progress*, the monthly journal of the American Federation of Arts. In 1914 Phillips included both essays as the first chapters in his *The Enchantment of Art*, although he retitled the second essay "What Impressionism in Painting Really Means." Both make clear Phillips's initial difficulty with Monet's work in particular, which he then believed emphasized only outward appearances.

At the time, Phillips's interpretation of "impressionism" was about the "expression of the individual soul" of the artist. In his understanding "impressionism" could be found in the work of artists from the past and the present. In this category he included the Venetian painter Giorgione (c. 1477–1510), the Spanish painter Diego Velázquez (1599-1660), the Dutch artist Rembrandt van Rijn (1606-1669), and the French artist Jean-Baptiste-Siméon Chardin (1699–1779), as well as the contemporary work of the American impressionist painter Julian Alden Weir (1852–1919). Phillips believed Giorgione to be the first modern master, a reflection of his reading of Pater's "The School of Giorgione."[9]

As David W. Scott has pointed out in an insightful essay, by 1927 Phillips felt it necessary to concede that his original interpretation of "impressionism" was really about "expressionism."[10] This explicit acknowledgment of his lack of preparedness in the early 1910s for the newest styles of European painting was forthrightly expressed in his introductory essay to the revised and expanded edition of *The Enchantment of Art*. "Fifteen Years Later" is reproduced in this volume along with the 1927 revised version of "The

---

9. Walter Pater. *The Fortnightly Review* 22, n.s. (October 1, 1877): 526–38. Duncan Phillips, "Giorgione: The First Modern Master," *Yale Review* 2 (July, 1913): 667–80." See Lane, "Duncan Phillips and the Phillips Memorial Gallery," 114 n.16.

10. David W. Scott, "The Evolution of a Critic: Changing Views in the Writings of Duncan Phillips," in *The Eye of Duncan Phillips*, 18.

Impressionist Point of View" that expunges all of the original 1912 text that "quarrel[ed] with the great and other dashing French innovators" whom Phillips characterized as "men improperly called impressionists."[11]

Although Phillips's changing aesthetic ideals shifted in the early 1920s, through much of the 1910s he was still educating himself, his views firmly rooted in the belief that recognizable subject matter was essential to meaning. In 1917, he joined the Century Association, an invitation-only men's club in New York City that focused primarily on culture. It included both critics, academics, and American artists such as Weir, Gifford Beal (1879–1956) and Augustus Vincent Tack (1870–1949), the artist who sponsored Phillips for membership as a Centurian. Each of these men became important friends and even family when Phillips married Beal's niece, the painter Marjorie Acker (1894–1985), in 1921.

One of the critics Phillips met at the Century Club was W.C. Brownell, literary advisor to Scribner's publishing house, who advocated for maintaining the classical tradition and striving for the eternally beautiful in art.[12] Brownell's belief in high ideals and connoisseurship adhered closely to Phillips's own belief that tradition was important to painting and stylistic anarchy unacceptable. It is not so surprising then that Phillips's essay "Fallacies of the New Dogmatism in Art," his last critical writing against the European modernists, was published the same year he joined the Century Club.[13] In this essay, Phillips restated his firm belief in the importance of tradition and connoisseurship.

In the mid-1910s, Phillips published several essays on American painters whom he believed to be especially important. His 1916 essay on Albert Pinkham Ryder (1847–1917), who died the following year at the age of seventy, should be understood as an homage to

---

11. Duncan Phillips, "The Impressionist Point of View," *Art and Progress* 3 (March, 1912): 510.

12. Lane, "Duncan Phillips and the Phillips Memorial Gallery," 116.

13. Scott, "The Evolution of a Critic," 14.

a unique American artist whose radical yet wholly romantic work would provide a lasting legacy for future generations of American artists in the twentieth century. With considerable insight Phillips characterized Ryder as an artist "indifferent to the world's opinion," an independent creator in whose work one finds a "spiritual loneliness" in compositions that are "simplified recreations of his dream." These comments characterize Phillips's lifelong championship of artists who refused to follow popular trends for their own sake and, instead, chose to stay true to their personal inner vision. Ryder's work struck Phillips most profoundly at the 1913 Armory Show where he was especially entranced by the small, mysterious, and romantic *Moonlit Cove* (early to mid-1880s). When Phillips set about making lists of artworks between 1919 and 1921 that identified what he most wanted to acquire for his new museum, *Moonlit Cove* was on the list. Phillips was ultimately able to acquire it for the collection in 1924.

Around 1919, Phillips began plans for a second book (to be titled *Representative American Painters of the New Century*), intended to bring recognition to contemporary American painters—a group that Phillips believed were overlooked and underestimated by critics and collectors alike despite their increasing representation in the New York galleries.[14] While the book was never published because the publisher wanted a more general history of American painting, Phillips directed his energy to creating publications at his newly established museum.[15]

Phillips's advocacy for contemporary American artists was new for the time.[16] Two of the artists he held in highest esteem were the conservative Weir, who was one of the original American impressionists of the 1890s, and the romantic painter Davies, who was aligned with the radical ideals of European modernism. Weir, whom Phillips came to know through the Century Club and whose

---

14. Ibid.
15. Ibid., 15 and n. 36, which is the 1919 letter from the publisher Harpers.
16. Lane, "Duncan Phillips and the Phillips Memorial Gallery," 21.

work he collected in-depth from 1916 to 1921, embodied for the young critic and collector a certain ideal of connoisseurship that emphasized the importance of tradition and recognizable subject matter conveyed with sincere emotion. Davies, despite his advocacy for modernist painting, was one of Phillips's ideal artists in the 1920s with whom he was personally close and whose symbolist works he acquired in-depth for his museum. While Phillips had originally planned essays on both Weir and Davies for his rejected book project on individual American artists of the twentieth century, he turned his essays on these seminal American painters into independent publications of the newly launched Phillips Memorial Gallery in 1922 and 1924, respectively.[17]

Another 1922 Phillips Publication was devoted to the nineteenth-century French artist Honoré Daumier (1808–1879), whose painting *Three Lawyers* (c. 1870) Phillips had acquired in 1920 for his new museum. The Daumier essay reflects Phillips's aesthetic growth as he eloquently lays out an argument for Daumier as an artist on par with Michelangelo and thus a great artist who has been undeservedly overlooked by contemporary critics such as Brownell. At the end of this extensive essay Phillips proclaims Daumier "the pinnacle of French genius" who "conferred upon the world a language which is, in the most profound sense, our universal heritage." Phillips's belief in Daumier's exceptional achievement never waned. Over the course of the next thirty years Phillips and his wife Marjorie grew their Daumier holdings to include two watercolors, forty-eight lithographs, and, most significantly, a total of seven oils, including *The Uprising* (c. 1848–60, acquired 1925)—the largest Daumier canvas in North America.

---

17. *Julian Alden Weir: An Appreciation of His Life and Works*, Phillips Publication No. 1, New York, 1922. This book was first published in 1921 by the Century Association with essays by Phillips and six other Centurions. Phillips took over the copyright. *Arthur B. Davies: Essays on the Man and His Art*, Phillips Publication No. 3, Washington, D.C., 1924. See Appendix B, Years 1922 and 1924, *The Eye of Duncan Phillips*, 676.

THE 1920S AND PHILLIPS'S MATURING AESTHETIC PHILOSOPHY

Phillips's growing acceptance of abstraction in the early 1920s followed his loss of interest in American impressionism as a collector and a critic. He acquired very few American impressionist canvases after 1923 and began to consign and sell others as early as 1924, yet the American impressionists whose work he had collected played an important role in his growing appreciation for abstraction. In varying degrees, the work of Childe Hassam (1859–1935), Maurice Prendergast (1858–1924), and John Henry Twachtman (1853–1920) that had captured Phillips's imagination during the 1910s reflected a sophisticated interest in color, abstract design, patterning, silhouettes, asymmetry, flattening of space, and surface.[18] His personal relationships with the artists Davies and Tack, and his marriage in 1921 to the painter Marjorie Acker, were equally important to Phillips's shift away from representation to an understanding of how it was possible to be "abstract in style" while still maintaining one's self identity.

As Scott has pointed out, Phillips shed the pejorative associations of the word "abstract" around 1924 as he began to see abstraction in the visual arts as analogous to music.[19] The painter Augustus Vincent Tack's decorative abstractions were especially key to this shift in Phillips's thinking.[20] He acquired a first Tack abstraction for the collection in 1923 (*Storm,* c. 1922–23), followed by four additional

---

18. See the discussion about the importance of Duncan Phillips's collecting the work of the American impressionists Hassam, Maurice Prendergast (1858–1924), and John Henry Twachtman ((1853–1902) from 1915 to 1923 relative to his greater sensitivity for abstraction in contemporary American art in the mid-1920s in my essay "A Personal Vision: Collecting American Impressionism, 1915–25," in Susan Behrends Frank, *American Impressionists: Painters of Light and the Modern Landscape* (New York: Rizzoli International Publications, in association with The Phillips Collection, 2007), 58.

19. Scott, "The Evolution of a Critic," 16.

20. David W. Scott, "Mutual Influences: Augustus Vincent Tack and Duncan Phillips," in Leslie Furth, et al., *Augustus Vincent Tack: Landscape of the Spirit,* exh. cat. (Washington, D.C.: The Phillips Collection, 1993), 79–80.

ones in 1924, which Phillips associated with music in an accompa-
nying catalogue essay.[21] A decade earlier he could not have imagined abstraction as either spiritual or emotional. By 1928, Phillips
had become so enamored with Tack's approach to abstraction that
he commissioned the artist to produce a series of twelve lunette-
shaped decorative abstractions and a single monumental canvas
titled *Aspiration* (1931) for permanent installation in the museum's
wood-paneled library (now the museum's Music Room). The exhibition of those panels in 1930 was accompanied by a significant
Phillips's essay, reproduced in this volume, that opened with the
assertion that "great compositions in music" and "great compositions of color" by a painter are both expressions in different media
of an "artist's abstractions."[22]

Phillips's new appreciation for abstraction allowed him to embrace American artists who transformed their direct experience
of nature into highly personal compositions. For example, Phillips
began acquiring works from the Alfred Stieglitz Circle in 1926 and
the Phillips Memorial Gallery became the first museum to acquire
the work of Arthur Dove (1880–1946) and Georgia O'Keeffe (1887–
1986) that year, as well as the first American museum to acquire
works by John Marin (1870–1953).[23] Phillips soon became the

---

21. Duncan Phillips, *Exhibition of Recent Decorative Paintings by Augustus Vincent Tack*, exh. cat. (Washington, D.C.: The Phillips Collection, 1924).

22. The thematic plan for Tack's room of paintings was likely developed in
conversations between the artist and Phillips, wherein Phillips conceived of the
cycle as unfolding through space, unified thematically by a mystical sense of
transcendence and universal order. See Leslie Furth, "Landscapes of the Mind:
Augustus Vincent Tack's Decorations for the Phillips Memorial Gallery," in *Augustus Vincent Tack: Landscape of the Spirit*, 81, 84, 95–97.

23. In 1907, John Marin was in Paris and exhibited at the Salon des Indépen-
dents in the spring and at the Salon d'Automne in the fall. That year he also sold
his first work to a museum, an oil painting titled *Mills at Meaux*. The French government acquired it for the Musée du Luxembourg. See Barbara Rose's essay in
John Marin: The 291 Years, exh. cat. (New York: Richard York Gallery, 1998), 14. In
1926, the Phillips Memorial Gallery acquired two Marin watercolors, becoming

most important patron for both Dove and Marin, providing material support, not only in the form of financial assistance, but with
acquisitions and exhibitions at the Phillips throughout each man's
lifetime.[24] This volume contains Phillips's memorial essays on each
man. In his 1947 tribute to Dove, the year after the artist's death,
Phillips acknowledged that his evolution as a critic and collector
was very much related to the discovery in Dove's work of a "sensuously visual" evocation of "painterly equivalents" that captured
the "essence of nature's reality."[25] In his 1955 essay on Marin, Phillips celebrated the artist for his controlled "calligraphic rhythms,
crosscurrents" and "explosions of line" that can be understood as
"experiments on the frontiers of visual consciousness," and ante-
cedents to the post-war abstract expressionists.

During the 1910s and 1920s, Phillips read contemporary criticism, often making marginal comments and notes in these books
that assisted in the formulation of his aesthetic opinions.[26] As he

---

the first American museum to acquire the artist's work and the first to acquire
his watercolors.

24. Beginning in 1930, Phillips provided a monthly stipend for Dove that last-
ed till the artist's death, allowing Dove to quit his commercial work and devote
himself exclusively to his art. Phillips added more than forty-eight works by Dove
to the museum's collection and in 1937 gave the artist his first museum retrospective, the only one during the artist's lifetime. Phillips demonstrated a similar
loyalty to Marin, whom he also regarded as an American genius. In the depths of
the Depression in 1938 Phillips, through Stieglitz, paid Marin a monthly stipend
of one-hundred dollars. Phillips also acquired more than twenty-three works in
all media from all periods of Marin's career and gave the artist nine exhibitions,
including his first solo museum show in 1929, which Marin attended, marking
the beginning of a close friendship between artist and patron. It was the closest
friendship Phillips had with any of the Stieglitz Circle artists.

25. Duncan Phillips, "Arthur G. Dove, 1880–1946," *Magazine of Art* (July 1947):
194.

26. Phillips was a perennial maker of marginal notes in books that captured
his intellectual attention—his manner of creating a private dialogue with the
authors. The Phillips Collection Archives have Phillips's original copy of Clive
Bell's *Art* (New York: 1913) with its marginalia. The museum also has Phillips's

continued to educate himself in art criticism during the museum's early years, he delved ever more deeply into the writings of the English painter and art critic Roger Fry (1866–1934), especially focusing on Fry's 1920 book *Vision and Design*.[27] Phillips's personal copy of this book is in the museum's archives and is heavily annotated with his pencil underlining and marginal notes. He also copied passages from Fry's "An Essay in Aesthetics" into a journal we can date to 1923–24 and separately drafted a manuscript titled "Notes from Roger Fry's *Vision and Design—Art and Life.*"[28] By 1924, Phillips's greater aesthetic maturity made him more receptive to Fry's view that it is an artwork's formal elements that convey emotional meaning, rather than recognizable subject matter. Phillips's immersion in the writings of Fry and his fellow Bloomsbury critic Clive Bell (1881–1964) gave him the aesthetic framework he was seeking to embrace abstraction from an intellectual perspective.[29]

---

personal copy of Roger Fry's *Vision and Design* (1920) with his marginal notes and underlining.

27. Harmondsworth: Penguin Books, 1920.

28. I presented a paper on "The Influence of Roger Fry's Vision and Design on Duncan Phillips's Aesthetic Vision and Exhibition Strategy for The Phillips Collection" at The Courtauld Institute of Art Symposium "Crossing Borders: Constructing Canons: Post-Impressionism in Britain, America and Beyond," London, June 10–11, 2021.

29. See Lane, "Duncan Phillips and the Phillips Memorial Gallery," 124–27. Lane highlights the shift in Phillips's aesthetic opinions that began to be more receptive to abstraction by 1920, arguing that the greatest impact on Phillips was his intensive study of Roger Fry's *Vision and Design* (1920) around 1924. By 1926, Phillips's distrust of abstraction had become understanding through his equally intensive study of the writings of Clive Bell (*Since Cézanne*, 1922) and Jan Gordon (*Modern French Painters*, 1923). This Anglo-American dialogue is discussed in the recent book by David Maddock, *Roger Fry, Clive Bell and American Modernism* (Oxford: Peter Lang, 2020). Maddock frames the dialogue about modernist abstraction as one that begins with Fry's 1910 post-impressionist exhibition in London and transitions to its interwar manifestation with Alfred Barr's 1936 Museum of Modern Art exhibition *Cubism and Abstract Art*. Maddock discusses the manner in which key aspects of the Bloomsbury aesthetics of Fry and Bell were taken up by American critics such as Sheldon Cheney, Albert Barnes, and Barr in the 1920s. Phillips is overlooked in the discussion.

Both Fry and Bell were formalists who shared a passion for contemporary French art nurtured by Fry's groundbreaking exhibitions on post-impressionism in London in 1910 and 1912 that included the contemporary work of Picasso and Matisse.[30]

In 1913–14, Bell published *Art*, his first book, which espoused his theory of significant form, which Phillips read and rejected in the mid-1910s.[31] Recent scholarship by Grayson Lane has pointed out that Phillips's acceptance of Fry's aesthetic theories in 1924 allowed the novice museum director to read Bell's 1922 book *Since Cézanne* with fresh eyes and an open mind.[32] Bell's theories, like Fry's, not only confirmed for Phillips an acceptance of abstraction, but also helped neutralize his inherent bias before 1925 against non-American art evident in his near exclusive commitment to the work of contemporary American artists.

Like Fry, Bell saw the emergence of Cézanne as important to the liberation of art from representation. Not only did Fry and Bell give Phillips permission to accept that an artist could use art's for-

---

30. The two exhibitions of modern art organized by Roger Fry that had a seismic effect on British art and the British public were *Manet and the Post-Impressionists*, Grafton Galleries, London, November 9, 1910 – January 15, 1911, that included not only the work of Manet but also that of Cézanne, Gauguin, Van Gogh, and Matisse; and the *Second Post-Impressionist Exhibition*, Grafton Galleries, London, October 5 – December 31, 1912, which featured the work of English, Russian and French exponents of post-impressionism, including Picasso's cubist works and the most recent painting and sculpture by Matisse. See Maddock, *Roger Fry, Clive Bell and American Modernism*, 91.

31. Bell's *Art* was published in New York in 1913 by Frederick A. Stokes Company and in London in 1914 by Chatto & Windus. Bell's Preface in the book is dated November 1913. See Phillips's 1928 essay "The Aesthetic Experience," reproduced in this volume, in which he describes *Art* as "pretentious" and how, before reading Bell's work of the 1920s, he thought of him as "intolerant and "pedantic." Sometime between 1914 and 1917 Phillips's wrote notes in the margins of his copy of *Art*. See Appendix B, 1913 Unpublished Writings, *The Eye of Duncan Phillips*, 675.

32. Lane, "Duncan Phillips and the Phillips Memorial Gallery," 129–31. Bell's *Since Cézanne* was published first in London in 1922 and then the following year in New York as *After Cézanne*.

mal language to express human emotion, spiritual essence, and an underlying universal order, but Fry's linking of styles through history was transformative for Phillips. Both ideas impacted his acquisition and exhibition strategy in the second half of the 1920s. The European modernists whose work he had so disparaged in the 1910s soon became the focus of Phillips's acquisition strategy in 1925 when he acquired the first of six works by Cézanne (*Mont Sainte-Victoire*, 1886–87), a first work by Gauguin (*Idyll of Tahiti*, 1901, deaccessioned in 1936 as a partial trade for Goya's *The Repentant St. Peter*, c. 1820–24) and a painting by Odilon Redon (*Mystery*, c. 1910). None of these artists had been on any of Phillips's lists of "desired works" in the years preceding their acquisition.

By 1926, Phillips's initial distrust of abstraction had gradually transformed into a new understanding, a fact made evident in his 1926 book *A Collection in the Making: A Survey of the Problems Involved in Collecting Pictures, together with Brief Estimates of the Painters in the Phillips Memorial Gallery*, the first catalogue of the Phillips Collection.[33] Along with short essays on 105 painters and black & white illustrations of 144 artworks, there was a preface and a major essay that described Phillips's evolving concept and mission for the museum, which relied greatly on the lessons he took from Fry's essays in *Vision and Design* regarding the viewer's opportunity to share in the artist's vision:

> To the extent that we enjoy pictures for their own sake and not because of their resemblance to or their reminders of the life and literature we leave behind, we are sharing a painter's point of view.

A Collection in the Making was a grand manifesto and mission statement for the museum setting out how the Phillips Memorial Gallery was to be different than other museums. It was Phillips's most important and comprehensive statement about his vision for the museum during the museum's first years of active engagement

---

33. New York and Washington, D.C.: E. Weyhe and Phillips Memorial Gallery, 1926 (Phillips Publication no. 5).

with the community. In the preface, Phillips articulated for the first time that the intellectual framework for his museum was conceived as an "experiment station":

> This is the record of the youth of an idea, the concept of a small, intimate museum combined with an experiment station, and it marks the first stage of our progress towards the realization of an ideal.[34]

Inclusiveness and openness to the art of lesser-known independent artists was to be a hallmark of the collection. The "quest of beauty" "under whatever auspices, ... tested or tentative, new or old" was a defining goal. Exhibitions were the means to explore and test the ideas of artists outside the constraints of chronology and geography in order to reveal that art is a universal language that defies time and place:

> I bring together congenial spirits among the artists from different parts of the world and from different ideas...Thus I demonstrate two things—the antiquity of modern ideas, or, if you prefer, the modernity of some of the old masters, and I prove in our Main Gallery and its union of old masters and modern painters that art is a universal language which defies classification according to any chronological or national order.

True to this articulated mission, Phillips gave support throughout his life to America's living artists through financial stipends, acquisitions, and exhibitions, recognizing the seminal role played by artists as diverse as Dove, Marin, O'Keeffe, Milton Avery (1885–1965), Morris Graves (1910–2001), and others in creating a new paradigm for American modernism.

---

34. Duncan Phillips, "Preface," in *A Collection in the Making*, n.p. In 1927, Phillips wrote a letter to the *New York Herald Tribune* proposing his approach for other museums, especially the Metropolitan Museum of Art. With no New York museum committed to the work of living artists in 1927, Phillips was outspoken in his belief that an institution like the Metropolitan should follow his example and set aside a space, a curator, and a small purchase fund to "experiment with vital works of art." Duncan Phillips, Letter to *New York Herald Tribune*, February 10, 1927, The Phillips Collection Archives.

In addition to his support for America's modern artists during the interwar period, between 1925 and 1930 Phillips acquired more than 50 works by School of Paris artists, including major works by Pierre Bonnard (1867–1947), Braque, and Matisse, making The Phillips Collection the only American museum actively acquiring the work of the French moderns in the 1920s. Not until the Museum of Modern Art was established in 1929 would New York have a voice in the modernist revolution to rival that of The Phillips Collection.[35] Bell's *Since Cézanne* singled out Bonnard and Matisse for special attention, which Phillips read in the mid-1920s and took to heart. We celebrate the fact that The Phillips Collection is the first American museum to acquire the work of Bonnard and Braque, in 1925 and 1927, respectively, making note that the Phillips has the most extensive collection of Bonnard's work in North America. Included in this volume are Phillips's essays on Braque (1945) and Bonnard (1949), each of whom was given the special designation of a "unit artist" within the Collection with their work collected to reflect nearly all facets of their lengthy careers.

In 1927 and 1928, Phillips dramatically changed his exhibition strategy as he began to organize installations around the formalist ideas he had assimilated from Fry and Bell. In the October 1928 exhibition titled "Art is Symbolical," the museum's El Greco, *The Repentant Saint Peter* (c. 1600 or later, acquired 1922), was the centerpiece and its influence traced through nineteenth-century French paintings in the collection, including the museum's 1886–87 Cézanne landscape *Mont Sainte-Victoire*.[36] Fry's essay on El Greco in *Vision and Design* was especially important to Phillips who underlined numerous passages that put El Greco's art in

---

35. This period of Phillips's collecting is discussed in detail in Elizabeth Hutton Turner, *Duncan Phillips Collects: Paris Between the Wars*, exh. cat. (Washington, D.C.: The Phillips Collection, 1991).

36. Phillips acquired his second Cézanne in 1928—an 1878–80 *Self-Portrait* that was the first self-portrait of the artist to enter an American museum.

perspective with other artists, including Cézanne.[37] Bell's *Since Cézanne*, by contrast, attempts a history of Cézanne's legacy after 1904 with evaluations of contemporary French artists in which Matisse and Picasso are identified as "the protagonists of the heroic epoch (1904–1914)" after Cézanne, different directions by two very different artists.[38] Picasso, the theorist, and Matisse, the expressive Fauve.

Thus, one begins to understand how and why Phillips's 1929 essay "El Greco—Cézanne—Picasso," included in this volume, opens with a shout-out to Bell's *Since Cézanne*. The essay was written soon after Phillips acquired his first two Picassos for the museum—*The Blue Room* (1901, acquired 1927),[39] a Paris Blue Period work, and a later small cubist picture *Abstraction, Biarritz* (1918, acquired 1929). In essence, Phillips's essay linking El Greco, Cézanne, and Picasso was his response to the two Bloomsbury critics. Phillips carved out a space of his own wherein he declared that Cézanne would not have approved altogether of his disciple Picasso and that "of the three baroque painters only Greco and Picasso are of the same Gothic family."

Phillips revised and retitled this essay as "Research and Stylism in Painting: El Greco—Cézanne—Picasso" when he republished it in 1931 as part of his book *The Artist Sees Differently: Essays*

---

37. See Lane "Duncan Phillips and the Phillips Memorial Gallery," 129 and 129 n. 64, which identifies the source of Fry's comparison of Cézanne and El Greco as Julius Meier-Graefe, which then was repeated by Maurice Denis in his 1907 article on Cézanne in *L'Occident* that was translated by Fry for *Burlington Magazine* in 1910.

38. Clive Bell, *Since Cézanne* (London: Chatto & Windus, 1923): 14–19.

39. Phillips originally called the painting *Early Morning* until changing the title permanently to *The Blue Room* in 1939. For discussion of *The Blue Room* in full see my essay "The Blue Room Reconsidered," in *Picasso: Painting the Blue Period*, edited by Susan Behrends Frank and Kenneth Brummel, exh. cat. (Toronto: The Art Gallery of Ontario and DelMonico Books-D.A.P., 2021), 24–51.

Based Upon the Philosophy of A Collection in the Making.[40] In the revised essay, he moderated his position on Picasso, admitting that Picasso and Cézanne share a romantic nature and also something Gothic. Phillips admitted that it is the "hieroglyphics of Cubism at its most abstract" that challenges him as he feels it "is an aesthetic style in the making, like the chaos beginning to take shape before creation."[41] He sees something of this also in the late work of Cézanne. It is a distinct shift in tone and judgment about Picasso's Cubist work that separates the revised essay from its earlier version with the 1931 text exhibiting a more generous understanding of the young Spaniard's contemporary work.

Between 1928 and 1931 Phillips continued to read contemporary criticism in his quest to refine his aesthetic views and thoughts about modern art, writing a number of significant essays that laid out his views with increasing confidence.[42] "Art Is International," a 1928 essay, expands on an ideal that Phillips introduced in *Collection in the Making* and made a pillar of his aesthetic position— that art is a "universal language breaking down artificial barriers of nationality and race." In this essay, Phillips applied this ideal to American art, stating that "the whole world is to be found in the United States" and, thus, "American art means international art." He explored this position more thoroughly in his 1944 essay "The American Paintings of the Phillips Collection," also included in this volume.

The 1928 essay, although focused on confirming American art as part of the world community, made clear the larger goal for Phillips, which is that "the essential universality of art, regardless of estranging local currencies and languages, can yet unify all man-

---

40. New York and Washington, D.C.: E. Weyhe and Phillips Memorial Gallery, 1931 (Phillips Publication No. 6; 2 vols.).

41. See Duncan Phillips, "Research and Stylism in Painting: El Greco—Cézanne—Picasso," in *The Artist Sees Differently*, 1:77.

42. To the works of Fry and Bell we must also add Jan Gordon, *Modern French Painters* (New York: Dodd, Mead and Company, 1923), which Phillips read in 1927. See Lane, "Duncan Phillips and the Phillips Memorial Gallery," 131.

kind." The essay affirms in absolute terms that art is a "universal language" through which there can be a "fusion of differences in a common ideal" that rise "above the tribal feud and the herd mind" to become an "ideal of international cooperation."

Another 1928 essay, "The Aesthetic Experience," is Phillips's attempt to clarify some of the issues raised by contemporary critics on the subject of art and aesthetics.[43] Expanding again on an idea introduced in *Collection in the Making,* that the artist's point of view is a special perspective that the public should seek to understand, Phillips elaborates here that "Artists can only be encouraged to be loyal to their own ideas" and "let us all cultivate tolerance of the many significant differences with which artists see."

It is this essential idea that the artist must remain true to himself that guides Phillips throughout his career. He explores this idea more fully in the lead article to his new museum publication, a little magazine initiated in 1929 titled *Art and Understanding* that was intended to sketch out his aesthetic credo, along with "the philosophy of open-mindedness and tolerance" that Phillips's personal and social idealism embraced. In his editorial "Art and Understanding," Phillips acknowledged that he was "striving year after year to interpret...not only *the* artist's point of view collectively, but also *an* artist's point of view." Phillips makes a point of emphasizing that an artist's point of view is distinctive to the individual in the same manner that speaking and handwriting are. David Scott interprets this essay as expressing Phillips's goal to bring the public and the artist closer together through increased mutual understanding.[44] Phillips here laid out his lack of sympathy for artists who conform to group ideals and styles in their ambition to belong to the "band wagon of modernity." As noted by Scott, Phillips had a growing suspicion that modernism could become cult-like or, in Phillips's

---

43. Phillips organized his commentary around a select group of critics and their books: Jan Gordon, *Modern French Painters* (1923), Leo Stein, *The A-B-C of Aesthetics* (1927), and Clive Bell, *Since Cézanne* (1922).

44. Scott, "The Evolution of a Critic," 19.

words, a form of "group consciousness" that would impose limitations on independent spirits in the same manner as academicism.[45] This became a major issue for Phillips, reinforcing his determination to support artists whom he believed were true to their own artistic credo independent of the group mind. As he first did in *Collection in the Making*, Phillips reaffirmed in this 1929 article that

> The Phillips Memorial Gallery…stands for a definite policy of supporting many different methods of seeing and painting, avoiding partisanship and propaganda for any one point of view, seeking the best of each, trying to understand what may be all the more significant and worthy of study because it is strange and new.

He concluded the editorial stating explicitly for the first time that while "the artist must understand and be inspired by the world…the world for its own part must understand and be inspired by the artist" and "meet him more than half way." Phillips's idealism was expressed in his fervent belief that "art is the greatest unifying and it is also the greatest clarifying force of the universe" and should not be "regarded as merely a racial or national expression."

The 1929 essay on "The Many-Mindedness of Modern Painting" focuses on those European and American artists whose work Phillips had added to the museum's permanent collection by that time. In his discussion of the four "pioneers" of modernism—Cézanne, Van Gogh, Gauguin, and Seurat—Phillips makes clear that he is not a believer in the doctrine of the "modern movement of art" as "a cleavage, a sudden and revolutionary break in the link which connects the present with the past." Phillips had addressed this idea initially in *Collection in the Making*. In this essay, however, he argued more distinctly that the initiation of the modern era in painting "was not a revolution but simply a pivoting by a few artists of restless and daring minds on the axis of their own period in order to look out over a new prospect." For Phillips, the transition was a gradual one from Impressionism to a mode of picture making that

---

45. Ibid., 18.

emphasized moods, exaggerated intensities and artistic introspection. Phillips circled back to one of his recurring themes—that artists must be true to themselves. In thinking about the state of art at the end of the twentieth century, Phillips speculated that

> the trend in art will be toward a fusion of Orient and Occident, of Europe and America...Unification through a great universal stimulus and a common aspiration to world peace...but not at the cost of a required conformity.

"Modern Art, 1930" was the lead article in the second issue of *Art and Understanding.* It not only summarized the current "epoch-making" art scene in New York but allowed Phillips to give his own critical assessments of the contemporary artists who were then represented in the collection, paying special attention to Matisse and Picasso, who were considered artistic leaders "attuned to their time."[46] Written soon after the Museum of Modern Art's wildly successful inaugural exhibition *Cézanne, Gauguin, Seurat, Van Gogh,* in November 1929, Phillips remarked on the "respectful" public response to the MoMA show compared to the raucous one received by the Armory Show in 1913. Phillips judged this "sudden reversal in taste" as a byproduct of a "steady stream of propaganda and publicity." Rather sarcastically, Phillips declared "At last we know what it is to be modern and what is to be our style for the first half of the Twentieth Century." Acknowledging the pleasure he took with his "experiment station," Phillips cautioned that "Modernism" as defined by the work of Matisse and Picasso was now accepted as a "fait accompli," recognizing that MoMA's inaugural show had created a watershed moment in the American understanding of "modernism."

What Phillips abhorred about the general acceptance of this definition of modernism was that lyrical and independent work by non-conforming artists such as Bonnard in France and the Americans Marin and Tack were being overlooked by the critics and dealers and, thus, also by collectors and museums. Three years earlier,

---

46. Ibid., 19.

in 1927, Phillips had successfully brought together the oil paintings of Bonnard and other contemporary French painters with the watercolors of Marin in the museum's Main Gallery in a multi-part exhibition intended to demonstrate the universality of art as a formal language shared by artists of different origins. Phillips wrote in 1927 that Bonnard and Marin were "the two most fascinating temperaments in contemporary art."[47] Tack was also a key figure in that 1927 exhibition. In Phillips's view, which he hammered home at the conclusion of "Modern Art, 1930," these three non-conforming modern artists—French and American—were great individualists who would not only stand the test of time but ultimately be understood as "the genuine modernists."[48]

In the essays "A Collection Still in the Making" and "The Artist Sees Differently," Phillips continued to develop and drive home these points. In his 1930 assessment of the collection as it entered its second decade, Phillips reminded the reader that "[his] own special function is to find the independent artist and to stand sponsor for him against the herd mind." He went on to declare that "the true artist needs a friend and the true patron of art has nothing better to give the world than the helping hand he extends to any lonely, lofty life made perilous because a free spirit cannot or will not see eye to eye with the crowd." His stated intention is to keep his museum "open to all works of art which seem in any way true or beautiful, by whatever method they come, tested or tentative, traditional or experimental." Phillips emphasized again his "interest in experiment" and openness "to change and progress in art as in

---

47. Duncan Phillips, "Sensibility and Simplification in Ancient Sculpture and Contemporary Painting," *A Bulletin of The Phillips Collection* (February and March 1927): 12. The other contemporary artists included in the exhibition were the French artists Edouard Vuillard (1868-1940), Matisse, Albert Marquet (1875–1947), André Dunoyer de Segonzac (1884-1974), Maurice Utrillo (1883-1955), and the Americans Tack, Edward Bruce (1879-1943), Karl Knaths (1891-1971), and Marjorie Acker Phillips (1894-1985).

48. See Scott, "The Evolution of a Critic," 19, who also emphasizes this aspect of Phillips's essay "Modern Art, 1930."

science," proclaiming once again that he stands "for open-minded-ness and tolerance of different points of view." Even so, he admits that he has "strong likes and dislikes" and is not trying to include in the collection everything of quality being produced by contemporary artists. The emphasis on "true" and "beautiful" is notable as it reveals a continued preference for work that conforms to an essentially romantic ideal. The article emphasized again what had become Phillips's recurring refrain of the "universality of art as a unifying spirit" and the assertion that "Art is part of the social purpose of the world" where "a gallery can be a meeting place of many minds."

"The Artist Sees Differently" explored further Phillips's concerns about the tyranny of the crowd and the "furies" of the herd mind that would "lead to the lowering of standards and the gradual extinction of distinguished individuals." First published in *The American Magazine of Art* in February 1931, the essay became the introductory chapter to the two-volume *The Artist Sees Differently.*[49] Of note, Phillips wrote how much he "resent[ed] the idea that the art of an age of machinery should be itself mechanical." He singled out the work of the French painter Fernand Léger (1881–1955) as an example of an artist whose work was dehumanizing and mechanistic, describing Léger's palette, for example, as "soulless" as the paint applied to "metal for our motor cars and buses." Phillips never acquired an example of Léger's work for the museum.

It is revealing that Phillips turned to Fry's *Vision and Design* for reassurance that "the artist, on his way through the world, really takes time to look at it with rapture and wonder." Phillips deeply believed throughout his life that "Artists see differently not only

---

49. The second volume included 244 illustrations. The essay "The Artist Sees Differently" evolved into a slide lecture that Phillips gave many times between 1931 and 1934, including one version delivered as the Trowbridge Lecture at Yale University on March 20, 1931. There are twelve versions of this slide lecture in The Phillips Collection Archives, which gives weight to the significance of the topic for Phillips. See Appendix B, 1931 Unpublished Writings, *The Eye of Duncan Phillips,* 677.

from other types of humanity but each from all the rest" and that "art is not authentic unless it is also an expressive creation...an intimate personal message." He again reminds the reader in this essay that "open-mindedness" is intended to allow one to find the best examples in a world of "conflicting purposes, contrasting temperaments and creative cross-currents." He asks that the spectator "open their minds to each work and to each human being back of it." In so doing, he assures the reader that the spectator and the artist can share "the unity and the harmony of art" which "are recognized as the very goal of the soul's adventure."

THE 1930S

Phillips's belief in the transformative experience of the work of art by the spectator is one that he developed further in the 1930s, along with his increasing advocacy for the individualism of the artist independent of the "herd." What bothered Phillips by the 1930s was the developing aesthetic orthodoxy that an artwork should be understood as an isolated object of transcendent pure form. Phillips was more of the mind of Alfred Stieglitz and his circle who believed art to be an expression of the artist's individuality, a manifestation of the artist's inner "essence."[50]

In 1934, Phillips read John Dewey's *Art and Experience* (1934). The American philosopher and educational reformer took a more structured approach to the idea of artistic individuality. In his copy of Dewey's book, Phillips made marginal notes and extensive underlinings of specific texts.[51] As pointed out by Scott, Lane, and more recently Mary Jane Jacob, Phillips was drawn to Dewey's idea that works of art bring together form and experience through identification with "the Artist and his inner life."[52] Dewey linked

50. Lane, "Duncan Phillips and the Phillips Memorial Gallery," 145–47.

51. A photocopy of Phillips's heavily annotated copy of Dewey's *Art and Experience* rests in The Phillips Collection Archives. See Appendix B, 1934 Unpublished Writings, *The Eye of Duncan Phillips*, 677.

52. See Scott, "The Evolution of a Critic," 20; Lane, "Duncan Phillips and the Phillips Memorial Gallery," 148–51, 149 n.133; and Mary Jane Jacob, "Not the Eye

art more closely to the artist's inner world and outer existence than did Fry or Bell. Dewey's point of view and argument resonated with Phillips who was already open to the ideas because of his sympathetic response to the artists in Stieglitz's circle, especially, Dove, O'Keeffe, and Marin. Phillips appreciated especially that Dewey's point of view affirmed that all aesthetic experience can be evoked by the artist's internal and external experience no matter its style (abstract or representative) or source (nature or life experience) as each artwork reflects an artist's entire life experience, not just the exterior expression of an artist's emotions in an object. In other words, art is not created in a void and artists draw from their experiences in the world at large, as well as from nature. Not only did Phillips advocate aggressively for the importance of personality in art, for which he wrote a three-part article in 1935, but throughout the 1930s he gave lectures based on the theme of personality in art, including one on Marin and another on the Swiss-born German artist Paul Klee (1879–1940), whose work Phillips first acquired in 1930.[53]

But the Beholder: The Shared Vision of Duncan Phillips and John Dewey," in *Seeing Differently: The Phillips Collects for a New Century*, edited by Elsa Smithgall (Washington, D.C. and Lewes, U.K.: The Phillips Collection in association with D Giles Limited, 2021), 33–41. See also Duncan Phillips's paraphrase of Dewey in "Personality in Art: Reflections on Its Suppression and the Present Need for Its Fulfillment, Part I," *The American Magazine of Art* 28, no. 2 (February 1935): 84.

53. Phillips published his essay on "Personality in Art: Reflections on Its Suppression and the Present Need for Its Fulfillment" in three parts: *The American Magazine of Art* 28, no. 2 (February 1935): 78–84; no. 3 (March 1935): 148–55; no. 4 (April 1935): 214–20. From 1936-1942, The Phillips Collection Archives have eight versions of a slide lecture titled "The Expression of Personality Through Design in the Art of Painting." The file includes drafts on Marin, Klee, and Knaths. See Appendix B, 1936 Unpublished Writings, *The Eye of Duncan Phillips*, 678. Dewey's lecture to the Washington Dance Association at The Phillips Collection on November 13, 1938, was titled "The Philosophy of the Arts." See Jacobs, "Not the Eye But the Beholder," 41n.36. Phillips acquired a first work by Klee in 1930, *Tree Nursery* (1929), which developed into a full-fledged passion for the artist's work between 1938 and 1948 when he aggressively assembled a group of thirteen mature works by the artist and installed them at the museum in their own room in

Scott makes the observation that Phillips's agreement with Dewey in the 1930s is uniquely positioned during a decade when the debate about modernism in America pitted cubism and formal abstraction against realism and regionalism.[54] Dewey's argument countered the growing orthodoxy of modernism as abstraction, which Phillips believed was a constraint on the individualism and independence of artists. Dewey's philosophical framework embraced all sides of artistic creativity without contradiction. Phillips immediately recognized Dewey's point of view as sympathetic to his own. Thus we can find in this volume Phillips's essays on artists in the collection whom he valued for their independence and their vision as diverse as Bonnard, Braque, Dove, Louis Eilshemius (1864–1941), Lee Gatch (1902–1968), and Giorgione, among others.

Phillips pursued his passion for Giorgione in the 1936 essay "The Leadership of Giorgione," included in this volume, where he described the artist's work as "hypersensitive lyricism, tinged ever so lightly with sadness." In the foreword to the essay's publication the following year as a separate book, Phillips reiterated his conviction about the historic roots of modern artistic concepts, writing "Giorgione is the first single-minded Independent in the history of pictorial art and the first proponent of art for art's sake."[55]

THE 1940S THROUGH THE 1960S

Although Phillips had laid the essential intellectual foundation for his museum's collecting philosophy by the 1940s, he continued to read the work of later formalist critics. Of greatest importance to Phillips was Henri Focillon's *La vie des formes* (1934; published in English 1948),[56] which is a discussion of the art-historical problem

---

1948 where they became a source of inspiration to artists for nearly forty years.

54. Scott, "The Evolution of a Critic," 21.

55. Duncan Phillips, *The Leadership of Giorgione* (Washington, D.C.: American Federation of Arts, 1937), 11. See also Passantino and Martin, "Chronology," 39.

56. Henri Focillon, *The Life of Forms*, translated by George Kubler (New York: Zone Books, 1992 [1948]).

of style.[57] Phillips's interest in Focillon reflects his ongoing commitment to a measure of formalist critique during the interwar years. While Focillon's philosophy emphasized form as the essential quality in art and style as its treatment, he provided a theory for how art forms change styles throughout history, and go through phases that can be understood as experimental, classic, refined and baroque. Focillon's idea that style is cyclical helped Phillips understand more fully the variety of modernist styles appearing in twentieth-century art, which had always been a serious hurdle for the collector and critic. In his 1952 Introduction to a new collection catalogue, Phillips wrote "To Henri Focillon I am indebted for the clearest statement on the transitional stages in the life of forms."[58] With form and style as the primary considerations of art, Focillon also believed that museums should organize their collections by stylistic temperament rather than chronology. His philosophy thus validated Phillips's own ahistorical museum practice, which embraced the primacy of artistic temperament as the basis for exhibition and permanent collection installations.[59]

As Scott observed, the war years of the 1940s deepened Phillips's commitment to individualism and the universality of expression.[60] In 1944, during the midst of World War II, Phillips proclaimed in the essay introducing his exhibition "The American Paintings of

---

57. See the insightful discussion about Focillon's ideas and Phillips in Lane, "Duncan Phillips and the Phillips Memorial Gallery," 139–40.

58. Duncan Phillips, *The Phillips Collection: A Museum of Modern Art and Its Sources* (New York and London: Thames and Hudson, 1952), ix. See also Lane, "Duncan Phillips and the Phillips Memorial Gallery," 139 and n.104.

59. Focillon gave a lecture on "Goya to Daumier" at the Phillips Memorial Gallery on April 18, 1940. At the time, Focillon was an exchange scholar at Yale University escaping occupied France and in residence at Dumbarton Oaks in Washington, D.C. In her memoir, Marjorie Phillips remembered that her husband revered Focillon's *The Life of Forms* and that both men shared a great admiration for Daumier's painting *The Uprising* that is in The Phillips Collection. See Marjorie Phillips, *Duncan Phillips and His Collection*, 216; Passantino and Martin, "Chronology," 40.

60. See Scott, "The Evolution of a Critic," 21.

the Phillips Collection" that America's heritage was "a fusion of various sensitivities, a unification of differences." This is an important essay and its inclusion in this volume reflects its historical moment. Expressing in its fullness his belief that art is an international, universal means of expression that crosses boundaries of race, and language, Phillips celebrated in this essay the fact that his collection included naturalized Americans from Russia, Hungary, Romania, Italy, and Japan, among others, for it meant that American art was truly an international art. He embraced the diversity of American art, declaring that "all the world contributes to our spiritual and creative resources since all the world is contained in our United States." It was a bold statement then and is still so today.

In the 1940s and 1950s Phillips wrote a number of important tribute essays that recognized the passing of seminal figures in his personal journey as a collector and critic, such as the critic Focillon, the photographer-gallerist Alfred Stieglitz (1864–1946), the Stieglitz artists Dove, Marin, and Marsden Hartley (1877–1943), and the European artists Bonnard and Klee. It was a time of reflection and summing up. A number of these significant essays are included in this volume.

While New York took the lead in the new American art in the postwar era, The Phillips Collection still played a seminal role in bringing contemporary art to Washington audiences well into the 1970s under the leadership of Marjorie Phillips after her husband's death in 1966 and their son Laughlin Phillips. Phillips continued his search for new talent, writing in 1954, at age sixty-eight, that he was "attracted to qualities of contemporary art precisely because they thrill me with refreshing differences."[61] It speaks to Phillips's continuing engagement with the art of his time that major works in the collection by artists as varied as Josef Albers (1988–76), Richard

---

61. Duncan Phillips, *The Phillips Collection and Related Thoughts on Art*, brochure, 1954, unpaginated; originally presented as a radio talk entitled "The Pleasures of an Intimate Art Gallery," Washington, D.C., WCFM Radio, February 24, 1954. The printed essay is included in this volume.

Diebenkorn (1922–93), Sam Francis (1923–94), Sam Gilliam (1933–2022), Seymour Lipton (1903–86), Robert Motherwell (1915–1991), Rothko, Clyfford Still (1904–1980), Mark Tobey (1890–1976), and Bradley Walker Tomlin (1899–1953) were acquired from exhibitions organized at the museum in the 1950s and 1960s. Phillips clearly favored the poetic and lyrical side of postwar painting that seemed alive with light and movement and often related to the museum's great modern colorists, like Bonnard and Matisse.

Throughout his career as a critic and collector Phillips remained highly suspicious of art that he believed to be dehumanizing. He was anti-mechanistic in the same spirit as the critics and artists in the Stieglitz circle. Evident in Phillips's early critical reviews and then more explicitly as his aesthetic judgment matured in the 1920s it is clear that he believed most fervently in those artists whom he perceived as true to their inner selves despite the pressures of what he thought would be passing stylistic fads. Phillips's preference was always for expressionist art in many forms that looked to nature for inspiration, championing artists who were individuals, not followers. Klee's art, for example, with its spiritual overtones and his individuality of personal expression was seminal to Phillips's commitment to this German artist. It is the same wellspring from which Phillips's lifelong commitment to Tack and Rothko springs. In a similar vein, the work of Morris Graves appealed to Phillips because its humanist message transcended cultural barriers.[62]

Over the course of nearly fifty years, Duncan Phillips assembled a collection of modern painting that is substantially different from that of his contemporaries as he was interested in connections between works of art across time and geography and he was willing

---

62. Phillips was introduced to Graves's work in 1942 at the Museum of Modern Art's exhibition *Americans 1942: 18 Artists from 9 States*. Graves exhibited thirty works and received positive reviews. Between 1942 and 1954 Phillips acquired ten works by the artist for his museum. See "Morris Graves," in *The Eye of Duncan Phillips*, 577 and 798 n.1.

to take risks that other museums with conservative directors and trustees were reluctant to take. He supported artists of diverse aesthetic temperaments and collected works that were important on their merits, not because they illustrated schools of thought, were faddish, or were by famous names. In his 1954 essay "The Phillips Collection and Related Thoughts," reproduced in this volume, he expressed those principles for a new generation:

> What I delight to collect…are the world's wonders of personality—not what can be put into a picture but what cannot be left out—that quintessence of self—captured in some expressive correspondence of aesthetic form.

—⁓—

DUNCAN PHILLIPS
WRITINGS ON ART

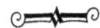

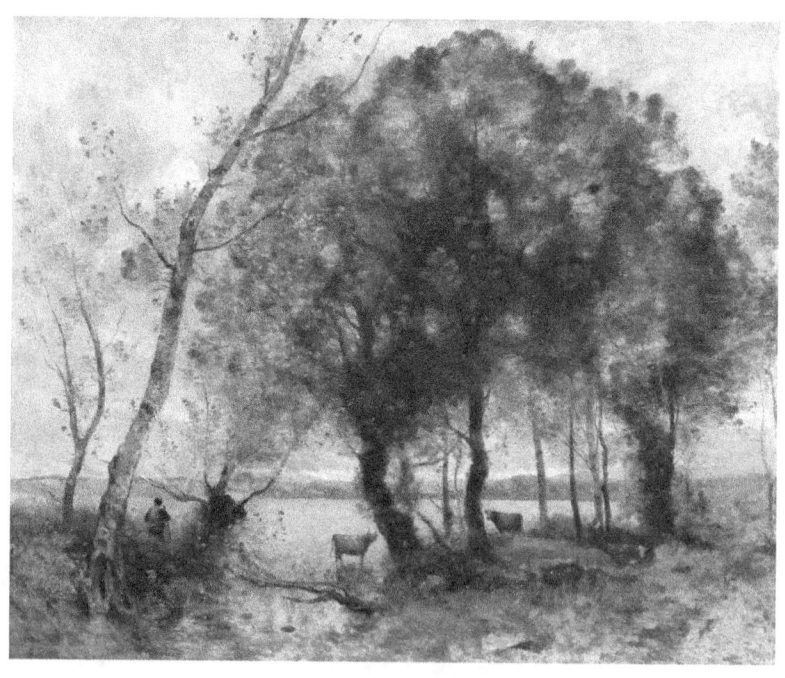

Jean-Baptiste-Camille Corot
The Lake, 1861
Oil on canvas
The Frick Collection, New York
Henry Clay Frick Bequest

COROT

(1906)

BECAUSE some landscape painters copy nature coldly while others mischievously exaggerate their impressions; because some lack poetry and others sense; because some fear to be thought odd and others dread to be rated conventional, many a picture of marked ability has turned us away, dissatisfied or disgusted. Happily for art, there are painters who have learned that the secret of success with landscapes is to interpret as well as to copy Nature, and to blend the personal and the impersonal, the romantic and the real, by drifting down the stream of dreams until the "genus loci" descends to crown a labor of love. Look at almost any of Corot's canvases, and feel not only the spirit of the pictured spot, but the very mood in which Nature is plunged at the chosen hour of night or day. Look at the more characteristic of his paintings, and if you love poetry you will fall easily under the spell of moist dawns and twilights in the woods, during those still hours when Nature is drowsily awakening or gently drifting into her long sleep.

From that of many landscape painters, the temperament of Corot is unique. He is often associated with the Barbizon School, but unlike him, they did not paint—as Dupré himself expressed it—with wings on their shoulders.[1] He has also been compared to Constable, for their names have been linked together as the two supreme masters of wind-stirred foliage and glistening dew. But Constable's temperament loved the heat and bustle of noon, while Corot's sought the dim light before and after the brilliancy of midday. Constable found his most cherished opportunities in the angry clouds of a summer storm, the sun breaking through, and the many colored beams of

First published in *The Yale Literary Magazine* 72 (November 1906).

1. [The painter Jules Louis Dupré, one of the leaders of the Barbizon School, is said to have remarked that Corot painted with wings on his back.]

the rainbow. But Corot waited patiently for the storm to subside, for the clouds to dissolve, for the rainbow to fade, even for the sun to set, and then in the restoration of stillness and quiet color, he was happy. Finally, Constable loved to put into his canvas touches of everyday life—a homely woman under a red parasol taking a constitutional on Hampstead Heath, or a small boy lying face downward, drinking out of a wayside brook. Corot's world, on the other hand, is the fairyland of his own fancies. He no sooner sketched a forest glade than wood nymphs, the radiant children of his dreams, came forth from every side to people the lovely shades of his creation, and dance with the joy of sunrise or the glamour of moonrise.

These unearthly nymphs, forever dancing, amuse us, just when, sobered by the beauty of the pastoral, we do not wish to be amused. We do not see why the charm of the forest depths would not be more charming still in a complete solitude, or one broken only by the gentle presence of a timid fawn, starting at the least wind whisper. Even the most enthusiastic of Corot's admirers, and it must be acknowledged that these are more ardent than numerous, must view these dream children with a smile. Yet, after a study of Corot's joyous and naïve character, ever longing to put into some definite form the overflow of ecstasy with which the intoxicating freshness of Nature always filled him, we begin to realize that the classic, rhythmic maidens are the personification of his own feelings. Then our smile becomes one of affectionate intimacy and understanding.

A point frequently raised against Corot is his continued sameness of subject and sentiment. Color chords in silver and dark green; the whisper of the willow at the water side, and the essence of all that is mellowest in sunrise or nightfall—that is the entrancing vision, but the one and only general impression that the name of Corot conjures up. It is true that in his *Macbeth and the Witches*,[2] he has pictured with all the mystery of his favorite hour, the tragic destiny of the man. You catch the gleam from the armor of the two horsemen as they ride down from the depths of the black woods, and you shiver as

---

2. [1858–59, The Wallace Collection, London]

you look on the three gaunt hags outlined against the moonlight sky. Then, too, he has painted a few summer sketches where we languish in the quivering heat of a drowsy midsummer afternoon, and he has rendered the destruction of Sodom with the doomed city blazing in lurid glare. But these are among the rare exceptions. Few artists departed more reluctantly from their favorite themes than Corot. The cavilers will insist that in this age of mercenary specialists he was one of them, sacrificing to Mammon all hope of versatility that he might spend his time only on what he was sure would win public approval. No motive was ever farther from his mind than this. He painted forests and streams during the hours when the world is asleep because the poetry and serenity of the time and place enthralled his soul and swept it to inspired expression. The woodland quiet was to him what the laughing eyes of Lady Hamilton were to Romney[3]—a master passion.

If you would know the real heat of this passion, listen to his own excitably enthusiastic description of sunrise as it appears to the waiting artist:

> Nature lies beneath a white veil. Everything trembles under the first a wakening breath of dawn. The mists of night lie silver white on the cool grass. At the first ray of sun the flowers awake, each bathing in its drop of pearly dew. The birds twitter their morning prayer. One sees little, yet all is there. Now the meadows—the cottages, and the ever receding horizon appear, for the sun has risen. Everything sparkles—glistens. All is in full light, still and soft. And I paint—I paint. But now the sun begins to scorch, the flowers droop, and the drone of toil sounds from the village. I must go. I see too much and my imagination has no play. Work, my friends, and I will dream, and later I will paint my dream.[4]

It is quite as essential that an artist who would portray nature should dream well, as that he should draw and paint well. All the

---

3. [*Emma Hamilton*, c.1765–1815, National Portrait Gallery, London]

4. [*Corot raconté par lui-même et par ses amis*, edited by Pierre Cailler (Paris: Vésenaz-Genève, 1946).]

really great landscape artists have been dreamers,—though men of
erratic genius like Turner are subject to occasional nightmare. Corot
never painted nightmare. It was not in his scheme of things to perpetuate ugliness. His world is a pale ethereal dreamland so exquisitely lovely that one does not wish to wake. And the secret of this
magic dream likeness is the hush. In *The Goatherd*,[5] all the radiant
Italian valley and the distant city flushed with the glow of sunset
seem to be listening breathlessly to the sweet notes of the shepherd's
pipes. In *The Lake*,[6] there are two notes only, a dark bister and a
pale silver, yet it is a harmony in a minor key, producing an effect
of haunting and delicious melancholy. You feel the softness of the
air. You hear the rustling of the leaves. You see the ripples play on
the face of the still stream, and it all floats away in mist until it is lost
in the dim horizon. Surely, if the aim of landscape painting be to
communicate the artist's own dream visions of natural beauty, then
Corot's symphonies fulfill every requirement.

The genius and enthusiasm of Corot worked many wonders. The
scenery around Corot's home at Ville D'Avray is commonplace in
the extreme to the average eye. Yet under this poet painter's loving
touch it is transformed into a very Arcady. To my mind, this idealism
of Corot's was his crowning glory. He kept the fire of his youthful
enthusiasm burning brightly to the end, and this was greatly due to
his absolute absorption in his life work of finding and musing over
the serene aspects of the world's beauty. Though most of his days of
activity were spent in Paris, that most exciting of cities, and at a time
when political uprisings, tumults, triumphs, and vicissitudes made
life vivid, this dreamer of dreams went his way undisturbed and
totally detached from the world about him. Learning from a visitor
to his studio of the Revolution of 1848, which for a time caused the
upheaval of all Europe, he remarked abstractedly as he continued
painting—"It would appear then that some people are discontented."

---

5. [1872, Scottish National Gallery, Edinburgh]
6. [1861, The Frick Collection, New York]

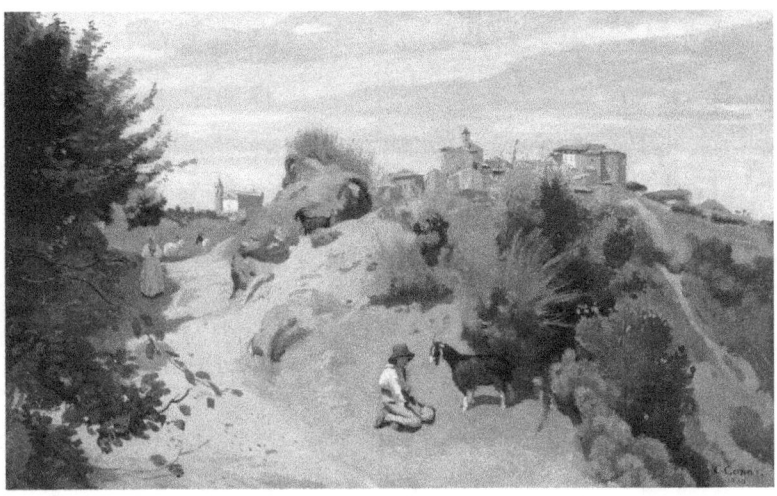

Jean-Baptiste-Camille Corot
Genzano, 1843
Oil on canvas
The Phillips Collection, Washington, D.C. Acquired in 1955

All the while that volcanic France was seething with eruptions, good old Corot was dreaming of his pastorals and keeping his heart fresh and young. To us it seems that this narrow outlook, this placid oblivion, disqualified him for a full-blooded manhood. Yet his art flourished, and the enervated world should be grateful for the breath of pure air that stirs his feathery lacework of spring leaves. The appeal of Corot the dreamer and idealist is not extended alone to those who can enjoy the woods and fields to their heart's content, but to the jaded toilers of the city streets. He calls them away from their surging, sweating thoroughfares to rest with him awhile in lovely byways where Nature gives her peace and plenty. At least to all, his call does not appeal in vain.

MEISSONIER'S NAPOLEONIC CYCLE
(1908)

AT this late day in the development of the art of painting, since we have learned the value of synthesis, and even gone to the extreme of tolerating many extraordinary experiments in Impressionism, the work of Meissonier is veritably a red rag to the art critic. Admitted by all to be a superb draftsman, he is credited by some writers with about as much soul as is required by the newspaper reporter assigned to the job of describing the gowns at the Opera. Unquestionably Meissonier's methods were not generally poetic, nor his ideals high. Instead of expressing his impression of a scene or a sitter, he minutely copied everything within the range of his vision. So all-encompassing was his observation, and so skillful his execution, that the perfect illusion of reality which he created left no more room for the imagination than the congested facts upon the face of an accurate photograph. The perfect analysis and reproduction of details being his avowed aim in painting, it is little wonder that he chose, for the most part, trivial subjects and diminutive canvases. His miniatures were profitable. Prosaic souls who imagined that accurate imitation was the highest reach of art, raved about him, while connoisseurs lingered fascinated over the brushwork of this incomparable copyist, whose anatomy was so faultless, and whose truth-telling devices established him as perhaps the greatest genre painter of all time. Yet we have outgrown such art. We expect at least a dash of the artist's ego, at least a suggestion of the poetry which pulsates through the prose of life. That is why indifferent and today the life-like boots and buckles of his cavalrymen and to the laces and breeches of the eighteenth century gentlemen, upon which this courtly French painter lavished his laborious genius.

Meissonier's career, however, had one great inspiration, and it sufficed to sufficed to lift him, in of spite of adverse temperament

First published in *The Yale Literary Magazine* 653 (May 1908).

and training, to the higher realms of art. This fashionable miniaturist was inspired with the seemingly vain ambition of depicting no less emotional and colossal a subject than the rise and fall of the great Napoleon. What is known as his Napoleonic Cycle is a series of three paintings following the Emperor down the tragic path from Friedland to Elba. The sentimental and romantic vein, in which he treated this Idol of all true Frenchmen, may serve to transform, for future generations, Meissonier the clever craftsman in oils, into Meissonier, a national painter-poet.

1807[1] is one of the most popular of all battlefield pictures. The artist, after careful development of the theme, declared it to be his masterpiece. Had he spent upon it days hot with inspired haste, instead of years cold with deliberate tinkerings, the essentials of the pictures, namely the movement and magic of the moment, might have been more vividly rendered. As it is, the artist's chronic realism was not damp enough to chill the glow of his own emotion, and the result is truly splendid.

Napoleon is presented at the crest of his glory, and the artist wishes to testify to the adoration of the soldiers for their great Captain, who had led them to victory, who was their very god, for whose triumph they would gladly die. The battle of Friedland has just been fought and won, and the genius of the conqueror has set in motion the irrepressible spirits of the French warriors. Boundless, fiercely excited hero-worship, this is the keynote of the scene. The canvas is bathed in sunlight and dazzles with the gleam of gay uniforms. The violence of battle is only suggested by the overturned cart and the hoof-trampled grass. No colors are bright enough for this triumphant moment. No shadow falls upon the Imperial figure to detract from its epic character. Napoleon, the master of Europe, is reviewing the charge of his Cuirassiers. Behind him stands the Old Guard, grim and proud. Before him a tide of cavalrymen sweeps in whirlwind circles. One rises to his full height in his stirrups, raises his

---

1. [*1807, Friedland,* c. 1861–75, The Metropolitan Museum of Art, New York]

helmet in salute, and we can almost hear his "Vive l'Empereur" as he gallops by.

Contrast the keynote of this scene with that of the second of the Cycle.[2] The soldiers, once so wild with enthusiasm, now stagger through the snow, wrapped in the gloom of a gray midwinter evening. The cheeriest are growling, the bitterest cursing; all are broken and exhausted in strength and spirit, their faith in their supposedly invincible leader shattered. their minds tormented with thoughts of dead comrades left upon the snows of Russia, or of dear French homes they have desolated in order to swell the armies and mold the fortunes of a headlong "Corsican Adventurer." And in the foreground ride the embittered Marshals, and the pale, defiant Emperor himself.

The third picture of the Cycle is called merely *1814*.[3] On a bare white hillock around which storm clouds are gathering, the Emperor has brought his white horse to a stop. The technician's instincts tempted him here to dwell, at the expense perhaps of proportion, on the physical aspect of this horse; slender legs that stand their ground, resolutely. head held erect as if expectant, as if defiant, bright, restless eyes, nervous, distended nostrils, every muscle taut and eager and ready. No such alertness burns in the bearing of the rider. Through a rift in a black sky, a weird white light falls upon the pale face of a genius. The fire has gone out of the eyes. Infinite weariness, despair unutterable, may be detected through the fixedly calm countenance. And as around the bare, white hillock the storm clouds gather and rumble, there seems to hover before the eyes of Napoleon a memory of Moscow and a vision of Waterloo.

At last we find in the art of Meissonier something above and beyond the skillful drawing and painting—an emotional strain which transcends the rich technique.

⸻⁓⸻

2. [*The Campaign of France, 1814*, 1860–64, Musée d'Orsay, Paris]
3. [1862, The Walters Art Museum, Baltimore]

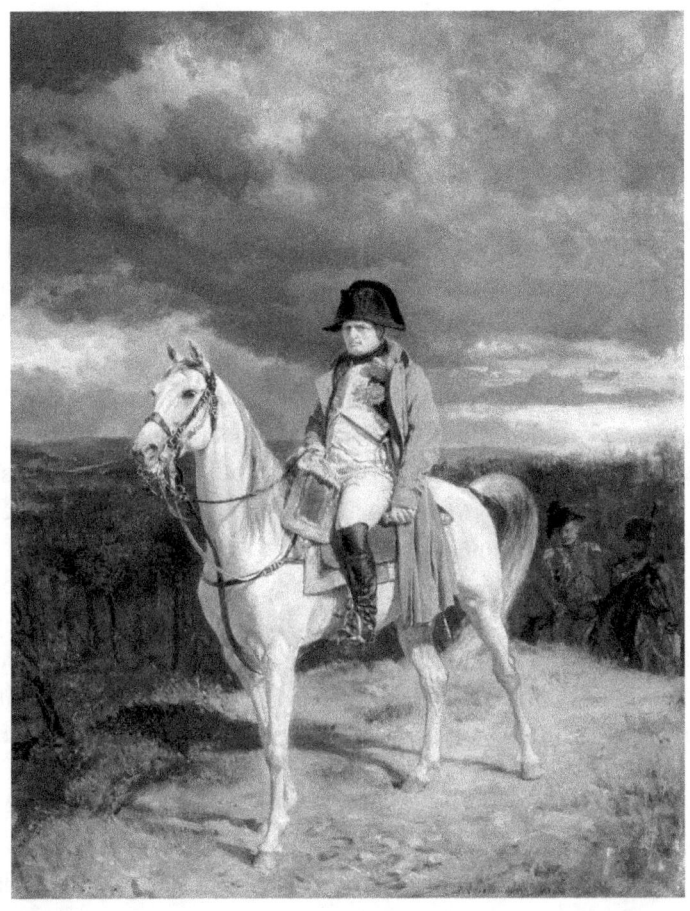

Jean-Louis-Ernest Meissonier
1814, 1862
Oil on panel
The Walters Art Museum, Baltimore

WHAT IS IMPRESSIONISM?
(1912)

WHAT does Impressionism in painting really mean? After some forty years of agitated discussion, there exists in the public mind a confusion amounting to bewilderment in regard to the proper answer to that question. The reason is not far to seek. Critics have been provocative and entertaining, according to their fashion, with a truly journalistic contempt for any short cuts to the truth. They have played with their subject as a cat will play with a mouse to prolong the pleasurable excitement. George Moore, for instance, pounced upon the truth when he said that Impressionism penetrates all true painting and only "in its most modern sense [signifies] the rapid noting of elusive appearance."[1] Yet he allowed the thought to escape that he might play with it upon another occasion. What is the result? Ask the average well-informed man you meet what Impressionism in painting really means, and he will reply somewhat as follows: "Oh—it's a new-fangled French way of painting everything light and airy, and of spilling all the colors of the rainbow—helter-skelter—into the same picture."

While resenting the flippancy of the gentleman's manner, the most enthusiastic critics of the new spectral vision could hardly quarrel with the truth of this statement. When urged to a definition of the same subject, Camille Mauclaire proceeds to industriously describe the technique of color spots invented by Claude Monet in his attempt to render the shimmer of aerial vibration. Now this method is a typical achievement of the modern mind. Suffice it here to say that, successful as it has been in producing upon canvas subtle verities of light and air, it is at best a brave but crude beginning and only an experiment in the evolution of realistic painting.

First published in *Art and Progress* 3, no. 11 (September 1912).

1. [Quoted in Jean N. Oliver, "Monet and His Art," *New England Magazine* 32, no. 1 (March 1905): 66.]

So engrossed is the painter with his melted outlines, his divided tones, his colored shadows, that his picture too closely resembles a scientific demonstration. "Coloured stenography," Huneker called it.[2] It seems hardly credible that learned critics can present any one technique as the embodiment of Impressionism, and to the average mind the word seems altogether too big for mere technical adventure, however important. Yet by the common consent of painters , critics and public, Monet, Degas, and the rest of that group are *the* Impressionists. The perplexing question is, wherein lies their right to a monopoly of the title? Opinions, moreover, seem to be divided whether these artists are Impressionists because of their methods or because of their motives. Most writers agree with M. Mauclaire[3] that the innovations of palette and brush have earned them the distinction, for these, at least, are indisputably new. Inconveniently however, the methods of the several painters, in variably grouped together, are widely dissimilar. Some laid their paint on in gobs, others in shrill, thin washes. If *Pointillisme* be Impressionism, how can Degas and the earlier Manet claim kinship with Monet, Renoir, Sisley, and Pissarro? If, on the other hand, this little band of men are Impressionists because they have been drawn together to ex press, each in his own way, transient aspects of contemporaneous reality, how can we forget that the expression of contemporaneous reality has been the unchanging purpose of true realists from the very earliest day? As for the "transient aspects," the new regard for effects of life and light in passing, these things constitute one of the valuable contributions of modern art. But the realistic principle dates back to Giotto. Can it be that learned critics, in cramming Impressionism into a new, small, pigeon hole, have only thickened the fog of misunderstanding that envelopes the name?

It is the general belief, a belief difficult to wholly eradicate, that Impressionism is peculiarly modern, and that, being modern, it con-

---

2. [Camille Mauclair, *L'Impressionisme* (Paris: Librairie de l'Art Ancien et Moderne, 1904).]

3. [James Huneker, *Promenades of an Impressionist* (New York: Charles Scribner's Sons, 1920), 241.]

sists very naturally of egotistical specializations, and adventurous experiments in technique. Now, in the first place, we forget that other times besides our own have possessed inquiring minds. It is inherent in the nature of man to be curious and experimental. He begins in the cradle by investigating the mystery of his toes, and he ends by dabbling with Nature's elemental forces, also with philosophy and machinery and art. Da Vinci wrote learnedly about perspective and colored shadows, and for him, as Pater observed, "the novel impression be conveyed, the exquisite effect he created counted as an end in itself—a perfect end." What could be more "modern" in subtlety of suggestion than the *Mona Lisa,* with her watchful eyes, her slow, disquieting smile and that fantastic background of blue-green rocks and interminable rivulets? As for Rembrandt's soul-searching shaft of golden light, that is but another early instance of the craftsman spirit delighting in the production of "effects," a spirit destined in our time to become so dominant and so contagious a force. But. in the second place, the true Impressionism is not solely concerned with technique, nor is it the gospel of either "art for art's sake" or "truth for truth's sake." In the last analysis, it is the soul of the painter that counts. Here imitation, be it ever so perfect, will result in a statement of fact such as we may find in any book of reference.

The personal and spontaneous impression, therefore, is requisite in realism no less than in romance. A painting may be a perfect marvel of realistic imitation—yet unworthy to be called art because lacking the artist's testimony of impression.

In the Walters Collection in Baltimore we may see side by side two small but characteristic canvases by Alma-Tadema and Jean-François Millet. The former is entitled *The Triumph of Titus.* It is a triumph of technique. The cold and lustrous sheen of the marble stairs and the variegated textures of apparel and ornament are copied in detail with unerring exactness. The imitation is astoundingly perfect. The adjacent Millet represents a flock of sheep, huddled by night, in their fold. They make but a shimmering blur under the misty moon. Nothing is described, nothing defined. And yet, somehow, we can see the restless stirring of the sheep, we can

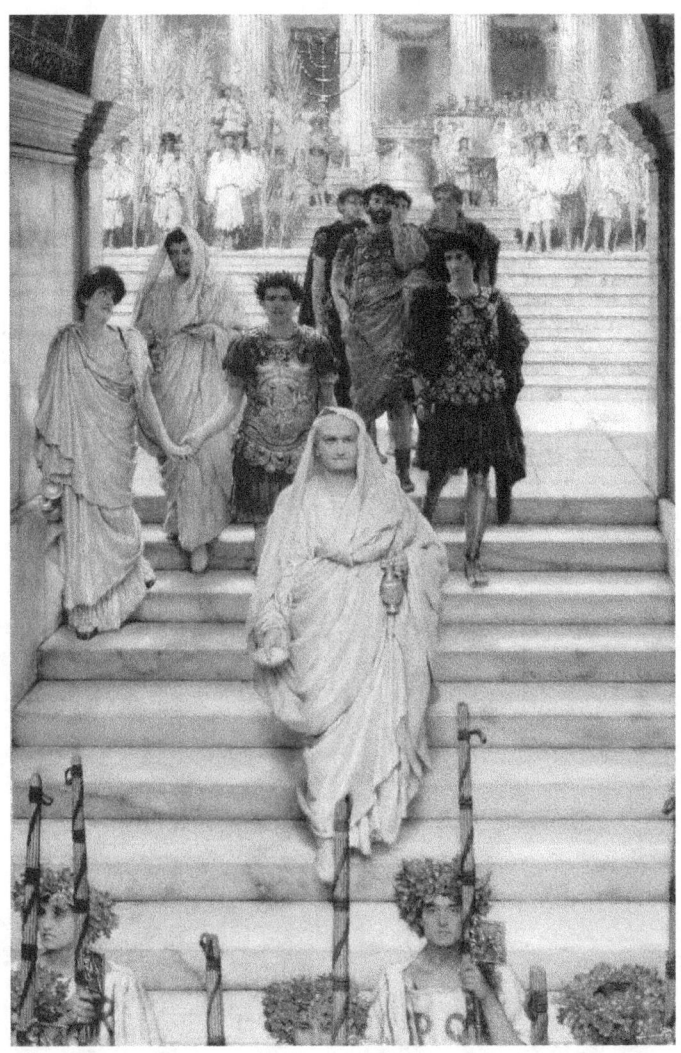

Lawrence Alma-Tadema
The Triumph of Titus: AD 71, The Flavians, 1885
Oil on panel
The Walters Art Museum, Baltimore

feel the chill of the air, and we are deeply impressed by the poetic illusion. Now both these pictures are realistic, each in its own way. The way of Alma-Tadema was an elaborate and painstaking prose, whereas Millet's picture is endowed with the directness and simplicity of poetic inspiration. Alma-Tadema arrived at his knowledge of Titus and his time through toilsome years of study; Millet saw his vision of the sheepfold one night and transcribed his impression before his brain was cool. Alma-Tadema employed the facts he found in books, Millet the secrets he learned from Nature. Alma-Tadema, the scholar, has painted with fastidious precision colorful chapters of ancient history; Millet, the poet-painter, transcribed with spontaneous and sublime carelessness the peasants from whose midst he came, their fields and flocks, their labor and their love. Both men may be counted realists, but Millet was also an Impressionist.

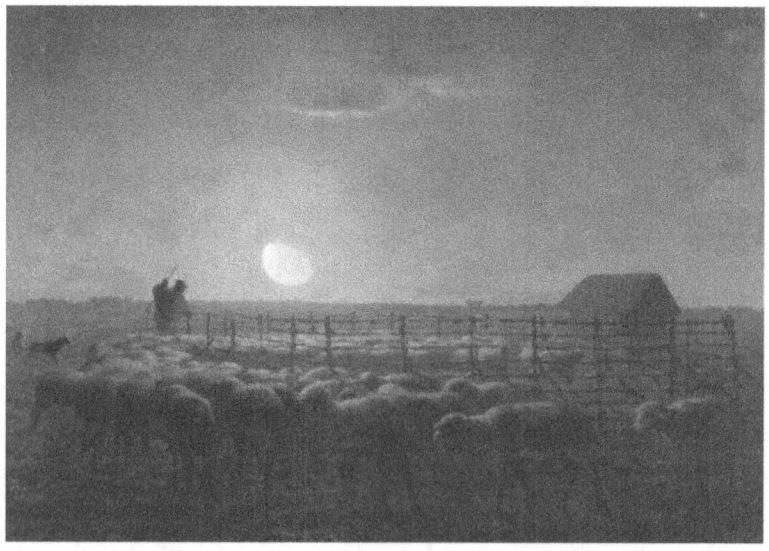

Jean-François Millet
The Sheepfold, Moonlight, 1856–60
Oil on panel
The Walters Art Museum, Baltimore

It is my firm belief that Impressionism is not a transient technique but an ancient and abiding faith, not merely the sensational production of some revolutionary modern painters, but one of the basic principles—I might say the one true philosophy, of all painting. As many as are the eyes that see, the hearts that feel, the brains that formulate their conception of visible or in tangible things, so many are life's real Impressionists. The value of their impressions varies according to their understanding. Even among those whose talents seek expression in the arts, there are all kinds of Impressionists, from the men of lofty genius on the mountain peaks of inspiration, the Michelangelos, and the Rembrandts, to the horde of petty craftsmen who labor in sterile moorlands with an unavailing and uncouth endeavor. Midway upon the scale are the radical, experimental Frenchmen we have been discussing, artists who are so enamored of the appearances of objects under diffused or conflicting lights, so absorbed in the striving to render visual sensation, that nobility of theme seldom concerns them. They are Impressionists to be sure, but they represent merely the most recent stage in a gradual and logical development.

That astute critic, R.A.M. Stevenson,[4] was, I think, the first to point out that Impressionism in the sense which is commonly accepted today received its original impulse from the supreme Velázquez. To him is attributed the practical demonstration of that vital principle which ordains that objects should not be painted as they are known to exist, but as they appear to the momentary and more or less abstracted gaze, under ever-changing conditions of light and air. As a definition of the Impressionism of nineteenth century realists, we shall see how this utters indeed the last word. How ever, if the critic had regarded Impressionism as an eternal principle rather than as a modern practice, he would have taken for his model not merely the brilliant advances which Velázquez made upon the knowledge of his time, but the complete genius of the man, inclusive of those instincts

---

4. [R.A.M. Stevenson, *The Art of Velasquez* (London: George Bell and Sons, 1895).]

for decoration and self expression which he inherited from his pre-decessors. His Shakespearean immensity lay in his perfect mastery of the dual nature of his art, the decorative and the representative, both, interpenetrated by his own taste for color and line on the one hand, and his own vision of his model on the other.

Let us, then, formulate new conclusions, at the sacrifice, perhaps, of favorite theories. In the first place, Impressionism can not be said to represent any one technique nor any one way of viewing nature, but, rather, all artistic achievements, whatever the method, in which sincere, spontaneous and forthright impressions are convincingly expressed through the art conceived by the brain, and the craft designed by the hand. In the second place, Impressionism is by no means solely concerned with the naturalistic portrayal of "transient aspects of contemporaneous reality." It is quite as high an art and a much more difficult one to give form and substance to one's fleeting impression of intangible beauty; to sound with Whistler a chord of color; to incarnate with Watts a powerful thought; or to perpetuate with the painters of old Japan a vanishing dream. Romance yields her impressions no less than realism. Thirdly, Impressionism is not

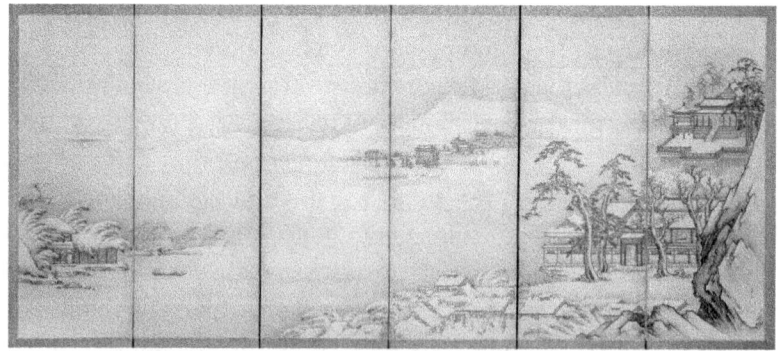

Kanō Sansetsu
The Ten Snow Incidents
Japanese Edo period, first half of the 17th century
One of a pair of six-panel folding screens; ink and light color on paper
Museum of Fine Arts, Boston

new and strange, but marvelously old. Stevenson said that to visit Velázquez at the Prado was to shatter one's faith in the modernity of modern painting. He might less cautiously and quite as accurately have stated that several centuries before this great Spaniard lived, far back in those dim ages of aesthetic dynasties at the other end of the world, there existed, in China and Japan, an art of landscape painting which contained the essence of Impressionism; that is an art in which the means of expression were harmoniously adapted to the artist's original emotion. For, after all, Impressionism is synonymous in equal measure with art itself, which is purely technical, and the artistic impulse which is, or should be, inspirational. In its only logical sense it means the giving of definite color and form to single, personal impressions. In this sense, then, have not all truly great painters been more or less Impressionists and should not the significance of the term be widened rather than restricted?

The
Enchantment of Art

As Part of the Enchantment
of Experience

Essays

By

Duncan Phillips

*With Frontispiece in Colour
And Eight Reproductions*

*New York: John Lane Company
London: John Lane, The Bodley Head
Toronto: Bell & Cockburn :: MCMXIV*

FROM **THE ENCHANTMENT OF ART**

(1914/27)

I

FIFTEEN YEARS LATER
INTRODUCING THE SECOND EDITION

AS I turn back to the essays of *The Enchantment of Art*, written from twelve to fifteen years ago, I am embarrassed by some of the premature judgments of my youth and envious of its genuine ecstasy. The book seems to me today the work of another person, and because of my curious sense of detachment I can and I must write about it with the sympathy and with the divergence of opinion which I would impose upon the confidences of a young friend. To be sure, this is a record of beauty which I myself lived through and at a most impressionable period. All the world was young for me because I was young. Art was a wonderland wherein I could expand my own experience. That charming essayist, [Edward] Sill, once wrote that the aspiration for more and ever more *life* is man's one permanent and paramount desire. "To be alive in every faculty; to have the greatest possible total of conscious being," in physical, intellectual, and emotional fervor, how and "where is there to be found a perpetual source of this power and activity" to supplement the limitations of our circumscribed existence save "in the expressed power and activity of other human spirits?—and that [of course] is art."[1] It was, at any rate, to this aspect of art that I was enthralled when I wrote my story of enchantment. Art was the more excellent world of truth and mean-

First published in *The Enchantment of Art as Part of the Enchantment of Experience: Fifteen Years Later* (Washington, D.C.: The Phillips Publications, 1927), a revised and expansed second edition of *The Enchantment of Art as Part of the Enchantment of Experience* published in 1914.

1. ["Principles of Criticism," in *The Prose of Edward Rowling Sill* (Boston: Houghton, Mifflin and Company, 1900), 145–46, quotation emended.]

[19]

ing within the outer world of facts. At the threshold of this realm of spiritual significance I stood expectant and exultant. In Italy, I wandered as under a spell which cast over my studies and appreciations the glow of a rather irresponsible but altogether delightful state of mind. This joyous mood I would gladly regain if only to compose once more with that "first, fine, careless rapture" which comes spontaneously only to those who seek adventures of the mind in the delectable country of youth. With disarming innocence I discovered for myself what was, I suppose, quite generally known. At any rate, I had to set it down, to tell of my discoveries, even as poets tell of their by no means unusual affairs of the heart. The mistakes of judgment which I made were after all no greater, considering the abandon of the outpouring, than the mistakes I make today. To be sure, I liked extravagantly a few painters and writers whom I now consider mediocre, and I did scant justice to other painters and writers who now seem to me great artists. Many of the ideas I was then eager to oppose I am now no less eager to uphold. Post-impressionism had upset my newly acquired and profoundly cherished standards of value, and I was not yet mentally prepared to make room for both subtlety and extreme simplification, for both veiled and glamorous content on the one hand and austere intellectual structure on the other. Rhythm I loved, and I practiced it in my prose, but to me it was a bounding pulse from the heart of everything, and I did not understand that it must be valued also as a logic—a mechanism, or more accurately as a functioning and instantaneous animation of parts, as the *means,* in fact, to produce the very emotions which had stirred me to the depths.

I no longer hold that "Impressionism is the function of all true pictorial art"—not even in the broad sense in which I used the term throughout this book. It seems that I was strangely agitated, fifteen years ago, because the modern French painters of atmospheric color and changing lights, of the passing show and of the passing moment, had appropriated the sobriquet as a description of their special innovation, whereas I was apparently embattled for the idea that impressionism means all potentially aesthetic sensibility and all

FROM THE ENCHANTMENT OF ART

responsiveness to creative impulse. To be more specific, I wished to
call attention to that unity of effect in the mind, or at least that rapt
focusing of attention, which the impulse of art can give to our broken, scattered, and imperfectly comprehended aesthetic thrills and
imaginings. I was right to the extent that there is not, and that there
well might be, one big word to define the elementary function that
the sensitive artist shares with the imaginative child and the wholly
sentient "man in the street" when all three encounter the experience of being suddenly transfixed with an idea or a mental picture
so that they must put it down in some enduring form before the dis-
tracting pressure of life pushes it out of their consciousness. What
I meant by impressionism is true to a greater extent of what is now
called expressionism. In other words, the urge to unburden oneself
of beauty applies less to the sensations themselves than to arbitrary
and unrepresentative concepts based on the sensations. However,
I wasted my time disputing the established monopoly of the word
Impressionist by artists who specialized in one chosen aspect of life
closely observed—who were interested in the local, the particular,
the evanescent. The revolt against all this has set in, and is now at
its zenith. To reflect an effect in nature is regarded as a question-
able practice unless one's reflection partakes of a childlike fantasy
as in Pierre Bonnard. If I had known the work of Bonnard when I
wrote *The Enchantment of Art,* I would have responded to his appeal
as to no other modern artist, for his is precisely the spirit of mingled
impressionism and expressionism—of the miracle of truth and the
romance of personal vision, which prompted me to a book in praise
of mingled conviction and enchantment. In reprinting so tentative a
work, I can only plead as an excuse the feeling I now have that I was
groping in the dark for a very important switchboard, which might
flood the consciousness of almost anyone with illumination about
the essence of art. I offer the book now, not at all as a piece of work
consistently in the realm of aesthetics (I have a book of that kind
smoldering at the back of my mind), even less as a contribution to
criticism or to art history, but as a youthful exercise in expressive
sensibility—with sensuous reactions to effects in art corresponding

to the painter's reactions to effects in nature—with a joy in finding nature in pictures analogous in kind with the painter's when he finds pictures in nature. I warn you, therefore, whosoever reads this book, not to expect much scholarly information, and technical teaching. I give you only a very personal document woven of delights and dreams into a harmonious fabric. And I hope you may find in it some heart-warming stimulation to the enjoyment of what artists have enjoyed in their first glow of imaginative conception. The emphasis is always on the source of art in life. The analysis is always of the effect on uninitiated minds rather than of the cause found in professional methods. The recreation of the artist's impulse by the impressionistic critic may be very different from what the artist himself intended but at least it is made out of the same dream-stuff and admits us into the same sanctuary of creative sensibility. Who could be exacting with a young appreciator's exuberant zest?

In spite of the fact that in these later days I plead or tolerance and the ventilation of the mind to all the winds that blow, yet I do not hesitate to republish these essays even though they are not entirely free from prejudice. To the charge of inconsistency I plead guilty, but it does not trouble my conscience. Consistency from youth to middle age is at best a stiff-necked virtue. Let me be tolerant then even of my own early intolerance, trusting that I may persist in this faith so that when I am sixty I may look back without too much confusion on what I am now writing at forty. However loosely constructed my early essays, and however weak the link between its two parts, and its commentary on two arts, yet the book somehow hangs together by reason of its imaginative and philosophical threads woven into a consistent pattern. Nor would I alter a line of the pages in which beauty and the relation of art to nature are candidly considered. They seem to me, from this middle milepost, immature yet essentially sound, and even fairly reliable as guides. And the faults of the volume proceed logically from its chief merit, its whole-hearted enthusiasm for the artistic life. With all its faults, therefore, I comply at last with the many urgent requests which have come to me for a second printing. What I have pruned away are the more conspicuous blemishes of careless thinking, ill-considered judgments, verbiage, and redundancies. In their place I have added one or two sober second thoughts, with the dates marking these revisions of opinion; also several critical papers hitherto unpublished except in magazines, including an analysis of the mind and art of George Moore, who wrote the finest literary impressionism, and an appreciation of Maurice Prendergast, which, although a comparatively recent piece of work, belongs with my essays on romantic comedy.[2] The dates which I have appended to each chapter tell the tale of a book which harvests the thoughts of a good many years. It has been my idea in this way to suggest the gradual unfolding of critical faculties. From a desire merely to communicate to others my own special and limited enjoyments I have in due time graduated to a sharpened consciousness of the need for understanding the artist's methods, and the even greater need for an open door of the mind to many different kinds of aesthetic expression.

---

2. ["The Spirit of Romantic Comedy" and "Romantic Comedy in Early Italian Painting," in Duncan Phillips, *The Enchantment of Art As Part of the Enchantment of Experience* (New York: John Lane Company, 1914), 206–41.]

II

THE IMPRESSIONISTIC POINT OF VIEW

I love all beauteous things,
I seek and adore them;
God hath no better praise,
And man in his hasty days
Is honoured for them.
I too will something make
And joy in the making;
Altho' to-morrow it seem
Like the empty words of a dream
Remembered on waking.

ROBERT BRIDGES[3]

"ART, I suppose, is all very well for those who like it," concedes the scoffing materialist, "but what is the use and what is the excuse for art criticism? What do you mean, to begin with, by the words art and beauty?"

Well, let us be humble about language and consider what we do mean by these words art and beauty. Even in the haziest of our human conceptions, art is associated with the idea of beauty, and beauty is a word we use to acknowledge those pleasures in our lives, pleasures partly sensuous, partly spiritual, which have lifted us, in a sort of ardor of appreciation, out of our self-centered habits of thought. *Beauty, then, is a special kind of pleasure or ecstasy which stirs and grows within us when, through contemplation of nature or experience with the products of life, we live more intensely outside of ourselves. But art we know is more than mere beauty in the abstract. Art implies, not necessarily the seeing of beautiful things, nor even the making of beautiful things, but the seeing or making of things beauti-fully; in other words, in a way to enlarge our experience and to sharpen and intensify our perceptions.* However, much work that is beautifully done is not art but skilled labor. The beauty that is given to a work

3. [*The Shorter Poems of Robert Bridges* (London: Geo. Bell & Sons, 1896), 67.]

of art means much more than mere creation, however successful, for a creation only becomes a work of art when it represents a genuine emotion on the part of its creator and is so conceived and so expressed as to communicate that genuine emotion to others. The craftsman turns out a beautifully made chair in accordance with a given pattern, but the thing has been done no matter with what emotion of joy, for the sake of the thing rather than for the sake of its beauty. It is a good job, but no more a work of art than the novel or play or picture that is made in the same purposeful and utilitarian way. Of course, if beauty were a fixed object that could be known and explored and described like a mountain, then we could all be artists. If there were such a thing as absolute beauty, it would be our duty to search for it until we found it so that we could apply it as a test to all and rest our minds from vague surmise and tentative theorizing. But frankly, beauty cannot be educed to any given formula, nor can it possibly be defined in words. It is not a matter of facts at all, but of concrete emotional perceptions often produced by sheer physical sensations. In dreams, we are at times conscious of a strange glamour that seems wholly unrelated to our experience, a veritable chaos of jumbled thoughts, colorful visions, forgotten images of the past, unspoken hopes and fears for the future, all in a setting that is the wildest of creative imagination. Of such personal and fantastically insubstantial dream-stuff is the mystery of life and its offspring, *the mystery of beauty, the mystery of what moves us spiritually in material things.* We can no more make all people appreciate the same beauty than we can make all people dream the same dream. Beauty is as vague and various and variable as human personality itself. *Emphatically, then, we cannot lay down laws for art, which is the human being's method for focusing and developing its perceptual sensibilities and for expressing its sense or conception of beauty, its detached and disinterested ecstasy.* But we can and should formulate rules for assisting us in the practice of the innumerable kinds of artistic expression demanded by the innumerable kinds of human mind and taste. And one truth at least is true for all people and at all periods. Art, to *be* art, must be sincere, and the expression not merely of sense, or sight, or sound, but, back of all that, the expression of the individual soul.

"But," shrilly protests the scoffer once again, "granted the artist, why the art critic?" Because the critic represents not only perception but appreciation, without which there would be no art. First of all there must be perception of that abundant beauty "in the rough," which, in our large way, we call by such names as reality and nature. The child sees beauty about him and loves it, although he does not know it for what it is. That is the stage of pure perception. Sooner or later to receptive souls appreciation comes, like a miraculous awakening to a life of new sensations. On the horizon of some lives this aesthetic radiance never dawns, and they are left in darkness, bereft of one of the richest joys of existence. To others, a mysterious power is granted to express their sense of beauty, to become artists. The majority of us are more truly artists in feeling what we cannot express, than hosts of expert craftsmen who glibly express, what they do not feel. Feeling is the soul of art. Technique is only its bodily functioning. It is, therefore, the appreciation of life which results in the expression of art, and to help us enrich our lives by the cultivation of our tastes and aesthetic faculties, that is the exalted purpose of all art criticism.

The *appreciation of life,* is not that worth while?—not life in the abstract but our *own* lives, our *own* experiences, our *own* moods and emotions. Stirred with very real reverence we are constantly exclaiming one to another—how wonderful is our world! Few are the scientist, few also the moralists, who fail to impress upon us our insignificance in the stupendous scheme of things. Of what avail are our petty strivings after this and that, our feverish desire for we scarcely know what. Every poet has urged us to come out into the night where stars that are changeless and serene preside over the mysteries of the dark. How all our vain philosophies are shamed beneath those stars! And how helpless is our knowledge and impotent our power while the storm god has his way with us and the chill wind of death blows wheresoever it wills!' Truly it is fitting that before Nature's god we should worship and bow down. But suppose that we carry this reverence to its logical conclusion. Suppose we say one to another—how wonderful we are, you and I! How wonderful that we have eyes to see the beauty of the stars, and ears to hear the terror of the storm, and souls which at the blowing of the wind of death are wafted all invisible into the dark beyond! Suppose we dwell upon our common merits as men, and our supreme fitness to inhabit and inherit the earth. Suppose, even suppose we admire our peculiar merits as individuals, the particular combination of opinions and beliefs, aspirations and passions, tricks of speech and habits of thought, which, distinguishing us for better or worse from any other mortals that ever lived, bear witness to the inscrutable miracle of personality. By all means, let us burn incense before all the shrines of nature, but in so doing remember that we are but fulfilling one of the thousand impulses of our imperious being; that we do not exist for nature, but nature for us, to give us something plastic to mold to our dream and to our desire.

The purpose of life, then, is the expression of self. In order to truly live, it is needful to freely give one's life, without pretense and without too much reserve. Doubtless the noblest expression of self is self-sacrifice. As for art, it is but one of the many channels for personal expression. Its function is to discover and celebrate beauty and truth, treasures that are supposed to abound on every highway and byway. But is it not now a truism that these treasures exist not without but within—within the seeing eye, the informing mind, and the mystical inner life of our sacred sensibilities? From the favored few consecrated to art, offerings of beauty and truth are prized by the world in proportion to the amount of personal taste with which they have expressed their sense of beauty and of personal wisdom with which they have been enabled to grasp and give forth truth. Individuality has been, and will, we believe, continue to be, the criterion for success in modern art. There is no statute book of truth, no positive definition of beauty. Both terms are relative, things of our own conception and of our own making. Unless we find in art personal testimonies and individual conceptions, beauty and truth may be stated with all copiousness and care, but to no greater effect than the repetition of the names we give to them. Unless we derive the benefit of sharing the personal vision of an exceptionally sensitive or original pair of artist-eyes, we much prefer to do without art and see the world for ourselves. And so we demand that art shall be the more or less adequately accomplished record of personal impressions. Otherwise the ablest craftsmanship that the schools can teach must be of little avail. And so we become, with reason, impatient and intolerant of painters who squander rich talent for the sake of display upon borrowed and labored themes for which they have the most tepid interest and in the production of which not a hint of their personal observation or emotion can be detected.

What is life? we ask. "Just one thing after another," says the Fool. "A series of definite and successive changes, both of structure and composition, which take place within an individual without destroying its identity," says the Wise Man. "A succession of vivid impressions," says the artist. That is what life means to him. The artist insists upon focusing his attention upon one thing at a time and everything else is a blur at that moment. As Walter Pater put it—he wishes "to define life, not in the most abstract, but in the most concrete terms possible, to find not a universal formula for it, but the formula which expresses most adequately this or that special manifestation of it."[4]

In another chapter of that remarkable book, *The Renaissance,* Pater says:

> Every moment some form grows perfect in hand or face; some tone on the hills or the sea is choicer than the rest; some mood of passion or insight or intellectual excitement is irresistibly real[...]for us—for that moment only.[...]We are all under sentence of death but with a sort of indefinite reprieve.[...]We have our interval, and then our place knows us no more. Some spend this interval in listlessness, some in high passion—the wisest, at least, among "the children of this world," in art and song[...]For art comes to you profess-

---

4. [*The Renaissance: Studies in Art and Poetry* (New York: Macmillan, 1904), ix.; quotation emended.]

ing frankly to give nothing but the highest quality to your
moments as they pass, and simply for those moments' sake.[5]

That is the best declaration I have ever seen of the motive which
governs and guides the representative arts, and as many also of the
presentative arts as either make their appeal directly to the senses
like color, music and dancing, or strive solely for such concise and
graphic effect as we find in some lyrics, prose sketches, and stories.

"Our moments as they pass"—how we waste them! The beauties
that come and go with the moments—how insensible we are to their
coming and going! Once gone they may return to us in memories,
with the intensified emotion of dreamlike things. Yet in their turn
the memories fade and the beauties are no more. Art is a means of
giving permanence to our moods and memories, of restoring to us
something at least of the original charms of a thousand sensuous
influences that have touched our lives in passing. Most of us try to
see life steadily and to see it whole. The worth of the flying moments
may or may not have impressed us. At any rate it is the serious business of life which absorbs our attention, the "eternal verities, and
some or all of the separate standards. Meanwhile the artist is standing by, watching the world as it passes, appreciating time as it flies,
as responsive to every influence and experience as a violin to the
touch of a master, striving to give his sensations and his moods emotional unity in his mind and then artistic unity in his creation—in
short, to give definite form to each separate, personal impression.
That is the impressionistic point of view.

---

5. [Ibid., 249, 251–52; quotation emended.]

III

ART FOR THE SAKE OF TRUTH—AND BEAUTY

WE cannot properly appreciate that impressionism which is the function of all true pictorial art* until we have brought an open mind to the consideration of the familiar dogma of the modern studio—"art for art's sake." Windy wars have been waged because of it. How it wearies the mind to think of all the cross-purposes and jarring contentions! Art is certainly the richer for Whistler and his influence, but it is not because he wrangled and carefully recorded his quarrels with his critics, but because he painted pictures greater than his theories. That the seed of his aesthetic doctrines should have fallen upon inhospitable soil in Victorian England is not to be wondered at. Ruskin had taught his country either to copy Nature with painstaking fidelity or to embody exalted stories and senti-ments for useful ends. Then along came Whistler asserting (1) that the artist must pick and choose his notes from the world's key-board—that "to paint Nature as she is, is to sit on the piano"; (2) that subjects are of extremely secondary importance—that a mountain is not necessarily sublime if it is painted with banal sentimentality or photographic exactitude, and that a suburban factory chimney in the evening gloom is not necessarily prosaic if seen and rendered with the eyes of the poet. In short, he insisted that a picture must exist for its own sake—that

> [I]f eyes were made for seeing,
> Then Beauty is its own excuse for being.[6]

To us, this does not seem to be a very radical or unreasonable doctrine. Yet the Victorian critics blinked and sneered and the Vic-torian public stared and giggled. In his fight for painters' principles

---

* For my present opinion of this theory, see the introductory essay [above].

6. ["The Rhodora: On Being Asked, Whence is the Flower," in Ralph Waldo Emerson, *Poems* (Boston and New York: Houghton, Mifflin and Company, 1904), 49.]

Whistler was practically unaided in England. In France, however, the battle had been waged and won. The stilted academic standards had been assailed and shaken by the concerted action of artists from Delacroix to Monet. With increasing strength their spirits rose and in angry defiance of continued clamor for the subject in pictures many men went to sensational extremes. Art for art's sake was then popularly and quite justly interpreted to mean, no art for truth's or beauty's sake, but art for the sake of technique, art for the sake of canvas covered thus and thus, for the sake of pigments so applied from the tubes, and brushes so manipulated, art for the sake of absolute values, and refraction and vibration, and broken tones, and spatial extension and a hundred other technical terms that are secrets of the few, obscure and unhallowed mysteries to the many. Artists have been fairly rioting in revolution and proclaiming a new dogma of their own in place of the discredited ones of the *ancien régime.* It is no longer art for the sake of the Church, for the sake of the Court, for the sake of Greek marbles, for the sake of the school or fireside interest in literature and history, but art for the sake of the artist, art for its own sweet sake. In effect the painter has been saying to the public—"You have made us tell stories, now you can watch us dabble in raw materials, and take our pictures to pieces to play with the parts. Our experiments will be helpful to us and bewildering to you. We have long realized that painting was falling behind the times, that we were not reflecting the life around us, that the scientific enlightenment of our age had passed us by, as if we were not concerned with psychology and invention. Now we shall make up for lost time. As for you—it will do you no harm to regard art in a new light, as no longer a subservient thing, but independent of you and your ideas, with a point of view and a dogma of its own. For centuries you have made us come to you to serve you. Now we shall see and paint what we choose and as we choose. You may take us or leave us."

So rang the challenge, and strange was the result of it. For a while people laughed at the French innovators, labeling them fantastics and barbarians, and all his life Whistler had a lively time of it with critics and a public who believed that his art like his outer life was a studied pose and an ill-natured joke. But what obscurity had never done for their more conservative predecessors in artistic progress, notoriety secured for these radicals and their teeming progeny. With that ever-familiar, ever-curious irony of Fate, the pendulum of public opinion swung from one extreme to the other, and painters awoke to find the crowd they had affected to despise, swarming to their exhibitions and teasing them, like amusement-seeking boys, to be as unconventional as they dared. Soon the house of art became a vaudeville, a work hop, a lecture room, a laboratory, all too seldom a temple for the soul. As for the notorious performers known by various names from Post-Impressionists to Dadaists, their insincerities of extravagant distortion are evidently based upon the impudent opinion that people nowadays will tolerate anything provided its novelty is proclaimed loud enough. The truth is that whereas a hundred years ago painters were tinting Greek and Roman statues, because they feared to take any liberties with the decorous, timorous public taste that frowned on innovation, to-day we are suffering from an excess of public tolerance in regard to art, an encouragement of any hitherto untried experiment, the madder the merrier. One truth has been conclusively proved. The cavalier declaration that art could do without the public was either a blunder or a bluff. Almost from the beginning painters have protested against the prevailing popular misconception of what art ought to be.

Of course, there was a time when painting was but a step removed from penance and from prayer. At work in mystic consecration upon his wooden saints and madonnas, the friar in his cell was blessedly insensible to the impieties of beauty. Browning's Pictor Ignotus[7] thrilled to know that on his frescoes there was no suggestion of grace and charm, no figment of truth to life nor resemblance to that outer world whose vanities he had renounced forever. He rejoiced

---

7. ["Pictor Ignotus," in *Poems of Robert Browning*, edited by Charlotte Porter and Helen A. Clarke (New York: Thomas Y. Crowell & Company Publishers, 1896), 123.]

that although he might have won favor and fortune out in the shrill sunshine, his painted confession of faith would molder and fade away on chill monastic walls. But all this was before the Pagan spirit of art was born again. Soon enough a strange joy came to the friar at his work. Voices and scents were borne to him on the restless winds seeming to call him to that outer world. Browning pictured him in this mood, his [Fra] Lippo Lippi[8] hungry for life and love. We may see how this human passion passed into his altar-paintings in protest. The devotional piety of the Flemish and Italian Primitives was in many cases genuine and charming. But even in such a devout spirit as Memling, what I prize most is the lively enameled color and the little blue-and-brown peeps of tapestry landscape that the painter shyly introduced as background to indulge himself in a clash of self-expression. Giorgione was the first to completely break away from ecclesiastical domination, and it was he who originated genre and the idyllic sentiment for pure landscape. But few were the men who dared to do more than protest against the prevailing fashions as Watteau protested against the frivolity which he was forced to paint for a frivolous age. The really great artists who declared war against the teaching of the schools and the taste of the buyers were all but submerged in consequence. Witness the poverty of Rembrandt, of Millet, of Sisley. But today extremists reap the benefit of their epoch-making courage, and now that eccentricity is at a premium where in their day formula was law, the wildest ventures are more profit-able than was their noble moderation. Of course, the public does not change from age to age as much as these changes in artistic fashion would seem to indicate. The trouble is that there has always existed, through all the changes of thought and taste, throughout periods of slavery, prosperity and obscurity for the artist, the same total igno-rance of the conditions that govern and limit pictorial expression. Art cannot exist without some appreciative understanding. If left to himself, the painter goes to one extreme, the public to the other, and great is the confusion. Whistler then to the contrary—I hold that

---

8. ["Fra Lippo Lippi," in *Poems of Robert Browning,* 124.]

the critic of art who can appreciate both points of view, and act as mediator between them, performs an indispensable function. He it is who must see to it that the artist is fair to the world and that the world is fair to the artist.

But before either of these desirable results can be secured, the artist and the world must be equally well acquainted with the various channels of artistic expression, their individual capacities and limitations. They must know that painting cannot tell a story, that it can only represent a moment's situation. They must know that it may deal with thought or emotion, but only in so far as these things may be comprehended in the color and form through the direct agency of the uninstructed and unaided sense of sight. The defenders of the story-telling picture make much of the fact that Rembrandt depicted incidents from the Bible. But can they point to a single canvas in which documentary evidence of a scriptural or archaeological character has distracted the eye from the essential unity of aesthetic and emotional impression? At The Hague Gallery, David plays his harp before Saul. Although we may not hear the music, our sight comprehends at a glance the effect which the harpist is producing upon the mind of the King. Meanwhile, our eyes are feasting upon the dazzling iridescence of Saul's turban, its mingled tones of copper and bronze, scarlet and green and gold, and as we gaze a spell of sensuous witchery stirs us, like the spell of some soul-disturbing rhapsody of sound. As in all great subjective paintings, the title has been only a pretext. We have beheld the glamour and shared the passion of one of Rembrandt's passing moods. Then again consider the little *Supper at Emmaus* in the Louvre. The face of Christ oppresses us with a sense of sharp, familiar suffering and at the same time uplifts our hearts to a vision of Divine inspiration and spiritual perfection. We do not need to note the awe and worship of the disciples at this sudden revelation of their dead and risen Master, for do we not share their emotion; are we not also in the radiant presence of that incarnate goodness that lifts the burdens of the world? This is not merely Christ as He appeared at Emmaus, this is the Savior as the afflicted and inspired Rembrandt conceived Him for his own consolation, and as we in our sorrows would think of Him to the end of time. This is not a story nor yet an incident from a story. It is a vision and a strong, sweet thought. How wonderful it is that simple technical skill achieved this miracle of spiritual expression. The technique is invisible in the subject and the subject one with the sentiment. Such is pictorial art at its highest and best.

To the familiar dogma of our present epoch that the worth of a painting can only be estimated by its technical merits, regardless of

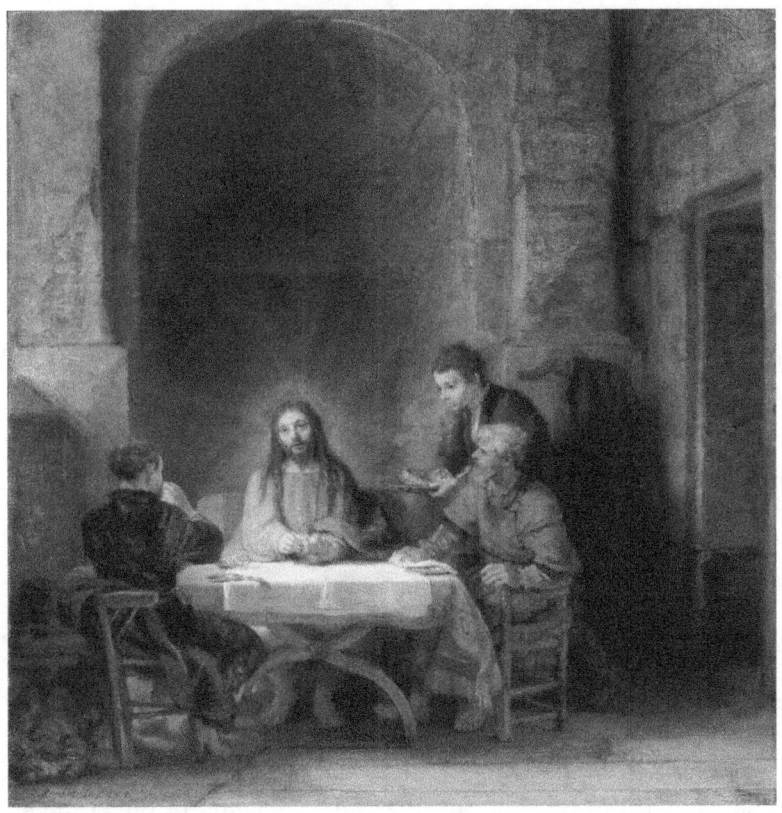

Rembrandt Harmenszoon van Rijn
The Supper at Emmaus, 1648
Oil on mahogany
Musée du Louvre, Paris

subject matter, Rembrandt's *Supper at Emmaus* is sufficient refutation. It reveals absolutely no technical feature which would give it any great éclat, not even this painter's usual dramatization of light. Its supreme mastery is evidenced rather in the amazing inspiration that brushed in that Divine face. It may be said that the picture is great because of the art that produced it, but how much less great that art would have been if the painter had not been inspired by a great subject. Unquestionably, a copper stew-pan by Chardin, true to life yet transfigured by his magical paint, is a nobler work of art than a head of Christ crowned with thorns in the cheap and perfumed style of Guido Reni. On the other hand, the unpretentious observations of copper stew-pans do not make for the very greatest art. The humility of such conceptions is in striking contrast to the philosophy of art as practiced and preached by the great stern symbolist G. F. Watts. By means of pictorial symbols, he sought to embody the inexorable mysteries of life and death, to reduce Creation to its primordial elements and to teach and preach the brave old moralities with that unself-conscious seriousness so characteristic of the Victorian epoch. Watts was born in the belief that art should be brought to the service of life, that art for art's sake is no better than ritual for ritual's sake. "The idea of following art through everything for itself alone," writes Gilbert Chesterton in his brilliant book on Watts, "through extravagance, through cruelty, through morbidity, is exactly as superstitious as the idea of following theology for itself alone through extravagance and cruelty and morbidity...The young critics of the [aesthetic school], with their nuances and technical mysteries, would doubtless be surprised to learn that as a class they resemble ecstatic nuns, but their principle is, in reality, the same."[9] Watts was one of those universalists who thought that just as the ecstatic isolation of the religious sense had done incalculable harm to religion, so the ecstatic isolation of the aesthetic sense would do incalculable harm to art. It was his firm intention, therefore, to present great natural truths and great moral ideas and

9. [G. K. Chesterton, *G. F. Watts* (New York: E.P. Dutton & Co., 1904), 22.]

it so chanced that to express these things he selected for his medium a pictorial symbolism of color and form. So perfectly did his symbols illuminate and exalt his noble though unoriginal ideas that they served his purpose in putting new vitality into venerable thoughts. His educational purpose was accomplished through the happy accident of a fairly original pictorial genius. There was a sublime unity to his conceptions, a unity into which vague, allegorical or topical allusions seldom intruded, a unity so clear that the world of abstract thought seemed to spring unlabored into shape and color beneath his brush. Pictures have no business dealing with symbols unless they can present them without the slightest infraction of the laws of pictorial unity. Furthermore, they must improve upon language as a means of conveying thought, else they are worse than useless. In some of Watts's pictures the colors are harsh and in others the meaning seems imprisoned rather than liberated by the design. As a rule, however, he was successful, notably in his deeply symbolical portraits of men and in such concepts as the picture entitled "Hope." How beneficently then an unsuspected power within an artist supplements and ennobles his limited intentions! Whistler proposed no more for himself than a decorative tracery of lines, an atmospheric valuation of tones, and a harmonious modulation of colors. In spite of his railing against subjects and sentiments, however, it is subject and sentiment rather than any aesthetic "note" that will cause his Nocturnes to endure, and in the best of his portraits he owed much of his success to the inspiration of his models. And so it was with Watts, whose art was conceived for the general good, but whose pictures are more likely to appeal to such critics of the subtler phases of beauty as can appreciate with what unique pictorial intuition and skill he gave original color and form to unoriginal abstractions.

It is quite true that the art of painting deals by preference with the concrete rather than the abstract, with the evidence of things seen rather than with any intangible fabric of thought. Watts, however, demonstrated that thought may be given a deeper and more intense life through concrete form and color than is the life of thoughts which, although forming and coloring the mind, have never found pictorial symbols identical with themselves. Now, even as Watts disregarded the rule that painting should avoid the abstract, so Rodin has been demolishing our traditional conception of sculpture as an art steeped in convention and remote from the life around us, a Greek or Egyptian world of embodied ideals and abstractions. That sculpture should be concrete and individual in character was a principle persistently accepted by the Gothic craftsman in his gargoyles and statued saints. What the Italian Renaissance then accomplished was to make sculpture pictorial and expressive of personal conceptions. It remained for Rodin to apply impressionism as well as imagination to the plastic depiction of life. Influenced by Dante and Donatello, he tries to reveal subtleties of sense and emotion, to give shape not to life's epic oneness, but rather to its dramatic manysidedness. Most sculpture is abstract and static, Rodin's is concrete and dynamic. Put his *Penseur* by the side of a marble Faun of ancient Greece and behold the difference between the virile animal body of Man, shaken with passion and aspiring purpose, and the serenely exquisite body of the old myth-maker's dream. Sculptors, following the archaic standards, convert life into structural, monumental art. Rodin converts the raw materials of his craft into a new creation, a re-shaping of his hired models so that they live again as in the flesh—quivering to the touch of love or under the lash of fear. Man is shown in his ugliness and splendid strength, his power and his pity; Woman, in her tenderness and irresistible grace, her yielding and withholding. And in leaving his creations unsevered from the mass of marble or bronze, he suggests the organic union of life and art, life that is the root of art, art that is the flower of life. All art is symbolical, since art can only appeal to the intelligence through signs representing a thought or a thing. But what a difference may exist between two symbols, both indispensable in their own way; for instance, between a peach imitated from life by Chardin and "The Mystery of Existence"[10] shaped in bronze by Saint-Gaudens. The

10. [*Adams Memorial*, 1886–91. Rock Creek Church Cemetery, Washington, D.C.]

mystery of existence in bronze, how vast the daring of it! You may see this nameless creation in a suburban cemetery near the city of Washington. A draped figure sits erect at the side of the tomb. The body is rigid yet under firm control. Only the face is bared and the lean, strong arm which supports it. The features also are fixed and the unseeing eyes gaze into infinity. This is neither Man nor Woman, for it is both. This is something sexless—universal—inscrutable. A figure of Grief one might divine, but grief seldom is so passionless. The eyes have the rigidity of eyes that can no longer weep, of a soul from which even hope has long since fled. Is this then "Despair"? Some have suggested "Nirvana," the oblivion for which the Oriental yearns. But the artist who made this thing would never give his symbol a definite title. Once only he is quoted as remarking, "What did I mean to express? Oh, I suppose, the mystery of the whole affair." One thinks of Shakespeare, of the significant lines—

> We are such stuff
> As dreams are made on; and our little life
> Is rounded with a sleep.[11]

To those, then, who claim that the pictorial and plastic arts are incapable of properly expressing thought and emotion, and should confine their efforts to the production of visual effects, aesthetic or scientific, there is only one answer. The painter has just as much right to describe his thoughts through color and form as the writer to describe his observations through language. The only rule that each must observe is—"To your own art be true." When the writer is attempting a landscape or a portrait he must keep his readers mindful that his pictures are only painted with words, literary suggestions of pictures, and when the painter is trying to express his thoughts, he must give them each a visual unity of conception so that, intent only on the colors and forms, we may look not for literary ideas but for the pictorial suggestions of ideas. Emphatically paintings can and should deal with the mind and the emotions, provided they act through the direct agency of the eyes. And so, if we are informed that

---

11. [*The Tempest*, Act 4, Scene 8.]

the subjects of pictures do not matter, let us merely point to Rembrandt's *Supper at Emmaus* and inquire wherein lies the greatness of this little canvas save in the inspiration the artist derived from his subject. And if they tell us that painting cannot embody thought, nor sculpture draw thought from substance, let us lead them to Watts and to Rodin and allow these giants to speak for themselves. Finally, if in turn we wish to demonstrate that the true artists among the advocates of art for art's sake do not mean all that they say nor practice all that they preach, we need to go no farther for an illustration than Whistler's portrait of his Mother. This is primarily a very personal, a very beautiful tribute to motherhood. Yet it is at the same time a decorative design of originality and charm. And here we may know the reason why Whistler is a greater painter than Watts. He was always true to his art, always decorative. For, in the last analysis, although painting may incidentally be useful, instructive, entertaining, edifying, or the reverse of these things, its original and fundamental function is not intellectual but aesthetic, not to criticize life but to decorate it, *"not merely to convince but to enchant."*[12] It may imitate a peach or express the sympathy of Christ, but in either case its highest purpose is to create a thing of beauty that shall be to us a joy forever. Life indeed contains all that we need of beauty, the constituents of all color, the materials of all form. But alas, while a wonderful accident of light is for a moment transforming our earth into a realm of enchantment, we are thinking of the price of a certain commodity in a certain market, or of what we said last week and wish we had not said. And verily we have eyes and see not and the beauty of the moment passes as if for us it had never been. But the true artist and the genuine lover of art, the creator who finds pictures in Nature, and the critic who finds Nature in pictures, they have eyes if they have nothing else. They may be without the price of a meal ticket, but they possess the sense of beauty, and as long as

12. ["And this is the particular crown and triumph of the artist—not to be true merely, but to be lovable; not simply to convince, but to enchant." "A Gossip on a Novel of Dumas's," in Robert Louis Stevenson, *Memories and Portraits* (New York: Charles Scribner's Sons, 1911), 227.]

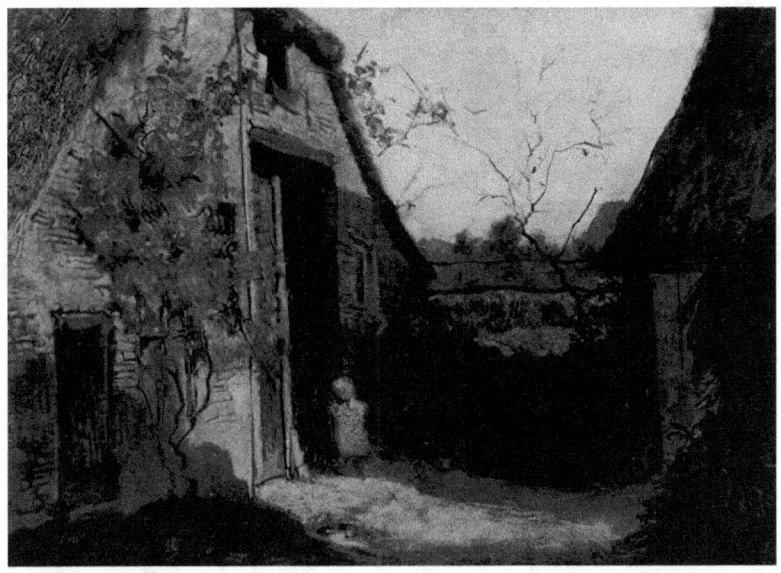

Matthijs Maris
Landscape with Barns, c. 1860
Oil on paper
Kunstmuseum Den Haag

they nourish and cherish such a living joy in their hearts, life may be
tragic or sordid, but never uninteresting. The ascent of the mountain
of endeavor may seem to them a particularly steep and arduous pilgrimage, but they will never be blind to the beauties on the way, they
will always find time to draw deep breaths of tonic air and enjoy the
view. And whether or not they scale the mountain to its cloudy pinnacle, as long as they breathe the air that is made of dreams there is
nothing so real but shall have a fascination, and nothing so strange
but imagination can make it real. And the creators who see beauty
and feel it, and then through a mystical wizardry of their own, record
it with a new glamour which, but for them, we should never have
known, they are the harps played over by the winds of all experience.
The influence of great art upon receptive spirits is as great as any
influence on earth. Great art passes into our consciousness, there

to abide. We may no longer see the morning sunlight stream across a space of bare white wall or fall upon a piece of deep blue velvet without thinking how Vermeer could quicken the pulse of aesthetic pleasure with his transcripts of just such simple things. We may no longer feel the spell of woodland twilight when the dew silvers the tremulous dim leaves, and the apricot glow of dawning or departing day flushes the far horizons, without summoning the joyous spirit of Corot and entering once more that spirit-land from which it is such an effort to awake. I remember a little picture in Amsterdam, by that unique painter, Matthijs Maris, which stirred me strangely when I saw it, and which haunts me yet. It was a subtle effect of atmosphere, a village street in partial shadow, its quaint gray houses dark against a sky all flooded with white light. Somewhere I had seen just such an effect. Suddenly a lost moment was restored to me and recorded on canvas, a rare, rich moment of unusual perception selected from ten thousand by a man who knew how to see, by an artist who could give his vision permanence. That is pictorial art in its essential relation to life; art for the sake of nothing save only Beauty, and for the sake of that incomparable joy with which Beauty thrills the soul.

CHARDIN

(1916)

IT is the paradox of Chardin which puzzles us in attempting to estimate the importance of his achievement. All those who understand the qualities of supremely good painting invariably become noticeably exhilarated over the mere surface of a little masterpiece by this most subtle of "Little Masters." Of course, as also with Vermeer—it really isn't little work at all. It is big, bold painting by a knowing brush which left enduring beauties where it passed. And there is big human feeling in it, too, expended (more's the pity if you will) upon a kitchen kettle or the corner of a sideboard. And the color! Fresher, finer color the world has never known. In the Louvre—Salle La Caze—the Chardins fascinate. From the sensual, sentimental, fashionable attractions of Greuze, Boucher, Nattier, and the rest, one must return again and again to the mellow warmth of Chardin's peaches and the lustrous coldness of his grapes to the depths of ruby wine in his old dusty bottle, and to the tender blue of his house keeper's apron, to the rich brown of his kitchen tiles and the fiery gleam of his copper cauldron, more than anything else to the wonderful way the colors play together, catching each other's influence, all in the harmony of daylight so diffused as to mingle the various subtleties of tone. And yet—there is good reason to check our enthusiasm and consider the man's limitations before we have exalted him to the highest rank. There remains a disturbing paradox about Chardin. Very curiously his choice of subjects reveals him as both the most humble and timid and as the most proud and independent of painters. The French people have a word for the domestic routine which Chardin so persistently represented. When they speak of an "interior" they refer, not merely to the inside of a house but to the intimacy of a household. All his life Chardin was content to paint the *intérieur* of the *bourgeoisie,* the daily round of small concerns

First published in *The American Magazine of Art* 7, no. 5 (March 1916).

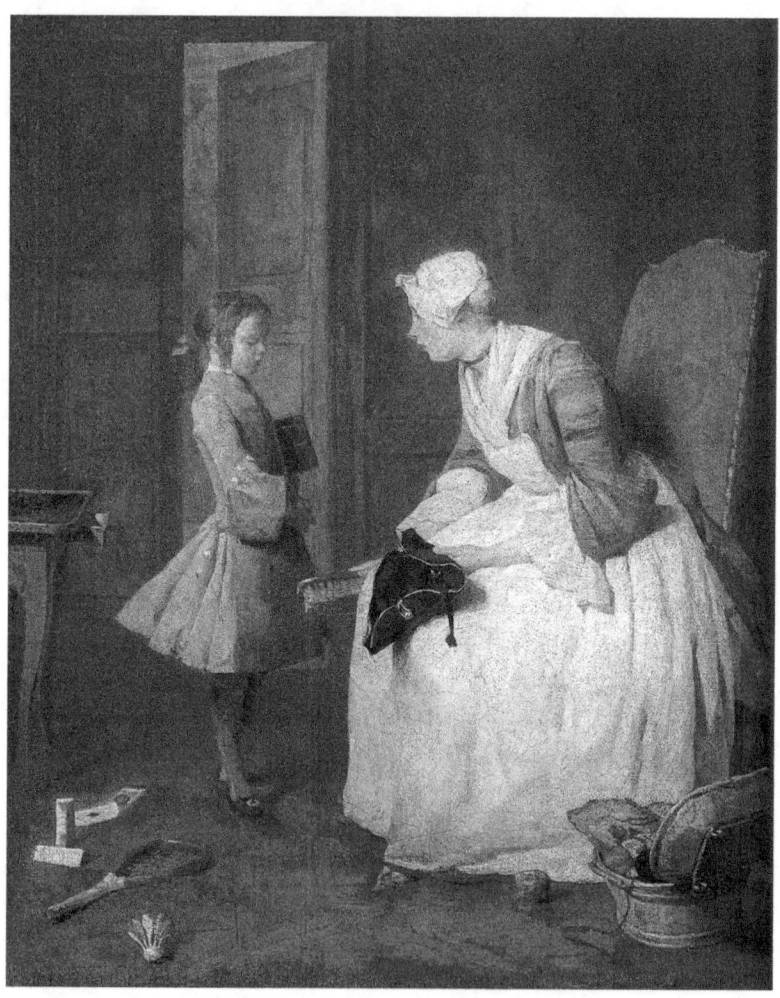

Jean-Baptiste-Siméon Chardin
The Governess, 1738
Oil on canvas
National Gallery of Canada, Ottawa

which make up the uneventful existence of the middle class house-keeper. The so delightfully this artist's delight, was spontaneously affectionate and in rendering the appearance walls and furniture. His empty whether they are neat or in disorder, immediately suggestive of the have just gone out and will soon Particularly we suspect Chardin passion for the pantry. To appreciate amiable weakness one needs only adventurous explorations of childhood into the risky region of appetizing odors. I cannot be convinced that Chardin only cared for Still Life because of its paintable surfaces and textures. For all his sure sense of the beauty of truth, citizen Chardin was no aesthete—"the world well lost" sake of arbitrary "arrangements." Had he been a seeker after effects of abstract beauty he would no doubt have followed Watteau's example and willingly furnished the world of fashion with flattering fantasies upon its palace gardens and gowns of rare brocade. Instead, we suppose that he associated imagination in art with the prevailing snobbery and artificiality of court life, against the standards of which, in his own unassuming way, he rebelled. Call him what you wished—he preferred to stay at home. Quite frankly there was all the beauty he needed—right there. *Voilà tout!* He liked to paint what he pleased, and as he pleased, taking as long to do it as ever he chose. He liked to watch the small children on his street, so quaintly well behaved and yet so much absorbed in their own devices for killing time. He liked to amuse the good woman, his neighbor, by occasional raids upon her larder. What *Nature morte* could he carry off this morning? A basket of peaches? No? He could have a few eggs and a slice of fried ham from last night's supper. *Bon!* that would do for his picture.

So easily satisfied for a subject! Surely it argues a lack of courage no less than a lack of imagination in the good man. But does it? Consider the aesthetic traditions and standards of the age and the city in which he lived, and had to make a living. Did he supply a demand? Not he. He knew himself and he knew that lots of other people were like him. He depended upon eventually creating a demand for the sort of thing he could do. The patricians were enslaving the artists, compelling them to refine upon their refinements, to celebrate their celebrity, to idealize their amours. Because one had to make a living, the artists made the best of their lot by painting just as well as the bad taste of their patrons permitted. After all there was so much that was picturesque and even personal about the Ovidian allegories and the Romanesque fantasies which were the fashion in pictures that their servitude was not as galling as it might have been. But Chardin apparently disliked caprice and realized his lack of imagination. He was not the kind of man who rebels conspicuously against authority or invents anything new and startling. He was not a rebel. He was a philosopher. He knew what he could do and what he couldn't—or wouldn't, it was the same thing. His young wife died four years after their marriage and left him alone with their child of three. His own wants—so simple, and his family—so small—was there any need to make money at the expense of one's sincerity? For him there was no use painting unless things were made to look natural. He would paint for his own class of people, scenes familiar to his life and theirs. Engravings could be made from them and sold cheap to everybody. People would be less satisfied if they could see beauty as he saw it, all around them, as the Dutch people had learned to see it from their painters. For always there was the Dutch tradition back of Chardin. In our admiration for his courage and independence we must remember that if it had not been for the precedent established by the genius Vermeer, Maes, and Pieter de Hooch, he might never have undertaken to paint at all.

And yet what really splendid courage it did require to be a Chardin, in spite of all that was going on in Paris!—to be an artist and yet to renounce the dramatic world that survived Louis Quatorze, the gorgeous pageantry, the historic backgrounds, the mythical disguises, the portentous significance of poverty being neglected to spare the pride of pomp: to renounce all this for the look of little shadowy rooms where the light came in so softly, where everything happened from day to day just as everything had happened long before these children of the painter's brush were born, one day exactly like its neighbors, familiar ways settling soon into habits. And so—quite unintentionally—the courage of the man's point of view changes our conception of his homely prose. It seems somehow poetic. The fruit heaped up for dessert in that bowl of flowered china becomes a symbol of the meals at home, and the young housekeeper[1] just back from market with a leg of mutton and a crisp brown loaf, she, too, becomes a symbol of the wholesome beauty that was his portion any day. And then there was the little boy blowing his soap bubbles,[2] building his card castles,[3] pouting because the governess reproved him for no longer playing with his toys. The good Père Chardin was never bored, like the little boy in the picture in Vienna.[4] He had a pair of wise and wonderful eyes with which he could see, in the loveliness of daylight and its diffusion, a certain delicacy and refinement even in the look of common things. Lacking in imagination and in invention he was richly endowed with a genius for painting and with something very much like a genius for philosophy, As Brownell has written, "There can rarely have been such an instance as he affords of an artist's selecting from his environment just those things his own genius needed, and rejecting just what would have hampered him or distracted him."[5] Painters shall always have much to learn from Chardin.

—*∿∿*—

1. [*The Return from the Market*, 1738, National Gallery of Canada, Ottawa]

2. [*Soap Bubbles*, c. 1735–40, National Gallery of Art, Washington, D.C.]

3. [*The House of Cards*, c. 1737, National Gallery of Art, Washington, D.C.]

4. [*The Governess*, 1738, National Gallery of Canada, Ottawa (formerly in the Liechtenstein Collection, Vienna)]

5. [W.C. Brownell, *French Art: Classic and Contemporary Painting and Sculpture* (New York: Charles Scribner's Sons, 1892), 38, quotation emended.]

ALBERT RYDER

(1916)

RYDER is unique among the painters. In the history of his own art there is no chapter in which be seems to belong. Although at first impression his figures look a bit child-ish and his vision appears to have the naive directness of a child, he is not a Primitive for be is too mature in his synthesis of effects and too incurious about the actual world in all its bewilderment of detail. What he loves best to paint are his visions of romantic beauty, the *Flying Dutchman,* the Forest of Arden, St. Agnes's Eve, the Rhine Maidens. An Oriental Encampment. His conceptions are intimately personal and his effects suggestive less of Nature than of other arts. As we study Ryder, we realize that his directness is a quality for plas-tic design, in spite of its apparent simplicity, is a pattern carefully wrought out of carefully made texture to convey a subtle emotion to the mind. If he is not a Primitive, he is even less the type we asso-ciate with the security of the so-called Masters, old and new, the great men whose art is a language for the many, and therefore suave and sound and sane. There is a spiritual loneliness in the work of Ryder and that slight divergence from the normal consequent upon an absolute indifference to the world's opinion. This quality is what also separates him from the rebels of art. Of course, it is easy to see how glad the Modernists would be to claim him, pointing out his independence from all tradition and pictorial formula, his intense inwardness, his simplification, his abstract expression of mass through color. All this is unquestionable and I believe that without any bluster of self-advertising this great man has done what all the little revolutionists keep pretending that they are preparing to do. Ryder has always despised publicity, has had no theory to advance and no desire to start a revolution. His self-sufficiency and devotion to his inward vision do not constitute him a Futurist, nor indeed a

First published in *The American Magazine of Art* 7, no. 10 (August 1916).

representative of any group or school. Fundamentally, he is much farther removed from these so-called Futurists and their propaganda than from the genuine Primitives and the established Masters. If we were compelled to put him in a pigeonhole it would be with the romantic painters DeCamp, Monticelli, Matthijs Maris, and George Fuller, and with the greatest of the English romantic poets, Thomas Coleridge. What Coleridge achieved in words, Ryder has crystallized in pigments.

We are inclined nowadays to lament the fact that Ryder has given his pictures literary titles, thus making them tribute-bearing illustrations of standard poetry instead of epoch-making creations of original painting. Personally, I like the titles, because they are characteristic of the man. No stories are told in these little pictures. They are not elaborations of a poet's theme, but simplified recreations of

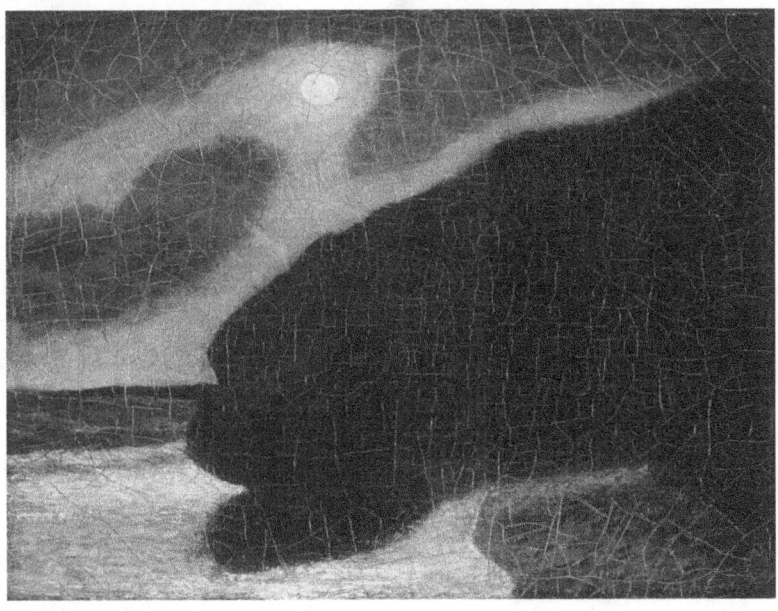

Albert Pinkham Ryder
Moonlit Cove, 1880s
Oil on canvas
The Phillips Collection, Washington, D.C. Acquired in 1924

his dream in a different medium. Ryder is himself a poet and be sees no reason why poetry should not furnish the inspiration for painting, even as painting has so often illumined the torch of poetry. Being both a poet and a painter, he knows how closely related are the dreams of mind and eye. He knows that the emotional mood of poetry can be the very soul of painting and that the decorative charm of painting is often the true purpose of poetry. If he is inspired to express in his own art the emotion with which the "Rime of the Ancient Mariner" has excited him, isn't this emotion apt to be quite as personal and rather more poignant than the emotion Cézanne experienced in the presence of a potato, or contemplating a bouquet of paper flowers? Ryder's literary titles simply show that he is well aware that if his art is incapable of adding new beauty and distinction to an old theme, whether selected from Nature or from another art, then it must be a very inexpressive language and certainly incapable of making its way in the world alone. Now Ryder's art is not dependent upon literature. He has painted barnyards with chickens, and stables with horses standing in their stalls, and I remember one very engaging picture of a wee dead bird. When his aesthetic themes were selected (childlike) in the stable, they received the same inspired distinction of style which he conferred upon his lyric dreams. The domestic and pastoral subjects are curiously attractive in the hands of Ryder. We did not know that the silhouette of a horseman against the afterglow could in itself suggest a thrilling adventure, that a hay-loft could be a thing of sensuous beauty, and a rooster a personage of romance, and that an evening light over a familiar cow-pasture could evoke a thought of curfew in Old England. And yet of course the painter's favorite dream is more compelling to the imagination, with its lonely voyager floating on a silver sea "beneath the cold glare of the desolate moon." Ryder dreamed this dream so often that it became a part of his inner life, and the acme of his inspiration.

There are two lines in the "Ancient Mariner," which might well have inspired the complete art of Albert Ryder:

> Alone, alone, all, all alone
> Alone on a wide wide Sea.[1]

The two lines contain only four words, which seem to occur involuntarily and inevitably; only four words, and yet so intensely effective is their combination, their spacing, their repetition, that the tragic meaning is flashed like an apparition before the mind, and we receive such a shock as we would feel upon hearing an outcry of panic in the night. These lines seem to me to contain not only the passion, but the aesthetic principle of Coleridge, Poe, and Ryder; their simplification of style for the realization of supernatural subjects, purposing in the words of Coleridge to create "a semblance of truth sufficient to procure for these shadows of imagination that willing suspension of disbelief."[2] This is easier to perform in prose than in verse and in pictorial drama it is easiest of all. Here then is the justification for Ryder's transposition of Coleridge's theme into his own art. The very colors described in the "Ancient Mariner" are the colors of Ryder's palette:

> About, about, in reel and rout
> The Death-fires danc'd at night;
> The water like a witch's oils,
> Burnt green and blue and white.[3]

Also, there is in this greatest of all ballads the possible origin of Ryder's gorgeous dream of the night sky:

> The thick, black cloud was cleft and still
> The Moon was at its side.[4]

And the very weight of Ryder's pigments, enameled tone laid over enameled tone, producing at last a wonderful, somber richness, even this unprecedented technique may have been suggested by the lines:

---

1. [Samuel Taylor Coleridge, "The Rime of the Ancient Mariner," in *The Ancient Mariner*, edited by Andrew J. George (Boston: D.C. Heath & Co., 1897), 12; quotation emended.]

2. [Samuel Taylor Coleridge, *Biographia Literaria*, edited by J. Shawcross, vol. 2 (Oxford: Clarendon Press, 1907), 6; quotation emended.]

3. [Coleridge, "The Rime of the Ancient Mariner," 7; quotation emended.]

4. [Ibid., 14; quotation emended.]

> For the sky and the sea, and the sea
>   and the sky
> Lay like a load on my weary eye.[5]

However intoxicating the delight of the color, however intense the joy or terror of the vision, it is always with the "weary eye" of the dreamer that Ryder approached his inspiration.

But although I seem to find in Coleridge a precursor of Ryder I am not sure that the painter is not, at least, the more consistent artist. "The Ancient Mariner" is a perfect achievement, a marvel of long-sustained inspiration. In every other poem by Coleridge, however, there is a surfeit of ornament, a wordiness which corresponds in painting to the preciosity of excessive indulgence in color or line. With Ryder, the color scheme is always a single chord of music and the color masses are composed in such a way that their outlines of dark against light and light against dark make the music of the picture, color and mass, and light functioning together, and all giving a sense of dramatic intensity. *Moonlit Cove* is one of the world's great romantic pictures—high tide and the glare of the moon. Something is soon to happen in this black corner of the coast. We *know* this, although we only find, dimly, in the shadow of a great rock, an empty deep-bottomed boat which casts its own shadow across the glistening, seething surf. The shape of the boat, the blackness of the shadow behind it, suggest a luxury of danger. And the man in the moon stares curiously down from among fantastic clouds.

In every picture there is some magic of rhythmic arabesque, some strangely solid mystery of color, some thrilling whisper to the imagination. We think by turns of dramatic folksongs, of Kōrin's designs in lacquer, of the tone poems of Coleridge, Keats, and Poe, of Wagner's operas of the Northland, first and last of music. And this subtle blend of enchantments constitutes the unique quality of the art of Albert Ryder, an art of imagination all compact and of romantic emotion in its most secret mood.

—⁓—

---

5. [Ibid., 11.]

FALLACIES OF THE NEW DOGMATISM IN ART
(1917)

I

AT this thrilling hour in our history as a nation when, in his luminous language, our President has called us all to patriotic service, it is difficult for us to concentrate our thoughts on matters merely aesthetic. Even those of us who, in days of peace, keep art uppermost in our minds, are uncomfortably aware that at a time when we are called upon to do our share "to make the world safe for democracy," art seems to be a comparatively unimportant topic for discussion. However, this is a natural reaction against the luxury of aesthetic pleasure—a part of the big, vague emotion which makes us all restive and absent-minded in any work or thought unrelated to the great war. We should not allow such a mood to throw us out of balance. Art is not as much unrelated to the present war as we might suppose. To study history—ancient, modern, or contemporary—in the searching light of art is to see into the souls of civilizations. If a nation enjoys depictions of cruelty and all kinds of violence and vice, there must be something organically wrong undermining that country. Of course, there are depraved minds at work in every virile nation, but they are powerless to poison a national state of mind which holds them in contempt. When we learn that Franz Stuck, whose pictures celebrate brute force and primitive passion, far from being discredited in his own country is regarded as a representative Prussian painter high in favor at Court, we seem to see the cause of the present war explained in terms of art. We all know how the silken seductive sensuousness of the arts of Louis Quinze

---

A paper read at the Eighth Annual Convention of the American Federation of Arts, Washington, D.C., May 16–18, 1917. First published in two parts in *The American Magazine of Art* 9, no. 2 (December 1917) and no. 3 (January 1918).

explain the French Revolution and how the proud unfeeling Neo-Roman arts of the Consulate and the Empire express the vanities of Bonaparte and the Neo-Roman wars of Napoleon. Art has been described as "a sensitive barometer of a nation's spirit." It may be more definite, in its exact indication of a nation's corruption or idealism. Since our contemporary civilization, as it was before the war, will be judged some day from symbols and symptoms discovered in contemporary art, it is a very sensible thing to do, in the stern seriousness of war time, to reflect upon the permanency of values in the works our artists are creating. It will also enable us to see ourselves as future historians will see us.

As a matter of fact, American art at its very best, in the work of such as J. Alden Weir, is something of which we can be unreservedly proud. The contemporary world boasts nothing finer or nobler than the art and life of Mr. Weir, and there are many other American painters secure of enduring fame. And yet I shudder to think how the mind of the United States might be misjudged by a visitor to the show of pictures and sculpture recently exposed at the Grand Central Palace in New York.[1] It stunned me to realize that at a time like this Americans have been committing these nuisances, creating these images both grotesque and indecent, mixed up on the walls with many other pictures merely pretty and stupid and shop-worn. As I hurried up and down the aisles of that vast place trying to find my way out of that maze of madness like a dreamer imprisoned in a chamber of horrors, I kept repeating, and I must have said it out aloud, "War is a good cleanser. We need war."

For if war is itself a madness it is also a cure for madness. In the humility of service and in the fires of self-sacrifice, cynics will often repudiate their disillusionment and acknowledge that mockery is a mean business, that sham is a damned disgrace, and that, judging from queer feelings in the heart, God's in his Heaven

1. [The Society of Independent Artists' first annual exhibition took place in 1917 at the Grand Central Palace in New York City. The Society was formed the previous year to give artists of any backgrounds or level of professional success opportunities to show their works.]

even when there is Hell on earth. Self-indulgent dilettantes rejoice at this moment to show their courage and give voice to exultation. In the present war there is the case of the young American poet, Alan Seeger, who at Belloy-en-Santerre kept his rendezvous with death.[2] A finer poet, Rupert Brooke, seemed to enjoy the war's liberation of his own idealism which he had hitherto concealed in true British fashion.

> Now, God be thanked Who has matched us with His hour
>   And caught our youth, and wakened us from sleeping,
> With hand made sure, clear eye, and sharpened power,
>   To turn, as swimmers into cleanness leaping.[3]
>
> Blow, bugles, blow! They brought us, for our dearth,
>   Holiness lacked so long, and Love and Pain.
> Honour has come back, as a king, to earth,
>   And paid his subjects with a royal wage;
> And Nobleness walks in our ways again;
>   And we have come into our heritage.[4]

The two ideas of glad release from self and purification through self-sacrifice recur in the imaginative writings of all those who have faced death in battle. And so we find that although art reveal, the symptoms of the social and political maladies which make men kill each other, it also reveals the personal chivalry and courage and the poignant sense of pity and even affection kindled among fighting men. When the sufferings of war have in their inscrutable way ennobled what remains of humanity, art is sure to appear more human, more humane, more inspiring, above all more sincere and contemptuous of sham. Art may be at a standstill in Europe today, in this country tomorrow. Yet for the arts everywhere there is a good time coming.

---

2. [The American poet Alan Seeger died on the battlefield on July 4th, 1916. His poem "I Have a Rendezvous with Death" is included in *A Treasury of War Poetry: British and American Poems of the World War, 1914–1917*, edited by George Herbert Clarke (Boston and New York: Houghton Mifflin Company, 1917).]

3. ["Peace," in *The Collected Poems of Rupert Brooke* (New York: John Lane Company, 1918), 107.]

4. ["The Dead," in ibid., 109.]

For some contemporary writers, Modern Art begins with the Christian Era, for others with the earliest years of the Nineteenth Century, for critics of the Post-Impressionist faith with Cézanne. There is no criterion certainly as to what constitutes modernity since every age has its own perspective, and its own perception of what seems new. And although artists in every age have yearned to add something new to the stock of the world's creations, they have usually only succeeded in repeating remote instead of recent ideas. Is there anything in the art of today that has not been done before unless it is the tall building we call the skyscraper? And even this, of course, is not so much an original creation as a novel adaptation to meet new conditions. We think of realism in painting as a modern achievement until we read of the famous still life by the Greek artist, Zeuxis, whose painted grapes tempted the birds to peck at them. We think of the depiction of sunshine and atmosphere as a modern achievement until we come upon the rainbows of Rubens and his effects of overhead light. Desperate in their desire to exhibit something new, Modernists have experimented with various methods and patterns only to he met by the critics with the comment that they have simply skipped over a dozen centuries or more and gone back to Giotto, to Byzantine mosaics, to Egyptian low reliefs, to Assyrian tile paintings, to Polynesian potteries and textiles. When they throw overboard art history entirely and seek to forget that any picture was ever painted, and try to paint as if with a mind wiped clean of all preconception, they are not yet worthy to he called original for then we accuse them of copying the "barbaric designs" of babies. The Post-Impressionists indeed no longer pretend to conceal this source of their inspiration and are proud to imitate the child's or child-man's unschooled conception of form. They dream of ultimately absorbing the primitive form of view wherefrom to begin all over again with the lost thrills of the first artists. This longing explains the deliberate savageries which Gauguin attempted to create in representing the exotic charm of the red natives of Tahiti. The fallacy of the philosophy which would urge us to renounce all that we have gained with civilization and maturity is too obvious to need discussion. In renouncing what we have gained we are not going to regain what we have lost. The simplicity of Matisse when imitating a child of three is about as simple and lovable as the simplicity of a soubrette talking baby talk to her partner in vaudeville. Whether it is the pseudo-savage or the pseudo-infantile matters little. In either case it is a lie. Even the originals which these modern fanatics imitate are wholly outside the realm of art. The phrase "savage art" is in itself an anomaly. Art is more than instinct, more than the mere impulse to create. Art implies knowledge, taste, selection, skill. We must conclude then that the extravagant Modernists in the arts are neither worthy to be called artists, nor are they genuinely modern.

But the Cubists and the Futurists, they at least have done something never done before? Yes, granting that we understand just exactly what they are doing. I am unable to throw any light on the perplexing subject of these atrocities enclosed in frames and christened with titles. The Cubists claim Cézanne as their ancestor because of his oft-repeated emphasis on suggesting the third dimension, and his trick of constructing objects by means of color-planes giving the impression of depth. They have his own words to justify their propaganda. One day, Cézanne remarked to an admirer, "Don't make Chinese images like Gauguin. Everything in nature is modeled on the lines of the cube, the cone, and the cylinder. If you understand how to paint these simple forms, you can paint anything. Contrasts and modulations of tones—there you have the secret for drawing and modeling."[5] There indeed in his own words we have a clear expression of the theory which makes Cézanne interesting to faddists. I shall want to speak again about this unique but over-rated painter. The point now is that the extremists who try to make a

---

5. [Here Phillips conflated several sources into one: "Treat nature by means of the cylinder, the sphere, the cone...You have the understanding of what must be done and you will soon turn your back on the Gauguins and [Van] Goghs," Letter from Paul Cézanne to Émile Bernard, 15 April 1904, in *Paul Cézanne: Letters*, edited by John Rewald (New York: Da Capo Press, 1995), 301; "Gauguin wasn't a painter. All he did was make Chinese pictures," in *Conversations with Cézanne*, edited by Michael Doran (Berkeley: University of California Press), 63.]

new art language out of a welter of geometrical forms were inspired by Cézanne's more or less facetious reference to cubes and cones. Cubism calls itself a systematic use of planes to convey a sense of weight and thickness. It has other intentions. Cubist pictures are not painted as often in cubes as in acute angles, swirls, and semi-circles. A characteristic Cubist canvas looks as if anyone of us in an absent-minded way had been making all kinds of zig-zags and criss crosses on a bare surface, jumbling the forms and inextricably confusing the out lines. If such a page of irresponsible scribbling and scrawling can move us to ecstasies of emotion then there must be something in Cubism and its orgies of unrepresentative form. Otherwise it is just what it appears—gibberish. We are told that the Cubist in blocking out details leaves only "significant forms" which contain the essence of the ideas expressed. To illustrate this idea, Arthur B. Davies recently took my education in hand and gave me an elementary object lesson. He brought out a framed picture of a young girl playing a violin—one of the exquisite things of his early period. On the glass he marked in chalk the contour of the masses and then removed the glass. The diagram was not unlike a Cubist masterpiece. And Mr. Davies said in all seriousness that this skeleton of form contained all the aesthetic emotion suggested by the subject, but now the rhythm. was released from all extraneous interest, from all sentimental irrelevance. We are told that a Cubist picture is like a world rising out of chaos. "The law of order is seen in the act of working itself out. We see a confusion of planes agitated apparently with life movement." For it is a paradox of the Cubist mind that although brooding upon the ideas of stability and permanence, of formal relations and static structure, principles which make geometry the logical vehicle of illustration, the Cubists are nevertheless tormented by the desire to express what they call "movement values." With the Futurists the craving for the expression of movement is allied to a desire to control, the element of time. They dare to depict on a single piece of canvas, past, present. and future, as they exist for instance simultaneously in a state of mind confusing all memories, sensations, and anticipations. In their field, the mental crowds upon the

visual. This implies "a simultaneousness of imagery, a dismemberment of objects, a scattering and weird fusion of details." As portraits of our overcomplicated modern consciousness—gorged on
sensations and undigested impressions—these Futurist pictures
are suggestive caricatures. But nothing uglier could possibly be
imagined. They make us think more promptly if sleepers struggling
with delirious dreams or madmen in frenzies of delusion than of
normal states of mind under the healthful stimulations of life. They
certainly have nothing to do with art. They have interest only for
students of pathology.

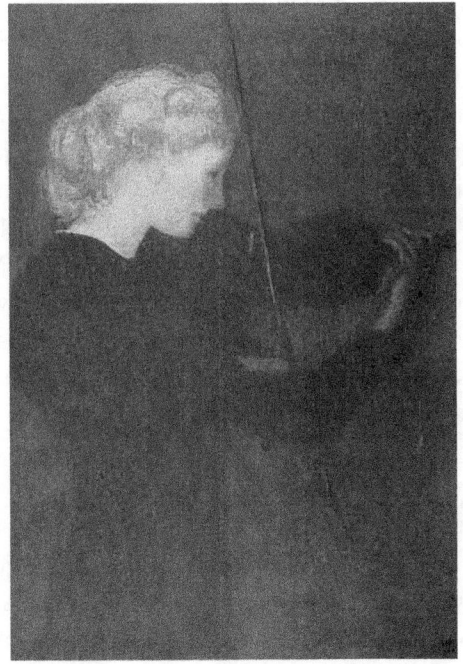

Arthur B. Davies
Violin Girl, 1898
Oil on canvas
Whereabouts unknown;
formerly in the Collection of Lillie P. Bliss

And now let us try to arrive at some conclusions as to the causes of the obscure malady which has produced in our day and generation debased aesthetic standards. The malady is most apparent in the thousands of so-called artists, yet it is also a public affliction. When we say that the new movement in art is sensation-seeking and hysterical and admit that the contagion is spreading and someone asks us innocently why we endure it, that someone has said the one wise thing there is to say. For we, the public, are responsible if the Cult for Matisse is taught in schools and if Paranoiacs are at large in our midst. We are too easily bored by monotony, too exacting of novelty, too restless for change and any sort of excitement. It surprising then that the side-shows of modern art pitch their tents in the midway of our lives and invite us in to gape and grin at their pretensions? Charlatans and false prophets are the natural consequence of a public curiosity about being "taken in." As a mere matter of policy Originality is at a premium so the exotic plant is forced, in season and out of season, into a profuse growth, rank in odor. We did not know that originality could be forced, but we live and learn. Mr. Brownell recently remarked that the boast of the Modernists to give us unprecedented emotions[6] was far from a benevolent one, for unprecedented emotions are apt to be bad for our health. Yet novelty we crave and demand, and this accounts for the success of the Modernist propaganda.

We cannot so easily explain the psychology of the sincere eccentrics and shrewd charlatans who make their success out of our demand for sensation. Our psychology is obvious enough. We want to be amused. We were children once and we still enjoy a circus so we set them up, these Cubists, outside of their tents, to advertise their sideshows. But the Cubists, do they regard themselves as our hired entertainers? Not for a moment. On the contrary, they take themselves very seriously. The prophets are making a new world out of chaos. They have a mission on this earth. But even the charlatans are serious—serious in believing that the crowds they draw are

---

6. [W.C. Brownell, *Standards* (New York: Charles Scribner's Sons, 1917).]

captivated and convinced simply because they seem hypnotized and non-resistant. Of course, they are the real victims of their own hypnotism and in time they no doubt come to believe their own theories. These extremists win the notoriety which above everything else they seem to want, yet their material fortunes are at best precarious, and many of them starve in allegiance to the cause they have espoused. So we cannot dismiss them lightly as wholly insincere and commercial adventurers. It must be admitted that they really cherish their propaganda. The bond which holds together the motley army of iconoclasts is the common desire to overthrow the established standards taught in the schools and respected in the homes. They wish to revolutionize modes of thought, life and language by making new measures of value. They wish to make art as democratic as the circus by making it as easy as any other kind of unskilled spontaneous expression—the nonsensical prattle and scribbling of very little children, for instance. A dread of hard work, a hatred for culture, and a passionate desire to be different—these, far more than any desire for material success are the incentives of the hitherto hopeless failures who could not compete with the past, but who now hope to become fashionable Futurists. Brownell believes that the underlying cause is "the immense extension in our time of what may be called the intellectual and aesthetic electorate."[7] Our specialized and elective system of education inevitably tends to indulge the susceptibilities at the expense of the intellect and results in making specialists, most of them insensitive to arts and letters, who sneer both at artists and scholars, yet who cultivate, as a supposed asset, a superficial veneer of culture. Thus we create just the sort of intolerant yet arrogant public which the Modernist can mold to his purpose, since the culture which he sells exacts from artist and public alike, neither pains of toil nor poise of judgment, neither knowledge nor taste nor skill, simply the dislike for platitude and the appetite for novelty.

It is very important for us to realize that we, the public, have a great deal to do with making the artists what they are, and therefore that we have a grave responsibility in the matter of establishing or

---

7. [Ibid., 21.]

discarding aesthetic standards. Brownell thinks that "the growth [of art] has been governed by demand not less than by supply, since however much the artist may have stimulated demand he is himself a product. It is plain, accordingly, that in the main a public gets not only...the newspapers it deserves but the art and letters it appreciates."[8] If today the artists are proclaiming rebellion, they must be deriving their rebellious spirit from us. Art is the barometer. If it is true that we can best study history in the light of art, it is no less true that we can best understand contemporary arts by considering contemporary manners, customs and conversations. We are now, however, in a period of transition when the old order is dying hard and may soon make a successful defense and refuse to surrender to the new dispensation. After the war we shall see what we shall see. At this point I wish to emphasize that the rebellion of the Modernists against tradition is nothing new, but simply the repetition in our era of a phenomenon which history repeats over and over, in every age, in every nation, almost in every family, the phenomenal uprising of each new generation against the standards of the old.

It seems certainly as if no more insolent challenge to established standards could ever have been issued than the outrageous manifestos in the field of art which we have witnessed in the last ten years. But we forget. In their days the Impressionists were supposed to be quite outrageous, and not long before the Romanticists seemed to have no reverence in their souls for the gods of Greece and the wisdom of the academies. In each of these interesting periods the great idea of Democracy was gaining ground in Europe, consequently the people had a good deal to say about art as about everything else. But in the matter of art they could not grasp the idea all at once. Interest in art was wide spread and this popular interest had in creased the number both of those who practiced and of those who professed to know about things artistic. The conservative majorities of those days exerted a great deal of influence and succeeded in making the painters and sculptors do pretty much as they wished. In other words, the majority of artists brought their own standards down

---

8. [Ibid., 13.]

to the standards of the crowd. There was a referendum to the half-instructed crowd which neither knew nor cared to be told what art is, but which had its own notions nevertheless-the idea being that pictorial art should be imitative. Now every Tom, Dick, and Harry, and every Amelia, Charlotte, and Jane, who thought about the matter at all, agreed that although they might not understand all there was to music without taking lessons, yet in painting at least they could certainly get all there was to be got. Didn't they have eyes? Well then, was not their opinion about what was true to life just as good as anybody's? This attitude persists to this day just as it has always done since primitive men whittled and carved their first crude imitations of reality to the dissatisfaction of their less creative tribesmen. In my least hopeful moments I assume that it is the misfortune of the pictorial arts that the same attitude must continue as long as the human race. *It is against this arrogance of the uninstructed public that painters have always protested and revolted sometimes in crowds, more often as lonely rebels. With liberties of color, with individual eccentricities of form, with over-accentuations of the inevitable conventions of their particular mediums, individuals and schools have tried to impress upon the public that pictures must be more than mere imitations.* It is only, however, in our own lawless day that the idea of abandoning the representative function of art has been, not only seriously entertained but aggressively undertaken. And so, because of the stupidity of the more conservative part of the public as well as because of the appetite of the new generation for new sensations, we have on our hands and on our conscience the Post-Impressionists, Cubists, Futurists, Vorticists, Orphists, and Heaven only knows how many other kinds of performing pet. Art is the barometer, and it is very quick to register the reaction of mood to public encouragement or aggravation which we carelessly call revolution of idea.

II

CIRCUMSTANCES and conditions change but certain fundamental characteristics of human nature remain as they were, and result in repetitions of the relations of artist and patron, similar reactions resulting everywhere from similar causes. In every age we find that a work intended to be regarded as a work of art is a revelation of an individual's personality, of his state of mind, perhaps also of his state of soul. When we detect among artists a uniformity of mood or purpose, a certain contagion of attitude toward the subject in art, or toward the patron or public. or toward life in general, we may call it either a tradition or a movement. A movement may or may not become dogmatic. *Strangely enough dogmatism in art results either from too much autocracy or too much democracy, from either too small or too large an electorate, from either meek submission to domination imposed upon the servile worker from some formal power of Church, State, or Academy, or else from violent rebellion against such autocratic authority—a rebellion so eager to substitute a whole new set of ideas that it simply offers a new dogma in place of the old.* When art is a matter of endowed patronage and when the public neither knows nor cares to know about the matter, then the so-called artists serve the Pope, or king, or patron, and the dogmatism of the minority prevails. And when art is a matter of such general interest that academies are supported by public subscription to maintain established rules and traditions, and, with increased familiarity, the public becomes at last arrogant with its little knowledge, dictatorial in exacting from the artist what it likes and what it is accustomed to get, then the so called artists serve the crowd and the dogmatism of the majority prevails. When at last in such democratic civilizations more liberal ideas are born, more revolt against established standards, more emphasis on license, liberty, and egotism, then violent reactions of anger against the dogmatism of academies and crowds make a new minority of ferment threatening change and even revolution, but fighting with the same weapon—the dogmatism of fixed idea. Stressing the need for self expression, originality, and untrammeled liberty from conventions, the Modernists of every age let themselves go beyond the borders of sanity, and even of decency, and become fanatical impostors often self-deceived. Rebellions against authority usually result in a throw-back to an idea long abandoned, which in its age was regarded as reactionary, or in proclaiming the initiative of some lonely, outstanding independent who was in his day antagonistic to all "movements" and happily unaware of what would be said and done in his name.

There have been many great artists who have rebelled against existing standards. Michelangelo felt himself a giant in the midst of uncontrolled pygmies—a Prometheus bound to Earth. Tintoretto was impelled to express a sense of life as drama. He felt surfeited with the sensuousness and sweetness of life and longed to start a new reformation, to hurl a thunderbolt of terror and excitement into the complacent vanities of Venice. His influence on modern art has never been properly estimated. Here was the beginning of the spirit of *morbidezza,* which he communicated to his pupil El Greco. The spirit found many followers among the passionate gloomy Spaniards, culminating in Goya. We find it again in Delacroix and Daumier, becoming violent again in Cézanne, Van Gogh, and Gauguin, and reminiscent of Michelangelo mannerism in Rodin's vivid "sketches in stone." When we think of Titian and Shakespeare and Velázquez, we know that the most sublime genius is poised and sane. But in the case of such great artists as Tintoretto and Rodin, and of innumerable individualists of lesser stature; it is not too much to say that "genius is oft to madness close allied." Many artists let themselves go and yet manage to stay on the safe side, but others pass across the border. It will not do to stress too much the need for untrammeled liberty and non-conformity in art. When we find imitations of such works of genius as are tinged with madness, we realize how easily acquired is the madness and how rare a thing is genius. Rebellions in art may be infinitely wise and productive of imperishable good, or they may be unbelievably mad and productive of incalculable harm. It all depends upon the people for whose pleasure and by whose

consent art exists. The lonely creators who work for their own satisfaction and pleasure only, seeking higher ideals than are recognized
in their day, are often the greatest artists of the ages, for individuals
are always greater than schools with their systems and revolutions.
But the great period of art is one which, while cultivating and cher-
ishing freedom of individual expression, yet maintains its function
of responsible sponsorship by exacting from artists that they cling
to certain principles and aspire to certain ideals. In the violence
of the present movement against representation in painting, great
masters are toppled from their pedestals and unsuccessful iconoclasts are exalted to heights they never dreamed of reaching. Only
an age which holds high standards in scant reverence, which loves
to be shocked with new ideas and amused to use new measures of
value, and which cultivates violent views on everything, would tolerate such vandalism.

Today the cult of the archaic is predominant and this dates from
Cézanne. He inherited it from a remote ancestor—El Greco. Roger
Fry states that Cézanne learned how to escape from representation
into an art of direct decorative expression from a hint El Greco threw
out about the fascination of Byzantine mosaics.[9] Clive Bell, a learned
English antiquarian, has lately written a clever book in which he
labors to make us learn that art has nothing to do with life and its
labels of meaning and sentimental association, but is merely an
arbitrary arrangement of significant forms which possess in themselves the power to move us to a state of ecstasy.[10] Applying this theory to the history of art he finds that the most significant forms were
made on the Oriental mosaics of Ravenna, and that only in Cézanne
has this quality of sublime beauty been brought forth once more.
Unquestionably, Mr. Bell has caught the contagion from which both
El Greco and Cézanne suffered so poignantly. Now it seems to me
that art never was more bored by its own existence, never more imi-

---

9. [Roger Fry, "Introductory Note to Maurice Denis, 'Cézanne,'" in *The Burlington Magazine* (January 1910): 207–8.]

10. [Clive Bell, *Art* (London: Chatto & Windus, 1914).]

tative than in this Byzantine period when an alien craft was transplanted and forced to grow because there was no native art which cared to live in the arid soil of enthroned asceticism. The unnatural contemporary love for the Byzantines and their borrowed abstractions seems to me to indicate a profound ennui and a passionate desire to be simple, austere and ascetic in protest against the complexity, the sensuousness, and the materialism of our times. If there were today a restoration of belief in the mystic virtues of ascetic religion, we might see the appropriateness for a Byzantine revival. But the need is now based on aesthetic rather than theologic craving and it is there we seem to feel that the reasoning is warped, for the Byzantine workmen were probably utterly "incapable of receiving and consciously expressing that "special kind of pleasure" we call beauty.

In the later years of the Nineteenth Century, the Impressionist painters were very busy making charming pictures of the modern world. They reveled in new subjects found in familiar corners and drawn from the moment's sensation, and they tried out new methods for calling our attention to the infinite variations of visible effects under the influence of changing lights. In short, they made realism more fanciful and flexible and at the same time more closely in touch with the latest researches of science. Meanwhile, a cranky well-to-do *bourgeois* by the name of Cézanne, who had a hobby for painting, became interested in the new palette and the new theology of art for art's sake—but he was temperamentally out of sympathy with the gaiety of the Luminarists and their pursuit of what seemed to him the evanescent and ephemeral. After experimenting with the color designs of Delacroix and passing from the note of exaggeration in the powerful drawings of Daumier to actual distortions on his own account, and finding himself most content with the solidity and stolidity of Courbet, he looked back where El Greco pointed to the formal architectonic grandeur and immobility of the Byzantine primitives and decided "to make out of Impressionism something durable like the art of the museums." What appealed to him about Impressionism was its fluent use of color which he considered the essential medium of painting. But Monet and Pissarro used broken colors to give sensations of momentary effects of light, and by means of color to "particularize" as Paul Dougherty expresses it, "luminous revelations of form." Cézanne claimed that in Impressionist paintings forms were altered by every change of illumination, so that one never felt a sense of the eternal structure of nature. His idea was to draw with color, suggesting depth by a trick of shifted planes, "a series of color touches following each other by contrast or analogy according as the form was to be interrupted or merely varied." In other words, modulation of color was used for modeling of form and at the same time the colors were employed as formal patches in a pattern of abstract decoration. If a tapestry effect was all that Cézanne wanted, he can be written down as a moderately successful decorator. He painted a few landscapes and even still life arrangements wherein he employed such subjects effectively as means to the end of giving

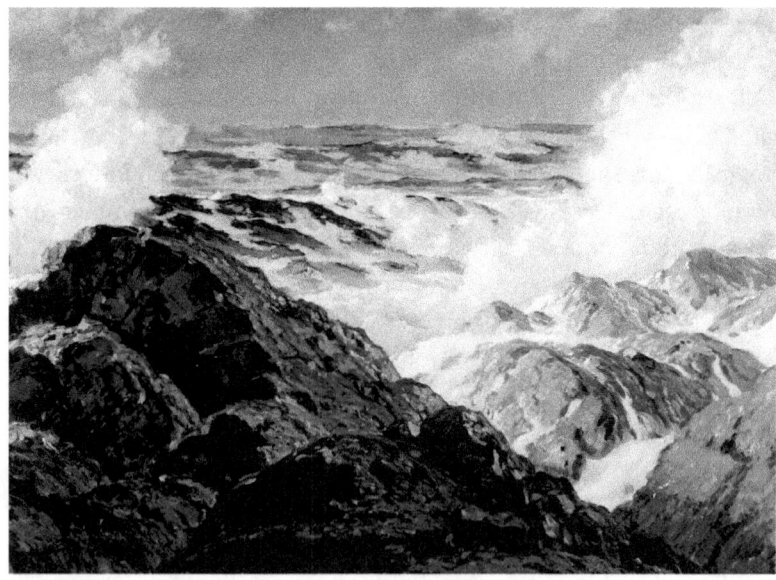

Paul Dougherty
Storm Voices, 1912
Oil on canvas
The Phillips Collection, Washington, D.C. Acquired in 1912

the limited pleasure we derive from tactful architectural details. But the writers and painters who exalt Cézanne nowadays seem to feel that he wrote a constitution for a new republic of painting and that no one before him ever suggested solid form. This stress upon the importance of Cézanne is one of the curious phenomena of criticism to be found in every age. In most of his portraits and landscapes he was both theoretical and awkward—a bad combination. Some of his most widely advertised studies of still life are as ugly in color as they are substantial in form and pretentious in style or manner. That they have a style or manner of their own is undeniable, but this is not in itself a virtue since some styles are without taste and some manners offensive. The significance of Cézanne is simply this—that like Van Gogh and Gauguin, who differed from him very widely in their separate aims, he was an independent thinker who reacted against both the romanticism which overemphasized the literary interest of subjects in painting, and the impressionistic naturalism which made representation more and more concrete and particular instead of making it, as he thought it should be, more abstract and formal.

That Cézanne, the austere, dogmatic advocate of pure painting, and Van Gogh, the wide-eyed dreamer frenzied by his own intense symbolism, and Gauguin, the uncouth savage who really belonged with the naked people of the South Sea Islands—that three men as different in aim, as unique in temperament—should be grouped together as propagandists, is proof enough of the lack of intelligence among their disciples. In temperament they were all nonconformists, with a mutual dislike for schools and movements and the complexity and scientific specialization of the age. In a sense they were all genuine primitives, and I do not doubt that they were all sincere. But the time was ripe for impostors. Democracy had made us all more or less educated and more or less anxious to have emancipated opinions about everything including art. The spirit of revolt against authority and of skeptical challenge to established standards which made science shake theology to its foundations and which made pictorial art purge itself of preaching and story-telling to illustrate the new dogma of art for art's sake, turned in time upon science itself and art itself and started a new cult for the simple life, for the primitive mind, for simplification and abstraction in art with the abolition of hitherto re respected standards. Out of this movement emerged Matisse who, unlike the sincere Independents, Cézanne, Van Gogh, and Gauguin, is a deliberate fakir. Out of Matisse swarm the spawn of Post-Impressionists, Cubists, and Futurists, who would not have become so fashionable with the faddists of our enlarged electorate if the eccentric men of genius whose leadership they claim had only lived a little longer to repudiate such contemptible followers.

The best way to resist the deteriorating influence of low standards is to have high standards, and the best way to have high standards is to think of art as something rare and fine and worthy of all reverence, instead of as something frivolous and notorious. In order to respect art, how ever, we need to be sure that it is worthy of respect. Art does not thrive on superstitious adulation but on the understanding criticism of friends. *The only way to answer the Post-Impressionist when he asserts that representative art is made impossible because it is supposedly comprehensible to everyone and so everyone is self-constituted to be a critic, is to make the knowledge of what representative art really is, and can be and should be a part of the compulsory education of every boy and girl, future artists and future appreciators alike. The only way to create not merely a few accidental artists of genius but another great period of art is to enlarge the knowledge of our enlarged electorate in regard to what art is. Democracy and high standards make art that is worthy of immortality. Democracy and low standards make art "the talk of the town."*

You may be wondering why I am so much engrossed with the work of extravagant fools? You may be thinking that I advertise them by my indignation. Why not overlook and contemptuously disregard them? They will be silenced by neglect. It is true that if we would all agree to pay no attention to them no matter how loud their publicity men scream for our attention, and if we would look in another direction no matter how curious we really are to see just what forms of mania their famous freaks are showing, and if intelligent people would cease to learn their dogmatic heresies and blatant half truths, then indeed we might be free of all the nuisance. But I wonder whether the time will ever come when grown folks no longer enjoy a circus. What I am most anxious to help in bringing about is an enlightened public opinion which will keep the performing painters. in the circus and be proof against taking seriously the quack arguments of their advertisers. Half truths so often sound convincing and theories seem. at times so unanswerable, making us search for rational qualities in things where none are to be found.

For instance, the Modernists have made it fashionable to talk about rhythm in art. Now rhythm is the beginning and the end of art. There can be no art without some element of rhythm which is, of course, the ideal of nature never entirely realized in a world of elements ever at large and at strife. *Any work which possesses none of those mysterious relationships of part to part and of part to whole, of the balance of contrasted elements, of the subtle sense of scale and tone, of the wave-like recurrence of mysterious pleasures induced by sound or color or line, is not a work of art. And yet we hear about rhythm as if it were a new invention by this man Matisse.* This painter (I quote from Mr. Caffin) in making a symbolical decoration of the dance is interested only in suggesting "the movement within the forms," so he gives his figures "something of a primitive suggestion," simplifying them "until…they convey no other impression but that of the elemental fact of bodies, organically related to one another in a unity of rhythmic movement." Thus, he is said to attain a symbol not merely of what is local and personal, but of what is permanent and universal in human instinct.[11] It sounds very well. But why must he make his symbolical abstraction out of forms crude, violent and revolting instead of out of forms which please the eye. Personally, I do not believe that simply because our sense of rhythm is an abstraction the forms or symbols in which the idea is expressed must also be impersonal and conventional. The abstract idea is always what makes the concrete impression interesting. But when we stop to analyze it we lose the pleasure of the moment. Under an

---

11. [Charles H. Caffin, *How To Study the Modern Painters* (London/New York/Toronto: Hodder and Stoughton, 1914), 211–12; quotation emended.]

[71]

arch of falling water or watching a drift of moonlit clouds, or the play of healthy, happy little children, we feel rhythm without needing to make for it any other image than the concrete sight we see. *The trouble, it seems to me, with the modern movement is that it is really reactionary in idea. It would make Egyptian hieroglyphics, algebraic or geometric symbols to emphasize the obvious fact that art is a matter of decorative convention.* Instead of art concealing its workings for the sake of greater subtlety, we are asked to admire the raw material and the crude workings which might be made into a work of art if an artist instead of a child or a savage had the impulse. Matisse calls our attention to his method of drawing like a child or a savage to show us how symbols can be simplified until we realize that if this is art then every fool can be an artist. He is even more crude in his obviousness than is Miss Amy Lowell[12] when she calls attention to her unrhymed cadences, stressing her accents by means of metrical arrangements until all the mysterious subtlety of the ancient music of rhythmic prose has been spoiled and sacrificed. *The argument that good drawing is not anatomically correct drawing but emotionally expressive use of line is undeniable.* No distortions are necessary to prove the point. All great artists from Botticelli to Whistler have deliberately taken liberties with nature for their aesthetic purposes, but they resorted to this expedient to prove the existence of unusual beauty. They did not resort to ugliness and malformation to prove the theory that nature is out of place in art. And so in this matter of the abstractions for symbolizing rhythm—rhythm which moves men gloriously to love and war, fraught with all the energy and the joy of living—why must we think of the hideous dancers of Matisse with their gross insistence merely upon the elemental fact of moving bodies, when we can dream of Tanagra statuettes and their influence upon Whistler, of the Winged Victory of the Louvre, of that processional rhythm of excited heroes and horses sweeping on its triumphal way along the frieze of the Parthenon?

---

12. [Cf. Amy Lowell, *A Dome of Many-Coloured Glass* (Boston and New York: Houghton Mifflin Company, 1912).]

Why this pursuit of the primitive instead of the perfect? Greek civilization was characterized by its devotion to the attainment of earthly perfection. The Greeks went at the business of making their own minds and bodies as perfect as possible in order to meet the need of making laws and institutions, sciences and arts, which also would at least aspire to perfection. The meaning of the present conflict in Europe is that two standards are embattled-the standard of primitive society with its superstitious fatalistic dogmatism and its unashamed brutality, and the standard of a civilization aspiring, foolishly perhaps, yet sublimely, for the perfection of its dream. Art must be the priest of this new faith in perfection. The very existence of art hangs today in the balance. Its life alone is worth fighting for since it corresponds to our inner life—our spiritual vitality. The Modernists in making art appear as mere aesthetics unrelated to the emotions of life, are making it unworthy of our devotion at this solemn time or at any other time. Patterns of unrepresentative ornament are invaluable for interior decoration subordinate as they are to the noble art of architecture, but to deny representative painting its ancient function of pleasurably appealing to our "emotion of recognition" and thereby intensifying our joy in life itself, is to emasculate the idea of aesthetics altogether and to make it impotent and devoid of life enhancing value. I would be the last to deny that every work of representative art *has* been great, not because of its subject, but because of its style. Whatever it has had to say *has* been said by means of the color and form. When, however, the philosophy of the pattern as an end in itself is applied to pictorial art the effect is as austere and as fossilized as an effect of pseudo-classicism. We see into a world within, and yet apart from the world of our normal human experience, a world freed from the arrogance of humanity, a world where ignorance is apparently not only bliss but wisdom worthy of all reverence, a world where egotism, as innocent of wrong teaching as a savage or a child, egotism pure and undefiled, enters into its own and is glorified. Aesthetics may be rational in reducing art's emotions to their abstract elements, yet art is personal, art is passionate, and its fundamental purpose is to communicate the gift of pleasure.

[73]

There is no more respect due to an art or to a religion which considers itself superior to the emotions of life than to an embittered cynic who despises humanity and shuts his heart to every influence which might make him human. Art can be the very flower of life, but the flower owes everything to the seed and the soil, and Nature is the source for art's flowering. And life itself—physical, mental, and spiritual life, is the meaning and the purpose of it all. What is ecstasy—who can tell? Save that it is all that ever thrilled us in a moment of bird song or of magic light and color, or of the passing scent of flowers and grasses, or of the touch of air and water. Joy of the dream-days of children, joy of the friend ships of men, joy of an ideal to fight for and a fight to the finish, joy of our lungs in the mountains, joy of high pastures under the clouds and the sun, joy of a swift horse galloping, joy of a boy and a girl on a beach at night, joy of the stars above them, joy of their hands entwined—such is ecstasy, the joy of rhythm in our world. And pictorial art, by means of its glories of color and line, can suggest all this to its vast advantage, can convey this ecstasy, since art and ecstasy are identical. It is the ecstasy of rhythm in art which makes life so glorious for many of us. It is the ecstasy of rhythm in life which makes art so necessary to our self-expression.

ART AND THE WAR
(1918)

IS art a luxury that should be discarded in wartime? Is it only a means of providing pleasure of a particular kind to a fastidious few? Or is it only a means of providing livelihood for men and women with no economic utility who had better at all times be employed in some useful occupation and who in wartimes should not be tolerated to continue their pleasant dalliance with aesthetic, delights but who should be turned into soldiers and sailors and munition makers?

Recently I heard of an artist who is worrying himself sick because he imagines that he is of no use to his country in the present war. That such a fine foolish thought should occur to him as it has occurred very often to a great many of us, is evidence of the overpowering effect of war, which, with austere command, consecrates us to a stern business and a solemn purpose. It is proof that in wartime we are apt to think more sentimentally than clearly. Art is not a luxury in spite of the fact that, according to its nature and function, it exists to give us "a special kind of pleasure."

There are two reasons why the conservation of art at its source—in the heart of the artist—should be an important part of our war preparations. In the first place we need the pleasure which the beauty of art can bring to refresh us when we are tired and to cheer us when we are dispirited and discouraged. Men cannot "keep on keeping on" at an alternately menacing and monotonous business, enduring hardships, facing death without some relaxation of mood. And back of the fighting lines the families of those who fight must relieve the strain of their recurring hours of dread by whatever means can be afforded to give them temporary pleasure. At all times and in all ages Art, like play and worship, may be a refuge. (I remember what Direc-

First published in *The American Magazine of Art* 9, no. 8 (June 1918).

tor [Edward] Robinson of the Metropolitan Museum said recently with great earnestness. He had seen, during the first year of the war, in the picture gallery of a small town in Belgium outside the Vandal's line of march some poor women feasting their eyes and resting their tormented hearts. He resolved there and then that if the United States became involved in the war, he would keep the Metropolitan Museum open if he had to keep it open alone, and make it as attractive a haven as possible for all who might come to it for relief from the relentlessness of their lives.) Art ministers to distress of heart with its balm of beauty.

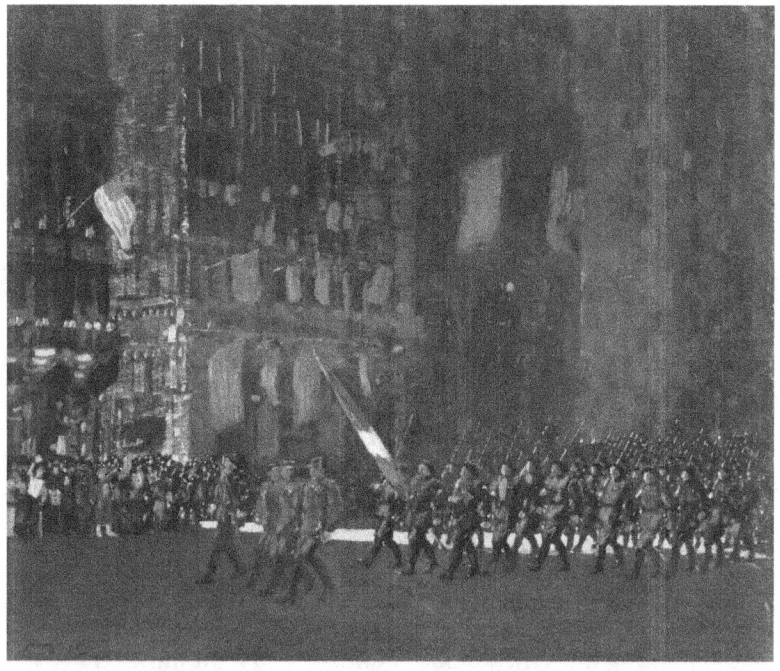

George Luks
Blue Devils on Fifth Avenue, 1918
Oil on canvas
The Phillips Collection, Washington, D.C. Acquired in 1918
[included in the exhibition *Allied War Salon;* see note 4 below]

There is, however, another reason why Art should be zealously maintained as an asset to a nation at war—and now I am speaking particularly of pictorial art. Pictures are painted to give pleasure, not merely to the eyes but to the functioning minds and hearts which may recognize their significance and suggestion. By means of pictures we may command attention which we could never hope to secure by means of printed words. "Seeing is believing." The artist exists because that old saying is so true. How often we admire and applaud the logic of a lengthy editorial in a morning newspaper—only to forget by afternoon the points which the editor so painstakingly made. Whereas the crude cartoon which embodied the same idea in its vernacular of exaggerated drawing—that cartoon made the idea more clear than the editor's two columns could make it. The cartoonist goes straight to the point. He is convincing but also concise and captivating-in other words an artist. There have been many artists who have exercised an impressive influence by means of cartoons, we think of Raemaekers today but behind him are Goya, Daumier, Gavarni, Leach, Charles Keene. Emphatically, Art is an asset for potential usefulness in time of war because truth somehow never seems so true as when we take a sensuous pleasure in recognizing its truthfulness and spiritual beauty, never seems so poignantly appealing as when we apprehend it by means of sense—whether of sight or sound. Whenever a man can make us take a sensuous pleasure in recognizing a truth or in apprehending a beauty, that man, whether teacher or preacher, has a gift of expression essentially artistic. It is a talent which we need just now in this year 1918. We need Art in our business of winning the war. We need Art to clarify our understanding of the ever-changing situations of the conflict. We need Art to help us create a single mind out of the many minds which confuse our country. We need Art to sustain us in pursuing a single minded and unchanging purpose to the war's successful conclusion—and after.

Our national emergency then demands of artists that they continue to do the work for which they are best fitted, striving insofar as they are able to help us win the war. The cartoons of the inspired

Hollander, Louis Raemaekers, are proof that a picture may be a powerful weapon in war both for offense and defense. Was it not Maxi-
milian Harden the fearless German editor who declared Raemaekers worth at least two army corps to the Allies? His, indeed, is the
spirit of a Dante guiding "the conscience of [civilization] through an
inferno of wrong."[1] And his is the glory of a St. George riding full tilt
upon the loathsome dragon which menaces the liberty and purity of
the world. To study his portraits of the Hohenzollern tyrants—father
and son—and their Prussian officers in spiked helmets—gross, cruel
barbarians all—directing their devilish work in the name of the
Christian God—is to feel a Crusader's hot blood surging through
one's veins, urging immediate consecration to our cause. Much may
be done by contrast. The drawings of Lucien Jonas which are now
on view at the Library of Congress at Washington are entitled as a
series *Les Grandes Vertus Françaises,* and they show that war may
bring out the best as well as the worst in a man. It all depends upon
the motive which has been instilled through many generations into
the soldier as be goes to war. Has he been trained to believe that
in war moral law may be held in abeyance and that in war the passions are let loose by consent of the Most High? There is an illuminating drawing by Lucien Jonas which contrasts the souls of two
Prussian officers and a young French *poilu,* their prisoner, "Gott be
thanked," to do with as they will. Facing the inquisition of two Prussian tormentors—facing a revolver held close before his candid eyes
by a leering assassin, you see the French boy's anger, and your heart
leaps to his as he answers, scornfully, but calmly enough, "Je ne dirai
rien." The incident is not unusual. It is one of the commonplaces
of war that civilized soldiers regard heroic death as desirable and
betrayal of trust as damnable and that seasoned soldiers cannot be
shaken by any gust of panic. But is it not well for us to be thrilled by
a realization that our own boys are capable of making such a choice
in emulation of their British and French Allies. A picture of the inci-

---

1. [The *Boston Transcript* quoted in *The War Cartoons of Louis Raemaekers*
(New York: Brown Robertson Co., 1917); quotation emended.]

dent which I have just described thrills us as we need to be thrilled; whereas in print we may or may not pause to reflect again how close to God is man. Through inspiration and through indignation, the pencil of the draftsman may be a powerful weapon in mobilizing for aggressive warfare.

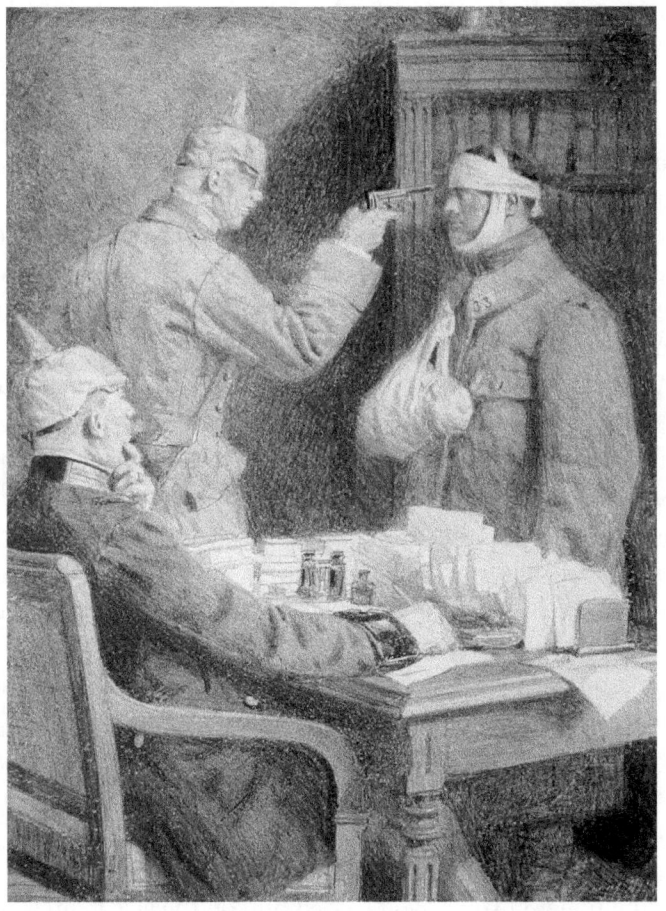

Lucien Jonas
Je ne dirai rien!! (I will say nothing!!)
From *L'Œuvre de Guerre* (Paris: Editions d'Art Guerrier et Moderne, 1918)

As a defensive weapon also Art can exercise a wholesome and corrective influence. It can defend us against ourselves—against our unpreparedness—let us not be afraid to say it, against our inefficiency, against our lingering apathy and our dangerous sense of detachment. It can shame us out of our selfish clinging to habits of other days and out of our selfish complaining about sacrifices and hardships which all must make. Art can save us alike from the enervating effects of depression and the injurious relaxation of overconfidence, stabbing us into full understanding of the enormous task which we have undertaken, a task from which there can be no turning back until the shattered world has been indeed remolded nearer to our heart's desire. Art can exhilarate us with such a tonic of determination and consecration that we may be strong, if need be, for a long war—strong to resist the peril of those pleasant thoughts of peace and ease, while yet peace and ease are unthinkable with an unconquered Prussia plotting for world power.

My readers, I can hear you complaining that I am saying undisputed things, that the dynamic powers of pictures may be taken for granted, that somebody will surely do something about it. In that case, my friends, you no doubt can tell me what is being done by means of pictures in this country to help us win the war. You answer, if you are well informed, that there is a Division of Pictorial Publicity charged with the responsibility of getting posters turned out to advocate the buying of Liberty Bonds and Thrift Stamps, to urge conservation of food and fuel, and to encourage enlistment. There are two effective posters which you remember. You have more than once noticed that cute girl in a sailor suit drawn by Howard Chandler Christy who pouts so prettily on many a billboard, repeating archly her little speech, "Gee I wish I were a man—I'd join the Navy." And you may have felt embarrassed when your Uncle Sam pointed an accusing finger at you as you passed him on the street, presumably shouting, "I want you," which, of course, is perfectly true, but much more could be said on the subject. If you think that the Poster adequately meets the entire need of the nation for patriotic expression in paintings and drawings, then I must respectfully disagree.

The Division of Pictorial Publicity is trying to do what the Parliamentary Recruiting Committee and other agencies for publicity have done in England, but England has not confined its wartime art lo posters. England has sent her best artists, Muirhead Bone and Augustus John, McBey and Nevinson, with commissions to the Front to make records for history. The recent exhibition in New York of British drawings and lithographs expresses Britain's ideals and efforts in the war and has revealed a new virility both of observation and of imagination developed in the artist through the new inspiration. These pictures are already being distributed in a systematic way by a government agency "over there," and our own Government should see to it that they are distributed to our own people "over here," together with drawings by Forain and Steinlen, which we can have from France for the asking. The need for pictorial propaganda is far greater here than it is in England where every air raid of the Hun keeps the Briton properly aggravated. We are not only thousands of miles away from the guns and the casualties, but we are as a nation made up of many unassimilated races. Our Aliens thought that in coming over to the United States they would be secure from the supposedly dynastic and imperialistic wars of Europe. Many of them frankly came to avoid compulsory military service. Our entry into the war and our call to them to join the colors awakes in them no ardent response. They are not so much pro-German as constitutionally spiritless and unpatriotic, and our unscrupulous demagogues as well as our peace loving nuisances can mold them to their cowardly purpose. Such men are busy with insidious propaganda which it is often difficult for us to defeat because it does not often come out in the open or take definite shape. The only way we can fight anarchist and pacifist propaganda and save ourselves from sad experiences with our own Bolsheviki—is to carefully and studiously distribute from a Government Department of Exhibitions educational and inspirational material wherever special kinds of appeal are most needed. More important even than the issue of pamphlets which the Committee on Public Information is already dispensing, more important than the war photographs supplied by the Divisions of Films and Pictures is the distribution of original drawings, paint-ings, and prints which minister to the morale of our people. Even from such propaganda as produces subtly beneficial effects not easy to calculate, appropriations must not be withheld, for the spirit of the nation ill its main spring in action. We must reach our fight-ing men. They must be made to feel that the nation is solidly back of them. And we must reach our industrial war workers. They must be given a new pride in their work and sense of patriotic participa-tion in the war for democracy. Most of all we must cause a change of heart in our pacifist intellectuals, our shirkers and slackers, and our Aliens or so many races and prejudices, creeds and clans, all or whom must be made, and if not now then never, Americans in fact as well as in name.

The Four Minute Men[2] are doing splendid work along the lines I have indicated but they have no funds to enlarge their efforts. Why not give them pictures to show in tho theaters where they speak? Why not make them the orators for our pictorial propaganda? These outstanding opportunities for arousing and educating our people about the issues or the war must not be neglected or we shall some day suffer in open sedition the consequences of our carelessness. We must not waste the wonderful Raemaekers material but we must use it with thoroughness guided by discretion. Lantern slides and post-cards of the most helpful cartoons should be supplied to distribut-ing agencies in different cities for moving picture theaters and small shops everywhere—North, South and West as well as East. Organi-zations like the National Security League are already sending out lecturers, as well as pamphlets but their lecturers should carry lan-tern slides and convert their lectures into patriotic mass meetings with organized singing of rousing songs. But even more effective

---

2. [The Four Minute Men were a group of 75,000 trained volunteers from lo-cal communities, established by President Woodrow Wilson in April 1917, after the US declared war on Germany and Austria-Hungary, to give brief speeches on various topics provided by the Committee on Public Information at movie theaters across the country during the four minutes it took to change film reels.]

than any efforts too obviously labeled propaganda will be the insertion of a few slides with a punch or a thrill in every moving picture program. Slackers seeking only amusement, yet in a receptive mood, will get an infusion of patriotism and an awakening to what is going on in the world, in spite of their indifference. The newspapers in the villages and the small towns should also be supplied with such pictures as have something instructive and inspiring to say and patriotic prints and posters should be the war time decorations for the walls of all our public schools as well as the Red Cross workrooms where they are usually seen. The first thing to be done, let me repeat, is to create in Washington a department for pictorial propaganda, at which headquarters the morale of the country would be studied in every section and the sectional needs met by a proper distribution of the pictorial material which would be continuously collected for the benefit of all the people. Money should be spent freely for this vital purpose. Plans have been submitted and I hope that the Department of Exhibitions may soon be realized at Washington.

Art is the universal language in which can be written the most authentic history or the mighty days through which we are passing. Our nation, from the very beginning of its physical participation on the battlefields of the war, should have artists at the front to represent it and to collect for its archives standardized pictorial records. General Pershing has asked for American artists and the men who compose the Division of Pictorial Publicity have already, with the authorization of the Government, selected eight artists to sketch what they see on our sector of the Western Front. It may be wise to send more artists later on, but the quality of the work they would do must be the first consideration and a few artists of brilliant talent for vivid artistic expression will meet the need of the nation for pictorial records better than four times as many mediocrities, however excellent their intentions and ambitious their efforts. To mention only one of many artists whose temperament and talents are of the type we need at the front, let me call attention to the drawings of Mahonri Young—better known, to be sure, as a sculptor of laboring men but also a gifted draftsman and watercolorist who has given us the quintessence of the Far West and of the big simple live of the Plains. Perhaps his drawings would perpetuate a typical American reaction to the grim landscapes of the front as those of Muirhead Bone have perpetuated the emotions of a typical Briton.

Much is made of the horrors of war. We hear constantly of outrages and agonies and we see photographs which make our blood run cold. It is well for us that we should see these sights so that in our comfort and security at home we may reverently remember those who suffer for our sake—who need our support—whose necessity is so much greater than ours. Yet too much emphasis may be placed upon the horrors of war. The sweethearts. and wives, the mothers and daughters—yes and all those who go to meet an unknown fate need to be comforted and cheered by the thought that in war there are fine companionships, hours of high-hearted camaraderie which in retrospect will seem delightful—marching songs which for all their banality thrill the heart with some rare invigorating beauty. We hear all too much perhaps of the horrors of the war—let us gladly think at times of the humor and glamor. The humor is to be found where one would least expect it. Man is a peculiar animal. He laughs so that he will not weep or cry aloud with exasperation and exhaustion. Look over the pictures of Bairnsfather and see how the "fed up" Tommies make the best of their lot even in the muddy "shell-'oles" of No Man's Land and afford unconscious amusement to thousands of unknown comrades whose hearts go out to them in recognition of their troubles with genuine tributes of understanding and respect. Why not send Briggs or Hill or some other humorous draftsman to the front to see and sketch the funny side of the lives of our soldiers for their own amusement? We supply them with books and magazines we try to coddle them, and they don't really like it—we try to distract their minds from the insistent pressure of their own lives and prospects, but it is no use. Soldiers will think and dream about those trenches. A sense of humor is ever the best safety valve for self-pity and a daredevil grin can quell a ghost of worry any time. I wish that all our soldiers could see that Statue of Cangrande at Verona,[3] a Knight of the Middle Ages in his full battle armor, ready for hand-to-hand conflict yet dedicated by he artist in the joy of a merry moment which he has snatched from the midst of the grim suspense of battle, his visor lifted and his whole face radiant.

But there are many of us who could never feel any humor in war who can respond glowingly to the spell of its glamor. To be sure, modern warfare has put on science and discarded much of the pomp and circumstance of romantic adventure. But what could be more incredibly romantic than aerial warfare? That pictures have been made from actual experience in the clouds depicting engagements between Allied and enemy airplanes, the mere mention of the fact is exciting. I was, therefore, eager in my desire to see the paintings by Lieutenant Farré, the French aviator of aerial warfare, which were recently on view at the Anderson Galleries, New York. Here, indeed, is the climax of all man's romantic experiences. We feel the ecstasy— the exaltation of flying and the tense excitement of strategy in the skies. The technical details of these pictures are accurate and the beauty rather hit or miss what appeals to me about these pictures is their power to stir the imagination. They are magnificent material for pictorial propaganda and I am glad they are to be sent around the country under the auspices of the Aero Club and insistent that at least the best of them must be reproduced in color on postcards and lantern slides so that as many Americans as possible may get the thrill of the wonderful tale they tell.

But more vital even than the record of sights is the record which art can make of the high-hearted emotions of this war against war— this desperate agonizing effort to clean the world and to make it over, with military autocracy destroyed by its own weapons so that future generations may be free to develop their best powers unmolested by dynastic interference with their right to life, liberty and the pursuit of happiness including the profound happiness of art. That is a cause for which artists can well afford to tight. The existence

---

3. [1340, Museo Civico di Castelvecchio, Verona.]

of art is at stake. The painters and sculptors can visualize—just as in a sense they symbolize the ideal for which we are fighting—the civilization which we intend to preserve: Robert Spencer, the contemplative poet-painter of New Hope, Pa., wrote me a long letter which showed that he had been pondering deeply the problem of Art in wartime and I must quote from it, for in this letter we are given to understand not only the artist's faith and courage about art and beauty but also his fervent response to the idealism which actuates the Allies in their defense of civilization and liberty. Incidentally, we are reminded that in wartime not only should the artist help the state, but the state should support the artist.

NEW HOPE, PA.

MY DEAR MR. PHILLIPS:

Thank you for your letter in which I am very much interested...This war is dreadful beyond thought but a necessity—a working out of destiny. The world will be more wholesome for it. It will help to wipe out degeneracy and give a new impulse to life the world over. As I see it–the fight is between Democracy and State Socialism. The Allies stand for the right of the individual to live and work as he sees it. German Rule and Socialism mean one and the same thing—the end of man as an individual—the most terrible thing that could happen. Imagine every act of the individual dictated by a government, every picture painted at government instigation subject to governmental censorship! The triumph of Germany, or of Socialism would mean the end of joy in work, the death of pride, effort, and ambition and, of course, the end of art.

I wish I could paint war pictures. I wish I had the power of the cartoonist. Germany has no more bitter enemy than I...But my point of view is too quiet. When I try to point a moral or adorn a tale I find that it is out of my game. So I really have to do my bit in another way. Yet if I can find a composition bearing on the war I'll try it.

When I think of war in these days, it seems almost a criminal waste of time for me to be peace fully sitting in the sun on a canal bank watching lazy barges floating by or noting the color and romance of mill hands coming out at closing hour.

Yet perhaps Art's pleasure is meant to give men's thoughts occasional relief. Perhaps the artists are the mental branch of the Red Cross. One cannot live in Hell all the time.

I wonder if collectors ever took how particularly hard hit painters are just now, especially those who depend on sales for their bread and butter. Buying seems to have stopped. The younger men can do something else. But the older men— what of them...Hundreds of them will go to the wall. Is it not worthwhile to keep artists alive for the sake of after time? The artist walks a straight path. Instead of living as the best sellers live, he is content to eat his crust and paint for posterity and the best there is in him. All true artists are doing just what the Allies are doing. They are fighting for future generations.

Sincerely yours,

ROBERT SPENCER

I quote this letter with Mr. Spencer's permission because I hope it will help others as it has helped me to keep art's vital function solicitously in mind throughout this crisis. We must see to it that artists are mobilized to make their willing contribution to the Cause, and we must also see to it that while they are heartening us as we carry our packs, we are sustaining them through the hard times for their own sake and for the sake of "alter time."

The National Arts Club's Exhibition of painting and sculpture by American artists which was conceived for the purpose of crystallizing American thoughts and sentiments about the war and of expressing our allegiance to the cause of the Allies will be open to the public before this article goes to press.* As yet I have not seen many of the works which I hope are being created in patriotic studios of America. Our artists unfortunately have, as yet, no contact with the actual shock of battle and they are too far from the sound of the guns to receive the great reaction. Nor have they yet experienced

---

* This exhibition has been unavoidably postponed as announced elsewhere in these pages. [The exhibition was postponed in May 1918 because of an insufficient number of works of merit being submitted.]

the personal losses which make them realize the depths of their own emotions about this war. They are thrown therefore upon their own mental and imaginative resources. Yet the war is shaping and coloring their every thought and observation, whether they realize it or not and some of them will find the inspiration they need. Some of the m surely will think of something to say which will help us to make the most of today and to face tomorrow unafraid. I have seen one small canvas, designed for this exhibition, which is very big in conception. It is by that idealist, Augustus Vincent Tack and is entitled *1918*.[4] A strong, yet haggard Cross Bearer labors up a steep hill,staggering under his load. Around him, a black storm swirls and rages, threatening to engulf him. His feet sink in the mire, his knees falter, his muscles ache, his back all but breaks with the agony of his effort. The burden grows less bearable every step and a persuasive voice from somewhere is urging him to drop his cross and run for shelter from the storm. But in the upper sky there is a rift through the clouds and a little space of wonderful blue, and the summit now is almost in sight, the summit of the questing hearts of mountain-climbing men. Triumph awaits him, if only he can hold yet a little longer. "Fortitude" might be the title or just "The Burden"—the old, old story of Man carrying his Cross. Yet for this crisis in world history—this year of climax in the drama of nations, the title is eloquent enough. The situation of the year 1918 stands revealed, and we feel a new significance to those splendid words of our fighting men: "carry on."

America's soul may be glimpsed in some picture or more probably in some work of sculpture at the exhibition. A few fine things which will add to our stock of courage and faith and enrich our spiritual inheritance will justify the purpose of the exhibition even if the

---

4. [*1918—Carry on.* The painting was included in the exhibition *Allied War Salon* at American Art Galleries in New York in December 2018, which was held under the auspices of The Division of Pictorial Publicity and to which Duncan Phillips was both a lender and a member of the Committee on Arrangements.]

majority of the work shown lacks adequate inspiration. At least the artists will show what we are passing through, how individually and as a nation we are nerving ourselves for our solemn hour to fulfill our destiny.

JULIAN ALDEN WEIR

(1921)

I

SINCE the passing, so recently, from our midst of J. Alden Weir, the best critical opinion, in his own country at least, has crystallized rapidly and acclaimed him with a remarkable degree of confidence as a man for the ages, as one who now enters upon a splendid destiny of imperishable and ever increasing fame. I do not feel certain that Weir will ever be one of the popular painters who are appraised at or above their real value by the general public. He never carried his heart on his sleeve, never painted pictures which correspond to "house hold words," never tried to entertain nor to educate the crowd, nor to organize a fallowing and start a "movement." He was contemptuous not only of sentimentality, but of sensationalism and of the notoriety which so often passes for fame, and in his own manner of painting, so marked was his restraint that he tended to an expression of unconscious austerity. Yet he was the most approach able and genial of men. The very essence of his art —what makes it great—what will make it immortal—is the warm and glowing lovableness which underlies the reserve. Weir believed that art does not deserve all the time and talk men spend upon it if it does not stimulate to finer issues our dormant faculties for living. If the value of art is measured according to its expressional power, then the art of Weir is very great even if it is not entirely easy of access. It is the pure gold deep in the earth which we must dig to find, not the cheap gilding on the gaudy surface of commercial ornaments.

We have lost in Weir a painter of a great tradition—an artist absolutely individual and independent of any School, yet one who

First published in *The Art Bulletin* 2, no. 4 (June 1920) and reprinted in *Julian Alden Weir: An Appreciation of His Life and Works* (New York: The Century Club, 1921).

belongs in the company of all those masters of truthful observation and personal expression in painting who have cared more for true and fine relations of color and tone and of light and shade, and for true and fine interpretations of beauty and character in the visible world, than for the formal analysis of abstract aesthetic principles and the repetition of formulas for classical design. Weir was beloved by all factions in the rather overheated air of disputation in which, strange to say, art seems to flourish. There never was any doubt where he stood. Although a member of the National Academy since 1885, and President of that body from 1915 to 1917, he was nevertheless an adventurous spirit himself, open-minded and sympathetic in regard to the adventures of the younger men, and frankly opposed to the tyranny of traditions and to all, dogmatic intolerance. His reasonableness was so sweet that *poseurs* were shamed to sincerity and extremists sobered to moderation by his influence, recognizing in him a spirit no less young than theirs, but mellowed by a big sincerity and a temperate and judicious poise and a loyalty to high ideals. In his own work there is fundamentally a selection and a fusion of what was best in the truly great artists of many centuries. However, so fresh was his point of view, so spontaneous and ardent his response to the stimulations of life, so self-reliant his character and so fond of experiment his boyish nature, that slowly, even laboriously, yet surely, he evolved and created for himself a technique which is his alone in the history of art, and the perfect medium for the expression of what he had to say. Old Masters as different as Velázquez and Rembrandt, Chardin and Gainsborough, Constable and Corot, would have recognized in Weir an artist of their unmistakable kind. Jean-François Millet stood before the prize-winning picture which Weir, a Beaux Arts student at the time, had painted for his landlady of the Inn at Barbizon, and exclaimed, "Tout a fait distingué." Where Corot, Monet, and Manet left off, Weir carried on.

I realize that I should not be hazarding an opinion nor daring to estimate the ultimate place in history of one so near to me in time and so dear to me in memory. I loved Alden Weir, and now that he is gone it is more difficult than ever for me to write of him as an artist in a manner altogether free from the bias of my affection for him as a man. Fortunately in this case the man and his work were one. It would be difficult to estimate the man and his own special and indispensable quality without reference to his work which perfectly expressed him. On the other hand, it would be most unprofitable to study his paintings from the merely technical standpoint, since there is no technical merit in his work, however great, that explains the enchantment of his art, which is absolutely a matter of personal charm; charm plus nobility breathed into his best drawing and pervading that unerring instinct for fine choices which we may call his taste, so that his art and his personality seem to be somehow compounded and inseparable, and his paintings the radiations of his own spirit, sincere, sensitive, almost shy, yet virile and joyous.

It seems to me that the two outstanding points that I wish to emphasize are, first, Weir's special capacity to make us see and feel that ordinary human experiences are desirable and delightful, and the world (to each his own world) full of places and people inexplicably attractive and worth knowing. Second, the personal independence which pervaded everything he did and found for itself a well-pondered and ultimately perfected medium of expression, so well adapted to it that it seems part of it, the spirit of the artist animating and refining the rather rebellious substances of the copious pigment which he loaded and manipulated mysteriously. There is a third point which I wish now to stress—his Americanism, his combination of certain traits which we like to think of as characteristic, not of what is common but what is best in the American. In this third aspect of his art we shall only be considering again the first and second, for they complete my very simple conception and interpretation of Weir the artist and Weir the man. His Americanism was, let me admit at once, of a special rather than a complete or composite character. As has been said of him, "From the America of immigration and quantity production he stood apart. His task was to fix the survival of the older America," the Anglo-Saxon America of the founders of our old families, more particularly yet, the America developed in New England and New York. Weir carried into American painting, writes Frank Jewett Mather in *The Review*, "a quality of aesthetic conscience akin to that of William Dean Howells, and Henry James in his earlier phase. [...] Whether his theme were a New England factory village, a bunch of roses, or or a finely bred American girl, he thought to tell the true truth of the matter [...] neglecting none of its finer shades and overtones."[1]

Now this subtlety of observation and this delicacy of feeling are not generally considered qualities either of American art or of American character, at least not by those who usually talk loudest and longest about what they call "the American note" or "the American flavor" in books and plays and paintings. There is a cult nowadays across the sea and among the European-minded art critics of our eastern cities for Americanism in art. Whatever good work is done that does not give the American flavor or sound the American note can be excused by these critics as an excellent by-product, but must be discouraged as liable to interfere with the production of the genuine American article. Indeed, the American article in art has become one of our successful industries. The continental relish for the American flavor is now catered to consciously and carefully by novelists, dramatists, musicians, architects, sculptors, and painters, impatient to acquire European reputations. To be sure, Walt Whitman, Bret Harte, and Mark Twain did not have Europe in mind when they created out of the raw fabric of their own experiences *Leaves of Grass, The Luck of Roaring Camp,* and *Huckleberry Finn,* yet even these great authors were subject to the lure of a foreign vogue for their native products, and they all lived to luxuriate in their own homely Americanism. Whitman especially seemed confident of his future influence with the European-minded critics. He was always arrogantly self-conscious in proclaiming that he thundered with the voice of a new continent and of a new evangel. Unquestionably there was in the man a glowing enthusiasm for the human species and a rapturous exaltation about the American social experiment.

---

1. ["Alden Weir," *The Review* 1, no. 32 (December 20, 1919): 675; quotation emended.]

The European-minded critics are certain that Old Walt represents what American art is or should be. They insist that America is not only frank and free and brave, but also vulgar and vain and fond of creating a sensation. Now it is true, perhaps, that our American symphony calls for a few blaring thrills of brass, but after all, the big bass tuba cannot speak for the whole orchestra.

The paintings of J. Alden Weir unconsciously express the reticent, innate idealism which guides and guards the better known materialism of America. It is an injustice to ascribe to the average American an indifference to that grace of spirit which we call refinement. We may be a shirt-sleeves Democracy, but we have our own standards. The attitude of the average American to that indefinable, unmistakable something which the old colored servants of the South used to call "quality"—the quality of their masters—curiously corresponds to that indefinable, unmistakable something in a. work of art which artists and critics also call quality, recognizing an air of aesthetic aristocracy. In the mind of Alden Weir the refinements of observation and emotion to which he was ever bringing his big, genial, whole-hearted tribute seemed to require from him also a technical language of similarly subtle and particularized distinction. He could suddenly become absorbed and fascinated by the momentary effect of a long familiar and unremarkable scene. I remember his picture of the corner of a high pasture, just a bit of sunshine playing along a stone wall and over a well-worn foot-path, and a silvery green tree outspread against a warm blue sky. The design of the picture I discovered later to be original and delightful, but my first pleasure was that of recognition. I seemed to have passed that way many a time, and to have noticed unconsciously just such an effect of light and color. Memories came back to me of walks in the country—of days on a farm. It is wonderful that some little songs and apparently casual little landscapes have such power to make the fugitive moods which come and go with the ordinary round of our days and nights almost haunting in their persistence and poignancy. So also with Weir's portraits. He could see distinction in an apparently ordinary model and make us see what he had seen to like and admire. Whether convinced or not, our hearts go out to him for feeling that way about people; for saying and believing and repeating that homeliness covers but cannot conceal the beauties which are real and endeared by association, and distinguished not by conventional comeliness but by essential character. Of such a kind was the idealism of Weir, and in spite of the European-minded critics, we know that this chivalry of thought and this idealizing love of familiar things are traits of the fundamental, the original American.

His themes were American, his. mind was American, his method was American, and he was American heart and soul. Many stories of his patriotism are told. Although forty-six years old at the time of the war with Spain, he volunteered for active military service. I shall never forget the fire in his eyes as he spoke of our national dishonor in the unhappy early years of the World War. Nor will the splendid memory fade of that inclement day when Weir, old and ill and lame, but buoyant, ardent, eager to show his colors, marched with the artists in the Preparedness Parade. It is only natural that' Weir's national spirit should have been strong, for the child is father of the man, and Weir's childhood was spent at West Point, where his father, Robert W. Weir, was professor of drawing from 1834 to 1877 in the U.S. Military Academy. J. Alden Weir was born at the Point, August 30, 1852, one of sixteen children. From all accounts Julian was a normal, active, athletic American boy and, needless to say, an imaginative one. I have heard an anecdote told of his childhood which shows his early initiative and enterprise. A friend remembers that one moonlight night he was found with some small companions, half-way up a very tall ladder which the boys had placed against the steep wall of an old barn. Julian explained that they were going to try to get up to the moon which, to their excited eyes, appeared to have landed big and bright right on top of the roof. There was nothing precocious either in his mind or in his talent in these early years. In fact, he showed no exceptional talent in the days when he first tried his hand at drawing, under his father's instruction, in that old barn back of the house. Nevertheless, the boy's enjoyment of pictures developed rapidly, and he was determined to become an artist.

His taste preceded his talent, and he showed very soon that art was his natural language, that the root of the matter, so to speak, was in him. Given this inherent, aesthetic instinct, and the patient, self-reliant tenacity of purpose which characterized him from the first, and sooner or later he was certain to succeed.

As a newspaper critic once shrewdly suggested—if Weir in his student days had worked in an intimate relation with some great artist who had been also a congenial spirit and who would have helped him to mature his individuality of mind and hand, a master who would have borne the same relation to him that Twachtman bore to Ernest Lawson, he would probably have arrived and found himself and formed his own peculiarly distinguished. style much sooner. The man who almost, though not quite, performed this service for Weir was the Frenchman, [Jules] Bastien-Lepage. Weir went to Paris to study painting in 1873 and was enrolled in the École des Beaux Arts under [Jean-Léon] Gérôme, the painter of large, historical tableaux which show infinite labor in archeological research and imitative drawing. Consequently the pictures young Weir painted during his first year in that studio were "a là Gérôme," and that means the antithesis of what he himself was destined to do. Although he never lost his admiration for Gérôme as a teacher and was always glad to have had such grounding in correct drawing and minute observation as the pupils of this stern old painter could not fail to receive, yet it was not long before the student saw the coldness and hardness of the method of his master, and even before he left the studio, other lights were leading his undecided steps in very different directions. Gérôme disapproved violently of Courbet and the Impressionists, yes, even of Millet and Corot, but to his credit be it said, he never interfered with the temperamental predilections of his pupils. He trained them conscientiously and solicitously in their drawing, but when they knew how to draw, he sent them on their separate ways with his warning. In 1873, Weir met for the first time Bastien-Lepage, and subsequently became the intimate friend of this brilliant young Frenchman who, like so many other artists destined to an early death, matured rapidly and achieved in early youth both a style and a reputation. Bastien at twenty-five seems to have been regarded as a leader, as a *cher maître* by the group of art students who gathered around him and were his comrades. Alden Weir was of this group.

In the book on *Modern French Masters,* which presented biographical appreciations by American painters, the chapter on Bastien-Lepage was written by Weir.[2] It is full of intimate talk about the subjects which were of supreme interest to the Parisian art student of his time. Many a pupil of Gérôme shared Weir's revolt against the artificiality and the perfunctory elaborations turned out with great effort in the name of art for the applause of the populace and for the awards of the Government. There was a great cry for a return to nature. At Mlle. Anna's restaurant, in the particular circle where young Bastien dined with his admirers, hung a picture of a French holiday in Spring, which he had given in payment of his account. This picture was decorated by the boys when Bastien failed to win the Prix de Rome with his picture of *The Angel Appearing to the Shepherds*[3] and not one of the group but felt assured of their wisdom as superior to that of the members of the academic jury who had so stupidly failed to honor themselves in honoring their idol. Bastien invited them all to visit him at his home in the village of Damvillers during the *fête* of the village, and Weir describes the experience with delight in the memory. As he says, "[w]e loved the man for his honesty, his truth, and his sincerity,"[4] and he always retained a good part, if not all, of his boyish enthusiasm for the French realist's art, with its genuine love of nature and human nature, its unaffected simplicity, its kinship of line to Holbein, its popular adaptation of the subjects of Millet and the true values of Manet.

I have touched at some length on the atelier of Gérôme and on the friendship with Bastien because there is something significant

2. [*Modern French Masters: A Series of Biographical and Critical Reviews by American Artists,* edited by John C. Van Dyke (New York: The Century Co., 1896), 227–38.]

3. [*The Annunciation to the Shepherds,* 1875. National Gallery of Victoria, Melbourne]

4. [*Modern French Masters,* 227.]

in the fact that, unlike so many others who felt the force of Gérôme's teaching and the charm of Bastien's friendship, Weir showed no lasting trace of the influence of either man. One of the few subjects upon which Weir often felt impelled in later days to speak with some severity was the tendency of teachers of painting in all periods to impose their own methods upon their pupils, thus encouraging them to become dependent imitators, and preventing the discovery and development of their own individual powers of observation and expression. I remember how proud he was of the success of one of his pupils whose method was in no way suggestive of his own, yet who had thanked him fervently for his instruction and inspiration, and the insight into his own special qualities without which he would never have attained self-realization. In his own student days Weir was unconsciously directing his own course and choosing to take to himself only what he would eventually need.

As a student Alden Weir painted genre, still life, portraits, and landscapes, and only his very earliest works, which he destroyed, showed the influence of Gérôme. I have seen evidences of his extraordinary versatility in these formative years; a charming head of a young Breton girl, a group of French children burying a dead bird, delicately drawn in a manner suggestive of Boutet de Monvel, a Vollon-like still life, a romantic figure composition with light and shade showing the influence of Italy, finally a bright and rather tight little landscape giving promise with its joyous intimacy of mood of the great landscape poems of later periods. The handsome young American evidently was adaptable, impressionable, responsive to many influences and all of them fine ones. But he had not found himself in those days. He was traveling pleasant ways, seeking beauty everywhere, searching for himself and exerting an unconscious direction over his search, but failing yet to find his own individual expression.

In 1876, he went to Spain, and thenceforth Velázquez became his God of painting. It was only after seeing Velázquez that Weir really caught up with the advances made in his own time by such men as Whistler, Fantin-Latour, and Manet. Returning to the United

States in 1877, he spent the next two years in New York in a sumptuously decorated studio in the Benedict Building. It was then that he painted *The Muse of Music*,[5] a very handsome and well-painted canvas in the grand manner, formal and not entirely sincere, for the grand manner did not come naturally to Weir, who was always what the French call an "Intimist."

In 1880, Weir won a medal in the Salon and went with Bastien-Lepage to Belgium. In the summer of 1881, he went to Holland with his brother, John F. Weir, and John H. Twachtman. This was the beginning of the intimate friendship of Weir and Twachtman. From all accounts, it was a delightful summer, and Weir grew to reverence Rembrandt for tone and poetry and Frans Hals for his bold mastery of medium, and as never before to love landscape motifs, the immense skies of Holland with their ever changing and never failing fascination of light. In 1883, Weir was again in Paris, and on this trip he was chiefly interested in the Impressionists, becoming so convinced of their importance that he purchased many of their works for Mr. Erwin Davis, who had commissioned the young American painter to buy for him some representative examples by the contemporary Frenchmen, relying upon his taste and his already celebrated eye for true quality in works of art. Fortunately, through Weir's influence, the *Jean d'Arc*[6] by Bastien-Lepage and the *Woman with Parrot*[7] and *Boy with Sword*[8] by Manet passed from the Davis Collection to the Metropolitan Museum, where they are monuments to the wisdom of Weir, and where they have exerted a powerful influence in the development of American art. By this time, Weir's taste was formed. It remained for him, however, to work out his own artistic destiny and save himself from the quicksands of eclecticism.

It is said that when Weir came back from Paris in 1877 he was in appearance, in taste, and in manner a charming Parisian. Although

---

5. [1882–84, Private Collection]

6. [*Joan of Arc*, 1879, The Metropolitan Museum of Art, New York]

7. [*Young Lady in 1866*, 1866, The Metropolitan Museum of Art, New York]

8. [*Boy with a Sword*, 1861, The Metropolitan Museum of Art, New York]

the years abroad had been for him a period of great inspiration and enjoyment, and although Europe had given him his education as an artist, yet he never seems to have even seriously considered the idea of living outside of his own country and, after his return in 1883, he married and settled down on a farm in Connecticut, exhibiting pictures with regularity in New York and Boston and becoming the most American of Americans. He made hosts of friends with his enchanting smile and his genial sportsmanship. One knew that under the surface there was rugged manliness which could be aggressive, but one knew also of the kindness and tenderness of the man and his

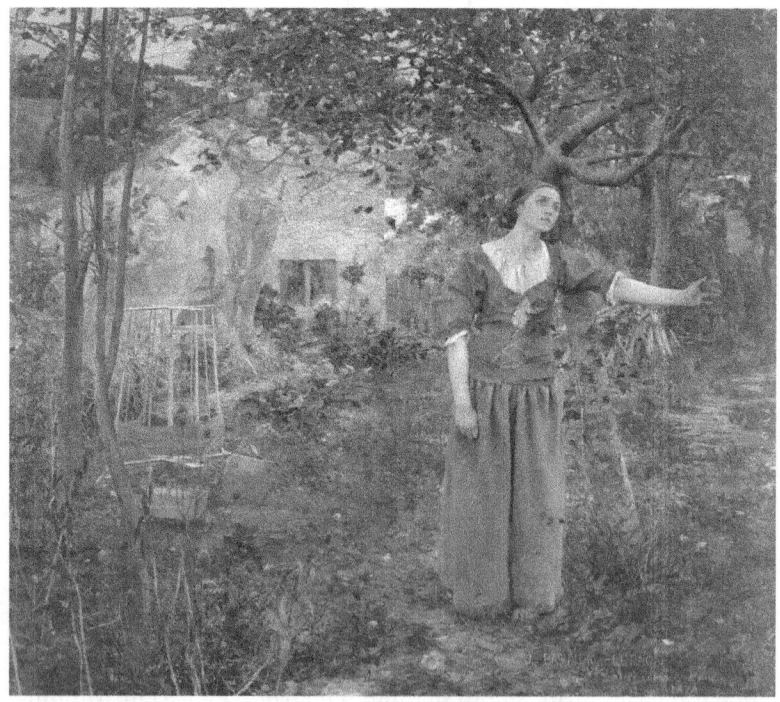

Jules Bastien-Lepage
Joan of Arc, 1879
Oil on canvas
The Metropolitan Museum of Art, New York

high ideal for art and conduct. He was soon elected a member of the Tile Club, which included among many of New York's most representative men in the various arts, William M. Chase, Francis D. Millet, Edwin A. Abbey, F. Hopkinson Smith, and Augustus Saint-Gaudens. During this period, his style was still in the process of being farmed through the knowledge gained by constant experiment. He knew what he wanted to say. The American portraits and landscapes which he wished to paint were already in his mind's eye, but at the exhibitions during the 1880s Weir was represented by pictures which won the praise of the more discerning critics for their quality rather than for their originality. He revealed what he had learned in Europe, and his aim seemed to he, what with Chase it always was, to show America *la bonne peinture,* the intrinsic beauty of surface obtainable in oil painting which ought to be cherished for its own sake. It was what America needed at the time, this emphasis of the young men upon art for art's sake, this insistence that in art, subject, however pretentious, is of no consequence without style which may dignify the slightest subject. Weir's still life of this period is as distinguished as that of Vollon and superior to what Chase and Emil Carlsen were doing then. Collectors are proud today if they have kept the luscious paintings of roses arbitrarily relieved against dark backgrounds, which they probably acquired without due appreciation of their historical importance. These things posses so delicious and unctuous a pigment, so charmingly rendering their subjects with especial regard to richness of tone and texture, that they would make Weir sure of a reputation as a painter's painter even if he had not gone on to greater achievements. While America was learning to recognize "quality" in painting through just such masterly works as these by Weir, the young painter himself was experimenting with new methods, new ideas, and a new palette. The portraits which he exhibited at this time indicate the chosen direction of his progress, but they were considered, and correctly so, inferior to his still life. They showed his desire to emulate the wonderful dull blacks of Frans Hals and Manet, and their even more wonderful flesh tones kept gray and flat by a diffusion of enveloping atmosphere rather than accented and modeled in arbitrary light and shade. But Weir missed the magic of these secrets known only to Hals and Manet, and today his early portraits seem rather dull and austere.

The turning point in Weir's artistic life came in 1891, when at the Blakeslee Galleries he showed for the first time a collection of landscapes in high key of color and with the transparent shadows of the French Luminarists. A second important landmark was the exhibition at the American Art Galleries in 1893 of works by Weir and Twachtman, together with pictures by Monet and Besnard, which were included for purposes of explanation. The newspaper critics, who had considerable influence at that time, applauded the celebrated Frenchmen so that their pictures were acquired by a few daring collectors, but these same critics lacked the courage to recommend the American disciples whose more conservative pictures failed to find many who were bold enough to either purchase or praise. Monet was purchased as a curiosity because of his foreign vogue. Twachtman, even more of a curiosity than Monet in his method, was utterly incomprehensible and, being an American, negligible. It must be remembered that during this period Americans were so much obsessed by foreign paintings that they were inclined to be dubious whether any art, good or at least original, could come out of their own country.

Weir was fond of telling a story about one of the few sales recorded at this exhibition. A certain collector over whom Weir had an influence, but whose admiration for Weir's work did not extend to Twachtman, was finally persuaded to buy one of Twachtman's landscapes which Weir had pronounced great and worth its weight in gold. Weir would not consent to sell this collector a picture of his unless he also bought an example of the art of his friend, whose work he insisted was finer than his own. The result was that Weir selected a picture for the collection, and the collector condescended to humor him and acquired it. Proud of his purchases and glad to appear to the two artists as a daring patron of their adventurous method, the collector invited both artists to his house to dinner. Weir arrived late and found Twachtman ill at ease and dejected. At the first opportunity he inquired the cause. "My God," growled Twachtman, "haven't you noticed? They have hung my picture upside down."

Weir and Twachtman had become zealous converts to this new style of painting; the application to canvas of broken colors which, by the demonstrations of Monet, had been proved capable of recombination, not by mixture on the palette but by juxtaposition, fresh from the tubes, so as to give a closer suggestion of light. Both had promptly set to work to study the great Out of Doors with new eyes. While still painting and exhibiting tonal pictures of most discreet conservatism, Weir and Twachtman were preparing to apply Monet's method to American subjects, and to carry it on with modifications which would make it more adaptable to individuality of expression and more amenable to beauty. No one else, perhaps not even the fact, Weir's earliest effects of sunshine were often weak, suggesting a sun trying to come out of a fog. The tonal harmonies were charming, however. The soft colors suggested to the contemporary critics the qualities of pastel. Weir had won a reputation. as an accomplished painter of still life, so the critics were on their guard against any hasty accusations of incompetence. But people said—yes, even some artists who should have known better—"Too bad; another good man gone wrong," and the critics damned with faint praise, and only one or two seemed to realize the tremendous importance of this forward march by two gallant spirits not, content to stand still. A little later, Childe Hassam and Theodore Robinson came back from France with sparkling rainbow palettes and began to paint with a greater facility in the new style, an earlier attainment of their full powers than the early efforts of Weir and even of Twachtman. But the two great American painters of spiritualized naturalism proceeded on their own way, showing the results of their study of Monet, but unlike Hassam, their intention to depart from his method and to adapt it to their own ends. What matters it now that those early landscapes of Weir were loose without much strength, transparent in the shadows but without much light? The important fact is that they were great art in the making. And they intrigue us! We are conscious of something very personal and somehow very original trying to get itself said in a language not yet entirely familiar. Occasionally, there is a wonderful work of art full of a touching poetry and of vividly remembered atmosphere; of impressions absorbed in moments of sensitive response and transferred to canvas with an art which seems, as yet, more a matter of lucky inspiration than of confident mastery of method.

I have a small landscape of about this time, a country lane in Spring with a glad sun shining and a hint of birdsong in the sweet, still air. There are radiant pinks and tender greens, an endearing touch, a lyric charm. Usually the sun in the early Weir landscapes did not shine so well. But they are invariably full of dimly lighted or partially shadowed places which are marvels of tone. It certainly is not difficult for us now to see the great Weir emerging out of these lovely pictures which in their day were accounted failures. Some critics had faith in them. Clarence Cook wrote in 1891, "Weir sees as the Venetians and Velasquez rather than as Raphael, Dürer, and Ingres, with their hard, precise, and analytic eyes. And these new works show no violent change. They are the logical outcome of Weir's artistic tendency since his return from Europe. Only the key has changed. The man is on his way." Here at least was one critic who saw that Weir was approaching, if indeed he had not already arrived at, that starting point of all the art that is truly great—when the method is discovered, and occasionally the scope and aim of it realized, thereby one's own innermost individual *Something* may be given to the world to add to the sum of the world's treasure.

II

SO, after ten years of experiment and cultivation, the art of J. Alden Weir came at last to fruition. He was destined to say in his chosen way something that needed to be said about his native land, and to say it more exquisitely, with greater delicacy of feeling and distinction of style, than lay within the powers of any other American. The large, formal figure compositions, the still life, rich in texture and very personal, the sombre, solid portraits, and such masterly landscapes, in the manner of Barbizon, as "The Old Connecticut Farm," were only practice for the ultimate themes. When he had thoroughly mastered his craft and learned from experience and won for himself a hearing and established a reputation, he then deliberately turned his back on everything he had done, disregarding the material success which could have been his for the asking had he continued along more traditional lines, and broke ground in untilled fields. Chalky, perhaps, and a little weak, the earliest landscapes in high key, yet they were eloquent nevertheless of the great American painter who had finally found himself and who could be counted upon for an ever increasing mastery of his method and for works of the most personal, inimitable artistry and the most sensitive and beautiful emotions. Having discovered and attained to his own predestined style, his work became, for the first time, the spontaneous natural expression of his own life and character. Thereafter his pictures form links of record of a rare personality devoted with single-hearted sincerity to the expression of the simplicities of life, the finer every-day experiences of which are revealed only to spirits of singular sweetness. The rare intimacy of the pictures of Weir, their true delight in little things and familiar surroundings, their wholesome joy in life's untroubled hours of serenity and health and genuine contentment, remind me of Chardin, the difference being that the Frenchman's special pleasure was in the domestic interior, whereas Weir's was out of doors, on the farm, in the fields and woods, and at the hospitable hearth only after nightfall. But both men wrote in terms of exquisite tone, color, and atmosphere their appreciation of the quiet joys of just being alive from day to day, with a chance to observe how lovely things really are if we know how to see. Velázquez had taught him how to see, how to find the elements of beauty anywhere and to make for himself, by means of exquisite craftsmanship, true patterns of form and line and texture, and of colors harmonized in light and air; a world of enchanting realities. It is, however, of Chardin's sensitively chosen scale of values, particularly his gamut of lovely grays and tawny tones, that Weir's palette reminds me; of Chardin in the portraits and still life and of Corot in the landscapes. Chardin, Corot, and Weir, they all had an intimacy of spirit which makes their art particularly ingratiating. For them art. became a part of their own lives and their way of conveying to others their satisfaction in life. From the time when Weir first began to exhibit his paintings in the new method there is no better way of knowing his Hf e than through his art.

Very personal also are the landscapes which Weir painted on his own farms. He spent six or seven months of each year in Connecticut, where he owned two country places, and where he hunted and fished in season. He would spend alternate summers at Windham and Branchville. The place at Winham is an estate of three hundred and fifty acres and has been in Mrs. Weir's family for one hundred and fifty years. A ball in honor of Lafayette was once given in this house. Each generation of Mrs. Weir's family has added to the original structure, until now it is large and rambling and full of quaint charm. There are ancient forest trees round about, which many of us know in the landscapes not only of Weir, but of his friend, Emil Carlsen, who lived nearby for many summers. The other place at Branchville is of two hundred acres, heavily forested with fine old timber. The old house has an immense living-room with an old oak floor, and its windows are quaint Dutch ones which Weir brought from Holland. Once, when a party of friends joined Weir for a week of fishing in the spring, three cords of wood were burned in two days in the two vast fireplaces at opposite ends of this room. Six-foot logs are offered up, and the sacrificial blaze is a roaring one. It is pleasant to think of Weir's handsome, silvered head in the firelight, his eyes merry with anecdote or softened with sentiment. He was a delightful storyteller and a great listener to the stories of others. His big laugh was of a kind that warmed the heart. His mind was alert and active, keen and shrewd in criticism, yet generous and tolerant, the mind of a big man. He loved animals, especially dogs. It would be hard to find pictures more intimate in their charm than the water colors he painted of his own hunting dogs asleep around his hearth after a hard day in the woods. Fishing was a passion with Weir. Recently I was looking over his scrapbooks, and most of the press clippings were not about art at all, but about "The Elusive Trout," "Beguiling the Tom Cod," "The Sensitive Salmon." It may seem rather surprising that among his landscapes we find few records of the sport he loved so well; no pictures of little rivers where he waded hip high, or of shadowy pools into which he dropped his tempting flies! Evidently he felt that art had no more to do with sport than with politics and business. It was his life work to search for beauty and then to express it. Sport was his relaxation, into which he could plunge with whole-hearted gusto, leaving art behind. There are two pictures entitled *The Fishing Party*,[9] both very lovely landscapes with figures enveloped in silvery sunshine, but they are for connoisseurs of rare beauty—not for sportsmen. He was fond of telling stories, but not on canvas. I do not remember a single story-telling picture from his hand.

One of the most charming and one of the most completely representative of Weir's paintings is *The Donkey Ride*,[10] showing his daughters, Dorothy and Cora, when they were little girls, mounted on dainty and demure gray donkeys against a beautiful background of hillside and summer sky. From a decorative standpoint, this picture is a thing of extraordinary loveliness. There is no modeling and

---

9. [*The Return of the Fishing Party*, 1906, High Museum of Art, Atlanta; *The Fishing Party*, c. 1915, The Phillips Collection, Washington D.C., Acquired in 1917]

10. [1899, whereabouts unknown]

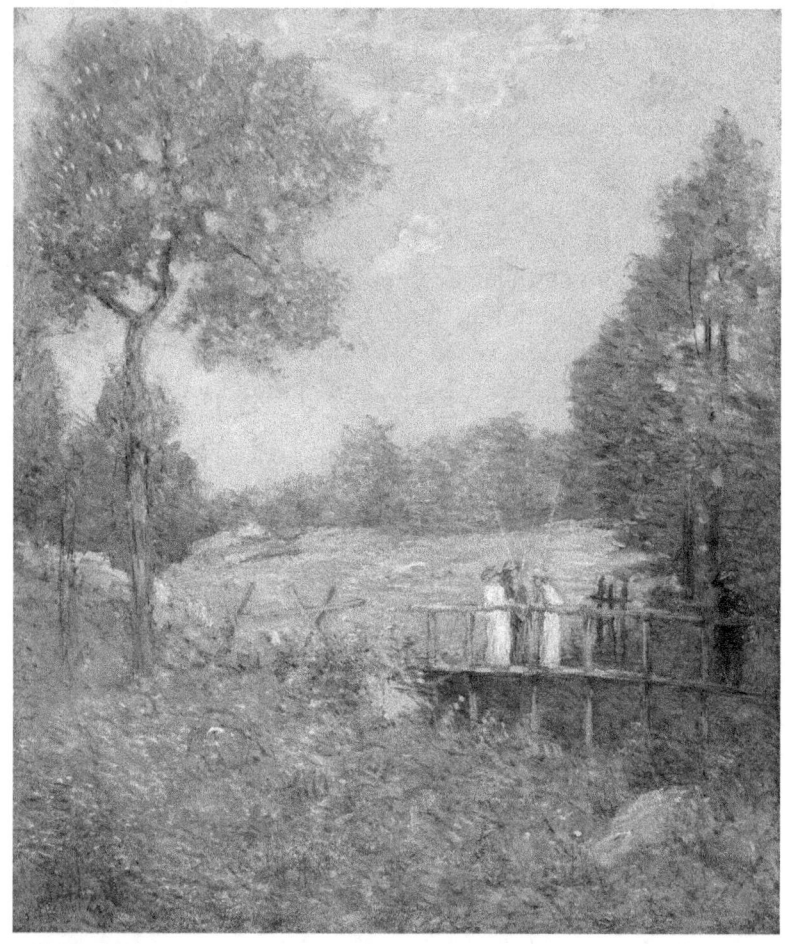

Julian Alden Weir
The Fishing Party, c. 1915
Oil on canvas
The Phillips Collection, Washington, D.C. Acquired in 1917

no atmosphere, for everything has been deliberately kept flat to convey the joy of a mellow old tapestry. The well-worn leather of the old saddle and the rough hair of the donkey are realistic in effect and tempt us to touch them, so wonderful is the *vraisemblance,* but these textures are lovely for their own sake and, although each bit suggests vividly the character of what it represents, yet there is an abstract beauty which ties every part together. Charming, of course, as a poem on all happy American childhood in the country, yet this picture is chiefly valuable perhaps because of its design, which is as fine as those by "old masters" of the Far East or of the eighteenth century, when Japanesque caprice rather than classic convention ruled. Often, by the way, we are reminded of the spirit of the eighteenth century in England. As Royal Cortissoz has observed, "There is the old English flavor of those winsome color prints, 'The Cries of London,'[11] in such a picture as 'The Flower Girl'[12]—a canvas which cheers and charms us like a quaint and ever refreshing song of long ago."

Scarcely less adorable than *The Donkey Ride* is the other donkey picture entitled *Visiting Neighbors*,[13] representing Cora Weir tying her donkey to a garden gate at about noontime of a summer's day. Whereas *The Donkey Ride* was not only a donkey ride but a decoration, this picture is first and last just a vivid glimpse of the real world at Branchville, Connecticut, and of a little girl who had a good time with that particular donkey, and who used to tie it to that particular rustic fence which her daddy had noticed took on just that grayish violet tone at that hour of the sun-flecked green midday. The quivering joyous languor of the hour is conveyed in the artist's most masterly manner. The tree trunks are rough and beautifully true, the texture of the bark suggested in striated brush strokes of violet and

---

11. [Francis Wheatley exhibited a series of thirteen oil paintings entitled *Cries of London* at the Royal Academy between 1792 and 1795. Stipple engravings made of Wheatley's paintings by Luigi Schiavonetti, Antoine Cardon, Giovanni Vendramini, and Thomas Gaugain, in both plain and colored versions, became highly popular and were among the first affordable works of art. See Royal Cortissoz, "The Eighteenth-Century Color Print and English Society," *The Century Magazine* 83, no. 1 (November 1911).]

12. [*Flower Girl*, c. 1900, Maryland State Art Collection]

13. [Now titled *After the Ride*, c. 1903, The Phillips Collection, Washington, D.C. Acquired in 1917]

brown. The drowsy gray donkey and the little girl are immersed in sun and air. As the little girl would say, "It's the good old summer time." There is, a monotony of content everywhere. How it stills the soul to feel a little breeze in one's hair, to stretch one's body till it thrills, to play with children and animals, to be a child again and follow the lure of one's own caprice in the great outdoors! Richard Hovey, poet of comradeship and the open sky, has put the mood into living language:

> O goodly damp smell of the ground!
> O rough sweet bark of the trees!
> O clear sharp cracklings of sound!
> O life that's a-thrill and a-bound
> With the vigor of boyhood and morning, and the
>   noontide's rapture of ease!

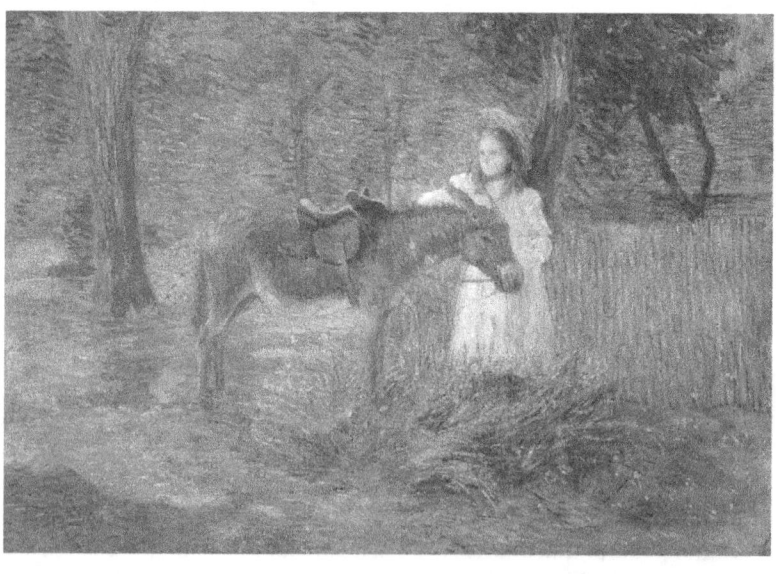

Julian Alden Weir
After the Ride, c. 1903
Oil on canvas
The Phillips Collection, Washington, D.C. Acquired in 1917

Was there ever a weary heart in the world?
A lag in the body's urge or a flag of the spirit's
    wings?
Did a man's heart ever break
For a lost hope's sake?
For here there's such lilt in the quiet and calm in the
    quiver of things.[14]

Back of the old farm-house at Branchville is the rocky hillside which Alden Weir has immortalized in that epic picture of the American farmer amid soil and sky entitled, *Plowing for Buckwheat*.[15] Weir did not want us to think that the frame for this picture would contain all that was worth transcribing. He wished us to understand that his viewpoint was more or less unstudied, that what he painted was a hastily selected part of the big world of cloud-shine and alp trees and fallow, fertile fields which stretched immeasurably above and beyond the borders of his canvas. This largeness of nature worship and this unconscious function he performed of painting American epic poetry accounts for what has been called a carelessness on Weir's part in composing his landscapes. We have seen that in *The Donkey Ride* he could satisfy those who require a pattern in a picture, but the essential Weir was more concerned with expressing the big though simple emotions which nature gave him, than with the patterns which could be arranged out of her raw materials. If you are a lover of open American hill country, not the culminating majesty of mountain peaks, nor the perfection of paradise valleys, but just nice livable, lovable farm land, neither too opulent nor too austere, then you will enjoy yourself in the landscapes of Weir. The season is usually summer, the hour morning or approaching noon, with overhead light in a pale sky. In the *Plowing for Buckwheat*, great, billowy clouds are crisply accented against the azure in silvered brilliancy. A drowsy heat pervades the air. It feels good to drop

---

14. ["The Faun," in Bliss Carman and Richard Hovey, *Songs from Vagabondia* (Boston: Small, Maynard and Company, 1905), 16; quotation emended.]
15. [1898, Carnegie Museum of Art, Pittsburgh]

down on some sweet-smelling hay under a friendly tree and look up. An imperceptible breeze stirs the upper branches. The distant woods are mellowed by traveling shadows. It is pleasant to watch the slow, brown oxen, the sunbaked hillside, and the farmer who turns from his plow with a friendly "how-d' do." In *The Fishing Party*, the sun under which we stand seems to silver the ferny foreground, the sky so subtly modulated in key from the horizon up, and the distant woods beyond the open fields. Across a little bridge pass the white-clad figures of friends going a-fishing. If only one could hear the hum of insect life and of incidental, unimportant human voices, the sensation-of any sunny summer day on a farm would be complete. And Weir was no more true in recording day than in remembering night. He fascinates with the exact effect of a spooky darkness as I fitfully glimpsed in the flare of a rusty old lantern.

In painting people instead of places, it is fascinating to see Weir's mind concerned with different problems and expressing beauty and character with a technical method of combed lines and varied surfaces for conveying a sense of flesh and fabric under diffused light, which is perhaps even more individual and distinctive than the short stroke, the embroidering touch employed so wonderfully for the landscapes. In the many paintings in oil and water color celebrating the charm of children, one is led to believe that Weir's genius was never more inspired than in the interpretation of childhood. Who can forget the sweet and demure little girl whose kitten slumbers in her gently folded arms? This picture deserves to rank among the great portraits of children. Even Sargent's *Beatrice and the Bird Cage*[16] is not more beautiful than the *Little Lizzie Lynch*[17] of Weir. Sargent became tender and reverent in painting children, but when they grew up he saw them in his worldly way, wisely and without sentiment. Weir's humanity did not stop with children. His imagination was deeply moved by the old-fashioned American girl as he loved to

---

16. [*Beatrice Goelet*, 1890, Private Collection]
17. [1910, whereabouts unknown]

think of her, in her sensitive, radiant youth, full of her sweet contradictions, free and frank and fine of body and soul, the comrade and playmate of man, yet more. puritan than pagan, with an inarticulate reserve coming up at the first hint of sentiment, to conceal depths of dear, mysterious, feminine emotion. All this we seem to know about Weir's young American woman without, of course, ever stopping to analyze her, which would be destructive of the charm the artist makes us feel in her presence. Weir was the inspired interpreter of a chosen American type that is marked by a penetrating sort of refinement which he reverenced and to which he could impart a charm through the chivalric graciousness and the Hellenic joyousness of his own mind. This refinement which he saw and sought to express was not at all a matter of class or race, although the New England woman of old Anglo-Saxon lineage was a favorite theme. In the portrait of Miss de L. at the Corcoran Gallery in Washington,[18] we feel Weir's interest and respect for a type which might be called middle class European. We rather think that she is a Jewess of European parentage. Perhaps she is a dressmaker or manages a small shop. She has been good looking, but years of drudgery and disappointment have exacted their toll. She is a brave woman. So it is always with the types chosen by Weir. He sets us wondering about them. The men also are interpreted with profound sympathy and understanding, their physical beings so suggested that we feel their living presence in the pigments. The portrait of his brother, Colonel Weir, is a masterpiece and, as the subject requires, is ruggedly painted in a style which would have done injustice to his gentler sitters. And the portrait of the great poet-painter, Ryder[19]—what a noble head! We know that this man is a genius, and that he lives in a world of his own invention. Weir was Ryder's guardian angel. Some day there will be a tale to tell, a revelation of all that the great-hearted Weir was to poor Ryder, and it will be the basis for a most beautiful legend. No

---

18. [*Portrait of Miss de L.*, 1914, whereabouts unknown]
19. [*Albert Pinkham Ryder*, n.d., National Academy of Design, New York]

two men could have been more different. There was never anything literary or mystical about Weir, and yet he understood Ryder's poet soul, and in his portrait we share his reverence for the superb intellect and greatness which animated the lonely dreamer whose eccen-

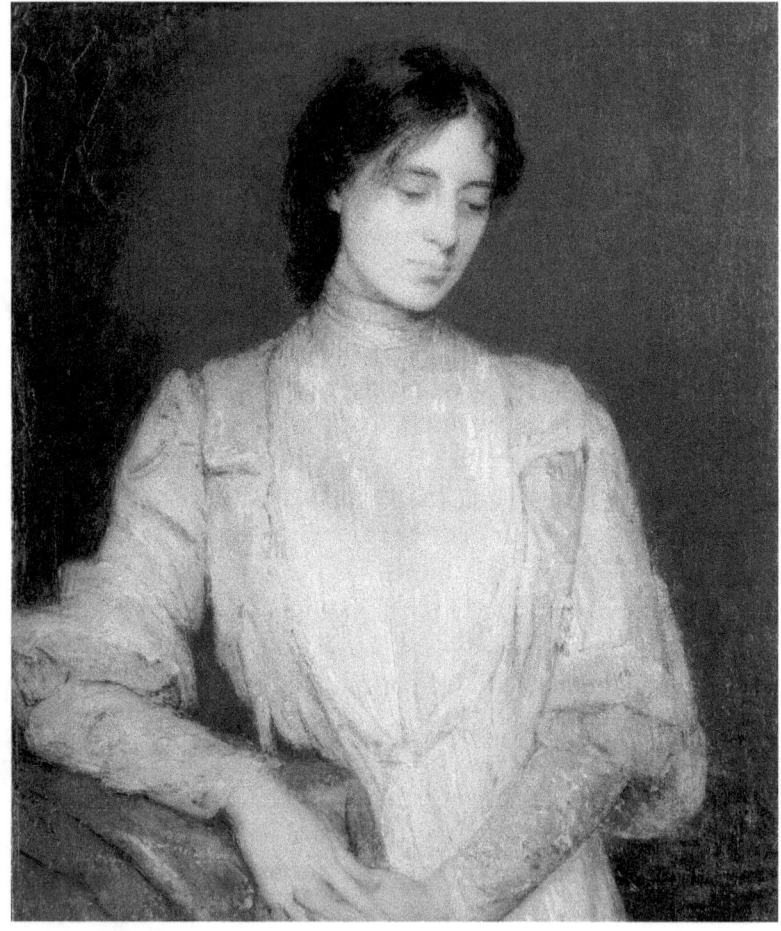

Julian Alden Weir
A Gentlewoman, 1906
Oil on canvas
Smithsonian American Art Museum, Washington, D.C.
Gift of William T. Evans

tric personality and shabby appearance might have attracted mere curiosity and pity from the casual observer.

Perhaps the finest of Weir's many interpretations of feminine character is *The Gentlewoman* of the National Gallery in Washington—a person of rather austere intellectual type, one might assume at first glance; yet soon enough we recognize that she is really a gentle, gray lady whose meditations are sound and sweet. It is delightful to remember her, the simple lines and colors of her dress, the unobtrusive dignity of her hands, the smoldering light in her downcast eyes, as of spent moments and bright memories. With infinite sympathy and admiration her youth has been revealed in the very embarrassment of taking leave of her for always. Yet we see that the art of living is ever at her command, and that the years will add to her exquisite distinction. Hers is a personality before which we stand uncovered, introduced by a very courteous gentleman who knows her worth, and whose praise is as fine a tribute to Woman as ever an age of chivalry could boast. The man who created this portrait was not merely an accomplished painter; he was a great artist and inspired by a great ideal.

If *The Gentlewoman* is Weir's masterpiece in the idealized naturalism of his figure paintings, *Pan and the Wolf*[20] may be chosen (it was his own choice) as his most important landscape. Certainly it is the most impressive, because of its classic grandeur of design. The artist seems to have said to himself, "Now, suppose I try a classic landscape as Corot would have painted had he lived a little longer." And so—there is the same glamour of twilight on the edge of a wood, of color lingering in the western sky, of the illusions that linger in a green glade silvered in dew-drenched dimness, of antique figures in a dreamy dusk. But now there is added pale air that trembles, transparent shadows on the rocks and jeweled gleams woven through the mystery of dark and light to make the Memory of oncoming night not only more beautiful, but more true. To challenge comparison with Corot was a daring thing to do, yet the comparison was

---

20. [c. 1907, The Phillips Collection, Washington, D.C. Acquired in 1916]

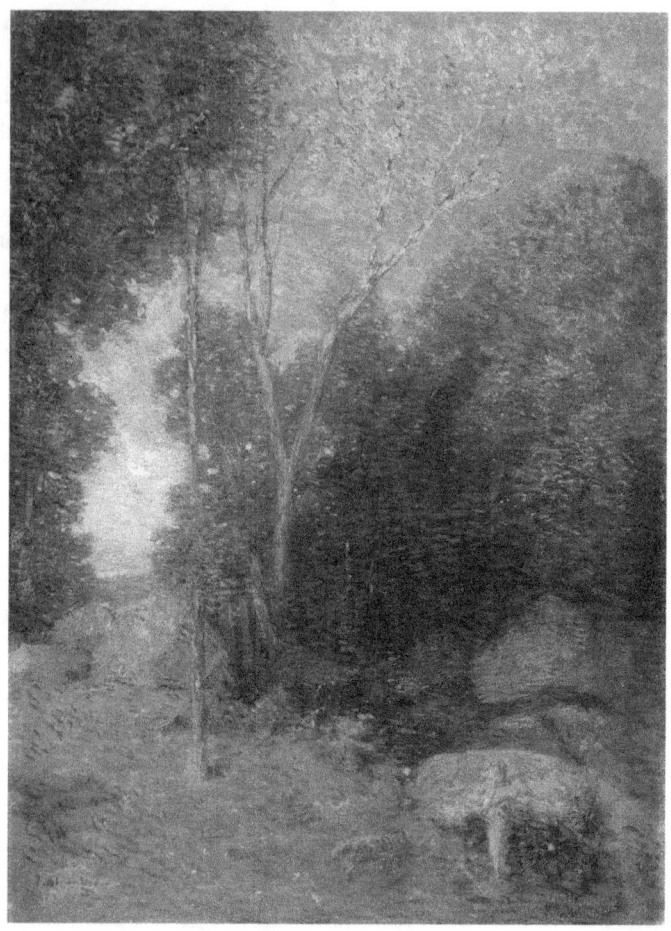

Julian Alden Weir
Pan and the Wolf, c. 1907
Oil on canvas
The Phillips Collection, Washington, D.C. Acquired in 1916

inevitable, nor does Weir suffer by it. The Frenchman may have been the greater master of design and the more perfect painter, but he confined himself to a much narrower range. Weir was incapable of repeating *Pan and the Wolf* as Corot repeated over and over his dance of dryads, or of Italianized shepherds in sylvan settings, where every tree is in its proper place. The two men were most alike, and most spontaneous and delightful, when they were content to represent the familiar scenes they lived in and learned to love. Corot pleases me most in his bright little *paysages intimes* of sunny country roads and his well-loved lake near Ville d'Avray. It seems to me that it is not the Weir of *Pan and the Wolf*, but of such landscapes as *The Old Connecticut Farm,*[21] *The High Pasture,*[22] *Visiting Neighbors, The Fishing Party, Plowing for Buckwheat, The Spreading Oak,*[23] *Birches at Windham,*[24] *Building a Dam,*[25] *The Hunter's Moon,*[26] *Afternoon by the Pond,* and *Woodland Rocks,*[27] who will live forever as the poet-painter who sang the song of spring and summer and autumn in the American countryside, the song of American sunshine, of sweet American breezes rippling through summer leafage, the song of American skies, and of New England fields, for all their stones, and of friendly woods, not in spite of but because of their slender second growth. Weir loved nature too much in particular places to alter the aspect of his familiar world. If an ideal loveliness is in his landscapes, it is the idealism again of the man's own nature expressing its joy in reality through a magic of beautiful painting.

Weir's wonderful versatility and courage for new experiments, the adventurous spirit of the man, continued into his old age, and it is a joy to record that, in many ways, his latest pictures are his best. There seemed to be an ever increasing mastery in his method of solving each problem. Never before had he been more certain to achieve beauty of texture and solidity of form, evanescence of

---

21. [*Connecticut Farm,* 1886, Princeton University Art Museum]
22. [c. 1905, The Phillips Collection, Washington, D.C., Acquired in 1920]
23. [c. 1910, Portland Art Museum, Portland, Oregon]
24. [*The Birches,* 1903, Private Collection]
25. [1908, whereabouts unknown]
26. [c. 1909, Private Collection]
27. [between 1910–19, The Phillips Collection, Washington, D.C., Acquired in 1920]

light and concealment of labor. The *Knitting [for Soldiers]* of 1918 has exquisite transitions of light and the most enchanting tones. The modeling achieves on a flat surface and without apparent effort a perfect realization of weight as well as of form. The drawing is profoundly sensitive and expressive of the subject, a wholesome American girl day-dreaming as she knits her helmet of gray wool for the boy who will fight for her rather more than for Democracy. In spite of fatal illness and failing strength, J. Alden Weir, in this affectionate tribute to the American woman in the war, did his bit with all his accustomed genius, nobility, and charm.

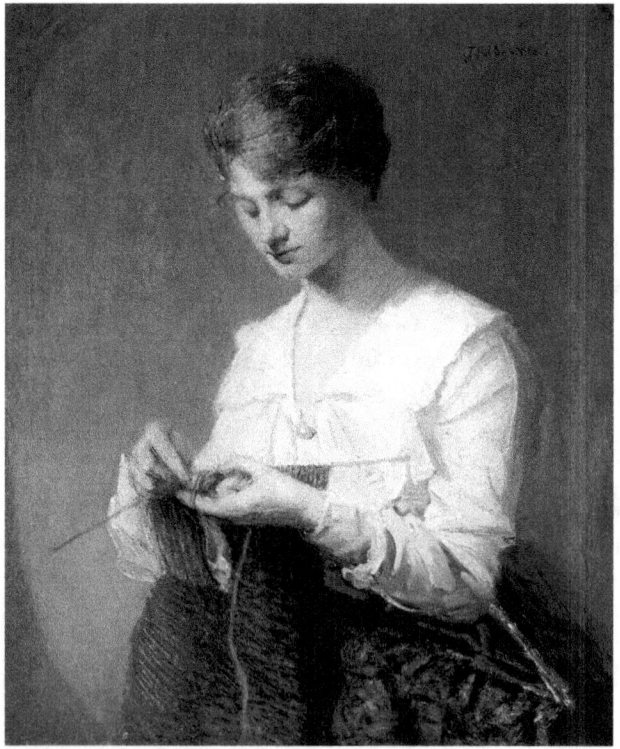

Julian Alden Weir
Knitting for Soldiers, 1918
Oil on canvas
The Phillips Collection, Washington, D.C. Acquired in 1918

On the 8th of December, 1919, Weir died of heart failure after a protracted illness, through which he had been inexhaustibly cheerful, patient, and productive. He will always symbolize for me in his life and express for me in his art the wholesome sagacity of choice, the nervous complexity of purpose, the high unformulated ideals, the. virile simplicity of soul of our own United States.

HONORÉ DAUMIER
(1922)

IN his day Honoré Daumier was celebrated as a caricaturist and only a few of the more discerning artists and critics realized that he was one of the giants of Art, one of the salient individualities of the nineteenth century. Of the Old Masters only Michelangelo surpassed him in giving to abstract thought plastic expression. The wonder is that he was able to do this, not from his inner consciousness in hours of deep meditation with the help of far sought models, but in the midst of his professional labors, from casual contact with the turbulent life of the streets of Paris, where he would see the drama of ordinary experience enacted on all sides and would seize the moments when expressive movements of forms full of character revealed to him meanings profound in their significance. Also he could suggest the rhythm of life itself in the continuity of his line. In this power he resembles Tintoretto and El Greco, as also in the way his figures are modeled in light which reveals their rotundity while accentuating their expression. It is of Rembrandt, however, that we think most often as we look at Daumier's greatest paintings, for these two artists were passionately solicitous for human suffering and with a keen sense of the beauty of tragedy.

Those of us who recognize in Daumier one of the world's great artists are inclined to shed biographical tears, when we speak or write about him; because he toiled for forty years as a caricaturist. It is sad to read of the contract he made with *Le Charivari* for eight cartoons a month, of the four thousand lithographs reproduced in that one periodical, while he was kept in a state, if not of actual captivity, at least of what amounted to servitude by his own specialized success, by the reputation he made at an early age for himself and his editors, by the joint forces of expediency and habit and popular

First published in *Honoré Daumier: Appreciations of his Life and Works* (New York: E. P. Dutton & Company, 1922).

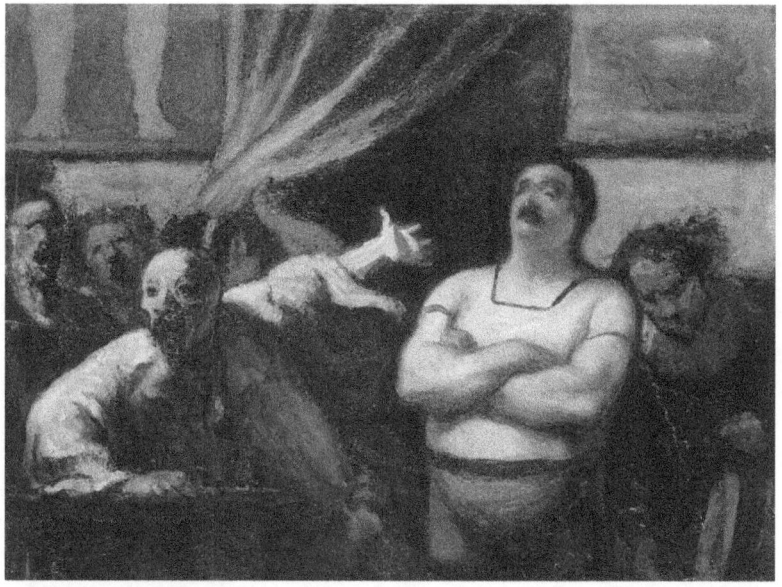

Honoré Daumier
The Strong Man, c. 1865
Oil on wood panel
The Phillips Collection, Washington, D.C. Acquired in 1928

demand. Knowing his seriousness and his ambition, we lament the fact that he never found leisure to cultivate the fruits of his spirit. We resent the constraint and the painful efforts to keep playing the part under which his work as a caricaturist must have placed him. We recall other instances of the curse of comedy, of the tragedy of enforced humor. We wonder how he found time to do the beautiful things he did, how he managed to make himself at the first possible moment not only a painter but a great one. The noble, monumental works of art which he might have painted torment us. Today we rank him with the greatest of the great. Is it only on the quality of his few paintings executed between 1850 and 1864, while taking a vacation from *Le Charivari*, that we are to estimate his place in history? Emphatically, no. The fallacy of our pathos is that the lithographs were not hack-work at all, but full of genius, not handicaps to his success but stepping stones to his complete self-realization.

The lithographs of Daumier not only constitute the bulk of his life work but express him more fully and freely than a life-time entirely devoted to painting would have done. If, like Millet, heedless of failure and reconciled to poverty and neglect, he had celebrated all his life long the heroic aspects of the lowly, or if, like Delacroix, he had been absorbed in technical experiments, and in romantic dreams, or if, like Courbet and Manet, he had been a "chef d'école" of realism, at war with the academies; if he had painted in any one such way or in each of them by turns to the limit of heart's desire there is doubt whether he would have achieved a more distinguished place in the history of art than we now accord to him for his life work as a satirical draftsman of the "bourgeoisie," who permitted himself one splendid digression into painting with results gloriously distinguished in style and all the more precious to us because limited in quantity. And the lithographs are inherently important. We delight in their unfailing observation of physical and mental absurdities, their amazing insight and intuition. Here are evidences enough of consummate genius not only for satire and for philosophical realism, but also for a pictorial style upon which the best contemporary art has been modeled. Daumier spoke, in his drawings as in his paintings, with the unmistakable accent of greatness, a sonorous language of balanced light and shade, line and mass. The art of the painter may be sensed in the lithographs with their rich velvety blacks and delicately modulated half-tones. His forte was the silhouette. What an affluence of these in the prints! And what a preparation for the paintings he received with his long practice of drawing from intensive observation and memory of only the expressive and essential lines. At no art school could he have learned so well what to eliminate, how to abbreviate, how to reduce a theme to its simplest terms. However, only a very few comprehended the art that was in the lithographs. Their success was due to their commentary on contemporary life and manners. Never have there been better caricatures, never pictorial satire more comprehensible and at the same time more profound. His world and his time needed the mind and the heart of this man, needed all it could get of him day after day, every flash of his wit, every spark from his spirit, every shaft of illumination he could cast on men and events. His paintings were scorned as negligible, since at that period it was taught that paintings should not descend to the level of actual life, especially the life of the lower classes. He might have changed all this, fought and won the fight for realism then and there, but that was the destined work for Courbet and Manet. Daumier inspired these men and forged their weapons. His fight was not aesthetic but philosophical. Drawing for the people in their own funny papers, he made them share his hate and scorn for injustice and cruelty and sham and called them to enjoy his good-natured teasing and mimicking of "Les bons bourgeois," "Les drôles papas," "Les bas bleus" and all the rest of the familiar Parisian types he lived with and laughed at and loved. If he had never been an illustrator the world would be the poorer for comprehensive and profound studies of human nature, for revelations of the master passions, the secret springs which control desires and destinies. He drew a veritable *Comédie Humaine,* the people revealing themselves as they do in the immortal novels. In fact the art of Daumier in his lithographs is the pictorial counterpart of the art of Balzac. There are of course, striking differences. Daumier had more sentiment, Balzac more daring. Balzac divined what he never witnessed and attempted to interpret every class. Daumier's drawings had an influence on the masses and came therefore under the control of the censor who compelled him occasionally to spare the Church, the Army and the State. As for the aristocracy, it was out of his range and even when visible he found it so schooled in reserve, so clever in concealments, that he did not attempt to penetrate its dis guises, pref erring to confine himself to classes wherein people are more inclined by temperament to spontaneous self-revelation. If it had not been for Daumier's contract with *Le Charivari,* we would never have suspected the range of his observations, the potency of his satire, the scathing power of his scorn, and, "au fond," the genial kindliness of his spirit. Through no other channel than journalism could he have been such a force for good, such a constructive, corrective influence. As a painter he was first and last an artist, scrupulous not to teach or preach where teaching or preaching are out of place. In his lithographs the artist was secondary to the satirist, the philosophical observer of the passing show, and gladly and eagerly he let himself go, rejoicing in the racy spectacle of human life and in the chance to draw a moral or adorn a tale and extract a joke. Make no mistake, Daumier was no victim of press and public. He was well content with his special field and proud of his power and supremacy therein.

Paternal influence had a great deal to do with shaping his career as a cartoonist and with reconciling him to the exacting demands of that vocation. Honoré's father was a glazier who once aspired to write verse. His failure to be taken seriously as a poet humiliated him and convinced him that art is a delusion and a snare. He bade his boy beware of artistic ambition as if it were a deadly sin. Honoré was therefore put to work running errands and later serving writs in a Court House. There he received vivid early impressions of "les gens de justice," and they seemed malevolent and sinister to him from that time on. His instinct for drawing was not to be denied and in the end Daumier *père* acquiesced. I suppose it was very constantly on the boy's mind to convince his father that he could make his living with his pencil. As a painter the boy would have had to laboriously make his way and fail to prove his point if he failed to hit the popular fancy. So he decided to study lithography and to draw cartoons which could be reproduced in periodicals. The editor of *La Caricature,* [Charles] Philipon, was a man of powerful personality. He fired his staff of young men with his own political principles and made them all ardent propagandists. Apparently young Daumier was genuinely interested in politics and with a strong Republican bias. Philipon made him into a furious fighter for democratic ideals, a formidable foe to Louis Philippe and his ministers. His portraits of famous personages like [François-Pierre-Guillaume] Guizot and [Adolphe] Thiers were carefully prepared. First he studied his victim with that penetrating all-seeing eye of his, then after fixing the man in his marvelous memory, he would model him in clay, the salient points of him at least, then he would fire away with his pencil and his drawings were full of the freshness of his first impression and the sense of volume gained through his practice with sculpture. In spite of the caricaturist's willful exaggeration, the likenesses were said to be startling. Philipon and Daumier became dangerous to the government and finally *La Caricature* was suppressed. With probable relief, Daumier turned to *Le Charivari* and drew one series after another of quietly humorous studies of plain people of many types. I have no space here to even suggest that quality of these famous drawings nor to describe their subjects nor to comment on their satire. They were caricatures of a familiar kind made for popular entertainment. But they were more than that. Human forms moved obedient to dominant instincts and the goads of special and secret desires. These forms were modeled in light and shade, the stone left bare for the strong lights, the dark notes laid in with a painter's sense for colorful mass. The line was alternately ludicrous and portentous, mock heroic, fantastic, deliciously comic. The harmless and amiable idiosyncrasies of the average middle-class person were as interesting to Daumier as the desperate ideas of the derelict and the devious wiles of the wicked.

The revolution of 1848 was a signal for Daumier to take up again the weapons of political satire but his heart was no longer in the work. Although he never tired of studying humanity yet he longed for leisure to paint from an artist's instead of a journalist's point of view. About 1850 he began to paint in watercolor and oil and to exhibit occasionally at the Salon. His work was received coldly with shrugs of faint praise covering general consternation or else with torrents of protest; meant to be friendly, against the abandonment of his special field in which he was the undisputed master. Daumier had discounted all this and he was prepared for misunderstanding, failure and neglect. He was painting consciously for posterity, as well as for his own pleasure and in justice to his own genius. About 1860 be resigned from *Le Charivari* to devote his time to painting while even his friends shook their heads with grave concern and warning.

They were right. Daumier could not sell a picture, and in 1864 he was compelled to return to his drawing board and his caricatures. He painted for a few years more when occasion permitted, but the approach of the Franco-Prussian war fired his patriot spirit and he felt that his country needed his powerful commentary. It was only when his sight began to fail that he gradually retired from his arduous professional labors to his little home in the village of Valmondois, given him by his friend Corot. He had saved little or nothing from his salary, having always been impractical and improvident and generous beyond his means. In the end, it was he who had to accept help from friends to save him from actual want. Although totally blind during his last years, and these must have been a premature death to one whose eyes had been so important, yet he was happy in the contemplation of posthumous fame, especially after the retrospective exhibition of his work at Durand-Ruel's gallery in 1878, when all intellectual and artistic Paris rendered homage to his genius, and even his paintings came into their own. He died the following year.

The paintings of Daumier may for convenience be considered categorically, according to their subjects. First there are the satires on the Law Courts of Paris. Ever since his experience as a boy when in corridors and court rooms he had gazed at the powerful, portentous personages in black gowns who held, it seemed, human lives in the hollow of their hands and human hearts under the lash of their scornful and remorseless logic, Daumier had promised himself some day to strike back at the bullies. and hypocrites of the law and to hit them hard. He fulfilled this intention and none of his satires seem more humane, more earnestly purposeful, than those in which he withers with scorn the contemptuous carelessness of prejudiced judges or the mock emotion of a counsel for the defense, working himself up to actual tears in his appeal on behalf of the innocence of a habitual criminal, or the grim and curious alliance of a stately and austere attorney with a degenerate and beastly client taking counsel together in whispers how they may evade the law, or the meaningful exchange of glances between two lawyers as they gather up their papers at the end of a trial, the successful veteran of many unscrupulous arguments enjoying his latest triumph and saying "I told you so" to a colleague who has just called him again a "clever devil." I could refer to many more of Daumier's celebrated exposés of the legal profession in the Paris of his day. The pictorial possibilities of these subjects appealed to him as a designer and especially as an emotional painter. He gave us the silhouette of the capped and gowned *avocats* against bare, illuminated walls, the drama of cast shadows, of dimly seen distances containing groups of figures vaguely suggesting tragedies of the kind we touch in passing, and that pale light which enters obliquely from unseen windows and diffuses itself with dreary and discouraging coldness over these scenes of intrigue and suspense, of turmoil and trouble. Especially beautiful are the black gowns and the white walls when daylight falls upon them for an accidental moment of beauty in the midst of cruel bleakness. Velázquez and Ter Borch never surpassed Daumier in revealing the sensuous colorfulness of luminous blacks and ivory whites, nor are the shadows of Rembrandt more mysterious or marvelous as envelopment for figures. It is real air we breathe in these court rooms of Daumier's, and the special odor of it we seem to remember.

In *Le Charivari,* one of the most popular of Daumier's series of lithographs dealt with the disordered lives of derelicts, drunkards, beggars, parasites and enemies of society. These he satirized with scorn which suggested that no civilization can be considered worthy of the name which permits such wretches to live at large and multiply their species. In his paintings he analyzed the vagabond instinct of man and found a class of Bohemians sharing the irresponsible waywardness of the utterly worthless, yet ennobled by qualities for which Daumier had special sympathy. In this class belong the professional clowns, wrestlers, gypsies, itinerant peddlers, fiddlers and nomadic adventurers of every sort—odd, eccentric, overgrown children who are the world's hired entertainers. They are the descendants of the jesters and jugglers of the Middle Ages, men whose misfortune it is that they cannot be taken seriously, but are set apart, by reason of their physical and mental peculiarities, to be buffoons. That such men have capacities for deep feeling and serious reflection, that they have the same problems, passions and sorrows as other men, personal troubles which. must be concealed lest they interfere with their destined work of making the world laugh, Daumier saw this truth and insisted that we should see it. Shakespeare, who conceived the character of the heroic Fool in *Lear,* diverting his royal master's tormented mind from its agonies by his antics, would have recognized in Daumier a passionate sympathy like his own for the poor chap who must jest though his health is spent and though his heart is broken. Our artist's personal tragedy is delicately suggested, his own subjection to caricatures, his impending need at the time to return to it since no one would buy his serious paintings. I do not mean to say that Daumier was ever in any sense a mere comedian, for I think I have made it sufficiently clear that in his caricatures he was a person of national power and importance and that he exulted in the exercise of his humorous faculties, putting much of his art into it as well. But the point of view of the artist was Daumier's natural angle of vision and the fact that this point of view had to be suppressed and that of the journalist substituted, this is a real tragedy and adds a poignant personal note to his paintings of professional entertainers who have to be funny because the world wills it and not because they are so inclined. It would be difficult to find a more haunting picture than that of the tired mountebank, resting behind the scenes. His gymnasts, wrestlers and boxers, for all their big muscles, are weary, body and soul. The choice of such themes was unprecedented. Daumier was one of the pioneers in depicting the gay and debonair heedlessness of consequences which charms us in the lives of gypsies and vagabonds, strolling players and street musicians, poets and artists who live gaily in garrets, wondering where the next meal is coming from, laughing and singing in the teeth of fate. Every adversity they turn into adventure to be met with becoming bravado. Our grim and sordid old world is their playground. The theme is as old as the troubadours and François Villon. It lived again in Murger's *Scènes de la Vie de Bohême,* in Stevenson's *Providence and the Guitar,* in Locke's *The Beloved Vagabond,* in Synge's *In the Shadow of the Glen.* Daumier saw the glamour, but being a realist saw also the tragedy. In one memorable painting fugitives are seen in fantastic silhouette against a fierce, lurid sunset sky as they hurry down a winding trail in a wild country, lashed by the wind, pursued by enemies, seeking escape, "anywhere, anywhere, out of the world." We recall Bret Harte's immortal tale, *The Outcasts of Poker Flat.*

In his paintings, Daumier was often a dramatist as well as a painter, but he was too much of an artist as well as too much of a humorist to ever paint melodrama or mere burlesque. He had caused so many sensations with his caricatures that he was cured in advance of any desire he might have have had to paint sensational canvases for the Salon. He had told so many grim and funny stories and preached so many sermons showing the horrible example and made so many grotesque images to lampoon the lamentable specimens of the human race that there was no danger of his deliberately diluting the pure aesthetic purpose which he cherished for his paintings with any such irrelevance as an infusion of the over-emphatic satire of his journalist days. This is something that Daumier's imitators would do well to understand. What they stupidly imitate in their paintings is the mere journalese of the master's caricatures, not the art that is in them and not the ancient and universal language of pure plastic beauty which he used in his paintings. To be sure he aspired to interpret modernity, but always through art which is ageless. Subjects drawn from the life of Paris, its river banks, its streets, its station waiting-rooms and railroad compartments, its theaters, and other places of amusement, where plebeian types congregate and reveal themselves so clearly—these subjects were dignified in Daumier's paintings by his unfailing respect for his aesthetic medium and by the principles of restraint and harmony which give to the true artist's observations of character some quality or other of beauty. Millet's attitude was much the same. What Millet did for the French peasant, Daumier did for the bourgeois of Paris. Both men use individuals as representative of classes and classes as expressions of ideas and ideas as the proper material for the painter in giving to particular aspects of the spectacle of human life some general and universal significance. This quality of observation in Daumier entitles him to higher rank as an artist than belongs to satirists such as Goya and Hogarth, who resemble him in many ways, chiefly in that they are all gifted with the flair for beautiful paint. But Goya's satire was a matter of satanic hate and morbid revery and Hogarth's of didactic discourse on the frailties of human nature, whereas Daumier, like Balzac, was conscious always of having to do with the epic of facts and with the beauty of truth, with some meaning perhaps which may become apparent, some gestures which may express states of soul if we study with sufficient sympathy the endless procession of life wherever we see it passing. Daumier, through his window, could see a splendid woman of the people bathing her man-child and her household linen in the river, and respectfully he watched her as she managed somehow to carry the bundle of wash while assisting her small son to climb the steep steps, one by one. Her strength, her adequacy for her task, all are revealed in the silhouette of her shoulders and arms against the white light shed on the river and on the row of vivid white tenements of the opposite shore. No sensationalism and no sentimentality here, only the beauty of truth trained to seek and find for painting what is bath picturesque and emotionally significant—in line, in light, in color, and most of all in form. When he painted a group of men singing in lusty chorus, watching their leader, the rollicking mirth of "close harmony" in their eyes, or else a party of hunters, thawing out with the help of pipe and bowl before a blazing fire, a faithful old hound in their midst, sharing the good cheer and delicious relaxation of the moment, Daumier was no longer a caricaturist looking for something to caver with ridicule but the artist citing two instances in which that blessed boon, good fellowship, may be sensed in all its heart-warming splendor. Then there are the paintings of artist life, and of that world where in studios pictures are born and where in galleries amateurs congregate. These Daumiers are perhaps the least important but they are the most personal of all. In them our artist pays a tribute of genuine sentiment and affection to that world to which he belonged but from which the exigencies of his career estranged him. All his life Daumier drew pictures which were successful exactly in proportion to their facility of comprehension by the public, but when his chance came to paint he painted for himself and for those rare

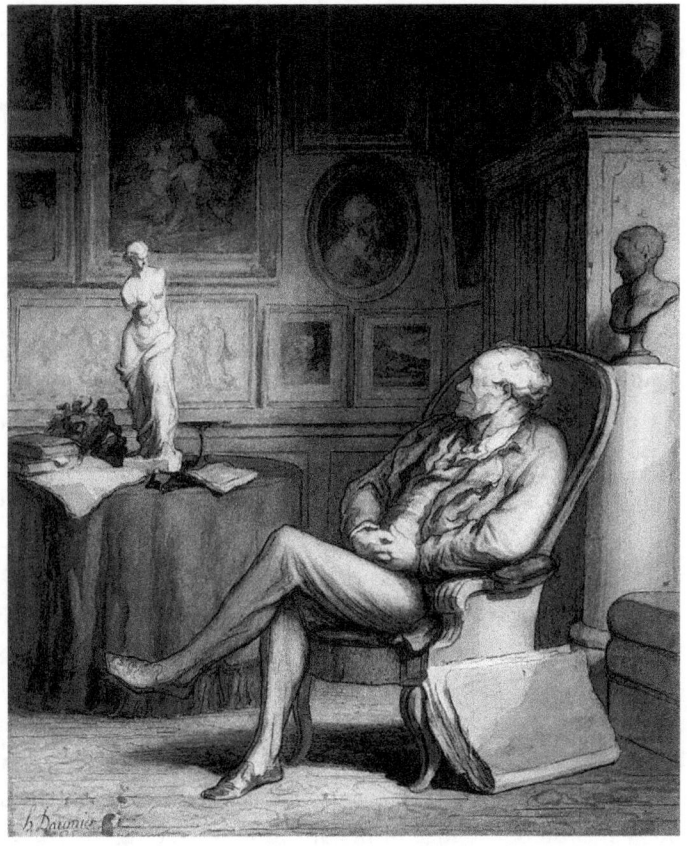

Honoré Daumier
The Connoisseur, c. 1860–65
Pen and ink, wash, watercolor, lithographic crayon, and gouache over black chalk on wove paper
The Metropolitan Museum of Art, New York. H.O. Havemeyer Collection, Bequest of Mrs. H.O. Havemeyer, 1929

individuals who care for aesthetic values. His heart went out with special affection to the patron of art and the friend of artists who helps the lonely creator in spite of the "world and his wife," and in spite of the dogmatism and stupidity of those in authority over him in his own profession. I love Daumier's watercolor of the Collector, alone with his treasures, lounging in his slippers and dressing gown in the depths of an easy chair.[1] He contemplates in contentment these spoils of the spirit of extraordinary men and he dreams perhaps of how he can communicate to the many who "have eyes and see not" the ability to appreciate the beautiful, to the end that artists may not be without reward in their own day and without honor in their own country.

Many men of special gifts were contained in Daumier. He was a caricaturist but he was just as much a mystic. He was at heart a romantic poet and he was actually a realistic painter. He was a patriot and therefore a propagandist, but he was also an artist and a technical experimenter far in advance of his age. He was celebrated chiefly for his scathing satire, but the works by which he most wished to be remembered were small, quiet canvases in which he revealed to kindred spirits his love and reverence for spiritual things, Few people know him as the painter of *The Good Samaritan*,[2] nor have I ever seen this painting, yet I know I would take off my hat to it as to the work of the real Daumier. Perhaps the most significant subject he ever undertook was *Christ Mocked*.[3] The head of the Saviour is seen in silhouette above the howling, gesticulating mob, very pale, showing a soul very sensitive to all these insults and yet proud and cairn and patient, victorious over the torments of the hour. Here Daumier expressed his inmost soul's protest against the mean business of mockery in which, because of his aptitude for seeing the ludicrous side of everything, he himself had been so much employed. Here he

---

1. [*The Connoisseur*, c. 1860–65, The Metropolitan Museum of Art, New York]
2. [c. 1850–60, The Burrell Collection, Glasgow]
3. [*Ecce Homo*, 1850, Folkwang Museum, Essen]

appealed to his race and fellow countrymen, begging them not to mock so much, to judge less harshly when they cannot see. Daumier had been a fighter but he had always played fair and had fought for the sake of an ideal. He had exposed base passions conscientiously but he had a repulsion for vice and avoided unnecessary indecency. In this he differs from Rabelais with whom he has been compared. Of his four thousand cartoons, there is not one that is unclean, an amazing record for a French humorist. Daumier's individuality was so marked, his absorption in novel subjects and great emotions so unmistakable that Mr. W.C. Brownell would not have accepted him as a representative French artist. That fine critic has convinced us that "French art does not contain enough personal flavor to escape conventionality." To be sure, exceptional personalities come to the surface and emerge "from the mass to which culture gives its conventional uniformity."[4] But these are the men of genius. The fact remains that mind is what counts in French art—not emotion. When the French enter the realm of sentiment they are in danger of becoming either fantastic or conventional. "[Their] technic itself is sapient rather than sensuous."[5] "The divinity which presides over every aesthetic shrine is Taste. [...] Naturally the rule of taste results in rigid standards following the tyranny of the mode. Nowhere, perhaps, is fashion so exacting. [...] Hence the development of schools, the erection of methods into systems."[6]

We are reminded of Athenian culture but the critic remarks that "the French have the antique sanity" but not "the serenity nor the spirituality of the antique world."[7] Agitated mind counts with them more than tranquil emotion. Their philosophy intrudes. Thus Millet's sentiment is mentally preoccupied by his pervasive interest in the French peasant. And if Brownell had chosen to bring Daumier

---

4. [*French Traits: An Essay in Comparative Criticism* (New York: Charles Scribner's Sons, 1919), 252.]

5. [Ibid., 151.]

6. [Ibid., 272–74.]

7. [Ibid., 160.]

into the discussion, he might have said that he also was too emotional to be a representative French artist and too much preoccupied (with his street types), too conscious of their background, in a word, too romantic, to be of the true classic breed.

Throughout Mr. Brownell's masterly analysis of *French Traits*, the name of Daumier is not once mentioned, and only a passing reference to him is made in the earlier volume, *French Art*.[8] This seems to me most strange, for I recognize in Daumier the French aesthetic genius, not at its most ordinary level, but at its best. Even with Daumier, mind counted more than sentiment, and to be precise, such emotion as he displayed in his art was philosophical and humane rather than poetic. Of course, his early adoption of lithography as a profession and his long continued career as a cartoonist left little time for the dreams and moods required by the poet. But this was not altogether a compulsion by circumstance. It was essentially his own choice. The caricaturist's habit of mind more or less clung to him when he later attempted flights of pure fancy, and his symbolism and his sentiment were accented with curiously fantastic emphasis. I have already stressed his philosophical solicitude. And objective pity it was, whereas Rembrandt's was subjective. I have noted his concern for form, for structure, for symmetry, his rather restrained palette. All these qualities are described as truly French in Brownell's analysis. But Daumier, of course, was one of the exceptional geniuses. He was certainly not consistently French to the extent of being like the lesser men, conventional, restrained, elegant and correct. He represents the classic virtues of French art at their crest when conventions can at last be overturned and new standards, new methods, a new viewpoint, established on the old foundations. His function in the history of modern art was to discover the romance of reality, to fuse form and color, style and character, to make men and women out of modernity instead of lay figures out of mythology serve as symbols of universal significance.

---

8. [*French Art: Classic and Contemporary Painting and Sculpture* (London: Charles Scribner's Sons, 1901), 98–99.]

Such artists as Meunier, Degas, Rodin, Forain, Carrière, Picasso, and Cézanne have at different times and in different manners, followed where he led, but they have seldom proved worthy of his inspiration. Behind the complex nineteenth century satire and its romantic ardors, and behind the thoroughly modern philosophical realism in Daumier was the classic spirit, not only sane, but serene in spite of its emotions, and spiritual in spite of its skepticism, seeking to symbolize with monumental, elemental forms and grandiose contours the significance of human life. It was his French logic derived from classic sources which made him the first painter to depict the lives of the poor on the streets of Paris and, through them, to suggest the essential meaning of everything. For is it not logical that a modern artist should interpret his own world and time, that he should use his own eyes to observe life at first hand, that he should prefer street types, unconscious of being observed and of a simple class whose gestures are unrestrained, to self-conscious studio models? And is it not logical that an artist should learn that first lesson of art which teaches a man to find out what he is and what he can do best, and admonishes him to pursue that course whether it takes him over some old trail or impels him to blaze a new one? After all, his fine logic makes Daumier bath French and Classic in spite of his passionate romanticism.

In conclusion I wish merely to express once more the hope that the dead are aware of what we think of them. It would be comforting to feel that Daumier, that great, good man, realizes how today we crown him a veritable king of art. He possessed in abundance just those qualities we prize most in an artist. His disciples are the most distinguished draftsmen, painters and sculptors of our day, and those who show his influence, in one way or another, are to numerous to mention. However much he may seem to us the very pinnacle of French genius, yet his gifts are of a kind which we may all claim, for he conferred upon the world a language which is, in the most profound sense, our universal heritage.

—◆—

ARTHUR B. DAVIES:
DESIGNER OF DREAMS
(1924)

DAVIES is already recognized, not only in this country but in Europe, as one of the few men of original and authentic genius among the painters of our contemporary world. Critics who are apparently impervious to his enthralling charm and baffled by his undeniable obscurity and extravagance of expression are ready to acknowledge his importance, seeming to sense the distinction of mind and eye and hand which manifests itself in his slightest sketches. Indeed, this magician cannot touch brush to canvas, cannot take on a new medium, cannot accept the challenge of any technical adventure without creating some rare felicity of contour or some passage of enchanting color, or some exquisitely evocative hint, even amid the bewildering maze of his late and unlamented Cubist preoccupation, of fair young forms and faces from out the dear forsaken ways of his earthly experience. His fundamental qualities of lyric inspiration and linear rhythm qualified him long ago for the Parnassus of painters and the Olympus of designers. Design is the one word no critic can leave out in writing about Davies. There is another necessary word to complete any appraisal of his genius and I think that word is fantasy. Language and legend and literature, however, are too obliging and offer too many verbal alternatives to make any choice entirely satisfactory. James Huneker resorted to fabulous imagery and called forth an exquisite Unicorn shod in ivory out of one of Davies's most characteristic and famous pictures to symbolize him. This required a further elaboration of his admirable idea and there was talk of "the impossible blue rose" of illusion as eternally opposed to the "rare roast beef" of common-

First published in *Arthur B. Davies: Essays on the Man and His Art* (Washington, D.C.: Phillips Memorial Gallery, 1924).

place fact.[2] And in one essay there was mention of Pan and Ariel and Puck and Shelley, and in another of Botticelli and Piero di Cosimo. No one has understood Davies better than Huneker with his love of all that is fantastic in the Arts. It is difficult; to do justice to artists of this type. Shall we improvise upon the theme of whatever it is they conjure up in our own fancy? Or shall we delve into the perilous depths of their complex personalities and analyze them, try to disengage their own special contributions from the wealth of beauty upon which they have drawn, so that they will stand out clearly from all the suggestive figures woven into the glamorous background of their culture? The former is the easier way and yet it has seemed to me that to evade analysis because of the peril of the process is to acknowledge inability to interpret clearly the artist's mind and purpose, which is, as I conceive it, the critic's true function.

Arthur B. Davies is of the intellectual rather than of the instinctive type of original genius. The instinctive artists need but little culture and are either immune to many influences or seek immunity through isolation. The intellectual artists, on the contrary, are alert to all that is, has been, and will be. They respond to many influences and experiment with many methods and depend upon rich resources of culture and contemplation. They need not isolate themselves for their originality consists in the way they assimilate beauty here, there and everywhere, and they are never more true to themselves than when opening their minds to others. In spite of this eclecticism they never stoop to imitation and they succeed in evolving out of all their research and adventure in the wonderful world of ideas an organized system of expression which is theirs alone, inimitable and unique, their credentials to immortality. Few artists since Leonardo da Vinci, perhaps only Delacroix and our own La Farge, have had such culture as Davies controls, such a range of extraordinary knowledge, such an ardent curiosity about beauty and the causes for its effects, such a tireless mind serving such a boundless

---

2. ["In Praise of Unicorns," in James Huneker, *Unicorns* (New York: Charles Scribner's Sons, 1917), 4; quotation emended.]

fancy, and so debonair a facility for varied invention. He started out to be a civil engineer and he might have become an inventor of some strange device which would have helped us to solve another mystery. He might equally well have been a musician of the type of Debussy or a visionary poet like William Blake. His mystical and imaginative Celtic mind sought expression at an early age in the making of pictures, and so remarkable was his talent for drawing and for dreaming that the scientist in him soon gave way to the artist. The dealer, William Macbeth, recognizing the romantic quality of his point of view, advised Italy and persuaded the art patron, Benjamin Altman, to send him on a pilgrimage to that. homeland of romance. He brought back such works as *The Throne*,[3] *Viola Obligato*,[4] and *Rose to Rose*,[5] ripe, glowing and mellow as the Venetian masters, and yet somehow fresh and original, the spontaneous expression of a mind acquisitive and retentive and yet somehow different from all its derivations. He suggested from the outset that he was capable of mental adventure and there has always been the spice of strangeness in the beauty that he served for aesthetic epicures.

The type to which Davies belongs is that of the alchemist whose imagination is always speculative and whose research is always romantic. The yearning to do something never done before is the besetting passion. This searcher, whether he be poet, musician, sculptor, or painter, cannot rest until he has achieved beauty of some new and vaguely apprehended El Greco's, of Nature's vast structural symphony. "All nature was to Dominico Greco as a Living Presence," writes a biographer.[6] In the intensity of his desire to express his sense of universal movement and aspiration he resorted to overemphasis, to icy color made to palpitate with fire from within, to forms willfully distorted by excess of emotion. If his experiments

---

3. [1895, whereabouts unknown]

4. [1895, The Phillips Collection, Washington, D.C., Gift of Mrs. Wendell T. Bush, 1942]

5. [between 1890 and 1900, Yale University Art Gallery, New Haven]

6. [Albert F. Calvert and C, Gasquoine Hartley, *El Greco: An Account of His Life and Works* (New York: John Lane Company, 1909), 158.]

with color-construction and color-refraction have proved to be even more significant for modern artists than his mystical point of view, that is because we belong to an age of rational science rather than to an age of fanatical faith. But his decorative convention, his sustained rhythm of design was the perfect expression of the rhythm of his soul. And the mysticism which he consecrated to a morbid theology has been adapted in our time by such pagans as Cézanne and Arthur B. Davies for the expression of their own cosmic emotion. The mutual indebtedness of Cézanne and Davies to El Greco, iconoclast, innovator and mystic, is the bond that unites these standard-bearers of opposite ideas, the lion and the unicorn of modern painting.

It is curious but characteristic of Greco and Davies, both starting from influences in romantic Italy attractive to their diverse temperaments, that Theotokopoulos the Greek should have evolved towards the abstract art of early Christian mysticism leaving Greece farther and farther behind him as he merged himself with the flickering candle light and intoxicating incense of the Spanish Inquisition, while Davies, the Welshman, by heredity and temperament a Celt, has evolved to the abstract art of the Pagan world through a persistent pilgrimage towards ancient Greece, with head averted, in recent years, from all the romantic incidents, Celtic in their appeal, which continue to beckon him along the way.

In his day Davies, like Greco three centuries before, was inclined to fret when he was told how Italianate he was, so he went farther south to Sicily and Greece and, by way of antique art, he found himself in a larger pantheism, in a more abstract way of seeing beauty, in a more impersonal admiration for the curves and planes of the human body, in a growing sense of the rhythm which pervades life and should be the soul of art. When I say that Davies has been in quest of the Greek ideal I imply that he has never yet been able to make it quite his own. A pagan in imagination, surely the Greek myths were made by such as he. Yet who can doubt that his mind is troubled with the vibrant nerves of the twentieth century and that he is tortured with a desire for an intensely individual expression as the poised self-disciplined Athenians never could have been. Even when he sounds the Greek motif we are reminded of renascent Italy, of that complex modern longing for beauty pure and self-contained which first became aware of itself amid the crumbling of ecclesiastical canons in the Quattrocento. It is significant 'also that his art has hitherto been inspired, not by the democratic and heroic Greece of the grand temples and statues, but by what Élie Faure calls "intimate Greece," the Greece of Pompeian frescoes, of the carved reliefs from Myrina, the terracotta statuettes from Tanagra (which also influenced Whistler), the painted or incised vases, and indeed all the exquisite luxuries created for the homes of art patrons by craftsmen who were also poets in their various plastic ways and who no doubt more truly resembled our modern artists than the great architects and sculptors of the time of Pheidias. The mind of Davies is wistful and daring, capricious and charming. None of these adjectives describe Praxiteles. To the loveliness rather of the delicately draped and nude figurines of Tanagra with their enchanting blend of intimate naturalism, with a romantic and none too robust aestheticism, and even more to the dancing figures on the vases with their "line as pure as the line of the landscape, as incisive as the mind of the race, and suggesting the absent modeling by its direction alone," to these decorative artists of intimate Greece, Davies has turned for inspiration again and again.

A French critic has written that if Plato had painted, his work would resemble Puvis de Chavannes. It would be at least as permissible to suggest that if Theocritus had painted, there would have been flashes of Arthur B. Davies. The pastorals of the Greek and Sicilian poet have bewitched the landscape painter in Davies and his response is to create color lyrics in which white becomes the "leitmotiv" of his rapture. We behold brown shepherds tending white goats silhouetted against wide blue distances. Or, if the tempo be more drowsy, in a dim, blue-green Sicilian glade dappled with dew-drenched early light, the goats will sleep or stir in opalescent shadows. When the Parthenon receives from Davies pictorial tributes of adaptation it is to some delightful detail that his drawing is dedicated rather than to the sublime and grandiose general effect. First Poussin, then Puvis created true visions of antiquity in which the excited heroes and horses of the Parthenon frieze gallop gaily across a beach of the deep blue Mediterranean, but perhaps the most original use of the oft-recurring vision has been made by Davies in a small canvas called "The White Horses of Attica," which pays its tribute with a capricious modern idiom of prismatic color and tremulous light. This idea of classic landscapes to serve as accompaniment for the melodic design of antique figures has stimulated Davies to his finest and most characteristic achievements, to such noble canvases as those entitled *The Unicorns,*[7] *Natural Law,*[8] *Leda and the Dioscuri,*[9] *As Movement of Waters,*[10] *Eurydice,*[11] and *Fantasy of the Vine.*[12] How the very titles of Davies's dream pictures recall their glamour once we have known them! In spite of this passionate preoccupation with Greek art and legend, Davies is classic by choice. rather than by instinct. The Florentines of the fifteenth century would best have understood his unrest and his search for strange gods.

Like the Greeks and early Italians, though unlike so many aesthetes, Davies is a lover of life. Just as in the landscape backgrounds of early Italian and Flemish painters, the joyous peeps we get of the real world transfigured by their wayward temperaments reveal these men to us under the disguises they had to wear of prescribed ecclesiastical subjects, so we know Davies for the very human person that he is in the fond reminiscences of what he has seen, in the tender transcripts of the real world, in the bits of it chosen with childlike whimsicality and inserted here and there in the most dreamlike way all through the chaos and confusion of his prescribed theoretical experiments. No matter how he improvises with discords, carries his

---

7. [*Unicorns (Legend–Sea Calm)*, c. 1906, The Metropolitan Museum of Art, New York]

8. [n.d., whereabouts unknown]

9. [c. 1905, Spencer Museum of Art, University of Kansas, Lawrence]

10. [1905, whereabouts unknown]

11. [*Eurydice–A Rendezvous with Death*, 1920, whereabouts unknown]

12. [1904, whereabouts unknown]

refinements to the perilous edge of preciosity and experiments with geometrical symbols, it is impossible to conceal the lyric poet and the charming man who loves children and dogs and trees. The bits of reality in Davies are all the more appealing for being enveloped in an atmosphere of illusion.

Perhaps the nearest Italian analogy to the romantic dreams of Davies may be found in the Allegories painted by the aged Giovanni Bellini after he had fallen under the influence of his brilliant pupil, Giorgione. Glamorous are those backgrounds of lonely mountain lakes agitated by the wind, of dramatic deep blue skies garlanded with little silver clouds, of far, majestic mountain tops sharply silhouetted in frosty evening air. The foregrounds are utterly incomprehensible—yet bewitching with their dreamlike semblance of confused reality. In the dreams of Davies, as of Bellini, there are the loveliest little children, and they are none the less the children of dreams for being dressed in frocks which they have worn in Central Park and on Fifth Avenue. Titles are often given to these fantasies and some may puzzle over them in vain. I never care to know what they mean—those reappearing forms of little girls at play, of stags and goats in woodland ways, of tall, pale dream-women beside the marge of streams. For me they are just music, faint melodies of flutes; music too far away to follow, yet vibrant with the rhythm which persists in silent places. Davies, at that best period of his career when radiant figures moved like music through his world of fancy, had reached his promised land, had attained abstraction without losing the human touch.

For all their witchery, the dream-children of Davies are vividly real and his many interpretations of child's play seem to me not only his most appealing because most human pictures, but also his finest expressions of rhythm and ecstasy. Twenty years ago, he was content to let the joy of living inspire his art. In one adorable picture of little, children playing in the woods, wild with delight over the return of spring, the twinkling little leaves seem to dance and sing while the rivulet scampers gaily over the rocks, and the tiny fish dart in and out of the shallows. Oh, to be a child again—like the little boy up the tree and the little girl rolling over and over! It is plain that the sophisticated esthete, A.B. Davies, was once a little boy. But the picture must be seen to be appreciated. It is entitled *The Springtime of Delight*.[13] Many lovely pictures of this period might bear the same title. They all show the mind of Davies at its purest and best. In one miniature landscape, truly an echo of a Giorgionesque *cassone,* we feel a sharp sense of spring, and of children merrymaking over the blithe blue hills that are ever so far away. The naivete is deliberate. The white horse is drawn like the horses we draw at the age of five. In fact children must love this sort of thing since it proceeds so genuinely from the child's own point of view. And yet, of course, the art of it is ripe and mellow and never infantile. The kiddies frolic and scamper and skip across the foreground making a frieze of delicate colors and gaily moving lines.

In spite of the Italian and Greek influences which, more than any other, have formed the art of Davies, the inspiration of some of his finest work has been the scenic beauty of his native land, especially the castellated mountains and giant tree trunks and paradise valleys of California. Such scenes call forth apparitions. Even when full of solitude we are thrilled in such pictures as *Before Sunrise*[14] and *Many Waters*[15] by a sense of awed expectancy, thoroughly in a mood to feel that anything might happen. He has not been blind to the beauties of the more familiar and intimate types of America,n landscapes, but if he has painted a woodland dell or a hillside pasture or a mountain lake, it has been merely to supplement and complete the meaning of figures which he wished to draw in a decorative and fanciful way. Whenever he has done this he has impressed me with his desire to suggest a mystical accord in the scheme of things and with his unerring skill in making the landscapes and figures interdependent and inseparable so that we have the sense of nature serving only as a poignantly felt background for human beings and their emotions

---

13. [1906, The Phillips Collection, Washington, D.C., Acquired in 1919]
14. [1905, whereabouts unknown]
15. [c. 1905, The Phillips Collection, Washington, D.C., Acquired in 1920]

or of human beings existing only as a symbolical foreground frieze for nature and her elements. This is distinctly more the point of view of the selective dramatist with his "unities" of time and place, and of the selective poet with his "pathetic fallacy" than of the landscape painter who is usually ready to humbly acknowledge that nature's spectacular aspects are too overwhelming, and that since he must select his own themes let them be the scenes he knows and understands from long and close association; the banks of his own river, the corners of his own farm.

Davies also has painted his own home country and with much fidelity to fact but with a difference from the ordinary sort of naturalism. *Along the Erie Canal*[16] is a fascinating picture because we cannot disengage the realism of it from the romance. It is said to be a portrait of the place so that it can be recognized even to this day, thirty years after it was painted. This is all the more extraordinary because when we study it we find no meticulous truth-telling in any part but only a romantic glamour. And the technique is an amalgam of the style of the Hudson River men, those worthy pioneers of American painting, with the landscape touch of the Florentine and Flemish "Primitives" whose work the young American artist had just learned to love. There are American landscapes by Davies which I like even better. Never shall I forget *An Idyll of the Harlem*[17] with its distant view of High Bridge in rosy evening light against a deep blue sky. There are children and Airedale terriers and picnic baskets in the shadowy foreground and over the enchanting scene there smiles a yellow moon.

This "Idyll of the Harlem" is intimate and personal, a canvas of no great size and absolutely no architectonic pretensions, just a happy little picture for one's home, yet the design is built on so large a plan, so nobly conceived and with so splendid a sense of space that it has somehow the qualities of great mural decoration. This is even more true of *The Fantasy of the Vine*, which is as serenely decorative a com-

---

16. [1890, The Phillips Collection, Washington, D.C., Acquired in 1920]
17. [n.d., whereabouts unknown]

position of figures in landscape as Puvis de Chavannes ever created. There are no capricious inventions here arid no fragments which fascinate at the expense of the whole. The composition is a a marvel of equilibrium. The artist once saw a sun-kissed vineyard high on a happy hill above Lake Cayuga. It was a magic moment when the water was steeped in deep blue shadow. A vision came to him of joyous girls and boys out of old Greek legends, gathering grapes with ceremonial dignity, their beautiful bare bodies gleaming in the fitful light, all rosy golden against the clouded jeweled waters of the lake. The song is of all our human joys and of all the golden lights that come and go. It is unbelievable that we have not given Davies vast spaces to decorate for he might have been another Puvis had we recognized and nurtured his genius for heroic design.

Then there are landscapes by Davies which reveal nature at dramatic and deeply significant moments. One of these is entitled *As Movement of Waters,* and it is superbly elemental. The waves are rushing on the land with the tireless rhythm of the tides, and the land receives them with the proud resistance of the rocks. The clouds which move across the jagged silhouette of mountain peaks rejoice in the exhilarating battle of the cosmic forces. In the foreground one.

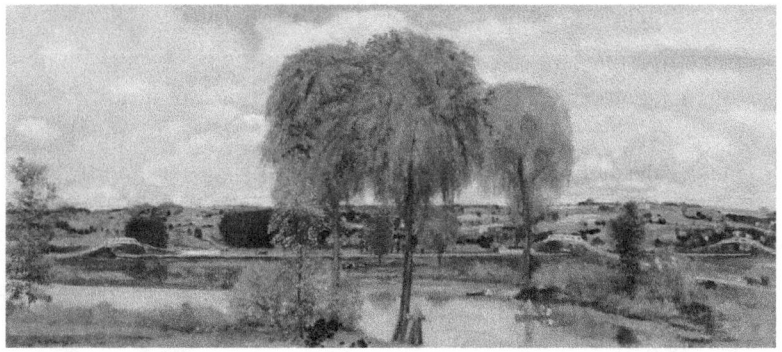

Arthur B. Davies
Along the Erie Canal, 1890
Oil on canvas
The Phillips Collection, Washington, D.C. Acquired in 1920

dimly sees human figures moving to rhythms greater than themselves, swept on by the urge of the elements to some obscure predestined purpose.

I could go on and on recalling paintings by Davies which I have
enjoyed. I wish I could dwell upon the delights of such unforgettable things as *Rose Garden,*[18] *The Throne, Breath of Autumn,*[19] *Four
O'Clock Ladies,*[20] *Hosanna of the Mountains,*[21] *Spring in the Valley,*[22]
Vanishing Mists,[23] *Sleep,*[24] *Alchemy,*[25] and *Unicorns*—especially *Unicorns,* one of the most original creations of imaginative art that has
yet come out of America. I have mentioned only a few favorites,
most of them from the Bliss collection, which contains an amazing
and ever-increasing number of works by the Enchanter. There are
many other collections which contain numerous examples, for it is
true of Davies, as of Ryder, that as soon as one fine picture by him
has been acquired another is desired, and this in turn whets the
appetite for more until the collector enters in spite of himself into a
lively competition with all the other men and women who have had
the same enthralling experience.

Quaintness plays a large part in the compulsion with which the
art of Davies in its romantic earlier phase captivates and charms.
Time brings to pass many changes. Today, Davies could not possibly be called quaint but he is quite frequently called queer. The celebrated Armory Show in 1913 was the beginning of the new chapter
in Davies's career. At that memorable exhibition the imported cult
of the pseudo-primitive asserted itself aggressively. Although Davies
became interested about that time in African Negro carving, he was

---

18. [n.d., whereabouts unknown]

19. [n.d., whereabouts unknown]

20. [1904, whereabouts unknown (formerly in The Phillips Collection, Washington, D.C.)]

21. [1905, Hirshhorn Museum and Sculpture Garden, Smithsonian Institution, Washington, D.C.]

22. [1912, whereabouts unknown]

23. [n.d., whereabouts unknown]

24. [*Sleep Lies Perfect in Them,* 1908, Worcester Art Museum, Worcester, Mass.]

25. [1910, whereabouts unknown]

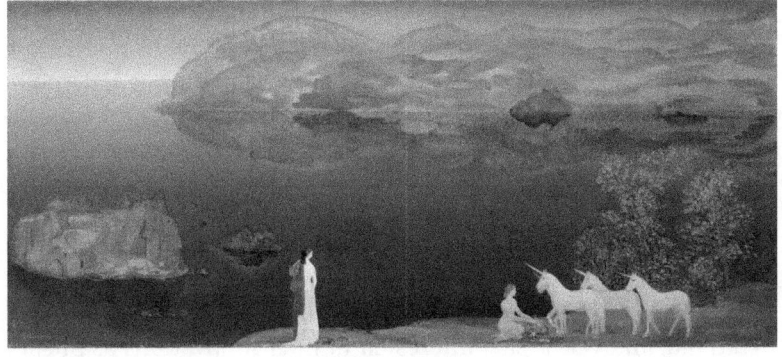

Arthur B. Davies
Unicorns (Legend–Sea Calm), c. 1906
Oil on canvas
The Metropolitan Museum of Art, New York. Bequest of Lillie P. Bliss, 1931
© The Metropolitan Museum of Art. Image source: Art Resource, N.Y.

never a pseudo-primitive in his own expression. He had loved childhood too well all his life to ridicule it in this way. Be that as it may he
recognized that those notorious painters known as "Post-Impressionists and Cubists" were after all rational enough in trying to build
upon the foundations laid by two pioneers whom he respected, two
insatiable searchers and daring innovators, artists who dreamed of a
new pictorial language of pure design, Cézanne and Seurat.

Taking stock of himself Davies had found that he was a master of
design and of linear arrangement but that his color lacked light and
vibration and that it was in no sense structural, and that his form
had been indicated merely by the direction of the lines for the sake
of the silhouette whereas now he wished to express, with his color
and light, his sense of roundness and weight, of depth, of movement,
above all of unity. Hitherto the lines and colors of his foreground
had made the melody and the sharply contrasted lines and colors
of his background, the harmonic accompaniment. Now, as Mather
points out in his masterly contributions to this volume,[26] he wishes

26. [Frank Jewett Mather, Jr., "The Art of Arthur B. Davies," in *Arthur B. Davies*,
45–58.]

to consolidate and to intensify his effects through the working of an all-pervading interior rhythm, to achieve envelopment not for the sake of naturalism but for the sake of emotional reinforcement and decorative unity. Hence his new enthusiasm for El Greco. Striving, at first obscurely, to this end, he began to experiment on his own account, never imitating either Cézanne or Seurat but quite frank in his study of these men and later of Picasso and Derain, and even some of the fanatical devotees of abstraction in painting. He knew that he was as remote from their cosmos as Shelley was from Walt Whitman, and yet he was interested in their innovations as Shelley would have been in old Walt's. His own purpose was to secure for painting the quality of abstract emotion which can achieve perfect conveyance only in music's self-contained expression of rhythm and ecstasy. He enlivened his color, made it sparkle with crystalline light, its deeper tones translucent as ancient glass. Abstract form became his obsession, and geometry was studied along with Egyptian art. In order to construct form into an organization it was necessary to destroy it in so far as it was representative. I remember well how depressing were the results to those of us who watched with suspense and alarm. His winsome world of make-believe seemed shattered as if at the whim of a petulant child. We said that his beautiful nude figures, checkered as they were with cubes and cylinders of light and shade, resembled harlequins. Affectations of pose which formerly had been but fugitive gestures now appeared to us petrified. He kept his effects so beautiful, however, at least in fragments, that he never lost his following of trusting devotees, though many of us wondered rather dubiously to what end he was drifting. Slowly, in spite of us, he evolved a distinguished personal style out of a theoretical impersonal formula. His friend, Miss Bliss, a musician as well as an amateur of painting, and a fellow searcher for jewels in the jungle of modernism, commissioned him to decorate a comparatively small music room in her home.[27] The result is astonishing. The

---

27. [Portions of the Lillie P. Bliss Music Room Mural are now in the collection of the Munson Williams Proctor Arts Institute, Utica, N.Y.]

unaccustomed eye sees details of charming human form arbitrarily embarrassed with a camouflage of transparent cubes which appear to be merely a superficial irradiation by prisms of light. There is a mild shock of angular lines and of dense dark spots introduced into the delectably luminous milieu. Gradually, we understand this aim of pure design, of vaguely symbolical pattern. One thinks first and last of ultra-modern music, of its curious intervals, its fused and fascinating dissonances, and this, of course, is what the patron and the painter desired. If we are properly on our guard not to look for literary significance we need not be confused by the complexity of design for the rhythms of color and of linear arabesque are actually restful, and the dissonances afford the relief of change. A considerable amount of mental preparation, however, and even of special instruction, is advisable, and how few of us take the trouble nowadays to remove our shoes, figuratively speaking, before entering art's temple!

The painter of romantic dreams and fantasies, the painter of adorable little children at play and of lyric landscapes of the mind, the Enchanter who saw beauty touched with strangeness all around him, and cast a spell over us in telling us what he saw, the A.B. Davies of long ago has changed, perhaps irrevocably. He is now an alchemist who repudiates representative painting and strives to transform the painter's art into something both scientific and emotional. He strives for the creation of solids and of synthetic unity, but these are the very achievements which too often escape his grasp. There are times, however, when he realizes his aim, when the modulations of his color define the structure and action of his forms and both elements convey the emotion desired. In his very latest phase, drawings in white chalk on black paper, the figures have returned to nature and to the Greek ideal of bodily perfection. Mannerisms have disappeared and, in such drawings as the one entitled "Constellations," there is a sublime sense of coordinate rhythm, a universal quality which transcends the personal charm.

To be categorical, what he *seeks* today are decorative experiments in the disposition of many figures all over a given space; the dynamic spark within the coordinated forms emanating from an emotional center at the core of the composition; continuity of line often edged with light; repeated accents of gesture and contour; lines and colors marshaled and moving in accord, then again in opposition, but always in ordered rhythm; design by planes suggesting depth and volume; rounded forms on a flat surface which remains flat; finally the spotting of darks and lights, or the mingling and modulation of tones, for the purpose of creating patterns whereby abstract emotions may be mysteriously aroused. Obviously if he *achieves* all this he will be among the Olympians of Art.

Music remains this painter's ideal, and to achieve for painting the condition of music, is positively his most constant aim and thought. The images and moods of music are vague at best. Vagueness is therefore the very essence of the painter's intention. It is foolish for us to quarrel with it. The construction, however, must be as clear as logic and the rhythms must have cosmic emotion. A single spirit must pervade and dominate all the lines, all the forms and all the colors. Davies has discovered in the greatest of the Greeks a secret for the expression of rhythm and ecstasy. He has found that their emphasis is on inhalation, on a focus of expression in the diaphragm. There, where we draw the breath of individual life from the universal energy we best express our emotion. From this focal point we give forth energy according to the amount we receive. In the master's studio are drawings which show a new and marvelous coordination of the action of many figures, all breathing in unison and expressing with their bodies that rhythmic continuity which is life itself. This indrawn breath of life at its moments of inspiration can be suggested in landscape as well as in figures. The trees in *Tissue Parnassian* [28] seem to breathe the life-enhancing air. Such a theory, implying physical fitness, mental and spiritual freshness, and a desire for life at its utmost, goes far to explain the relation of ancient Greek art to ancient Greek philosophy and the greatness of both. It may mark a new and more important phase in the development of the genius

---

28. [n.d., The Phillips Collection, Washington, D.C., acquired in 1923]

of Arthur B. Davies. The recently finished painting, *Tissue Parnas-sian* seems at first but a slight thing—a moment of light music or of dance, an experiment in combining distilled essences of Japan and ancient Greece. But soon we see in it an inspired expression of the thought Hellenic, of serenity and high ecstasy and the idealism of perfect poise, perfect adjustment of relations, as conceived through a pearly mist of modern longing. One thing is certain, these latest drawings and paintings convince me of what I have long suspected, that we must go all the way back to the Raphael of the Vatican, and back of him to the remote sources of our art in the mountain of the Muses to find the divinely beautiful possibilities of the human figure, considered singly and in groups, more admirably understood. There has always been a serenity, an incomparable, rare beauty in Davies' drawings of the nude, which, for all the seductive sensuousness, is not of this earth. In the last analysis it is the charm of Davies' fig-ures which makes us catch our breath, but it is not merely a charm of flesh but a spell like that of music or cloudshine or the ripple of wind in the leaves or the silhouette of mystical summits with dawn coming up again over the edge of the world.

There is a promise of great things to come in the latest creations by Davies, but so incalculable is his genius that it may be a promise unfulfilled. Caprice and curiosity are too inseparable from his mind to justify any confidence that he will cling to his present Athenian inspiration. After all, caprice and curiosity have characterized him throughout his adventurous pilgrimage in search of beauty and they will claim him to the end as one of the unresting searchers. They caused him to tire of his imaginative observation and lyric invention, and they lured him into the already overcrowded field of aesthetic speculation and experiment. The alchemist in Davies has always been associated with the poet, but in the earlier years the poet was making the alchemist serve his purpose, touching the imagination here and there with strangeness, whereas now it is the poet who serves the alchemist, lending to his strange experiments their subtle air of rare unearthly beauty. Even while enjoying his early work, we are often disturbed by an extravagance bordering upon affectation.

This temperamental tendency to surprise and shock has within the last ten years passed into a fixed habit of expression. Tired of looking about him for extraordinary bits of beauty, tired even of looking backward into the land of legend, or inward into the land of dreams, he has sought to pierce the veil of the unknown, to follow any imagined "gleam of that untraveled world whose margin fades forever and forever as we move." How dull it is to pause, to make an end! —And so, driven by ennui and by aspiration, he seeks, first in one way, then in another, to symbolize the vague summons of his soul.

He has symbolized this summons in many beautiful pictures. Perhaps the earliest was *Illimitable Dawn*.[29] Three young girls, hand in hand on a mountain top, overlooking a view of distant ranges, stand hesitant under the vastness of the sky, still dark with dissolving night, their lovely childish bodies tremulous with the wonder of the glowing light they see on the horizon's rim. One of them looks wistfully backward, but the other two face the dawning and the smallest one unconsciously bows before it, as if the thrilling meaning of her youth and the promise of abundant life and the possibilities of adventure had suddenly burst upon her with almost overpowering force. But the picture in which Davies has spoken most directly of his own emotion in his endless quest is the *Measure of Dreams*[30] at the Metropolitan Museum [of Art] in New York. A woman lost in sleep is seen passing from one dream to another. Pale waters and shadowy shores of the subconscious land, realm of the unwritten poems, the forgotten music, the spent delights, and all the fancies that break through language and escape—and through this drowsy land the dreamer still adventuring, lured on by curiosity and caprice, her languid limbs reluctant to be led. The picture sums up for us the career of this distinguished dreamer; the romantic beauty and the unconscious pathos of the wonder-working art of dream-haunted Davies.

---

29. [1903, whereabouts unknown]

30. [*Dreams (Measure of Dreams)*, 1908, The Metropolitan Museum of Art, New York.]

A COLLECTION IN THE MAKING

(1926)

MORE OR LESS AUTOBIOGRAPHICAL

I was born in a substantial old house of what had already become "downtown" Pittsburgh, where the gas-jets flared even on days when the sun could faintly penetrate the smoke. Looking back on my childhood in that house, I do not remember the pictures. I remember with a keen pleasure the appetizing odor of the bread box in the pantry, the unused room at the stairway-landing with a porch overhanging the back yard, and the top floor, a region boasting all the usual adventures of an attic. And yet the long and stately drawing-room contained oil paintings and many of them—"Hudson River School" landscapes and well-drawn, storytelling European pictures in gorgeous gold frames. I was constantly aware of them and more or less fascinated, but none too pleasantly. If my grandmother had made different choices, I might have found myself earlier, or given hints of my dormant passion for pictorial design so that I could have been better prepared for the work I am here to do. Having myself passed almost unscathed through a world fairly burning with pictorial beauty, glowing. with that sacred fire which warms one's inner life, I am enabled now to understand why so many people are turned to stone in the presence of works of art which the wistful artists made out of deep emotions. Perhaps these people have not seen paintings which are really works of art and consequently are led to believe that the painters have nothing to say to them emotionally. Perhaps they have seen many good pictures, but have been misled about the function of painting. If they are expecting pictures to be

---

First published in Duncan Phillips, *A Collection in the Making: A Survey of the Problems involved in Collecting Pictures Together with Brief Estimates of the Painters in the Phillips Memorial Gallery* (New York and Washington, D.C.: E. Weyhe and Phillips Memorial Gallery, 1926).

[153]

nothing more or less than accurate imitations of objects or illustrations of anecdotes, their "inhibition" to pleasure in the more important phases of design in the painter's art is no more to be wondered at than the severe judgments they express as a "defense reaction" when they do not find what they expect. Alas, there are as many bad pictures manufactured nowadays as there were in my childhood to postpone aesthetic awakening. And in this age of an enlarged electorate there are, I believe, more worthless opinions expressed than ever before, more intolerant prejudices aired, more unenlightened eyes comparing the object and its painted image with scorn for purposes other than imitation the painters claim to have. Truly the day of the public which really enjoys and which at least partially understands seems more and more an idle dream. Yet when I feel discouraged, I remember how wonderful the world was for me when at last the scales fell from my eyes and I could tell the difference between a picture the mere surface of which was like music—and another in which the paint was merely paint, spread thick or thin according to the "school," but in either case to no purpose of any possible consequence. What are we going to do about this unfortunate situation?

I for one might never have done anything if Fate had not forced my hand. There came a time when sorrow all but overwhelmed me. Then I turned to my love of painting for the will to live. Art offers two great gifts of emotion—the emotion of recognition and the emotion of escape. Both emotions take us out of the boundaries of self—the first cultivating our impersonal, detached faculties of delightful observation and the second stimulating our minds to flights of intuition, or sharpened consciousness of our capacities for imaginative pleasure. Then there is the immense relief of *Expression,* which is universal—which makes life tolerable for the artist no matter how much he suffers and which enables all of us who are sensitive to art to share this joy vicariously in sympathetic discernment of the motive and the act of creation. At my period of crisis I was prompted to create something which would express my awareness to life's returning joys and my potential escape into the land of artists' dreams. I would create a Collection of pictures—laying every block in its place with a vision of the whole exactly as the artist builds his monument or his decoration. I would interpret the artists in a style suggesting their own minds and methods. I would place their paintings in favorable light to speak for themselves when I had made it a little easier for them to be understood. I would live with such a Collection, learning from the mistakes I made—eliminating the dross—enshrining the pure gold. Why not open the doors to all who would come and watch the building of the edifice—watch the laying of stone upon stone—pass through the portals and share the welcome of art at home, art in its own environment favorable isolation and intimate.

So in 1918 I incorporated the Phillips Memorial Gallery, first, to occupy my mind with a large, constructive social purpose and then to create a Memorial worthy of the virile spirits of my lost leaders— my father, Major D. Clinch Phillips—an upright, high-minded, high-spirited soldier, manufacturer, and citizen, and my brother, James Laughlin Phillips, who was on his way to the heights when death overtook him—an idealist in politics and business—a keen student of men and social conditions—a broad-minded, warm-hearted, lovable and very noble American. Both of them had liked good pictures, and my brother would have been an enthusiastic and wise collector. No mortuary monument, remindful of the accident of death, would adequately commemorate two such men. Something of even greater practical helpfulness than art might have been more appropriate. But I needed to put my own best powers to a coordinated purpose. And I saw a chance to create a beneficent force in the community where I live—a joy-giving, life-enhancing influence, assisting people to see beautifully as true artists see. This aim of trying to understand and then to communicate the artist's point of view is made easier now through the life partnership I have formed with a painter. My wife helps me to build the Collection in the spirit of seeing beautifully with which she builds her own pictures out of the substance and romance of life.

THE POWER TO SEE BEAUTIFULLY

"THE power to see beautifully" is almost all there is worth bothering about in art. Certainly it is the one essential qualification of an artist. "How," we ask, "does an artist set about to see beautifully?" "There is nothing to be formulated about this process," answers the critic Royal Cortissoz, "[except that] in the glow and action of his genius [the artist] sees and feels with a supernatural intensity and the rapture of his vision passes into what he does."[1] In other words, beauty is ecstasy, and that is no monopoly of the artist. But where art and the handiwork of the artist are concerned, beauty is a special sort of ecstasy which has to do with such pleasure as we feel in the fitness and rightness, the dynamic smooth-running mechanism of things. When we feel the sense of rhythm in the universe and in ourselves, we can understand the artist's application of certain laws to bring his own sense of order out of the chaos in the visible world and thus to produce a new creation. We cannot all learn to be painters and sculptors with this great gift of creation, but we can learn the elementary principles of design and the point of view of the designer, his detachment from all that is unrelated to his problem of creating his own conception of beauty, his affirmation of the independence of the aesthetic sense from every other sense, of the artist's right to dominion in our imaginative lives free from the preoccupations and preconceptions of our actual lives with their non-aesthetic associations. We can all learn to see in that way—just as we hear in that way when we listen to great orchestral music. Roger Fry has pointed out that in life there is always something to do next which hurries us along, numbing our perceptions so that we never really look at the world to see how fair it is, nor to observe how accidents of nature, accidents of light—color—texture—and various elements in juxtaposition or fusion, may suggest to us, in art as in science, incredible inventions.

---

1. ["A Critic's Point of View," in Royal Cortissoz, *American Artists* (New York: Charles Scribner's Sons, 1923), 9; quotation emended.]

To have won the artist's point of view is to have acquired a resource within ourselves for resting our minds and souls with a complete change from our own affairs. Anyone who can appreciate beauty without any desire for possession is richer by many million heartbeats of delight than the covetous collector whose interest ends when his prize has been acquired. The mere possession of works of art never justifies itself unless the owners strive for genuine and joyous understanding of their treasures. Nor is the mere creation of beauty quite enough. Art is part of the social purpose of the world and requires appreciation and the bonds of fellowship with all who understand. Art is meant to give pleasure—but pleasure of the right kind. As Brownell has written, we need to know whether or not we are right when we are pleased. Each art has its own capacities and limitations and these must be recognized and respected. The appreciators must keep the artists true to their own special means of expression by evidence of their concern over the difficulties to be surmounted and the qualities to be achieved. To the extent that we enjoy pictures for their own sake, and not because of their resemblance to or their reminders of the life and literature we leave behind, we are sharing the painter's point of view. Pictures help us to live in complete possession of our sense of sight. However unrepresentative, they can train our observant powers by focusing them on aspects and effects; colors in their emotional action and refraction, with or without the flicker of light and shade; aspects and effects also of Line, of vertical and horizontal, curved and straight lines; patterns of forms in space; rhythmical arrangements of various kinds when every part functions to produce vitality, the very movement of life resulting, and the complex thus reduced to the simple by a unifying style. Pictures send us back to life and to other arts with the ability to see beauty all about us as we go on our accustomed ways. Such a quickening of perception is surely worth cultivating. I have devoted myself to the lifelong task of interpreting the painters to the public and of gradually doing my bit to train the public to see beautifully with a sublimated observation detached from self-interest and sufficient unto itself.

OUR SPECIAL AIM

THE Phillips Memorial Gallery differs from the usual type of public museum. My constant aim is not merely to exhibit but also to interpret beauty in art whatever the manifestation and to gradually popularize what is best, more particularly in modern painting, by novel and attractive methods of exhibition. I have conceived the idea that it is worth while to reverse the usual process for popularizing a picture gallery. Instead of the academic grandeur of marble halls and stairways and the miles of chairless spaces, with low standards and popular attractions to draw the crowds and to counteract the overawing effect of the formal institutional building, we plan to try the effect of domestic architecture, of rooms small or at least livable, and of such an intimate, attractive atmosphere as we associate with a beautiful home. To a place like that I believe people would be inclined to return once they have found it and to linger as long as they can for art's special study and its special sort of pleasure.

My idea is riot to show all our treasures at once but in ever-varied and purposeful exhibitions, arranging the Collection in units which are frequently changed so that the walls of the various rooms reveal interesting transformations. The critic Frank Jewett Mather, Jr., has written that a season of pictures at the Phillips Memorial Gallery should be as exciting to Washington as a season of opera. I maintain what I believe to be the highest standards. I purchase, or at least exhibit, works of art often a little difficult for the uninstructed public to understand. But by the air of comfort, ease and domesticity, by frequent changes of exhibitions in small rooms, the aim is clearly to popularize what is best in art without making concessions to the public taste. If visitors can be made to feel at home in the midst of beautiful things, subconsciously stimulated while physically rested and mentally refreshed, they will eventually absorb the point of view of the artist and remain thereafter on the same aesthetic levels.

Another way in which the Phillips Memorial Gallery differs from the usual museum is in the arrangement of the paintings. I avoid the usual period-rooms—the chronological sequence. That system is most necessary to illustrate the required books on art-history, but the Phillips Memorial Gallery is meant rather to supplement and illuminate the desired books on the theory and philosophy of art— on the ideas with which the artist has to do.

My arrangements are for the purpose of contrast and analogy. I bring together congenial spirits among the artists from different parts of the world and from different periods of time and I trace their common descent from old masters who anticipated modern ideas. Thus, our collection of French and American paintings of the Nineteenth and Twentieth Centuries really needs an El Greco—the founder of dynamic expressionism by means of a coordinated and emotionally effective use of form and color, line, and light. The idea of tracing the great rivers of artistic purpose back to their Primitive and Archaic sources, of suggesting their developing complexities, each tributary in its relation to the main stream, this perhaps is the most important work which teachers of art can already convey to their classes in lectures built around our exhibitions and our proposed exhibition units. Thus I demonstrate two things— the antiquity of modern ideas, or, if you prefer, the modernity of some of the old masters, and I prove in our Main Gallery and its union of old masters and modern painters that art is a universal language which defies classification according to any chronological or national order. As Courbet said, "There are no schools and movements worth a moment's attention. There are only true artists and pretenders."

DUNCAN PHILLIPS

OUR INCLUSIVENESS

THE Phillips Collection is based on a definite policy of support-ing many methods of seeing and painting. There are excellent reasons why collectors of taste limit themselves to one chosen School. They feel that its tenets express their personal preferences and convictions, and they fear that the admission of alien influences might disturb and distract them, introducing elements of discord into what had been a happy family on their walls. For a small collection there is no question as to the validity of such reasons for limiting one's choice to artists of closely related method and purpose. When, however, a large collection is formed we are dealing not with a family but with a world in miniature. To be sure, only what has been thought good should be introduced into this world, for art is nothing if it is not discriminating selection. Yet it should be the best of many different kinds of expression which the Museum or the large collection should delight to honor, provided that they are all sound and essentially sincere. Only on a most superficial view are differences of technique irreconcilable and impossible to fuse. The really good things of all ages and all periods can be brought together in one room with such a delightful result that we recognize the universality of art and the special affinities of artists. On the other hand, in the company of the true, the serious, and the more or less inspired artists, the works both of charlatans and of commercial picture-manufacturers seem conspicuously and disturbingly out of place. The Phillips Collection is famous for its inclusiveness, but at the same time for its atmosphere of aesthetic integrity. Those who fall out of our ranks have been found wanting, not in conformity to a set of rules, but in that unformulated inexplicable thing which differentiates pure gold from baser metals.

The bane of impassioned preference and convictions among artists, critics and collectors is the burning issue of intolerance. The traditionalist likes a picture for the very reason that a modernist despises it, because it is an echo of the more familiar past. Familiarity of aspect bores the champion of creative adventure, but is the very password to favor with the champion of a standardized art.

A modernist painter remarks that a beautiful landscape by Corot is very good considering the period in which it was painted. Such an attitude is only comprehensible to those who hold that the golden age of representative painting was really a period of almost total eclipse of the creative instinct, and that the recently recovered power of abstracting and coordinating the elements in Nature of the true and the beautiful acknowledges nothing to be legitimate art save only the Archaic and the Neo-Archaic; the carvings of the Congo or the pseudo-savageries of Rouault and Matisse. A broader attitude is that of Roger Fry who pays a reverent tribute to the old masters and selects a number of painters of the Nineteenth Century, preceding the epoch-making Cézanne, as entirely worthy of study and praise for important contributions to the recovery of our lost capacity for free and original creation. But even among the most tolerant modernists, who are not yet ready to destroy the museums, there is a persistent refusal to acknowledge that as the great representative artists of the past felt about nature so our contemporaries are still entitled to feel. As yet the photograph has been perfected by only one or two men, notably Alfred Stieglitz, so that the mechanical process truly serves the artist as an instrument sensitive enough for his personal expression. In the hands of less creative artists, the fact-finding camera may more and more be utilized as a source book of motifs for abstract design. Yet it is hard to conceive of the time when even the perfected art of the photographer will make us willing to dispense with the paintings of the colorful world as we enjoy its millions of poignantly lovely, transient manifestations. At least until that time when the camera, in its reproductive power, can replace the representative painting, most of us will find it difficult to see beautifully without some reference to the beauty which we still recognize in the world around us. My own love for the pure aesthetic emotion which, in music and in color organizations, lifts me out of myself on the wings of rhythm, even this predilection for abstract expression does not compel me to deny the ancient truth that the emotion of recognition is no less important to the artist than the emotion of escape.

The policy of the Phillips Memorial Gallery, then, is to choose the best representative painting as well as the best creative designing and to honor and to do reverence to both. For yet a little while it may be necessary to stress the tonic qualities of conventionalized simplification and the beneficent properties of abstract form and color. Soon enough, however, the Academy, which is hostile to a new phase of art only while it is new and unfamiliar, will come to recognize that these ideas somehow have taken hold of the popular imagination. After all, it will be a comfort to them that Cézanne, that celebrated free lance and hermit, was a stickler for system. Very well then, let his formula become the rule for the new Academy. Let the ceremony of his canonization proceed. It may seem fantastic to think that Academicians would ever come to it. But remember. The present fashions for Sargentism and Impressionism are only the latest fashions. Fifty years ago they were telling stories. A hundred years ago the tinting of Greek and Roman statues was the proper thing to do. Let no one be shocked at the suggestion that conventionalized simplification in the manner of Cézanne may be the next dogma prescribed by the Academic pontiffs for all who would be in good standing as followers of the established order. Before long the need for new life in art may cause the adventurous artists to plunge deeper and deeper into perilous regions of total abstraction where the cautious Academicians are less likely to follow them. The Phillips Memorial Gallery must guard its doors against the intrusion of wild, unbalanced radicals and of dogmatic; closed-minded conservatives, both standing for violent partisanship. We are hostile to the timorous Academy which, in every nation and in every age, represses originality while it is yet a vital force struggling forward in the world, but finally, in the course of time, standardizes whatever by-product of the original idea can be successfully manufactured and marketed. On the other hand we are equally hostile to the faddists of the latest Cults in art who squander their time and energy on propaganda and denounce as plagiarism everything that is not revolutionary. There is just as much sham and intolerance at one extreme as at the other. We stand sponsor especially for the lonely artist in quest of beauty, the artist backed by no political influence or professional organization, independent of all cliques and movements. However, we are willing to open our doors to all works of art which are true and beautiful under whatever auspices, by whatever method they come to us, tested or tentative, new or old.

Another difference from the usual gallery is that I purchase many examples of the work of artists I especially admire and delight to honor, even if they have not yet come into general recognition, instead of having one example of each of the standardized celebrities. I take any chance of being wrong. There are fashions in painting, and they affect market values, but the market values and artistic values do not always coincide, and I am interested only in artistic values. The test of artistic value is Time, and I shall not live to know whether the men in whom I have believed have justified my faith in their future. To stimulate contemporary artists by establishing personal contact and friendly relations, to win their confidence and to help them to understand themselves and to succeed with their own best methods and intentions, resisting the temptations to fall back on commercialism of one kind or another—such a policy I consider of the utmost importance. I have had more pleasure recently in discovering and helping some new men whose modest genius might have passed unnoticed, and others whose amazing originality is far in advance of their time, than from the rather exciting negotiations with foreign dealers to secure one or another of two master works by Daumier as a summit to our Daumier Unit. The Frenchmen for whom I am assembling exhibition units are Chardin, Daumier, Corot, Courbet, Monticelli, Fantin-Latour, Renoir, Monet, Sisley, Morisot, Cézanne, Puvis de Chavannes, André, and Bonnard. There will be others, but these are the artists on whom I have already made good beginnings. The Americans include Homer, Fuller, Inness, Ryder, Twachtman, Weir, Hassam, Prendergast, Davies, Tack, Lawson, Luks, Sterne, Kent, Myers, Speicher, Tucker, Robert Spencer, Gifford Beal, Preston Dickinson, Marin, Demuth, Dove, Karfiol, Weber, Hirsch, and others—always others. I am proud also to begin assembling the best pictures by my wife, Marjorie Phillips. Her vital assistance to me in forming the Collection since our marriage in 1921 makes her personality and point of view, as expressed in this group of her charming pictures, of special interest and significance.

The great artists represent what is permanent in the Collection. The lesser and younger men are undergoing an endurance test. If they can survive this test in proximity with the great they will be found in the ultimate, the permanent Collection, in the building which is still "a castle in Spain." The Phillips Memorial then is not a fixed, unchangeable institution. It acts promptly, seizing opportunities because it is one man and not a Board, with divided opinions and excuses for delay. Our purchases are not irrevocable. (1) We are a purchasing agency which pursues great outstanding masterworks by a few great masters chosen for our own educational reasons and an educational institution which plans to make these masterworks

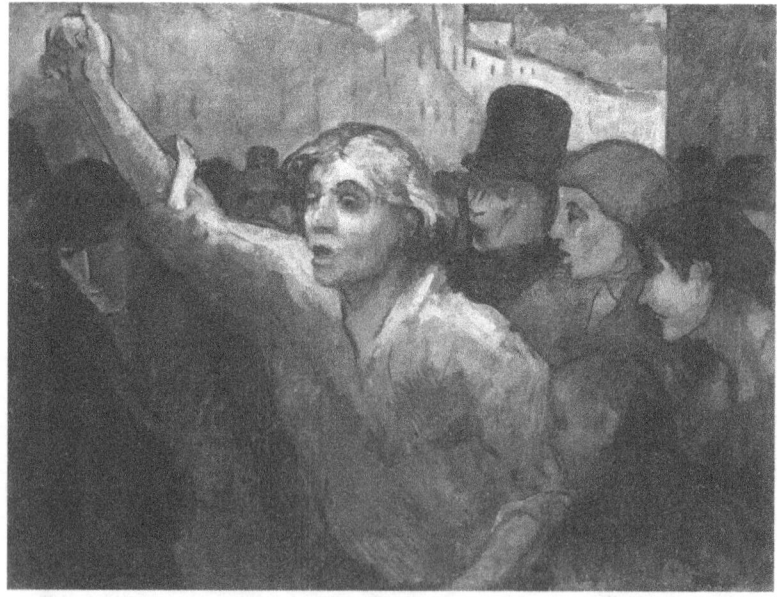

Honoré Daumier
The Uprising (L'Émeute), 1848 or later
Oil on canvas
The Phillips Collection, Washington, D.C. Acquired in 1925

a source of inspiration for living artists to aspire to as well as a pleasure for all, and (2) we are an agency for encouraging living artists when they give promise of potential distinction. I am willing to run the risk of overrating these young contemporaries by generously expanding the measure of my appreciation to the measure of their highest intentions as long as they continue to be true to what is best in themselves and to make some progress towards a high endeavor.

Then I wish to make our American art recognized abroad at its true worth. In our Gallery we consider it as part of the main channel and not as a back-water and we prove that the best American pictures of today stand the test of comparison with the great masters in our Gallery as many of the best foreigners fail to do. Therefore we should not tolerate the foreign attitude inclined to belittle us in all their books on art and to scorn us as a nation of materialists with nothing of our own to say in painting.

As we go to press with our first catalogue of the Collection, I realize only too well that many great artists are missing, while many others are inadequately or incompletely represented. We need an example of some great Primitives who worked either in the noble spirit and style of Giotto or the more intimate manner of Pisanello or Uccello. We need a Giorgionesque or Titianesque picture and something vital from the hand of Tintoretto himself as a source of modern romanticism. We need such Italians of the Quattrocento as Piero di Cosimo, Piero della Francesca, Botticelli, and Signorelli. We need masterful fragments or perfect copies of Rembrandt, Hals, Vermeer, and Velázquez. We need such Frenchmen as Poussin and Claude, and we need a sketch and a landscape by Rubens. We need Goya, Hogarth, Blake. We need an Ingres portrait, a colorful figure composition by Delacroix, a figure painting or still life by Manet, a scene from the race track, the ballet, or the workshop by Degas, and a monumental still life by Cézanne. Among the Americans I am waiting for a chance to acquire a great epic seascape in oil and more of the thrilling water colors by Winslow Homer, an ideal head by Fuller, a noble classic figure by Thayer, a solemn landscape by Homer Martin, a powerful and patient transcript of truth by Eakins, and perhaps an early portrait or genre by Sargent. A number of brilliant European modernists are as yet absent, but I wish to find examples of the inventive genius of Van Gogh, Seurat, Matisse, Picasso, Derain, Segonzac, Braque, and others. Meanwhile I prefer to show my sympathy with the gallant tentative modern adventures on new trails by buying the works of our American modernists who are not yet fashionable, sensational, and overrated. Of equal importance with the filling of these gaps is the carrying on of our Exhibition Units. No gallery in the world has a finer work by Daumier than *L'Émeute* [*The Uprising*] and a larger group of oil paintings by this, my favorite artist. It is my intention to continue in pursuit of great examples of his genius as a painter, a fact so long unrecognized.

THE NEED FOR A NEW PROFESSION

I cannot stress too much the eagerness of my desire to hasten the day when there will be in this country a public opinion more enlightened as to the significance and importance of beauty, the meaning and purpose of art and the special point of view of the artist. Commercial, or indolently conventional, or spitefully unsound, insincere, and sensational work by our professional painters will continue to be produced unless the people instruct themselves as to what is good and why it is good so as to insist upon high standards instead of being directly responsible for low standards. Open-mindedness must take the place of prejudice in regard to the "New Movements." If beauty is, as I believe, a vital element, then its expression in art will change as we change. It is certain that art would die if it should cease to be expressive of the changes wrought by Time in our consciousness. If art is ecstasy of expression then artistic creations are more likely to be inspired out of fresh and individual intensities of our own life and thought which seek their own fresh means of utterance than out of the arts of the preceding generation from which youth instinctively reacts. This fresh language may be entirely traditional yet revitalized and therefore truly a renewal of the power of the arts of the past. A renaissance of art is predicted to come in our time, but it must come, not from the ever-devoted few but from

the awakened interest, the unprejudiced catholicity and the enlightened patronage of the many.

I am still hoping that I shall live to see the day when no college
will be considered adequate which does not offer courses in the theory and philosophy of art and in the artist's point of view—courses
which should be part of the requirements for a degree. We make
compulsory courses which are far less practical and helpful in after
life than how to see. It is possible to know the names and dates out of
art-history and still to be in outer darkness as to the most elementary
principles of unity in variety and of rhythmical relations in design,
and without even a glimmering of what the artists and the critics
mean when they speak of" quality" in painting. A new profession will
come into vital activity whenever we see fit to incorporate the teaching of the painter's, the etcher's, and the sculptor's art into the public
schools as well as in the colleges. The intelligence for painting, to
speak consistently of my favorite art, is of a very special kind. Only a
few have it to a marked degree. These would be the ones who would
go out into the world to become active workers on the side of the
artists. These men and women of special fitness would be enabled to
take post-graduate courses in museum work or they would become
the teachers in the schools and colleges, or the reviewers for the
papers and magazines, and they could become really qualified dealers or, better yet, museum scouts, able to relieve the artists of the
need for selling their own works, able and willing to hold the artists
up to high standards, to encourage and support with helpful criticism, to offer exhibition space to all the artists in alternating groups,
to do away with the need for big miscellaneous exhibitions and their
unjust professional jury system for selection and awards. There is
nothing more detrimental to the state of mind which produces great
art than the clash of intolerant cliques among the painters and their
organized or unorganized herding together, the labor union idea,
with its intolerance of outsiders who almost invariably are the great
artists of the period. Trained critical minds among the laymen must
be best for the necessary task of comparative valuation because they
afford the most detached and disinterested judgments of pictures.

Such opinions moreover approximate to the judgments of posterity. And back of these trained experts would be a higher level of taste applicable to every home—a public opinion which would not only tolerate but appreciate and evaluate the artists and exert a wholesome corrective discipline in the same way that our electorate, more or less successfully, keeps itself interested in the honesty and ability of its public men. We should at least aspire to another Renaissance, another age of far-sighted patrons, of an enlightened public, of artists liberated by patrons and public but most of all by trained critics from the need of being organized manufacturers and self-advertisers of sentimental, standardized, smart, sensational pictures instead of fine ones. It is my hope that there will be other small galleries like ours all over the country—and around them art libraries and lecture rooms to develop and to train critics by contact with pictures thoughtfully exhibited.

SEASONS OF 1924–26

THE Season of 1924–25 seemed so impressive to those who followed our purchases and exhibitions that few would have ventured to predict that the Season of 1925–26 would even surpass it. In November 1924, we opened the Little Gallery for temporary exhibitions so that most, if not all, of our greatest paintings could be kept constantly on view in our Main Gallery for the benefit of the people of Washington and the pilgrims from other places. Last year's exhibitions in the Little Gallery contained paintings by Marjorie Phillips, Ernest Lawson, Childe Hassam, Arthur B. Davies, Kenneth Hayes Miller, Charles Demuth, and Preston Dickinson. The purchases for the permanent Collection were of the utmost importance, especially Daumier's masterpiece *The Uprising* of which Arsène Alexandre wrote, "There is no other picture of like importance that. we know or are ever likely to know of Daumier."[2] This is just as surely one

---

2. ["An Unpublished Daumier," *The Burlington Magazine for Connoisseurs* 44, no. 252 (March 1924): 143. Phillips's quote is a conflation of two sentences by Alexandre: "The picture is the most important and the most impressive of those

of the great pictures of the world as the more celebrated *Déjeuner des Canotiers*[3] by Renoir which we acquired in 1923. Another superb masterpiece added to the Collection last year was the *Rocks at Ornans*[4] by Courbet. Of the purchases during the Season of 1925–26, special importance attaches to the portrait of *Marguerite Gérard*[5] by Fragonard, *The Farm—Early Morning*[6] by Corot, *On the River Stour*[7] by Constable, *Mt. St. Victoire*[8] by Cézanne, *Early Spring*[9] and *Girl and Dog*[10] by Bonnard, *The Reapers*[11] and *Afternoon*[12] by our own contemporary Maurice Sterne. Our calendar of exhibitions in the Little Gallery was as follows: December—Bernard Karfiol; January—Group of American modernists, including Preston Dickinson, Charles Sheeler, Stefan Hirsch, William Zorach, Niles Spencer, and Charles Demuth; February—Group of American artists including Augustus Vincent Tack, Rockwell Kent, Eugene Speicher, Max Weber, Walt Kuhn, Marsden Hartley, Arthur G. Dove, Georgia O'Keeffe, Alfred Maurer, Vincent Canadé, Karl Knaths, together with *Mystery*[13] by Odilon Redon; March—Maurice Sterne; April—Marjorie Phillips; May—Group exhibition, including Berthe Morisot, Maurice Prendergast, Pierre Bonnard, Albert André, and others. Our new masterpieces by Corot, Constable, and Cézanne took their place in the

---

which we know or are likely to know of Daumier's. There is no work of his of like importance among those which have escaped the knowledge of historians and the zeal of collectors."]

3. [*Luncheon of the Boating Party*, between 1880 and 1881, Acquired in 1923]

4. [*Rocks at Mouthier*, c. 1855. acquired in 1925]

5. [*Portrait of Marguerite Gérard*, 1776, formerly in The Phillips Collection, Washington, D.C.]

6. [*Farm—Early Morning*, 1860–61, formerly in The Phillips Collection, Washington, D.C.]

7. [*On the River Stour*, c. 1834–37, acquired in 1925]

8. [*Mont Sainte-Victoire*, between 1886 and 1887, acquired in 1925]

9. [*Early Spring*, 1908, acquired in 1925]

10. [*Woman with Dog*, 1922, acquired in 1925]

11. [*The Reapers*, 1925, acquired in 1926]

12. [*Afternoon*, 1924, acquired in 1926]

13. [*Mystery*, c. 1910, acquired in 1925]

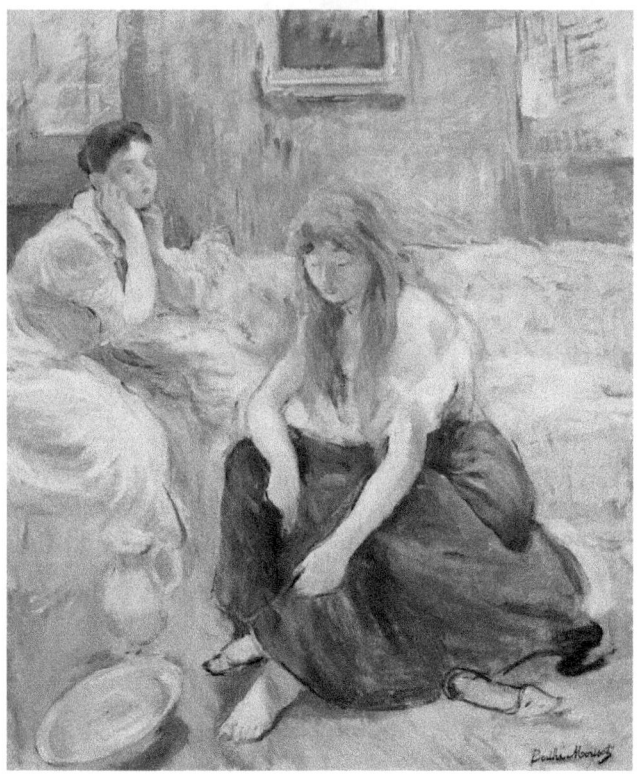

Berthe Morisot
Two Girls, c. 1894
Oil on canvas
The Phillips Collection, Washington, D.C. Acquired in 1925

Main Gallery as if they had always belonged there in that intimate association with El Greco's *Peter*,[14] Chardin's *Still Life*,[15] the groups of Daumiers, Courbets, and Chavannes, and the great Renoir.

This season of so-called Modernist exhibitions was carefully planned to give the people of Washington a chance they might not

14. [*The Repentant St. Peter*, 1600–1605 or later, acquired in 1922]
15. [*A Bowl of Plums*, c. 1728, acquired in 1920]

otherwise have had to see what is going on among the more adventurous artists of America, a ferment corresponding to what has been going on for many years on the Continent of Europe. To quote from one of my Introductions:

Our January exhibition revealed the fact that drastic modifications of the Cult of Cubism are being made in America, modifications calculated to reduce to a simplified clarity and pictorial style the complex of buildings constructed in straight lines with projecting or receding planes. The emphasis was on volume and on the conventionalized relations of colored forms in space.

The approach was intellectual rather than emotional, objective rather than subjective. In the February exhibition there is more lyricism of mood, more abandonment to the ardors of conception. The presiding genius is Odilon Redon whose ghostly symbolism might leave us cold if it were not for the stimulus to liberty of invention afforded by his discovery of the brooding mind of man as a rich vein of raw material for abstract art. He did not seek to intensify, as modern artists do, the realization of the foundation-facts of life. On the contrary he opened an avenue of escape. But it was an avenue of abstract design, and its spiritual adventure into Expressionism has had its direct influence, like the more profound and important inventions and imaginings of El Greco and of Blake, in launching the subjective branch of modern painting.

Such notes of interpretation, in our catalogues of the monthly shows, are intended for the possible use of our more open-minded visitors who may be baffled at first by an unfamiliar language, but who are anxious to learn this language so that they may enjoy the unsuspected beauty which it expresses.

IN CONCLUSION

$\text{B}\text{E}\text{C}\text{A}\text{U}\text{S}\text{E}$ our wall space at present is limited to one moderately large and one very small gallery, the monthly exhibitions are all I can do to practice what I preach about alternating exhibition units. Several sites for the Gallery are under consideration and before this book goes to press one of them may have been decided upon. Even after the time when we have increased the extent of our exhibition space, we shall continue our permanent and changing exhibitions at our present location, 1608 21st Street, Washington, D.C. Our visitors have been stimulated, and their horizons broadened. I have mingled with them enough to know that our work has not been in vain. We cannot accommodate crowds, and yet it is on record that on two occasions we admitted as many

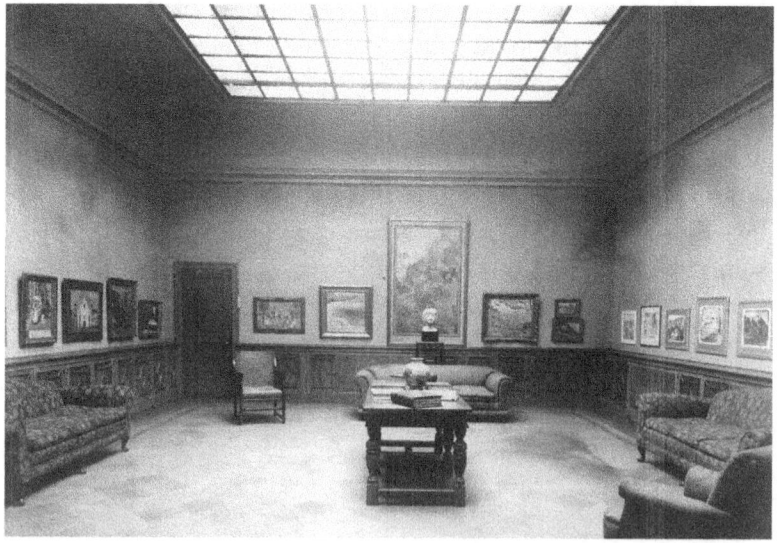

Main Gallery of the Phillips Memorial Gallery in 1927, with, among others, works by Vincent Augustus Tack, John Henry Twachtman, Paul Cézanne, and an Egyptian limestone head

as two hundred people during the course of one afternoon. The first occasion was the inaugural exhibition to the public of the world-famous *Déjeuner des Canotiers* by Renoir. Later in the same year we received approximately the same number of visitors on the day in which a lower gallery, not usually open to the public, was opened for an exhibition of large decorations by Augustus Vincent Tack, including loans from museums. I recognize a growing tendency among a few people to make visits to our Gallery an important part of the week's more vital activity. Earnest students, both artists and laymen, come and come again, bringing new friends whose names go on our mailing list. They linger for hours discussing the pictures with us or among themselves.

It is too soon to announce, too soon to do more than hint at, the educational plans of the Phillips Memorial Gallery. Suffice it to say that the publication of this book, and the purchase of land for our building will bring us to the end of our first stage of development. A few of our Exhibition Units are ready for installation, and in our Little Gallery we have demonstrated the manner in which they will be shown with catalogues containing critical aids to appreciation. A Bulletin of our activities containing special comment on our new acquisitions and a calendar of our monthly exhibitions may be published within a year, supplementing our monographs on the artists which are known to our subscribers as the Phillips Publications. The collection of paintings can now afford a fairly clear conception of the standards we wish to maintain in the future. We can therefore make our bow before the public as a special kind of educational institution, a sort of laboratory of art where at least two important groups of art students can be instructed. (I) We can awaken the aesthetic consciousness of boys and girls and guide them to such colleges as offer courses in the theory as well as in the history of art. We cannot only awaken dormant sensibilities but at the same time be instrumental in formulating a clear knowledge of what art is. Proof of this knowledge should be required from students before they can graduate from school and enter college. The artist's point of view is certainly as important a matter for study as the various college entrance requirements which also are cultural and not as "life enhancing." (II) We can do far more, however, for the matured post-graduate students of art who could be recommended to us by such famous art teachers as Professors Forbes and Sachs of Harvard, Mather of Princeton, Root of Hamilton College, and many others. Those who win scholarships from the Carnegie Corporation may think well of the opportunities of art study afforded by the Freer Gallery, the Phillips Memorial Gallery, and the Corcoran-Clark Collections of Washington. We wish to be a postgraduate supplementary school for students who are seriously planning to prepare themselves for art instruction. I can see the time when our Collection might be closed and all our resources devoted to a school for critics in a building where lecture rooms and research rooms, adjoining store rooms, would afford rich opportunities for the study of painting. I am anxious to be put in touch with serious young men and women determined to devote their lives and energies to the teaching of art principles, the conservation and proper use of art objects in museums and galleries and the encouragement and necessary assistance to creative work in the arts of design from the time a conception of beauty leaves the mind of the painter or sculptor in his studio to the time when it enriches a public gallery, a private collection or a home. Students can receive in our galleries, from their exhibitions of modern art with ancient sources, the basic idea of art as a universal language, breaking down artificial barriers of nationality and race, a language which never differs in essentials however varied the local, national, racial and historical manifestations. Lectures and informal talks can be illustrated with the actual paintings instead of with lantern slides and a course of conferences may be arranged for the season of 1927–28. An intelligent glance at our list of pictures will tell the tale of our scope and plan. We correspond to what in a curriculum is known as supplementary reading. My hopes, however, soar beyond affording knowledge or even giving pleasure to the people who need art to enrich their lives. I hope that our Gallery will furnish inspiration to creative artists, either starting or sustaining them on their thrilling quest. I hope it will eventually produce critics worthy of that high calling. I hope to gradually improve my plan for isolating artistic ideas in suggestive group exhibitions. Finally, I hope that through practice we may learn the art of popularizing a picture gallery without any lowering of high standards by means of intimate and illuminating methods of presentation.

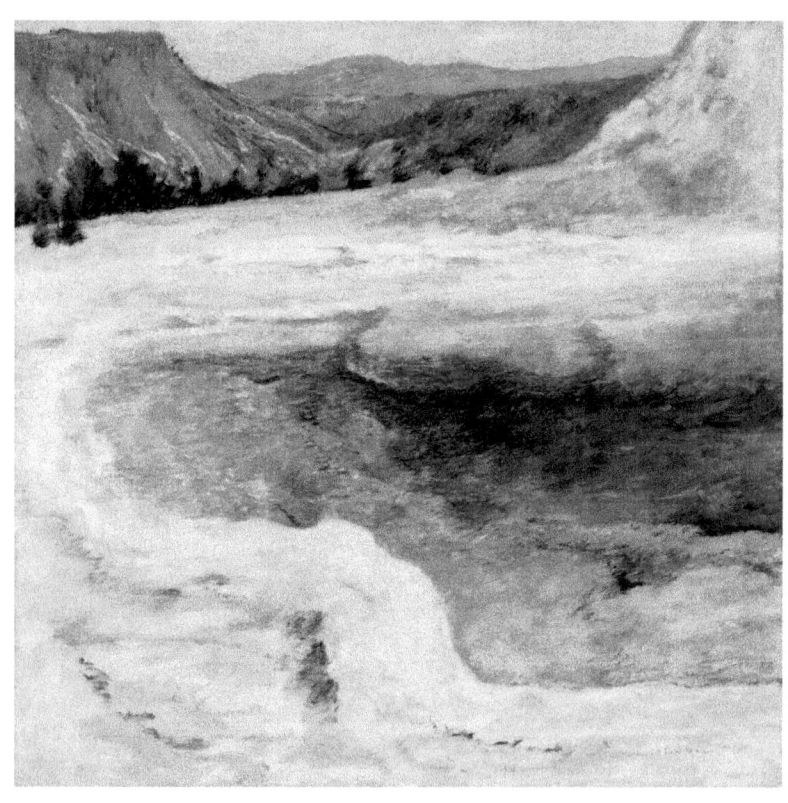

John Henry Twachtman
The Emerald Pool, c. 1895
Oil on canvas
The Phillips Collection, Washington, D.C. Acquired in 1921

ART IS INTERNATIONAL
(1928)

THE whole world is to be found in the United States. We may not like the idea yet we can no more deny than we can alter the fact. It is curious that a nation which seems to desire isolation above all things and which fears foreign entanglements as if they involved crime or inevitable calamity, should all the while be in itself the very symbol of unity in variety, of Cosmopolis. Nicholas Roerich, painter, philosopher, world traveler, and organizer, has chosen our country for his unique museum and university of East and West and of all the arts under one roof, because he sees in our union of all races and religions a symbol and a portent of world union.[1] Today, in New York at least, American art means international art. Foreign critics complain that our exhibitions are not different enough from exhibitions in Paris where also cosmopolitan culture with its variety of commingled racial ingredients almost obliterates the original French flavor. It is our pride that there are a few contemporary American painters who are persistently national and of our native soil. They paint as if they had never seen a foreign picture, as if their method had naturally grown out of their need for expressing an American mentality. If "local color" were the goal of art such artists would be the greatest. As it is they are certainly among the most vividly interesting. But should we isolate our artists to defend their Americanism against foreign influence? Is not this an unjustified assumption of their weakness? An artist may on his own account choose not to look in order not be influenced. On

First published in *The Art News* 27, no. 5 (November 3, 1928): 12–14. Reprinted in Duncan Phillips, *The Artist Sees Differently: Essays Based Upon the Philosophy of a Collection in the Making*, 2 vols. (New York and Washington, D.C.: E. Weyhe and Phillips Memorial Gallery, 1931).

1. [The Nicholas Roerich Museum and the Master Institute of United Arts were established by Roerich in New York in 1923.]

the other hand he may wish to learn all he can and use only what he needs. That is what our American Old Masters George Fuller and George Inness did on their foreign travels many years ago and it is what Arthur B. Davies was always doing from early manhood until his recent death while sketching in Northern Italy. Twachtman, Weir, and Eakins came home from their studies under academic French instructors to become thoroughly American in their expression. Twachtman and Weir adapted the high key of color and the divided tones of the French Luminists to American themes which they approached from the standpoint of lyric poets rather than of technical innovators. Winslow Homer was an artist of another kind, one of the men really immune to foreign influence. Of this type today are John Sloan, Gifford Beal, Rockwell Kent, Edward Hopper, Glenn Coleman, Charles Sheeler, Arthur Dove, T.W. Benton, James Chapin, and Charles Burchfield.

Nationalism as a quality in works of art has a racy tang for the civilized and unprejudiced foreigner and a romantic reality for the right-minded patriot. Its attraction is to the instinct which causes our pleasure in recognizing what we know from personal observation and experience and to that antithetical instinct which sends us out of our way in search of surprising peculiarities in the observation and experience of others. Nationalism in art is not a quality which can be cultivated. It occurs in its most pristine purity in a naive bourgeois, a Sunday painter of the people's amusements like Henri Rousseau, "le Douanier." It is an inevitable result of physical or mental segregation. When a whole nation is in a backwoods or in a backwater its art will naturally be different from a nation on the highways or seacoasts of trade and travel. When individuals have successfully isolated or immunized themselves against foreign influence or when they are overgrown children from some particular play ground of the world, like old Rousseau, their work will stand out and attract attention by reason of a disarming candor and innocence which atone for what might otherwise appear to be smugness and even ennoble what would otherwise be merely-quaintness. Such manifestations of so called "popular art" are important to us in our study of races in their holiday moods. The amateur painter of this type helps us to understand the effects of climates, customs and social conditions. This local color however is a consideration entirely distinct from aesthetic significance which may or may not be present in works of unschooled and unself-conscious spontaneity. Paintings which may charm and fascinate us with their local color, their sincere and unaffected nationalism may or may not be distinguished also by pure aesthetic qualities which are universal. There are instances of great artists who are both national and universal. Ryder was not interested in foreign art and lived a life of visions and of dreams. So truly cosmic was his imagination that he seems to have been oblivious of all nations near or far. In spite of this universality there is nevertheless something of New England, something I am told of New Bedford and its sea-faring folk, in his marines. It was not a matter of Ryder's wishing to be American but just of his inherent, inevitable integrity. As for John Marin he jots down original impressions of American scenes giving them specific titles such as "Bear Mountain," "Rockland County," "Deer Island," "New Mexico," "New York." Yet, as Ralph Flint expresses it, he appears to be transcribing stenographic notes at top speed from Divine dictation. Such vision is not geographical. The aesthetic qualities of Ryder and Marin are of worldwide consequence and transcend their unquestioned though unconscious Americanism. For myself I find that the charm and the fascination of art that is local rather than universal is chiefly a matter of rarity. If I encounter an exotic picture in a setting which sets off its strangeness I am more inclined to notice it with sympathetic interest than I would if it were surrounded by other works equally remote. This holds true no less of the work which I recognize as an unadulterated domestic product. What is more to the point, I can sooner separate the aesthetic qualities of either an exotic or a domestic picture from its extraneous interests linked up with associations, and I can more promptly judge it purely as a work of art, when it is contrasted with works which have little or no romantic appeal or local color.

There is a common mistake about the meaning of the word cosmopolitan. The finest cosmopolitan art is not marred by standardization nor is it a product of a composite and colorless fusion. Its essence is world-mindedness. Diversified elements are arranged and harmonized and respected in an atmosphere where each difference is noted and put to use for its own special qualities while each part contributes to the harmony and complex richness of the whole. That is the synthesis based upon analysis and respectful recognition of the fact that true artists see differently and when they come from different nations or races they may be expected to differ most of all. The essential universality of art, regardless of estranging local currencies and languages, can yet unify all mankind. Patriotism is an obstacle, especially when it is fanatical, breeding the boosting habit and a prejudiced intolerance o[all strangeness. Those of us who would break down barriers between races and nations must first see to it that we ourselves have left far behind us the belated minds of savages and that we have not only a tolerance but a taste for strangeness. And we must dislike uniformity and any codes, systems, or philosophies which would disregard racial pride and remove altogether the fascinating local color from life. International exhibitions are invaluable agents for exchange of knowledge and influence and for development of good will through mutual understanding. We have our exchange professorships to interpret nations and races to each other and we have our exchange scholarships which may be even more important. In time, there will be attachés for art on every staff of diplomats to balance the military and naval representation. These attachés will interpret the art of the countries whence they come to the countries to which they are accredited. Each nation should acquire for its embassies or legations abroad paintings and other works of art by its contemporary artists. Such a plan would not only afford support for native art and a recognition of art's importance as an educational force but the vast system of aesthetic exchange thus organized would inevitably lead to world-mindedness and a world-wide knowledge of racial character and culture. There must also be, as Roerich advocates, an international flag for art claiming and receiving the same immunity as the flag of the Red Cross during war's epidemics of violent insanity. Meanwhile we have the international exhibitions, sporadically at various world's fairs, and regularly at Pittsburgh and Venice. May they live long and multiply! I regret that the emphasis at these great shows is upon a non-aesthetic consideration, the artist's nationality. This is unfortunate as it leads to the competitive segregation of artists into geographical and racial specimens of the genus man. It is instructive, of course, thus to separate and observe and compare. Yet how much more significant it would be to combine and coordinate the artists of all nations into an international assemblage, a brotherhood of creators from all over the world, proud to have their works hung together without too much attention to the tags of nationality and school. Why should not these international exhibitions accept the fact that even as we in the United States mingle our foreign-born and make them into American citizens, caring less about their hyphens as labels for classification than as aids to learning about their racial and geographical backgrounds which we inherit, so the world-centers have a right to take stock of the artistic world-citizens, marking with interest and pleasure the significant differences but noting also, and employing to good effect, the affinities and harmonies of method and purpose. The only concern should be the beauty of arrangement of each wall's decoration. The walls must be composed as the painter composes his picture, rhythmically relating lines, colors and masses. National idiosyncrasies in juxtaposition would add to the piquant charm of varied styles and subjects. The aim of an international exhibition should not be to advertise the fact that ten or twenty nations are represented, nor to make it appear as if one federated state contained all this wealth of variety, much as we might like to hasten that far off consummation. The plan should be to make a stimulating blend and a subtle fusion of good pictures by artists of many nations and races. Of course one can make a different kind of effort and be a showman of racial idiosyncrasies but in that case it is impossible to attend to what I consider of far greater importance, namely the creation of an ensemble which, in shapes and lines and colors for the walls, is in itself a work of art, good in every part and especially good as a whole. Were I a showman I would select whatever made a sensation of one kind or another and the curiosity and entertainment of the public would determine my choice rather than my own sensibilities. As it is, the only question for me to decide is whether a work has artistic qualities of sufficient importance to justify inclusion. I have always felt that a large display of mediocre paintings or sculpture by a national group which is interesting only because it is a fragment broken off from the mass mentality of that nation is a sign of non-aesthetic motives in the organizers of the enterprise. Self-satisfaction in one national group tends to breed the same provincial complacency in others. In art at least there should not be unfriendly competition in mass production. Quality must count. Let us neither bring in foreign works of art just because they are foreign and seem to us novel and entertaining nor keep them out just because they are foreign and we have prejudices against invasions which might upset our self-satisfaction or prosperity. Let us sponsor foreign art only when it seems good enough to us as art and not otherwise. No genuine artist of this or any other country need fear to give the foreign artist his due share of appreciation. The dealers in and makers of American art who wish to keep out the best foreign art are as desperate in their sense of inferiority and martyrdom as were the artistic revolutionists of the earlier years of struggle who talked about destroying the museums in order that their new ideas might prevail.

Keeping out foreign rivals with a tax was recently the idea of a certain group of narrow-minded Americans who called themselves artists. Their appeal to the government for protection was fortunately denied when a storm of protest poured in to the Ways and Means Committee as it conducted hearings on tariff revisions. I am glad to say that the unorganized but self-respecting American artists and their patrons and champions were so vehement in their denunciation of the plea made by the American Artists Professional League that the honor of art in America was upheld. If there had not been vigilant and determined opposition it might have been made to appear to our legislators and to the world that art in Ametlica is regarded as a competitive trade instead of as a universal language

which knows no boundaries. A tax on contemporary foreign painting would have been followed in all consistency by trying to exclude
all especially gifted and creative foreigners themselves. Having thus
shut itself within a tariff wall, Democracy, with its love for the mediocre, would, as Forbes Watson expressed it in *The Arts,* have been
made safe for provincialism.[2]

I am tempted to tell what happened in Washington on a certain
day in February, 1929. The spokesman for the American Artists Professional League spoke in part as follows: "Thirty-five years ago I
was one of a group of artists who petitioned Congress to remove the
existing tariff on works of art. We did this because as a nation we
were in our aesthetic childhood. Children need to be educated. We
wanted to learn, so we asked that art be made free of duty that we
might see and absorb it. But conditions have changed. The child
has grown to manhood. We now have an enormous cultured audience. With this change in art appreciation has come an economic
change. Through unusual prosperity the scale of production in art
and industry has increased. The American artists are now asking for
an economic square deal as opposed to a theoretical advancement
of art in the abstract. We hold that the artist's economic position
has never been sufficiently considered." At this point he was asked
one embarrassing question after another. For instance, Mr. Aldrich
of Rhode Island interrupted with the following remarks: "The market for objects of art depends, does it not, on the taste of the pur-
chaser? Can a tariff affect that? American taste in certain instances
seems to demand the products of European artists." Mr. Rainey of
Texas followed with a bitter little speech substantially as follows: "I
want to get your position. A number of years ago you favored putting
artists' creations on the Free List, you wanted to develop art in this
country. Now it is your position that, your infant industry having
grown up, you ought to have a tariff because you have learned co
your grief that you are not strong enough to compete. Do you know
of any country in the world that has ever imposed a duty on the art

2. [*The Arts* 1, no. 2 (January 1921): 7.]

of other nations? I can answer. No nation ever has. Modern nations have developed their arts by drawing ideas from the arts of all other nations, by removing all possible barriers. That was the sound position for which you stood. Now you are cheapening and commercializing your art. I am ashamed of the artists of this country." Subsequently I presented the statement of a position to which many of my friends among the American artists had subscribed with letters and telegrams filed with the Committee. Part of my statement was as follows: "Any tax calculated to keep out of our country what might be of inestimable value in the art and thought of other countries in order to protect the weakest artists among us against the natural consequence of their weakness is a measure of repression against cultural growth worthy of the interior of China and its dread of "foreign devils." Since art has been on the Free List, American painters and sculptors have had the benefit of stimulation from new ideas and of inspiration to hold up their end at the international exhibitions. Are we now, for the sake of our weakest painters and sculptors, to deny to the American people their right to the art of all the world? And are we to misrepresent and humiliate the best and most self-respecting American artists who do not want protection and who do not need protection against anyone anywhere? For the sake of the argument I have been assuming that the purpose of those who would keep out foreign art would be successful. I doubt it. Such legislation would, in the words of a cablegram I have just received from the Honorable Elihu Root, "defeat its own selfish purpose, and seriously injure the best interests of the American people." It would not block the progress of art in this country. The museums and the connoisseurs would see to that. And the American collectors whose investments in art are made as shrewdly as in stocks and bonds would regard the most famous foreign artists as even more powerful and desirable than they are and assume that, tax or no tax, these foreigners represent a much wiser and safer investment than American art which is evidently a puny infant industry in need of much coddling and sheltering. The art lover cannot be turned away from a painting which he wants by something else said to be 100 percent American. Nor can art be reduced to the level of mass production by the machine. I protest against the proposed injury to the prestige and the honor of the best American artists by making it appear that they are so overwhelmed by a sense of inferiority that they must come whimpering to the government begging to be protected. Of what dread invasion are these plaintiffs so afraid? I assure you that outside of a few fashionable French painters the best American painters sell far better to the American public than do the foreign painters. This tax would only call attention to the acknowledged preeminence of six or seven celebrities who are apparently considered so strong that American art, in the opinion of these plaintiffs, is being crushed by their might. If this tax should go through American art would be made to appear almost worthless. Its prestige would suffer such a blow that I hardly know when or how it could recover." At the close of my address, Mr. Rainey of Texas exclaimed—with heat, "I am glad the gentleman who addressed us first did not represent the real artists of America," and I answered with conviction that "he represented a comparatively unimportant few."

As could be surmised from the quoted questions and remarks of two of the Congressmen on the Committee, the proposed duty on contemporary art failed to make an impression and modern art is still on the Free List. But the danger of a similar commercial spirit rearing its ugly head again must not be forgotten. An editorial writer of the *New York Evening Post* declared at the time of the Congressional hearing "Art lives and has always lived only because it knows no boundaries, national or mental. One would think the artists themselves would be the first to fight for an international solidarity of their kind but apparently this is not true." Alas, it is far from the truth! The nationalist point of view in art must be written down here in absolute frankness as a stupid and self-conscious one. We either overestimate or underestimate our own artists. We either neglect them when they are obscure and need our help or we coddle them with protection of their self-esteem, fearful of the foreign rivalry which would be the acid test of their worth and the incentive to their progress. And the artists, instead of feeling a solidarity as imaginative creators, a vast fellowship of constructors in a destructive world, a fellowship which could dissolve the ancient divisions of race, class and nation, melting them all in the enkindling warmth of universal aesthetic feeling and expression, instead of being the peacemakers of the world the artists too often are troublemakers with chauvinistic minds steeped in prejudice and spite. The brotherhood ideal perverted by fanatical nationalism can work havoc with the artists, reducing them to the level of any other self-glorifying tribe or sect. None of these local loyalties, these aggressive solidarities of artists according to nationalization papers instead of according to art itself can produce that unifying spirit in which the whole world must be reborn. It has been proposed that the artists shall point the way to peace through the disinterestedness of art and its universal language, through fusion of differences in a common ideal, through their representing civilization in a last attempt to rise above savagery, above the tribal feud and the herd mind. This ideal of international cooperation is on its way and nothing can stop it. World federation is now in process of becoming a practical realization in business, in science, in religion and in art. The foreign editor of *Le Matin* at the end of a pessimistic survey of failures by politicians to surmount such obstacles as trade rivalries, racial minorities and disputed boundaries, concluded with these words: "Fortunately the politicians are not the sole masters of human destiny. In the economic field a general organization is struggling ahead slowly but surely and in the field of intellectual and artistic exchanges each day brings closer together the nations which fought ten years ago. It might be said that it would be much better if the effort to organize world peace were taken out of the hands of politicians and confined to writers, thinkers, scientists and artists. Art is the especially appropriate rallying point for the determined efforts of the peoples of the world to impress their governments with the will to peace." As yet the artists have not caught the idea nor seen the vision. When it was proposed that they should form an international world center, if only as a symbol of the great advance, their general apathy only flared up in sparks of actual antagonism. It is one thing for an artist to be ahead of his time in art.

If he is stouthearted and strong in the faith he likes to be regarded as a progressive. But to be ahead of his time in human relations that is something else again and something suspicious.

The feeling against foreign artists undoubtedly arises from the fact that every nation, at one time or another, neglects its own as a result of foreign "high-pressure salesmanship" and propaganda. That is characteristic of the nationalistic point of view everywhere. America has in the past been neglectful of her artists and even today isolated instances of neglect due to overmuch foreign influence could be cited with proofs. There are contrary evidences of our cultivating a habit of mind indifferent to whatever is not American. But now I feel that we are in a period of ever increasing realization of that international fusion of many races which has marked us for ultimate leadership in art. There is noticeable now among those of us who care about such things an ever increasing pride in the way our artists are advancing to their destiny. Yet it needs to be said that our attitude toward our contemporary native art is still the usual biased nationalistic one. We are tao close to the artists of our time to judge them dispassionately and this is true no less of our attitude toward the works of foreign painters and sculptors. Nationalists, in other words people who are at all times flag-conscious and ill at ease in the world, are biased for or against the art of their own countrymen. Obviously the natural and the wholesome trend is to a partial and indulgent preference for the home product. Time was, however, and not so long ago, when Americans accepted the European contempt for the artistic efforts of the United States with meekness and turned to the Old World for art with a deference by no means based on intelligent appraisal of relative values. The explanation is simple. There is in the life of young nations a periodic though irregular oscillation between the inferiority and the superiority complex. Instead of the exaggerated humility as to our standing as artists which prevailed from 1870 to 1890, and even as late as the Sorolla and Zuloaga exhibition in 1914, we are now witnessing an exaggerated self-consciousness and bravado which challenges the world and resents the appearance of contemporary foreign paintings in our cities. It is sad to think of the neglect of our American Old Masters while nonentities with foreign names and medals were imported by our dealers and their products purchased for large sums by our prosperous travelers on their grand tours. And yet that was the reaction to the no less deplorable condition which had preceded it from 1830 to 1870 when our fathers or grandfathers, as the case may be, had felt no need for European culture and their so-called art, "free from foreign influence and competition," had grown smug and self-satisfied in a dreadful dullness. At the present time I am aware of the fact that in New York and Chicago press-agented exhibitions by foreign artists have resulted in many sales so that our hot-headed patriots have become alarmed. Protests have been made in timely editorials against any possible recrudescence of that cult of the foreign which has made our native artists miserable. The warning is natural and timely but the fear is unwarranted. We are learning about the eminence of great foreign artists whose work until recently we had not been privileged to see. It is well that we should know where we stand with men like Maillol and Matisse, with Bonnard and Vuillard, with Braque and Derain and Despiau, with Brancusi, Segonzac, and Rouault, with Sickert, Chirico, Klee, and Picasso, what we really think of them after the strangeness has worn off—how our best men compare with them on the same walls or at least under the same roof. Are we really neglecting American artists because we are also cognizant and appreciative of their outstanding foreign contemporaries, because we are developing in spite of ourselves an international mind? Let us suppose that any one of the men I have named came over and made his home with us. It might be that his inspiration would fail and his art crumble when uprooted in an alien land. But suppose that he was persistently a man of genius after becoming, by adoption, an American. How excited we would be! How likely it is that we would overrate him in patriotic panegyrics! Now, because he decides that, in spite of all temptations to belong to other nations he will remain, let us say, a Frenchman, why then must we be so sure that the praise of the foreign critics is propaganda and that the recognition of his genius before it is, too, fate by the American connoisseurs is aesthetic snobbism?

There is no danger now of a return to artificially inflated foreign prestige in art to the detriment of our own artists. We know our men too well. We honor them and we buy their works for our museums and our homes not just because they are American but for the far better reason that they are excellent artists worthy of our support and destined, we believe, to ultimate fame abroad. They are good workmen judged by ancient standards and ideals and all the better we think if they have been trained in our own schools and if they express our own characteristics and our own lives as Americans in the American scene, city or country. That is not provincialism. It is common sense. One paints best what best one knows, what one's roots ding to, what one grows out of, what one lives near and intimately loves. To maintain ideals for our art and to stimulate conditions favorable to its successful progress, this should be our only aesthetic concern as a member of the family of nations. In art as in everything else, let us make "America first" not a mere slogan but an actual fact. If we are world-minded and not stubbornly provincial, it can be done.

THE AESTHETIC EXPERIENCE
(1928)

FORM AND IDEA ARE IDENTICAL
IN PLASTIC ART

I have read so much that has been written on on the subject of art and aesthetics with a personal conviction that the issue has been clouded rather than cleared that it has seemed to me desirable to bring together a few current opinions which, taken together simplify the problem—if it is a problem. The old assumption that there is an absolute beauty, that "in art what is good for one is, or should be, good for all"-that there is an infallible criterion for the beautiful, seems to me untenable from the moment we recognize that essentially "art is the play instinct of humanity in making things," both the pattern and the picture. Every new method or theory of painting is either a new game which the artist, if he is free from interference, adapts to his own needs, imposing his own practical discipline, or, as it was in ancient civilizations, the game is for the artist to remain the anonymous instrument through which the age expresses the genius of its race and the spirit of its philosophy, using an ancient set of rules and code of conventions. The common purpose of the artist's play in every period is to make a symbol of correspondence between the thing or idea to be expressed and the means of expression. The form and the idea are identical in plastic art. When the mind changes the art must change accordingly. To one age, when group-consciousness prevails, under a dominance of imposed religious faith or fealty to a King or State, conformity to a set of rules in art is the great virtue. In another age, when individualism permits the play instinct to make its own discipline, beauty is various and variable, either formal or intimate and altogether impossible to

---

A revised and enlarged version of Phillips's review of Leo Stein's *The A-B-C of Aesthetics* in *The Yale Review* 18, no. 1 (September 1928), published in *The Artist Sees Differently.*

define. In an age of individualism, such as the late Nineteenth Century, nature's customary aspect must be reflected as in a mirror, for nature study is the absorbing interest of the majority. In reaction to this attitude the following socialistic period, such as our own, which is increasingly collective in its mentality, holds the reproduction of natural appearance in low esteem and sacrifices this imitative power to conventionalized symbolism, almost as it was when art was subordinated to royalty or religion.

Jan Gordon, in his excellent book *Modern French Painters*,[1] has pointed out that art separates into two almost antagonistic divisions, the imitative and the imaginative. The imitative came first. "Even the patterns on tattooed women of New Guinea, complex and handsome designs, are derivations from imitative drawings. This occurs all over the world. First the explicit pictograph—the imitation which is the first writing and the first science. Finally the Persian carpet and the pattern too beautiful to need its original script. For humanity has the patterning instinct. All legends have developed through the elaboration or simplification unconsciously given to the original stories. So with design. Starting as a fairly accurate imitation of an animal it develops further and further from nature tending more and more to become pattern." Picture-making grows out of pattern but as it is essentially representative it is a compromise between the scientific and the aesthetic.

What is the standard of art for one age is apt to be only a specimen for the archaeologist in another. If there were an absolute beauty either one or the other of two conflicting ideals and antithetical conceptions would be correct, like the answer to a mathematical problem. At the present hour, when we behold a survival of some other age, shall we decide that it is not valid art at all? The infinite variety of true artists and the unity of all art will soon be evident enough. The ends of the world, through conquest of space and control of time, are no longer isolated. Art, philosophy and religion of Orient and Occident already exchange influences. The day of universal art and

---

1. [New York: Dodd, Mead and Company, 1923.]

thought is no longer an impossibility. World-mindedness must first be extended from the few to the many. But for yet a while, the theory of the Absolute stubbornly returns to the minds of writers and artists who seem indifferent to the fact that along with it they should accept the smugness and blindness that it inevitably implies.

That beauty is subjective, that each of us makes his own beauty out of his inner consciousness is one of the two points which I consider essential to an understanding of the aesthetic experience. The other is that art, at least in so far as it is a science of the means of expression, is objective, that it can be learned like any other game, that it is impersonal, more or less disinterested, transcendent of self, in the exacting and exclusive task of creation. The artist seeks, more or less unconsciously, to survive himself, to continue to live down the centuries with whatever amount of life he can give to his work. It becomes his concern to study the life-giving elements of his particular art, each of which has its own organic peculiarities. The factor which assures life fair any art is rhythm or the coordination of parts, proportionately related one to the other in a functioning of order and movement, of continuity and consistency, of variety and unity. The artist is so exalted with his discovery that he can make a living expression by a chosen method that he is inclined to think that he has chanced upon the secret of extracting the beautiful or the eternal from nature. So close is he to his practical problems and so humble before nature, the source of his inspiration and invention, that he attributes to nature the beauty and the truth he feels in himself. This leads him to a passionate conviction that what he has discovered is right and that others who see differently must be misguided. If he felt any other conviction than this he might be a less consecrated and convincing priest of the beautiful. Since it is my purpose in this book, as well as in the collection of paintings which I am making, to stimulate interest in and to cultivate tolerance for many different aesthetic points of view, I have long recognized the need for facing the fact that the artist is not the best interpreter to the public of aesthetic intentions different from his own.

In agreement with this conclusion is the able American critic Virgil Barker from whose article on "Creation and Appreciation" in *The Arts* I am authorized to quote the following extracts:

> The making of art is a process of boiling down a great deal of life into the essence of art—a process of condensation. The appreciation of art is a process of living oneself out into its multitudinous separate manifestations—a process of expansion. For the artist, life is for the sake of art; for the appreciator, art is for the sake of life.
>
> As a consequence of the artist's necessarily intense feeling about his art, we must not be surprised if he is intolerant [...]
>
> On the other hand, as a consequence of the appreciator's demand that art add to the individual life, we expect tolerance of him. Indeed, he should not be merely tolerant but eager to discover new ways of exploration into nature and into the human mind. *If the lover of art allows himself to be persuaded into the belief that any one artist or school of artists can say the last word, he is merely selling his birthright as an appreciator for the mess of pottage which is the usual lot of partisan dilettantes.* In depriving himself of infinite possibilities of delight he simply limits his own development as a complete personality.
>
> This is why the pronouncements of artists upon the art they practice cannot always be accepted at face value [...] Any painter's judgment upon painting is decidedly worth having, as long as he keeps pretty closely to his own sort of painting. [...]
>
> Not merely the painters but the poets, the musicians, the creators in every art, are hopelessly divided among themselves; and to hear one set run down the others is to realize that finality of truth does not belong to any one group or method. If the would-be appreciator blindly accepts the dicta of any individual artist or group of artists, he thereby declines the very role he could play in the scheme of things. It is easy for the appreciator to be the follower of some prophet of art, it is easy for him to play the game of measuring all art by the foot-and-inch rule of artistic sectarianism. But in proportion as it is more difficult it is more worth while to comprehend the virtues of many different manifestations of art and pen-

etrate to the essential oneness which underlies all artistic expressions of the human spirit.[2]

As long then as humanity remains as it is, the essence of the aesthetic experience can be summed up in the line "It is in our life alone that nature lives." Beauty is in us, not in objects. Two works of art, at the opposite poles of intention, are equally valid-equally capable of becoming standards of great achievement. According to the range and scope of our understanding and appreciation of others we may extend our own horizons. To the statement that art is the play instinct of humanity in making things can be added the corollary that art-appreciation or, if you prefer, aesthetic contemplation is that other eternal play instinct for vicariously experiencing some or all of these transcripts, these identifications of man with nature, of idea with plastic form.

ART IS THE SYMBOL OF AN INTEREST

LEO STEIN's book with the somewhat misleading title *The A-B-C of Aesthetics*[3] is essentially a sound and sincere work. A man of ripe and seasoned scholarship, concerned with aesthetics all of his mature life, collects his ideas for our benefit. The intention is to clarify and to unify a mass of knowledge already familiar enough to most of us yet overlaid with fascinating considerations which are irrelevant, so that we miss too often the necessary discipline of thinking through to the true diagnosis of just what constitutes the aesthetic experience and the aesthetic object. Leo Stein is not altogether an art critic and only on occasions a psychologist. Nevertheless he is reputed to be one who speaks with authority on both these subjects and to whom one should listen with humility when he touches upon all matters involving either the perception or the analysis of aesthetic material.

---

2. [Virgil Barker, "Creation and Appreciation," *The Arts* 3 (January–June 1923): 413–14; italics added; quotation emended.]

3. [New York: Boni & Liveright, 1927.]

Twenty years ago, his championship of Post-Impressionist painting and especially of Cézanne, gave him, in spite of himself, the reputation of an advocate. I have no doubt that even then he denied special pleading and insisted that his absorbing interest in the movement of planes of color was focused upon this seeing habit of Cézanne's for the time only. A book even then was promised which would develop Stein's contention that not only is it less important what we see than how we see but that the capacity to see pictorially is in any case far more important than the seeing of pictures. Modern pictures are, in fact, of interest and value chiefly because they tend to isolate and exaggerate the aesthetic elements so that we learn to see in terms: of three or two dimensions, of line or light or sculptural planes or maps of flat color. All this has been the gist of Leo Stein and his talking and teaching for many years.

The long awaited *A-B-C of Aesthetics* reveals the defects of its conscientious and thorough method of preparation. To be sure the author maintains a consistent single-minded position throughout the work. But he spreads a simple thesis over too broad a field. He suggests that he is still discoursing to his disciples over the marble top table of a Paris café, talking without notes and starting many an idea when not in the mood to finish it or to connect it with a subsequent idea. Returning to it, as a later chapter requires, he makes us a bit breathless following his thought as it ranges forward and backward; far and wide.

The reviewer with such a book before him feels that he must know just how much ground has been traversed. For his own sake he must compress the thought, reduce it to its simplest terms and barest outline. In the case of this book of Leo Stein the process leads to the conclusion that the essay might have been a sufficient and more effective form. I have always felt that a review should furnish commentary which is primarily interpretation. It is only fair to an author who has meditated long and carefully on his theme to sum up for the reader the main points of the argument. I offer therefore a synopsis of Stein made out of paraphrased or his own rearranged sentences culled from widely scattered parts of his book. I earnestly recommend, however, that all those who appreciate authoritative opinion on aesthetics, and consistent, if not altogether clear or consecutive thought on the subject, should make the effort of reading this volume from cover to cover.

(1) The capacity to see pictorially is more important than the seeing of pictures, although of course one's capacity to see pictorially is nourished by one's familiarity with art. The aesthetic experience is a food to strengthen and sharpen the vision and to enrich the whole personality. Criticism is most useful when it leads to further and better creation and when it comes from one's own developed seeing habits. Connoisseurs who can distinguish between good and bad art are rare, like connoisseurs of wine. They are exceptionally endowed with the sense of quality and rarity but one can be nourished by art without this sense.

(2) Emotional excitement is not essential either to production or appreciation. If it were essential it would always happen. What really belongs to art always happens where art occurs. Beauty is not merely a special kind of pleasure in the contemplation of a thing for that might be characteristic of any other satisfactory result. *Aesthetics or the knowledge of beauty, has to do with knowing the objective quality of the thing.* All other properties things have belong to applied and not to pure aesthetics. An aesthetic object may be either a thing or an idea. Aesthetics is concerned with knowing the different degrees to which things or ideas have objective character. It has to do with quality and that means perception in relation to feeling.

(3) The pure aesthetic object, either thing or idea, has three properties: (*a*) it is known; (*b*) it endures; (*c*) it is unified. Other objects besides the aesthetic object have cognitive character. The instrumental object of science is consumed and does not endure. What distinguishes the aesthetic object is its indivisible unity. In science, which is also cognitive, the parts, taken separately, remain unaltered as atoms. Science infers one thing from another. It is inventorial, hypothetical, inferential. In aesthetics the parts interpenetrate—mix and change. Art is a complex of interdependent parts like any other organism in the physical world. Aesthetics discovers the character

of its objects singly or as unified wholes. The ultimate abstraction made by science is the atom—of aesthetics the symbol, expressing the singleness of the aesthetic fact.

(4) We make works of art symbols of our interests-seeing in terms of our recent seeing habits. Criticism of and pleasure in an object is of less consequence than its meaning for us as a symbol of something important to the artist. That art is best which adequately expresses the most of human values. But who is to judge what is most adequate? We must choose between different kinds of things. No picture is invalid if it represents any person's seeing. All we need to do is to put ourselves in that person's place.

(5) Both artist and spectator must have the capacity to maintain objective interest long enough to master the material and put it into form. Only continued interest and attention in the unity of see-ing as a whole will prevent inventorial or sentimental work. When once a picture is properly seen, it is finished. The thing gets a dia-grammatic fixity—which is the death of the pure aesthetic object for that individual. After that the work can serve only for applied aesthetic purposes—for stimulating aesthetic luxury and senti-mental revery—or else it can remain as a moment of the artist's or spectator's biography.

(6) The artist's field is the world seen through self. Aesthetics can-not give us anything more important than our Selves.

Seen through the semi-transparent medium of Self, which is a blend of many indefinite feelings and social contacts, the thing ceases to be just a thing and becomes an aesthetic object. Therefore this atmosphere of Self is an integral part of the aesthetic object.

(7) All things have their aesthetic aspects. Essentially the same kind of an interest that will make one person construct an ideal sys-tem in which everything is accounted for, from God to the atom, will make another try to get every stamp and all in perfect condition. The surgeon speaks of a beautiful operation and it is indeed aesthetic for him to recognize the conception and execution as the typical, classic, perfect expression of a felt interest. Aesthetic interest can be vital only where interest is genuine and extends beyond exploi-

tation. The new business man's religion of service can be aesthetic and its plastic material is the richest conceivable—men's human and social welfare.

Conclusion—pure aesthetics is a cognitive activity or attitude in which things are known as to their character and quality through the atmosphere of Self or Feeling.

Much of this argument is so convincing that it leaves me in a stupor of satisfaction, in a coma of conformity. I confess I was surprised by the prevailing dullness of the manner, the lack of zest in the presentation of so much celebrated research. Instead of illustrating and enriching the theme with allusions to individual works of art, the author drills his reader through setting up exercises in logic. For our entertainment we are given brilliant sentences and pyrotechnic paragraphs and occasional shocks, as when we are told that creative criticism is mere verbiage, or that the attempt to distinguish between good and bad in art is a waste of effort, or that art is simply a specialized activity and attitude so that "it is misleading to deny that something is the kind of thing it is when it is a bad specimen of its kind." There are times when I, for one, cry out in protest. I am not ready to put all this emphasis on pure aesthetics if it requires draining a work eventually of its power to please by learning it too well—reducing it, through this important knowledge of it as a whole, to such a finality of formal character that the doctor admits the pure aesthetic object cannot live thereafter. The author's own unhappy experience is an example of the tragic loss inevitably involved in being too penetrating, too persistent, and too pure an aesthete. It seems that Cézanne was almost worshiped by Leo Stein twenty years ago, and perhaps even earlier, at a time when to be aware of and interested in that obscure and eccentric artist was to be endowed with inspired insight and prophetic power. Stein seems to have grasped at once the significance of the pioneer-painter, realizing that his work was the symbol of a new and fresh interest which would teach men how to see in planes of col or as well as in lines and masses. The problem of deep space and Cézanne's discoveries of how to organize form within it organically, fascinated Stein and he fed upon this food until it became for him the bliss of solitude or as he calls it, "the power to see pictorially." At last his attention shifted to a new interest, and he discovered that Cézanne had become for him "more completely the squeezed lemon than any other artist of equal importance." Think of it, the impassioned philosopher Cézanne a squeezed lemon! Cézanne and his cosmos of plastic color relegated to the attic of the mind along with the algebra books after one's graduation from school! I respect the critic for acknowledging the limits of his temperament. His treatise becomes all the more valuable as a human document through such a confession. Yet I am not convinced by the argument that a work of art is just a means to an end, and that the end is just another bit of knowledge. Nor do I relish the idea that the aesthetic experience is less valuable for what it contributes to our pleasure than for its position as symbol of an interest which comes to a rather ignominious close when it has been completely studied and assimilated. From that time on we are asked to believe that art can be enjoyed, but only as a sensuous indulgence in the daydream or the imagined experience. I wonder whether what follows a completed understanding of the painter's point of view can really be either sentimentality or mere surfeit, requiring constant change. When I establish communion with the spirit of an artist through knowing his intention and recognizing the apt correspondence of his style to his idea my enjoyment grows richer with the passing of time. My pleasure is all the more dependable because my mind needs to make no further struggle. I can see more and more in a picture having already learned how to look at it. Poor Mr. Stein's enjoyment and even his interest have meanwhile breathed their last at the dread moment when the artist's interest in something has been accurately recognized, his mastery of his material placed, and the "aesthetic fact" clearly pigeonholed as a symbol.

As I write the spring of the year is at its old business of making the world over, with balmy air, vibrant light, odors of earth and growing things, movement of young leaves. There is a restless, whimsical tug at the vaguely troubled heart, and the mind is uneasy. At such a time it seems hardly sensible to be so much concerned, so gravely occupied with knowing beauty for what it is. One could find it for oneself in any flowery meadow or, for that matter, wherever the spring makes gay the corner of the street, whether it is the push carts of flowers or a bunch of bright balloons bobbing in the sunlit breeze, or the passers-by in their new hats and dresses. Yet for once, as part of one's education in art, beauty should be known for what it is and the aesthetic experience estimated consciously and at its true worth instead of dreamily and without intelligence. Otherwise, as Stein points out, the pleasure of the aesthetic experience would be on a par with any other situation satisfactory to our sense of fitness. To the end that we should know the aesthetic experience there is no better guide than Stein, unless it is Roger Fry himself.[4] There is no definition of beauty in Stein but "the aesthetic experience" as knowledge rather than mere pleasure is considered on almost every page. I dislike the disillusioned dryness of the logic while recognizing that it is unanswerable. We will be better for this book. It will help us rid our minds of dogmatism and of many fallacies. About absolute beauty, for instance: There is no such thing. What is good for one, is not, should not be, could not be good for all. This applies to art as it does to food and all kinds of merely material nourishment. "What is meant for one is poison for another." This is as true of one's aesthetic as of one's dietetic peculiarities. About rules in art: They are well enough, but only for games and sports, including the sport of technical devices such as painting. About abstraction: "There never was an art that was not abstract," but "the one hundred percent abstractionists have wandered by mistakes into the world of science" which deals with "atoms in relations" with "the atom instead of the symbol as the ultimate." About distortions in modern art: "They are only a recent case of the distortions implied in all art." About the role of emotion as a non-essential alike to artist and spectator: "Emotion is only the detonating amplifier to feeling and perception."

---

4. [Roger Fry, *Vision and Design* (New York: Brentano's, 1924). Duncan and Marjorie Phillips owned several editions of Fry's book.]

This last is one of the passages where the critic splits hairs and yet I do recommend it to your sympathetic second thoughts. After all, it will do us good to be disciplined with this drastic insistence upon knowing exactly the aesthetic experience as a food for the complete man—and more particularly as the recognition and expression of a felt interest. Whether or not there is emotional excitement, the discovery of the more or less personal symbol for the human interest, whatever it may be, is indeed the act or attitude which always happens where art occurs and which therefore undoubtedly characterizes art.

THERE IS NO OBJECTIVE BEAUTY

TO Leo Stein's assertions that we make works of art symbols of our interest, seeing in terms of our recent seeing habits, and that the artist's field is the world seen through Self, that all-pervasive atmosphere of each man's unique visual apparatus and mental preparation, it is only a step to the unflinching, important *Note on Aesthetic Theory* by W.M. Ivins, in *The Arts* for December, 1925, in which he declares that there is no such thing as objective beauty which can be set up as a standard: "one only knows objects [...] by their appearance; and as the appearance of an object is in us and not in the objects." Appearances are not only subjective but relative and they bring us back to ourselves. In art only qualities really concern us and these we can only recognize "by our [own] psychological reactions."[5] Stein tells us that to know the quality or character of an object is the function of the artist. Ivins adds that one never knows objects as such, but only by one's own impressions. And these we cannot clearly or completely convey to the outside world. There is no way for an artist to be sure that he has been accurately understood for his intimations and intuitions are often vague and his symbols of his interests may have no meaning at all for some and for others a different response than his own to the original idea or sensation. We

---

5. [W.M. Ivins, Jr., "Note on Aesthetic Theory," *The Arts* 8 (July–December 1925): 303, 305; quotation emended.]

can hardly wish that it should be otherwise for to make the imaginative inner life as demonstrable as a mathematical problem would
be to deprive art of its power to enchant as well as to convince. "In
everything that has to do with qualities, such as texture and color,
and all matters not of extent, or quantity, or time, or distance, or size,
or weight, but solely of intensity, like pleasure and pain, there is no
way on earth of measuring just what happens to us. We can arrive
in abstractions at quantitative measurements but we are utterly
incapable of measuring the psychological effects of qualities. To say
that it is impossible to make a qualitative measure is very different
from saying that there are no such things as qualities." But according to Ivins "it is very doubtful whether qualities are not among the
irrational things with which [...] analytical] thought [...] is unable
to cope." "[I]t would seem," he continues, "that all we can do is to be
honest, and when we talk about the qualities in art and whether or
not there is beauty in an object, always to preface our remarks by '*I*
think*' or '*I* feel.'"[6] Many people will have it appear to them in much
the same way and will not find it difficult to see and to feel likewise.
In time there will be an agreement that one work of art is finer than
another. That (says Ivins) is a matter for statistics or, if we prefer, for
historical record. However, "the man or woman who talks of 'eternal
verities' about art talks of necessity through his or her hat—for the
verities that any one can tell you about qualities in art are only valid
for himself and as eternal as himself."[7]

   It is, I hope, fairly clear from this reasoning of Ivins that he is
no apologist for academic dogma. In fact, he would seem to be giving aid and comfort to the enemy, to the "scab" artist who will not
accept the rules and regulations of "the Art Teachers' Union" but
would substitute merely personal discipline for the Academy's group
discipline and make an artist's honesty to himself the only requirement. Of the "people who find their greatest happiness in being as

---

6. [Ibid., 304, italics added; quotation emended.]
7. [Ibid.; quotation emended.]

nearly as possible like other people" he merely remarks that they should not make the "mistake to try to be individualists."[8] Theirs is the social function of seeing to it that group discipline, group consciousness and group taste shall continue to curb the excesses of temperament. But the Academy tries to do the impossible. That is the pity of it. It attempts to fix and to measure qualities as if they were quantities. It condemns a unique thing while it is still fresh and new to the world as a dangerous freak or at least an undesirable variation from the norm. Finally, it lays down rules for acceptable procedure according to the public opinion of the period—punishing non-conformity and independence from its own self-constituted authority. The purpose of art would appear to be the proficient and profitable manufacture of objective, external "beauty" in disregard of the fact that there is no such thing. Although the rules change with the changing modes the authorities set up by the popular taste continue to require conformity to the irrevocable dogma of the day. It is assumed that there is an absolute beauty, a standard implying that one thing should be the same as another thing and acknowledging a standard quality in all things which produce similar results, such as attracting purchasers. Ivins, having genially ridiculed all these antiquated but well preserved delusions, concludes with the statement that the genuine work of art is not what is like something else (that would make it a nullity) but rather that which is unlike anything else and therefore unique as individuals are unique. Thus he disposes of the attempt to apply the common sense of ordinary life to the uncommon things of extraordinary imagination and invention: He does not call sufficient attention to the fact that the rebels and the radicals of art are inclined to make the same mistake of thinking that there must be a common quality in all those works of art of which they approve. I would like to hear what Ivins would say of Clive Bell's "significant form" as it was set forth in his oracular little book entitled *Art*.[9] If significant form means simplification,

---

8. [Ibid.; 306, quotation emended.]
9. [New York: Frederick A. Stokes Company, 1913.]

organization and expression by plastic means only, it is easy to agree with him as to its being the acid test. But evidently it does not, for the author condemns many artists who simplified, organized and expressed themselves superbly but did not display and demonstrate what they were doing.

I have enjoyed *Since Cézanne*[10] and *Civilization*[11] so much that I have changed my mind about Clive Bell. He is not as intolerant and pedantic as one would suppose from reading his first and more pretentious work. Even in that manifesto he recognized no less than Ivins the importance of the third factor in the aesthetic problem in addition to the artist and his creation. That third factor is of course "the fellow who," in Ivins's words, "likes the object well enough to own it or to study it. Unless he can be found the object is not art at all, it is merely something somebody made. Now this appreciative person who turns the object into art likes that object for any one of a hundred million relevant and irrelevant reasons, of which the rules of the Art Teachers' Union is only one and the artist's expression of himself only another. He may like it because it is Greek or Egyptian or Chinese or because it was made in a certain place, or in a certain Century, or represents a certain thing, or for its color, or its pattern, or because it belonged to someone, or because it gives somehow a funny feeling of some kind." In the list, along with the ignorant, are included those who like the art object for the right and relevant reasons but who are inclined to be dogmatic in their opinions and overbearing in their tastes. Of this number is—or was—the famous Mr. Bell himself. Significant Form was for him the common quality existent in all objects which moved him in a particular way. But he was not so blind to the virtues of less valuable minds as to deny them their eligibility to enjoy the beautiful. He wrote charmingly of those who are sensitive, capable of responding immediately and surely to works of art but yet unwilling, perhaps unable, to analyze and examine their feelings when for them to feel is enough. Why should they

10. [New York: Harcourt, Brace and Company, 1922.]
11. [New York: Harcourt, Brace and Company, 1928.]

hunt for a common quality in all objects which move them in a particular way when they can linger over the many delicious and unique
charms of each as it comes. If such people write criticism and call it
aesthetics, if they imagine they are talking about art when they are
talking about particular works of art, if, loving particular works they
find tedious the consideration of art in general, perhaps, acknowledges the indulgent Mr. Bell, "they have chosen the better part, since
the starting point for all systems of aesthetics must be the personal
experience of a personal emotion."

Significant Form is a terse and comprehensive criterion for the
arts of design in their present state of rather self-conscious development. The trouble with the doctrine to which it was attached as a
slogan is the old trouble of a too narrow-minded application resulting in the apparent approval only of abstract art where the style is
stylistic and so formal as to be devoid of elusive and various appeal.
Art was like that whenever in past ages it was imposed as a rule and
performed as a ritual. The history of art is the story of how the artist
has rebelled and attempted to disengage and detach his personal
observations from the prescribed standards and philosophical dogmas based on non-aesthetic conditions of church, king and the
democratic rule of the majority. For the artist sees differently not
only from the man on the street but from his fellow artists. And even
within each art are separate states of the mind. And even within
each separate dominion every individual is a law to himself. As no
two human minds are alike so we may expect to find an infinite variety in the scale of creative conceptions and methods of technical
expression. All this makes for a clash of opinion which, in periods
when individualism is regarded with suspicion and alarm, results
in the subjection of the artist to a prevailing philosophy or code. In
self-defense, fearing the disapproval of the majority, the minds of
the artists meet in order to form Schools or Academies, representing standards for acceptable principles and practices. These institutions gradually build up aesthetic doctrine. Free and original artists
refuse to be bound and these are the lonely pioneers who blaze new
trails which must be beaten down by the feet of many intrepid fol-

lowers before the authorities recognize that new thoroughfares of art have been opened for traffic.

Science is a clear and constantly revised statement of something which matters more or less to us all. Art on the other hand is not a statement for all but a communication to a few, and to each of these with particular shades of difference. In that sense it is like great philosophic thought which we like or dislike according to our own philosophy. Art is the ancient language which the instinct of man devised, even before his intellect approved, to make articulate and social the inner and otherwise lonely imaginative life. One outstanding benefit of modernist art and the literature based upon it is its implicit isolation of the aesthetic sense from every other sense, its emphasis upon art as the expression of man's disinterested state of mind, of symbolical thought and vicarious emotion. as distinct from his actual life with its need for responsive action. The life of imagination is sharper in its emotions than the life of practical problems and concerns because there is concentration on the emotional part of seeing, hearing or whatever sense is acted upon by a given stimulus. The artist is the spectator who creates beauty from within himself for its own sake and with no circumstances impelling his creation other than his imperious inner need for imaginative expression. By reducing a picture to its diagrammatic structure and depriving it of its non-aesthetic human appeals and its reminders of ordinary experience the modern artist forces us to think about art as a complex organization which lives or dies according to its coordination or its lack of it. After we have learned a gain to recognize a work of art as something man has added to nature, as a transposition instead of as a mere reflection of nature, we are then enabled to regain our rights to the emotions of conceiving of reality and of escaping into dreams. But art must first be respected as a living, growing, changing child of man, having its own organic life, based on the same principles of rhythm and interdependence as those by which we live and with its own emotions in line, form, color, light, space, proportion, contrast, repetition, subordination, accent, continuity, harmony, unity and, in one word, *relations*. What is needed by artist and public alike is tolerance. Art is sure to be as various and variable as human consciousness itself and as relative to God the only absolute Beauty as is the individual's limited grasp of truth to God the only absolute Truth and his uncertain hold on goodness—to God the only absolute Good. Religion, Science and Art are all reflections of God who lives in us according to our aspirations. What we seek, whether we know it or not, is union with the giver of life and its rhythms, the energizing and enkindling force, the source in us of our divine discontent, of our creative impulses, our appreciative zest, our urgent need for understanding of and harmony with others and of knowledge of and peace with ourselves. We seem to be on this earth for some purpose and some of us wonder whether it might not be for our cultivation to the end that we could see God by breaking down barriers of selfishness and hate, apathy and passion and prejudice. The desire for more and ever more life to enlarge our own limited opportunities and capacities for living—this explains the indestructible power over us of Religion, of Science and of Art, all implying service and social adjustments and all baffled by our tenacious habits of intolerance. The exhilarating and revitalizing power of these fundamental currents of mind and spirit are only active and effective when in contact with the same forces in others. What we discover by research others may build upon. What we sincerely feel others can be made to fed if, being seekers of truth, we express ourselves with power to convince, and if, being intimates of beauty, we are given also the rare magic to enchant.

One word about an unnecessary conflict and embarrassment. The two functions of the same instinct for expression are so misunderstood that we often find critics and artists bitterly alienated. And yet, in the words of Havelock Ellis, "the aesthetic contemplation" is "the passive aspect of art," and art is "the active aspect of aesthetic contemplation."[12] To make the life-enriching endowment of sensitiveness to beauty the privilege and the opportunity of all, that is the

---

12. [Havelock Ellis, *The Dance of Life* (Boston and New York: Houghton Mifflin Company, 1923); quotation emended.]

only legitimate and worthy purpose of whatever is written about art. Much of it is of no value but the best of it aids both artist and public. The artist is made conscious of what he does in relation to what others have done and are doing and his point of view is patiently interpreted to the public to his own inestimable advantage.

Art is objectified beauty or aesthetic experience. And beauty is a subjective, cognitive, selective, and relative *interest* in some phase of life. For that interest art can find the appropriate symbol, to serve our need as a transposition from nature, or as the equivalent of life in terms of man's creation. Beyond that we are at liberty to speculate that the capacity for perceiving and appreciating beauty, in other words for experiencing aesthetic emotion, and for creating corresponding aesthetic objects as symbols, may be separate sparks of the divine and that both artist and critic are the consecrated ones who must keep the sparks alive both in themselves and in others like them. Sooner or later the most obscure and lonely artist finds his way to the two or three who, by their sympathy, will fully and beautifully complete his mission. If this appreciation never comes during his brief earthly pilgrimage he is consoled with the thought that some day, somewhere, his seed may bear fruit. It is my hope that we shall develop and train more interpreters of the *intentions* of artists who will not be too cautious and captious and quick to condemn if those intentions seem obscure to the public, untimely and unfashionable according to the taste of the times, and perhaps not adequately realized with technical success. Artists can only be encouraged to be loyal to their own ideas and to excel in their own, efforts through the assurance of sincere recognition and sympathetic interest in their intention. That is the source of all sound aesthetic pleasure and it can become a part of the spiritual progress of the world and the unfolding totality of existence. To that end, whether or not we are ready for enjoyment, let us all cultivate tolerance of the many significant differences with which artists see.

—⁓—

ART AND UNDERSTANDING

(1929)

THERE is nothing esoteric and beyond the comprehension of the average man in that incessant spiritual activity, almost as old as the human species, which we call art. The sense of well-being and enriched capacity for living which art can give, not only to those who create, but also to those who contemplate, is, I like to think, a privilege of the many as well as of the technically trained and sensitive few. The machine age promises to provide more and more opportunity for leisure. Those who tire of the accelerated pace of modern life and the furious tempo of its entertainments may turn to the fine arts for a cultivation of their vacant time. In such a belief I am striving year after year to interpret to people, distracted by more practical interests or more worthless diversions, not only *the* artist's point of view collectively, as a state of mind common to all true artists under the sun, but also *an* artist's point of view, whichever of the million and one I happen to be considering. Both have their origin in the childhood of the race. *The* artist's point of view begins with the first instincts to make things for any purpose at all. *An* artist's point of few comes with the first signs of individual divergence from herd consciousness and herd opinion. It is only when a sense of quality or pride of performance enters the mind that conscious art is born, yet anyone who has used initiative, ingenuity, and an elementary amount of invention and who has longed to have one or two congenial spirits notice and approve the job, has had enough experience to understand the artist's point of view and his inner compulsion to do a thing well. Art is the conscience of the creative instinct in man. It proceed from instinct which have led to our jobs, our games and our elves and our

First published in *Art and Understanding* 1, no. 1 (November 1929). Reprinted in *The Artist Sees Differently*.

desires to perfect the methods and the rules and to find the perfect application of the mean to a given end.

The difference between potential artists and conscious artists begins at the point where technic is recognized as such and degrees of excellence estimated in contemplation. The artist's point of view is an evolution from the primitive instinct to create for any one of many purposes, for instance to pray to and propitiate supernatural forces or to pass the time of enforced inactivity in caves. From such a utilitarian origin it seems an unimaginable distance to the ultra civilized isolation of the modern artist and connoisseur in their exclusive dogma of art for art's sake. And yet the evolution is clearly marked, from the Negro sculptors to Roger Fry who can tell us why these aboriginal artists carved better than they knew. The purpose of the self-conscious modern artists, as Roger Fry interprets them so clearly, is to create art not only for its own sake but for the sake of detached and disinterested states of mind so delightful and profitable to the inner life that they become ends in themselves, justifications of the long evolutionary experiment. But an artist's point of view has to do not entirely with the technical preoccupations which keep the public at a more or less disrespectful distance but with the universal stuff of personality, with idiosyncrasy of thought, vision, or touch, similar to a manner of speaking or of handwriting. Artists differ in this sense even as all men differ and such an individualism is an evolution from the first artists who broke far enough away from tribal domination and collective taboo to find instinctively the equivalents in color or line or dance patterns for their peculiarly isolated sensations and emotions.

As to what art actually is, distinguishing it from all the rest of creation, the answers to that question are many and different but they agree that art is the one method of communication which is also a symbol of life itself, of life with its rhythms and its complexity of interdependent relations, the absence of which in any work of man signifies that the living element is lacking, that there is perhaps an inventory of recorded facts but that the human consciousness has not flowered out of an organic coordination and unity of parts. Since art is as old as the human race and since it is synonymous with the proper functioning of human life it is a universal human concern. If the public has withdrawn farther and farther from the artists so that they have become more and more mysterious alchemists working for a few fascinated patrons, the fault is to be divided equally between the artist and the public. I hope to show that the world is in sore need of reconciliation between them, not altogether on the terms of one nor of the other but with mutual respect and understanding and exchange of influence.

From unknown beginnings down through periods of collective civilization like Egypt and Byzantium the individual was hampered by tribal control of his brain, by imposed traditions and conventions. It is only in modern times that the many-mindedness of art, left to itself without patronage and subsidy, has led on the one hand to much confusion of plan and purpose, and on the other co thrilling correspondence with intimacies of our personal experience. Even the recognition of strangeness in art helps to reconcile us to strangeness in life and in other people and to make the whole world kin. The Quaker of the oft-told story who confessed to his best friend, "Everybody seems queer except me and thee and sometimes thee seems a little queer," was voicing a psychological truth. There are queernesses about most of us in the eyes of the rest of us and only a few seem to understand how uniquely right we are in thinking and seeing precisely as we do. If it were not so there might be no need for arc since we would all see alike and think alike and what then would be the occasion for personal expression. Certainly there would be no ferment, no urgent passion to create. It is upon individuality, upon faith in and reverence for unfettered and fully developed personality that both Christian idealism and modern art are firmly based.

Frank Jewett Mather, Jr., was thinking no doubt less of our immediate period than of an earlier phase, when he wrote as follows: "Drive the doctrine [that the artist is free] to the extreme, and you make the artist more or less than a man. Nobody else is free; we are all trammeled not merely from within, through the bodies and minds we inherit, but also from without through the pressure of public opinion, the weight of custom, the compulsion of law."[1] This is a fine warning to the artist to avoid extremes both in life and art or to renounce the right to be called artists, since art is the cultivation of our sense of moderation and balance. It is also a no less timely warning to artists of the aesthetically snobbish type to avoid a total loss of contact with humanity since art is essentially and must remain eternally a means for intellectual and emotional exchange. The artist is indeed "neither more nor less than a man." He is man at his most sensitive spot. Is he not in a sense our barometer? If he rebels too recklessly and we applaud him, it may be a sign of our inner desperation. If he conforms too meekly and we like him meek, it may be because we are growing spiritless. We can diagnose ourselves and appraise our situation through understanding what the artists are doing and whether they are tending to conform or to challenge, falling back on tradition or enriching it with successful experiment.

Now there is a popular misconception that individualism is running rampant today. This was the case not so very long ago during a brief period of revolution when standards and values were successfully reversed and many extravagant theories were hurled like the sort of bombs which explode noisily but without damage. Today there is a profound change in the psychology of radical artists. Elie Faure has written that "of all the confused art movements one needs only to retain what seems to be the collective desire of which they are symptoms." There are eccentric individuals who continue to assume a look of singularity at all costs but when we have seen the most radical exhibitions in France, Italy, Germany, and Russia, it is easy to detect similarities of aberration and a general tendency to connect pictorial art with abnormal psychology and psychoanalysis. According to Élie Faure the total attitude of modern artists, including the conservatives, is to subordinate self to a collective stylization of one kind or another. He finds in this a protest of the painters and sculptors against the unquestionable excess of undisciplined free-

---

1. [*Modern Painting: A Study of Tendencies* (New York: Henry Holt and Company, 1927), 45; quotation emended.]

dom permitted to their work. It plainly means that, in the opinion of the studios, the public, which democracy has made important in art as in all things, is scornfully indifferent and not that it is increasingly tolerant. This indifference of the many, alarmed or antagonized by the hyper-aesthetic and the abstract, has served to stimulate the artistic encouragement of a patronizing few. These critics, collectors, dealers, and connoisseurs are acutely period-conscious and apt to be theoretical. As a result of their uncontested authority in the world of art a new ideal has been inscribed on the tablets of the law and the gospel for modern artists.

Impersonal Order, corresponding to our business organizations, is said to be the only proper concept of what the modern artist should strive for in his work. Architecture is proposed as the only legitimate art from this day forward. The other arts must be appropriately architectonic. Painters and sculptors must submit to group consciousness and invent an ideographic language of decorative conventions appropriate to the age of time-saving short cuts and labor-saving machines, conventions which in time all men will accept without question and even require from the artists. In other words, instead of the excesses of individualism of which Mather still complains, there are signs of an excess of impersonality leading to systems for collective expression similar to the Egyptian and Byzantine. The artists, baffled by public apathy, are in search of a style, in which form follows utilitarian function, to which the public can be made accustomed, and to which they can submit and subordinate themselves. Modern man feels confused and insignificant and inarticulate because of the continual hum and roar of the machines. Through his spokesman, the artist, he is reconciling himself to the idea that to be an individual no longer matters very much but only to adapt oneself to the new conceptual universe in which individual impressions are of little or no consequence. Since concepts are valued more than percepts and only the abnormal states of mind attract attention the artists of an individualistic bent are tempted to make eccentric demonstrations for the psychological clinic while the more rationalizing craftsmen make stylized decorations adaptable to objects of common use. Analyze the various new art movements since Cubism and their causes are found to be not excess of egotism but exasperated lack of self esteem and self reliance combined with a desperate desire to be noticed, if not individually then collectively, either as subjects for the research of psychology and other sciences or as timely and topical modes of new design for the new age. In short, the artists are anxious to be found on the band wagon of modernity as it parades the town, to get into the picture as an association of craftsmen since uniquely sensitive individuals are out of fashion.

I hold that what we need today is not less individual expression and not less cultivation of individual sensibility but more, to the end that the art of living will come back and with it the human joys of finding art to match our unique emotional experiences. The great humane individualists of art who lived during the unfavorable conditions of the nineteenth century conceived of art in this way and today we think of Constable, Delacroix, Daumier, Corot, Manet, and Renoir as artists who speak to us personally and directly instead of through a literature of propaganda and the arguments of professional advocates. When art was for the church it had an educated public. When art was for royalty the court and its academies set the superficial standards. Now that art is on the town the academy of the public and its enlarged electorate in artistic affairs represents the public lack of taste and whether there shall be progress from this low level is a question for the few critics and collectors and dealers who stand back of the progressive artists to decide. How fine progressive art will be must depend on whether or not its patrons tend to rise above mechanism, materialism, nationalism, the pseudo-classic, the pseudo-scientific, and other repressive forces of our time. And I would call the artists of the world to a higher destiny than to provide entertainment for a few of their protectors from public ignorance and indifference. I would plead with them not to follow but to lead public opinion in the fight against standardization, which will gradually dominate them unless they assert themselves. What the artists really need, what they really want, is an enlightened and sympathetic public which will take more interest in them as comprehensible, lovable, differentiated individuals with many fascinating minds and talents than in their formulation of their particular period or its self imposed doctrine or dogma. What they need and what they want, whether they realize it or not, is a new religion of humanity which will hold up to them higher ideals of cultivated personality and of personal expression.

Walter Lippmann, in *A Preface to Morals*,[2] deplores the lot of the modern artists. Bereft of faith, cut off from religious jurisdiction, called upon to substitute mere pictures for pictorial ideas or the telling pictorially of sacred stories, the duty of creation is thrust upon them. They are engaged in setting down a view of the world to replace the religious view of the age of faith. Every vision of the world implies some sort of philosophy. With the dissolution of the supreme ideal of service to God there is not yet an ideal which unites and regulates the separate activities of man. The modern artist has not yet discovered the ideal to organize his interest within the framework of a cosmic order. Granting the validity of much of this argument I contend that there is just such an ideal as Mr. Lippmann claims to be missing in the modern world. A new religion of reverence for personality and faith in and service to all men regardless of race, class or creed, to replace the old order with its emphasis on dogma and worship and the believer's individual salvation would bring Christianity appreciably nearer to the ideal of its Founder.

The artist can find the ideal as the scientists are finding it and as even the statesmen of the two countries which so recently were in a death grapple, Stresemann and Briand, are finding it around the table where together they plan for the gradual union and disarmament of Europe. The artists can find it if they will but open the doors and windows of their too exclusive workshops, if they will but be as much concerned with spiritual changes as with technical discoveries and their own professional politics, if they will but look out over the wide soul-stirring view of a new world in the making. It is an

2. [London: George Allen & Unwin Ltd., 1942.]

ideal of world peace, of world religion, of world federation, with the artists destined and equipped to convey the symbol of the new synthesis of Occident and Orient. I am not appealing for a painting that will teach or preach. The time has probably passed for acceptance of pictorial parable. Be that as it may, I believe in the theory that art is independent of all other activities and that it has its own pure and disinterested emotional significance. Nor can we hope for many inspired symbolists with a gift for embodying great thoughts and visions in abstract form and color. Let the artists be true to themselves. That is all that matters. As long as they are sincere about it and not merely submissive to current modes and schools, let them continue to create as they will in forms abstract or concrete, with local colors or with atmospheric colors. Let them go on with their intelligent and stimulating patterns and their plastic symbols for the constructions, the organizations and the simplifications of their complex age. The modern world at this period of transition and adaptation is so many-minded that art is bound to be confusing in its reflection of that strange variety.

The Phillips Memorial Gallery cannot in advance of the arbitrament of time claim to decide between conflicting aesthetic purposes. It stands for a definite policy of supporting many different methods of seeing and painting, avoiding partisanship and propaganda for any one point of view, seeking the best of each, trying to understand what may be all the more significant and worthy of study because it is strange and new. Out of the invigorating clash of all our differences will come a new age and perhaps a new art, rich and strong in its blend of opposites. Art has a mission for such a time as ours. Even as psychology is becoming the most important of all sciences because it deals with humaniculture, so art can be no less indispensable to the new religion of humanity and its constructive, unifying aim. For art also deals with humanity and is of personal expression the very essence.

To convey more perfectly than lies within my power the philosophy which I cherish for my collection I am authorized to quote at length from a beautifully satisfying essay on art by John Galsworthy.

And in the subsequent pages I invite you to a Symposium of distinguished contemporaries, an imaginary conversation between a few inter-creating philosophers out of which an appeal for independence and tolerance, open mindedness and world mindedness is developed as it relates to life and art. These men speak with their own words out of their own books, yet in building up one side of a debate through the contributions of individual points of view I have detached for my special purpose certain paragraphs and connected these with recurring considerations of the same themes so as to make a sequential argument. To do this I have had to take some liberties with the text, paraphrasing instead of quoting exactly. As Editor I call upon men of various types for views with which I am in agreement. The philosophical position from which many matters are observed and discussed is that of the detached and disinterested individualist who reverences human personality but not too much to analyze it and who claims that human life is sacred but that after ages of desecration it will cake all our wits and all our energies to conserve and cultivate it. Men of the most different kinds, for instance, John Dewey, Clive Bell, Dr. Fosdick, General Allenby, Havelock Ellis, arrive by way of widely separated trails at the same lofty lookout and my task has been to lead them on with the meeting of their minds as the purpose of the expedition. It seems to me worth doing, this reconciliation of alien standpoints. In fact, that is the very core of our contemporary problem.

My purpose, as it will increasingly appear in the following pages, is to affirm that the six qualities which I deeply desire for art, namely: cultivated sensibility, self reliance, self discipline, tolerant humanity, universality, and essentialism, are also the most urgent needs of modern life. The comprehensive meaning of my title, "Art and Understanding," should now be clear. The artist must understand and be inspired by the world and by the thought that a world society is on the march. The world for its own part must understand and be inspired by the artist and must try to give to his necessary innovations and inventions the same sympathy that it extends to other manifestations of vitality and progress. It must meet him more than half way so that he will not withdraw too far into himself or into abstraction. It must realize that his language can be learned and must be mastered if one would travel at ease in the expansive realms of art where nothing is impossible because everything is made new. Every artist is an isolated phenomenon and yet a brother in spirit to artists of his kind in all ages and of all races. Even his singularity is of short duration. For new modes of thought, belief and artistic convention have their difficult beginnings in isolated individuals or small obscure groups and thence extend gradually outward. Art is the greatest unifying and it is also the greatest clarifying force of the universe, and it is not for more than a moment to be regarded as merely a racial or national expression or the exclusive interest and business of a technically trained few.

THE MANY-MINDEDNESS OF
MODERN PAINTING
(1929)

WE are living in a complex period when the artists are acutely conscious of their background and of their need for simplicity. They are intensely anxious to be at one with the age and to express themselves in musical, pictorial, and decorative language as much attuned to it as the words of common speech. The adventurous zest of the Twentieth Century, its noise, its speed, its elimination of waste, its organization of effort, its emphasis upon system and its perpetual desire for innovation and invention, these characteristics inspire the artists no less than the concrete aspects of the modern world and the new materials employed in its service. If the modern movement in Art has done nothing else than reiterate such slogans as "Simplification, Organization and Expression" it would have justified itself and its spread of enlightened doctrine all over the world. Modernist art is not a revolution. It has evolved, like every other period, in a logical and gradual way. Its roots are deep in the remote past. Not since antiquity have the artists been so disciplined in theory to conform to the philosophy, the science, the tempo, and the very textures of the world around them. Period-consciousness is an interesting manifestation in art and its results are always traceable from cause to effect. Today, as often in remote centuries, we look at the world and at ourselves, not passively but actively, in search of what we set out to find in order to fit it to our theory, our preconception. Modern life is by no means as stereotyped and conventionalized as modern art. This no doubt was true also of ancient Egypt and its prescribed abstraction of Gad as Super-

First published in *Art and Understanding* 1, no. 1 (November 1929). Reprinted in Duncan Phillips, *The Artist Sees Differently: Essays Based Upon the Philosophy of a Collection in the Making*, 2 vols. (New York and Washington, D.C.: E. Weyhe and Phillips Memorial Gallery, 1931).

man and of ancient Greece with its ideal of perfect physical development for its divinities. Our age, like every other, has its significant
minorities, its non-conforming types, its contradictory and conflicting elements. What distinguishes the present period in art is the fact
that the preconceptions and the conventions are consigned to the
favorable few in defiance of the mockery of the many by the artists

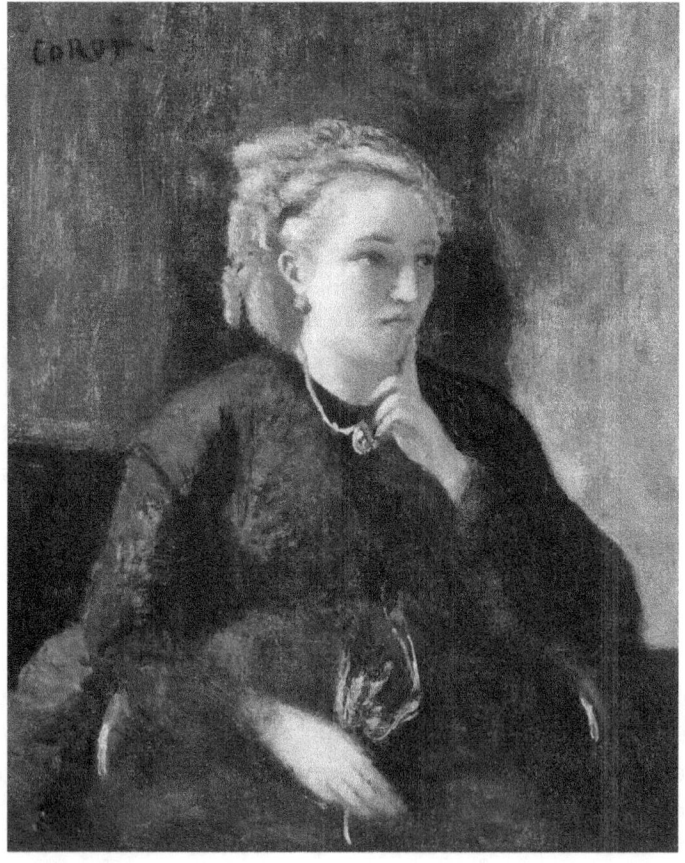

Jean-Baptiste-Camille Corot
Portrait of a Woman, 1870
Oil on canvas
The Phillips Collection, Washington, D.C. Acquired in 1922

themselves instead of being forced upon them by a despotic influence of church, court, or crowd, and its servile Academies. The public has not yet caught up with the advance of art; but at least it does not persecute those who run ahead of it, and it makes only a feeble protest against the aesthetic adventurers and their supporters. And the artists in rebellion against public opinion are more numerous and therefore more aggressive and independent than ever before. Not since antiquity has the aesthetic function become so specialized and self-sufficient, with style as its central idea and design as its primary purpose. So bracing has this new freedom been to the artists that their creative faculties have produced patterns almost unprecedented and possessed of freshness and vitality like nothing so much as the unschooled imagination of children and the instinctive designs of the childhood of the race.

This "innocence of the eye" is the quality which that sophisticated craftsman Henri Matisse frankly desired for art in general and for his own art in particular. His combination of elementary simplicity with utmost efficiency makes him the most characteristic leader of the new aesthetic movement. In the Fifteenth Century the thrilling herald of a new spirit was Giorgione. He was the first man of his time to revive with painting the pagan delight in material beauty for its own sake and to suggest the richness of the inner life of man in a world of mingled sensuousness and spiritual appeal. He came at precisely the right moment to awaken his contemporaries to their aesthetic need. The vogue of the young Venetian was enduring and made the Giorgionesque idyll a fashion down through the Eighteenth Century. What Giorgione was to his age of royal and aristocratic patronage in the glow of a renaissance of classic culture and pagan philosophy, Matisse is to our age of mechanical inventions, of widespread worldly wisdom, of technical triumphs, of labor-saving devices, of fads for savagery, and of Oriental adaptations. Matisse combines child and craftsman, fuses calligraphy ancient and modern, unites ideas of East and West in a style both simple and sophisticated, thus transcribing into a pictorial shorthand the qualities of the modern mind as he conceives it. That he was a shrewd prophet of coming events is now recognized. For a few years he was a storm center and brought down upon himself the lightning of abuse and ridicule by attracting it with extravagant discords and distortions. In due time it appeared that he was reducing all things with defiant bravado to the bare indication of the structure of their elementary forms and the calligraphy of their no less elementary colors as is intuitively done by children and savages. In the middle of the Nineteenth Century, design had become overlaid with so much irrelevance of subject-interest that Matisse set out to simplify the elements of design more startlingly than Cézanne and his contemporaries had dreamed of doing. Gauguin simplified boldly but his subject matter was so romantic that the innovations of technic and the attractions of ara-besque were not yet sufficiently detached from irrelevant interest. Matisse saw to it that no one could possibly miss the point. In a few years he had accustomed the eye to color-cacophonies and over-come prejudice to caricatured contours. What he made evident was a repetition of lines and colors in barbaric exciting rhythms. The similarity of "jazz" and modern dances is not to be denied. Matisse is the decorator of the age of "jazz" and of efficient "short cuts" like stenography. There have been so many cheap and gaudy imitations that the master may have become alarmed at his own temerity. He now modifies and envelops his pure color so that he is recognized as a man of taste, the graceful and elegant Whistler of the modern movement, propagandist, controversialist, but first and last the fine flower of intelligent eclecticism and of attractive periodicity. He expresses movement and character with the direct action of color and silhouette. He organizes his material with the executive ability of a modern administrator. He hints, with stripes and curves and color schemes, at the novel decoration of modern rooms. He is as effective as a smartly dressed woman of today boasting of her few concealments, managing her new illusion, in conformity with the prevailing mode for combined frankness and artifice.

Have we developed a Twentieth Century style in art? Yes, if by that we mean that respect for style has come back into its own so that all artists aspire to it and many of them achieve it. No, if we confuse style with either fashion or manner which tends to breed conformity and which can serve a general use. Style is an end, not a means. It is the goal of language or any other form of expression. It is what gives to the aesthetic language of any period its mark of enduring quality. The great American critic, Brownell, has written that style "has neither a system nor a method involving…any particular program," and should "be considered as that factor of a work of art which preserves in every part some sense of the form of the whole. An informing spirit…a theme through variations, it realizes relations…and is the agent that organizes variety into unity." Style interpenetrates any technic of any time "with its ideal."[1] There is style then and plenty of it in the best modern art but the style is this quality or that of the new craftsmanship, this virtue or that of the new method, never synonymous with any one procedure. It is more accurate to say that there is a modern aesthetic language containing many old and new, far sought and newly coined idioms and dialects, all adaptable to stylistic usage. It is a language like any other the new words of which we must learn. We cannot overcome its strangeness until we are thoroughly familiar with its vocabulary and grammar. The language is young and still in its self-conscious stage of rhetoric. Consequently it is of stylistic emphasis and coherence all compact. To serve all kinds of up-to-date people it is full of variations which, in the unfortunate ways of individuals, become too often mannerisms and which, propagated by cliques and schools, fall into one or another fashionable jargon, vulgar "slang," pedantic formula. Still life is the category of painting in which these may be best observed and this contemporary preference for still life is symptomatic. We are so proud of having recaptured the sense of design, long concealed under representations and illusions, that we practice the cult of the pattern for its own sake, caring not enough for our substance in our concentration upon style, which we make obtrusively technical. We not only simplify but systematize our compositions until something

---

1. [W.C. Brownell, *The Genius of Style* (New York: Charles Scribner's Sons, 1924), 15, 10–11, 19.]

clicks and invisible wheels are set in motion and we exclaim prag-
matically that "it works, it works!" Sensibility is subjected to the acid
test of surviving an automatic function. If it remains human and
concerned with anything outside of itself, then behind it must be
either a great artist, using abstract symbols as did Cézanne in his
monumental portraits, landscapes and still life, or else a diffused
genius for art. The Byzantine mosaicists, the Egyptian and Greek
builders created with symbols of almost anything a concept of the
world as architecture, vitalized by a passionate interest in formal
relations, in juxtapositions and proportions—such an interest as we
call the architectonic.

Still life today is hardly ever employed for the mere imitation of
objects. Often it is occult in some subtle suggestion as in the work of
Odilon Redon and his admirers. Often it is made a sensitive instrument responsive to personal taste. But the decorative convention
is insisted upon and the new technical devices are, more or less,
exploited. This phase of modern painting corresponds closely to
the fashions in dress and interior decoration. Those who follow, yes,
even those who set the fashions of today may be ludicrously out
of date the day after tomorrow. Yet even as no woman who shuns
the old-fashioned wishes to be out of date in her dress, so no alert
young artist feels that he can afford to disregard the prevailing
fashions in his profession. The changing conventions in painting
are the equivalent of the changing modes for dress. If there is true
style in new fashions, the art will live on into succeeding generations even as the style of an ancient literature keeps its hold on the
heart long after the words have become obsolete. The best artists of
every period are aware that the new fashions are adaptable to their
special skill but that their skill is not destined only for the display
of the new fashions. We are entertained with new lines, new colors, a new emphasis on planes, a new perspective as of one looking
down on objects tip-tilted at the outer edge or angle. Equally modern are the cults for the precise, ruled line with narrow black and
white edges placed together to clear up intermediate, closely related
tone-relations of austere yet fastidious appeal (Braque), and of the

heavy black contours to colored forms or spaces giving them the effect of leaded medieval stained glass (Rouault) or the swift calligraphic character and stenographic meaning of primitive drawing (Matisse). There are modernist painters who project their forms in a kind of sculpture (Derain) and others who shun solidity as only another illusion (Dufy).

Matisse is more interested in bizarre linear and color music which he has adapted from Japanese or Persian patterns than he is in humanity. Hindu and Negro sculpture give the clue to his. summary outline of the human form and its most striking lines and curves. He is overrated because he is so perfectly the man of the hour. Braque is a more aristocratic type, endowed with a more unusual sensibility. It has been his function to give to the bewildering innovations of Picasso the consistency and quality of the French genius for style in its broader sense. From nature Braque makes abstractions of reasoned relationships, of grained wood and veined marble, of lemon, peach, pear and plum colors, with accents of saturated whites and blacks, with curved lines and straight lines, with rectangular shapes, with clusters of grapes in clarities of light and densities of shadow, with tactile thrills of smooth or sanded textures. His formal arrangements, whether in the conventions of Cubism or in the more recognizable objects he employs today, are of such perfectly adjusted architectural structure and balance that no detail could be altered without destruction of the entire edifice. It is clear that with Braque, as with the scarcely less delightful artists Juan Gris and Marcoussis, we are dealing with classicists of a new type, men of pure proportions, of architectural feeling for projecting planes and their crisp recessions of cast shadow. Derain with his heads and nudes recalls Greco-Roman art; with his landscapes suggests a kinship to Poussin, early Corot, and Courbet; with his still life relates to Chardin and Cézanne. He has drawn from many sources, has been at school for man y years to modernity and its researches, making experiments in all the new manners. There was a time before the war when he wavered between Negro masks and dolorous medievalism as his chief influences. Since the war Corot seems to have become the paramount influence with Derain. Recently his work has become a fine example of French classic tradition ever renewing itself with fresh inspiration. His simplifications are now so ultimate, so inevitable, and so grand that they justify all the former eclecticism if it was needed to achieve this present authority. Picasso also

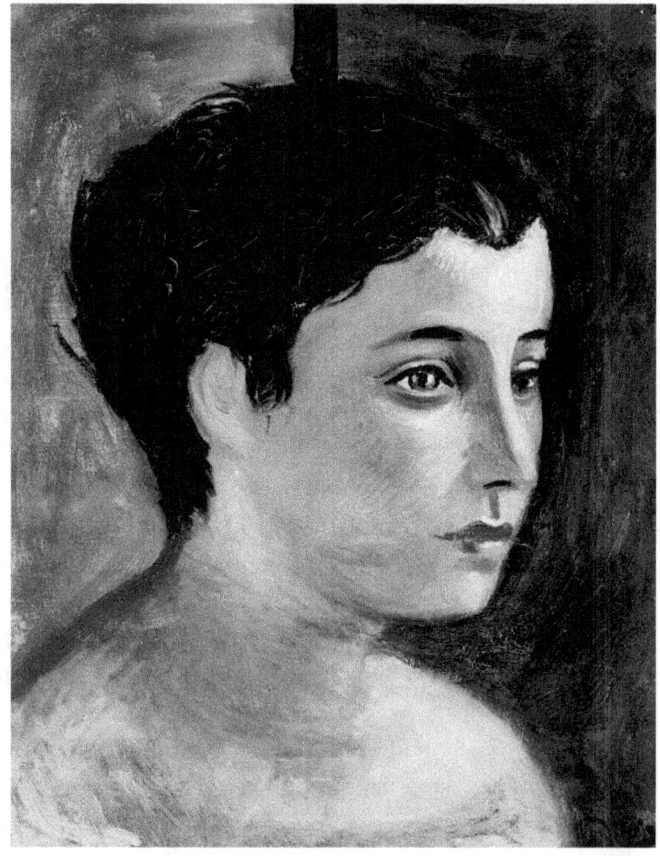

André Derain
Portrait of a Woman, n.d.
Oil on canvas
The Phillips Collection, Washington, D.C. Acquired in 1927
© 2022 Artists Rights Society (ARS), New York/ADAGP, Paris

is an eclectic and an incorrigible experimentalist. How this young virtuoso has bewildered the modern world with his fascinating feats of ranging all the way from romantic subjects in rich colors to geometric abstractions in monochrome! He reveals in his own career the restless, complex, inconsistent, modern mind, so eager for new sensations, so avid of influences, so gifted with cleverness and craft and culture, so insatiable in research! The pity of it is that his ideal seems to be crystallizing as the sterilization of style from any trace of personal expression. Yet this modern language of art was invented by great men with great personal conceptions and emotions, El Greco, Daumier, Cézanne, and Van Gogh. Cézanne, to be sure, kept his art impersonal and theorized while he experimented. But although he considered himself the primitive of the way he had discovered and was perhaps never a deft executant, yet not one of his innumerable followers has penetrated so far or climbed so high in his promised land. Just as Rembrandt was the first and remains the greatest of all Romanticists and Velázquez the first and perhaps the finest Impressionist and El Greco the earliest, and by far the most poignant Expressionist, so Cézanne, the later Cézanne of course, is not only the discoverer but the supreme master of the new classicism in painting which identifies drawing, form, space, light and pattern with color, the proper instrument of painting, in a grand classical or architectonic balance of every element, a new reading of the old Greek text, "nothing in excess."

And today what have we? We have an improved standard of taste both as regards artist and public. We know more clearly what art is about. We produce more inventive draftsmen on an average than any age since the Renaissance. There is a vitality and a vivid freshness in modern color and design which makes older fashions seem lifeless. But where are the passionate individualists, the keen sensitive temperaments of the Nineteenth Century? Today, with notable exceptions, such as Pierre Bonnard and John Marin, we must be content if the majority of first-rate artists give us brilliant craftsmanship, original invention in design and a reinvigorated body of clear and essentially sound doctrine. Picasso, Matisse, Derain, Braque, and in

America Sterne, Weber, Karfiol, Kuhn, and Kantor are important painters who possess sensibility and taste in ample measure and yet in their work either school explains or doctrine declaims too much. To be doctrinaire is to be dogmatic and I have long contended that the new dogmas are as dangerous to creative imagination and individual initiative as any of the ancient ones. There is, for instance, the dogma of what constitutes an authentic, orthodox modernist. One would think that a movement which began with four pioneers as different in their characters and ambitions as Cézanne, Van Gogh, Gauguin, and Seurat would a void this dogma, especially since the heroes of the movement today are all dissimilar and divergent in aim. If there is a single quality which is the criterion of what is modern it is applicable no less to every great period of art or at least to every great artist, so that it only leads to the conclusion that we are as we have always been, romanticists, realists, impressionists, classicists, natural primitives, as in every age since art began. It is less important for our artists today to take thought about expressing their period than seeing to it that their period shall express them.

What has kept me from complete sympathy with the doctrines of the modern movement in art is the organized intolerance of the preceding period and the claim that there has been a cleavage, a sudden and revolutionary break in the link which connects the present with the past, and marks the continuing evolution of the artist through the ages. It was Gauguin's saying that in art there is either revolution or plagiarism which started this fallacy. There was a distinct turning point toward the direction in which we are now traveling. It was not a revolution but simply a pivoting by a few artists of restless and daring minds on the axis of their own period in order to look out over a new prospect. They saw, they came, and they conquered, those four pioneers Cézanne, Van Gogh, Gauguin, and Seurat, leading ultimate unknown disciples on four different lines of adventure into unexplored country. A new period of painting is always launched in advance not only of the public but of the rank and file of the progressive artists themselves. Few of the Impressionists, who were the radicals of their time, really understood the seceding rebels from their camp. They regarded them as clumsy, unsuccessful Impressionists. And so indeed they were, until they acknowledged the fact and turned resolutely in a new direction. Impressionists however they continued to be, holding to all that they could develop further, abandoning only the scientific objectivity which seemed to them to have been completed. They felt the approaching end of the long period of nature study, the last refinements of visual examination and analysis. What happened at that crucial moment is now clear. From a habit of mind and sight which sought to surprise nature in the act of changing from one effect to another and which attempted to detect the cause for each effect, the pioneers of the present movement reacted to a concept of the world as architecture, and of the artist himself as the true subject for analysis. Man imposed himself upon nature to work his will after a fashion new and strange. Although united by a bond of mutual restlessness they failed to understand each other. They were all individualists and each of them had a different idea. And none of them were revolutionists; least of all Gauguin, who, judged by his own alternative, must be called a plagiarist like the rest of the human race. It was his particular plagiarism to steal a page from the remote records of Polynesia, to be aboriginal, whereas Van Gogh was by turns Japanese and Gothic, and Seurat was Egyptian and Byzantine, and Cézanne revered Greek order while grasping at Baroque suggestions. So it was with the rest, Signac, Toulouse-Lautrec, Denis, Vuillard, and Bonnard. All of them stemmed from Impressionism and its "mirror of the passing world," but they chose to be different. Signac tended to be even more scientific than Monet and his followers, the others less so, but all dared to be more or less *arbitrary* in the uses they made of Impressionist subjects and discoveries. Bonnard is the heir of Degas, Toulouse-Lautrec, and Van Gogh in his Japanesque caprice of composition, of Renoir in his subtle color reflections, of Monet and again of Van Gogh in his sparkling luminosities of landscape. But he was born a fantastic in his habit of observation and he carried on to a new art of orchestrated tones as subtle and indefinite as the elusive witchery of Debussy. Thus Impressionism consciously passed into Expressionism. The transition was so gradual that it was not clear that art was moving along with life and, as always, a little ahead of it. Impressionism was the end of one era and the beginning of another. Caught between the two, a madman to the old because of his utter abandon and a prophet of the new unrecognized as such until too late, was poor Vincent Van Gogh. But he is the proof that Impressionism contained in itself the germ of Post-Impressionism which was the reaffirmation of the aesthetic interest as an experience independent of all the other interests of life.

In pictorial art the Expressionist aims to do for the mind what the Impressionist is content to do for the eye and the visual memory. Both try to condense and intensify the aesthetic essence of a subject and both imply the elimination of non-essentials. The peculiar intuition necessary to the proper selection of what the artist desires to emphasize is as important to one as to the other. The difference lies wholly in the nature of the choice. The Impressionist responds chiefly to effects of light and atmosphere or to observed character in animated and fast changing moments of time. He makes a record of evanescent visual appearance, reviving our past experience or seeming to enrich our memory by admitting us freely into his own, so that we often feel we have lived what we have only seen and enjoyed in pictures, with the aid of the Impressionists' accurate, analytical perceptions. Then, too, scenes and effects which had always been familiar to us but never recognized as in any way of significance to art are brought vividly to our consciousness and we live more completely in the full possession and proper functioning of our senses. In transcribing not only what he sees but what countless thousands of others less sensitively endowed are capable of being helped to see, the Impressionist leads the public in its visual education. The Expressionist renounces all this power. When he looks at nature he is not interested in what appears at the moment for all with eyes to see but in what he alone is thinking about and in what equivalent images he can embody his concepts, exaggerated as they must be out of natural colors and shapes, distorted freely so as not to be mistaken for things instead of thoughts. His response is not to light and air as an end in itself but as a thought-compelling or mood-producing agency for emotional self-expression. The sub-conscious, the super-conscious, but most often just the self-conscious, afford the motif for technical experiment, as the inevitable next step in evolution after the triumphs of research in the outer world of objective facts.

There is a curious inconsistency about Expressionist practice which causes much difficulty and confusion. On the one hand it proclaims a passion for the impersonal—for the concentrated examination of the unchanging character of an object so that a clear-cut *concept* can be abstracted out of its familiar appearance. Any subject or none at all will suffice for this sort of a study of geometrical relations whether reduced to diagrammatic purity or symbolizing the same interests with architectural representations more or less literal though always divested of any personal reference to life. El Greco, in the year 1600, was enlarging his unit of design until every part of his composition was not only interdependent but a repetition in linear rhythms, brush strokes and color complexes. There was a rhythmic swirl which leaped and writhed like a central fire spreading to wildly associated lesser flames. This frenzied dynamism of El Greco's which anticipated by three hundred years the distortions of the subjective Expressionists of our day, seems to have little to do with the cold static calculations of our Post-Cubist composers, but in at least one sense it was also prophetic of this curious phenomenon of recent date. It affirmed the willful preconception and the "all-over pattern," and these principles were as applicable to a diagram as to a drama.

Cubism was invented by Picasso as a discipline for those artists who, like himself, were too susceptible either to romanticism or realism, too much drilled in the art of the museums, and who gave themselves no chance to develop the self-reliance necessary to the artist if he is to invent new symbols of art which grow out of the age and so become a part of it. The Cubists place overlapping planes, either flat or solid ones, across a space no deeper than the surface of the canvas. A sort of low relief is thus obtained and incidentally a pattern with mental implications through the dismemberment of objects and their rearrangement in fragmentary details seen from different angles. The assurance and facility with which, after twenty years of practice, the Cubist decorators hint at the organization and simplification, the structure and function of our epoch, and the decoration of its buildings, make it clear that Cubism is becoming a new order of design, adaptable to architectural detail, to stage settings, to sculpture, pottery, handicrafts, weaving, and all kinds of mechanical processes for making both ornamental and useful objects. Picasso has suggested that Braque should be secured to design wall papers, textiles, and tapestries. This suggestion reveals the fact that the trend of the Abstractionists in this utilitarian age is inevitably toward applied decoration. Meanwhile period-consciousness dominates those who wish to modify Cubism in order to reduce to a simplified clarity and pictorial style the complex of modern buildings. The emphasis is, of course, on volume and on spatial relations, but the facts are set clown almost photographically. It is contended that art must remain in the museum or else be insinuated somehow into the agencies of our active life. The artists, for our need, must find new elements of beauty in the new world of skyscrapers, steel mills, silos, grain elevators, oil tanks, machine shops, railroad yards, airplanes. Looking out of high windows at the setback terraces of our high buildings our young designers dream of the monuments of Babylon and the ancient instinct for conventionalizing form. Drilled in the calisthenics of Cubism the moderns have acquired training to compose forms in space. But Cézanne, who started the new classicism with his remark about the few underlying structural forms in nature, the cube, the cone and the cylinder, was far greater than all his followers because he was passionately moved by his conceptions and his cosmic and plastic philosophy. The contemporary approach is too theoretical. Stimulating at first, these pictures repel after a while by their hardness when once we have noted all their rather obvious relations.

There is more duration of pleasure to be found in "expressionist" pictures which are symbolical of moods, of abandonment to ardors of conception and to exaggerated intensity of technical means in precisely the revived attitude of El Greco. Whether they make introspective commentary from close observation of fragments of nature (O'Keeffe), or extemporize on their enjoyments of material textures for their own sake (Dove), or hint at racial and religious secrets (Weber), we are, in any case, lured into the inner life. Midway between the objective and the subjective modernists are a few realists who see what they want to see and who make their vision photographic, thus concealing the irony, the wit, the pessimism, or whatever it is which directs their observation. Often they have no reserves, no respect for closed doors and clothed minds, like novelists of the "stream of consciousness" school. But morbid psychology is not the only field. Whimsical observation of the drab, the commonplace, the painfully familiar, that is the starting point for Americans like Charles Burchfield and Edward Hopper. A preconceived attitude dominates the choice of whatever is to be exposed. Hopper proves that there is a way to intensify without needing to distort. Yet the cult of distortion is still much in evidence. It is freely employed to deal with fantasy, hallucinations and with involved imagery to symbolize other more or less subconscious states of mind. There is no need to write of Futurism, Dadaism, Vorticism. They are gone and almost forgotten. The latest thing, *Sur-Réalisme*—starting with De Chirico's dreamlike incongruities—has a philosophical or psychological base for its plastic imagery. Now that Matisse no longer distorts, there is a tendency to return to natural appearances but arbitrarily magnified under close scrutiny and arbitrarily simplified or developed into symbolical patterns. To sum up this survey, Expressionists are not inhabitants of any one country but of the misty realms of the subconscious or the cold clear climates where the mind takes stock of itself and puts its calculations to the test on the nearest convenient objects. It is often remarked that they are inclined to be too instinctive or too cerebral.

Both Impressionism and Expressionism are expressive of our psychology today. The people have only recently caught up with Impressionism and are now ready to understand and appreciate its purpose and meaning. And the radical artists, as is their custom, are refusing to see eye to eye with the majority. In every age the Academy represents the majority opinion. It follows instead of *leading* the public, and gives its official sanction to what has become general practice based on the successful advances of the preceding period. Unfortunately it is not content with performing the ceremony of canonizing what it once persecuted. It persists in despising and denouncing the new experiments which will be first permitted and finally prescribed by the pontiffs of the next generation. Artists are judged by academic juries of their own profession according to their technical competence and their measurable marksmanship in hitting the bullseye of popular favor. It is undeniable that the preceding period, against which the rebels of art are ever in revolt, is often superior to what follows. Evolution implies change and destined progress but certainly not a constant ascent to perfection. Regardless of the comparative merit of successive theories and practices it must be admitted that as men saw and felt in their youth so they can still be expected to see and to feel. This is especially natural when the view of the world reflected in paintings is suddenly changed from normal to abnormal. The ever-changing conventions of art, which seem abnormal only to an inartistic generation trained to photographic resemblance and the vision of the average man, can in time be relearned, can in fact become so pleasantly familiar that people will demand that their pictures remain conventionalized with clever artifice. It was difficult for our fathers, or grandfathers as the case may be, to recognize that they lived in a colorful world instead of a juicy brown one like their varnished brown landscapes. Now that they have learned that fresh, sparkling colors in painting actually reflect the world out of doors they are finding pictures in nature—seeing pictorially, which, according to Leo Stein, is the best thing to be gained by acquaintance with art and artists. There is so much endearing magic in the changing appearances of life which cry out for sensitive Impressionists to come along and give them permanence that I regret to see this vital movement commercialized as it so painfully is in the various national Academies. I predict that it will be rescued from these depressing institutions and go on to supreme achievements, following the inspiration of the whimsical, captivating Pierre Bonnard and of the Oriental tradition of self-effacing, mystical, spiritualized naturalism which our American poet of color, John H. Twachtman, carried to greater heights than any artists since the finest Chinese masters of the Tang Dynasty.

At the end of the century, I wonder whether the fashionable painters and sculptors and the schools they have founded on topical notions and timely innovations will seem as important as the work of isolated individualists who are being true to themselves and in that way true to their country, their period, and their ideal of style. A new world is in the making. The ends of the earth are coming together. The trend in art will be toward a fusion of Orient and Occident, of Europe and America. Prophetic of this phase is the symbolical color fantasy of Augustus Vincent Tack who, like Twachtman before him, is independent of schools and academies ancient and modern. A modernist who thought he knew just what one must do to be modern complained that Tack, like Rouault in France, is out of tune with Twentieth Century America—based as he was on Oriental and Medieval tradition. I asked him to tell me what is more of today, unless it be even more of tomorrow, than the art which hints at a universal aesthetic language, aiming at the universal, the far ranging, the broadly tolerant and humane trend of all liberal thought and aspiration.

And so, at the end of the Twentieth Century, I predict that there will be a revaluation of artists. What is called "the new classicism" will have reached its decadence and become academic. The young men of the advance will no longer be satisfied with the slogan "significant form." For the present, however, that phrase will do as well as any other to define the ideal of the contemporary movement in art if, by those words, it is understood that the form is the only part that matters, that the form, often identified with the color, is the one and only legitimate means of conveying significance, not only the symbol but also the substance of whatever is signified. The trend today then is toward a systematic reconsideration of all artistic work in the light of this doctrine and toward a codification of the new aesthetic so that the language will be available to all, as impression-ism is today, and applicable by all to the plan of their homes and places of business and the correction of their ways of seeing. The change from traditional habits is coming slowly in regard to interior decoration. In the home, men like to relax in a familiar atmosphere, to accept rather than to question the appropriateness of a picture to the age, of an arm chair to the period. However just what takes place when one language merges gradually into another can happen in the home. Good things of all kinds can be assembled in a creative ensemble of traditional style with the contemporary spirit increas-ingly dominant. Such associations of old and new, of Oriental, Euro-pean, and American, are true to our transitional period when influ-ences and idioms from all over the world are gradually portending a world culture which should reach its culmination in an American Renaissance. Unification through a great universal stimulus and a common aspiration to world peace is our urgent need but not at the cost of a required conformity. Our differences of nature and of race can be enjoyed and encouraged all the while that they are being related and blended. If there is stylization, it should be guided by that ancient principle of unity in variety which pervades every part with some sense of the form of the whole, interpenetrating every technic with this unchanging ideal.

EL GRECO — CÉZANNE — PICASSO

(1929)

CLIVE BELL, in his delightful little book *Since Cézanne*,[1] wrote perhaps the best, certainly the most compact and fluently phrased estimates of the contemporary French painters who are so much in vogue today. I feel that he makes the usual mistake of overestimating Matisse and Picasso. Yet he distinguishes cleverly between what they are acknowledged to be and what they essentially are. Bell adds astute commentary to the unquestioned correctness of our contemporary opinions that Matisse is a decorator with a very original and personal taste for color and line, and that Picasso is a bold yet cold doctrinaire or a peculiarly challenging type of schoolmaster. The art of Picasso to his mind seems more personal than that of Matisse and his taste more truly distinguished. Matisse is a pure artist, an esthete. Picasso is of the same type but he is something else besides, perhaps a mystic or perhaps only a necromancer. Matisse is single-minded. Picasso reveals a duality which makes him a more complicated theme for the critic. He has a passion for form, but he can stand away from his passion in apparent detachment and analyze it from every angle. His creative energies are not driven by boiling emotions but by the white light of incandescence which is none the less heat of a most intense and penetrating kind. "Picasso is not Spanish for nothing. He is a mystic." A foreigner always to the French, they are fascinated by him precisely because he is so unlike their traditional moderation. "It is in revolt against, perhaps in terror of, the profoundly un-French spirit [of Picasso] that the French artists are seeking shelter and grace under the vast though unconscious nationalism of Derain.

"For the French have never loved Cubism [...] How should they love anything so uncongenial to their temperament? How should

First published in *Art and Understanding* 1, no. 1 (November 1929).

1. [London: Chatto and Windus, 1922.]

that race which, above all others, understands and revels in life, approve [of] aesthetic fanaticism. [...] A French artist will never feel entirely satisfied unless he can believe that his art is related to, and justified by, Life."

Picasso, on the other hand, "was never satisfied with a line that did not seem right in the eyes of the God—of the God that is in him."

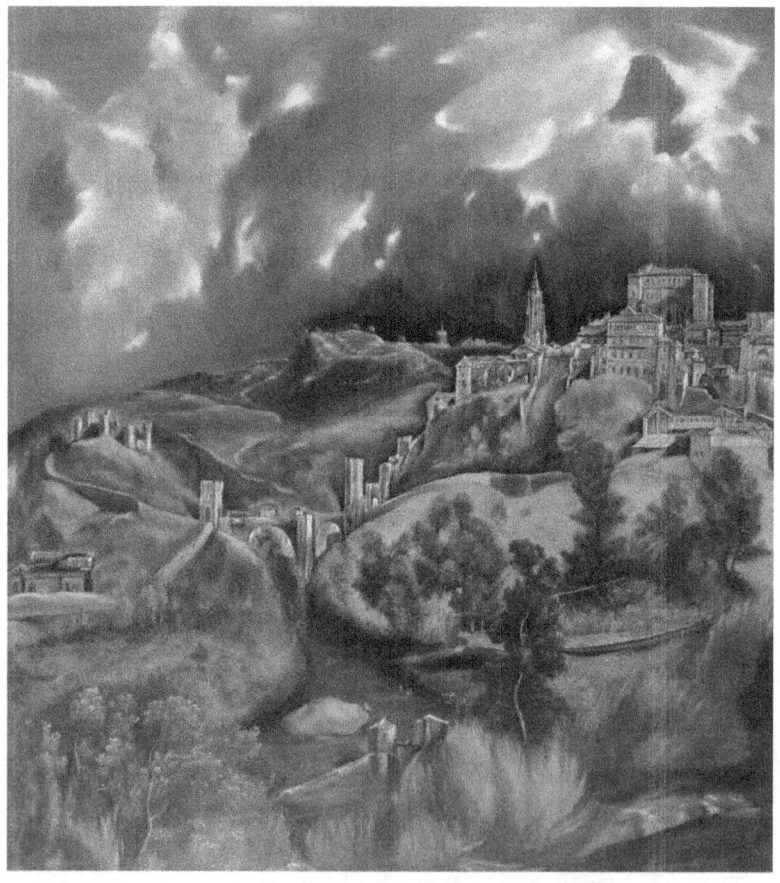

El Greco (Domenikos Theotokopoulos)
View of Toledo, c. 1599–1600
Oil on canvas
The Metropolitan Museum of Art, New York. H.O. Havemeyer Collection, Bequest of Mrs. H.O. Havemeyer, 1929

For him, life is only "the raw material of art" and specifically for his art. He is always "compelling his instrument to sing in unison with that pitiless voice which in El Greco's day they called the voice of God."[2]

This conception of Picasso by the brilliant English critic is reinforced by a German book, entitled *Picasso and the French Tradition.*[3] The author, W. Uhde, has long been a resident of Paris and an intimate friend of Picasso and his inner circle. The purpose of his authoritative work on the influential Spanish innovator is to assert that Picasso is a manifestation of the Gothic spirit. This, he labors to prove, grew somehow out of what was nostalgic and inventive in the Greek spirit as revealed in its mythology, its tragedy, and its Plato. The Greeks, according to Uhde, were never really serene in their sensuous pagan idealism but aspired to serenity and symmetry and order as a kind of discipline for their skeptical restlessness and vague yearning. Art for them was a sublimation for their natural conflicts of mind and spirit. Now the Roman-Italian culture chose to build upon the results rather than the hidden causes of the Greek unity and synthesis; upon the balance, the logic, the refined materialism, the systematic adjustments and the horizontal order of design. The essential genius of Italy as seen in Florentine paintings of the later Fifteenth and Sixteenth Centuries remained Latin rather than Greek. Yet the Gothic spirit was recrudescent. It had come, of course, from the Northern Countries. The Germanic races, including the Franks, had developed for their aspirations an order based on the vertical instead of the horizontal lines, and their trend in art as in everything else, was towards speculation and experiment. France was a battleground for the two ideals, but the classic, or Roman-Italian, gradually prevailed and even the French Gothic buildings took on a classic character, as we can see in Notre Dame Cathedral.

---

2. [Ibid., 205–7; quotations emended.]

3. [Wilhelm Uhde, *Picasso and the French Tradition: Notes on Contemporary Painting,* translated by F. M. Loving (Paris and New York: Éditions des Quatre Chemins and E. Weyhe, 1929.]

In the Italy of the Renaissance we know how very few great artists were rebels and radicals. Signorelli, Michelangelo, and Tintoretto stand out all the more strikingly because of the scholarly and worldly standards of the rest. To these passionate individualists, in rebellion against their period and their patrons, a young Greek art student in Venice by the name of Theotokopoulos turned with profound relief and affinity. Perhaps it was in recognition of his Byzantine background on the Island of Crete and of his Gothic mysticism that wise old Titian recommended this pupil of his to the Court of Spain. There the icy and flaming spirit of the Catholic crusade seemed to cry out for just such an icy and flame-like genius to portray it for posterity. In grim Toledo on the Tagus there was not yet a tradition which bound artists. They could make their own tradition out of mixed Occidental and Oriental contributions to Castilian culture. It was the time and the place for the development of a pictorial and plastic language to convey the theology of the Church and its aggressive advances into the unknown world. El Greco seemed just the man to create an aesthetic correspondence to the spirit of the times. Even the tortured inner lives of aristocratic individuals of court, church, and army needed such a dual nature as Greco's to interpret them to themselves. Of course technically he was far ahead of his period and, although tolerated, he was certainly not appreciated or understood even in the Spain he saw so profoundly. He would have been regarded as a fanatic to the majority of almost any date.

But I am getting too far away from Picasso's German friend Uhde, who hardly mentions the influence of El Greco and who has apparently never accepted the Oriental derivation of both men, since it interferes with his aim to prove that Picasso is by spiritual tradition a German. "It cannot be denied," writes Uhde,

> that Picasso's manner is sombre [...] that in his basic inspiration he is inherently tormented, [...] vertical in his general tendency, romantic as to tonality [...] It is, of course, always possible to plow up the question of race and to find Goth migrations to Spain [...] But suffice it to say that] Picasso's "blue kingdom" is veiled in [German] melancholy [and that] this romantic trait [...], manifesting itself [...] in sentimental

[...] fashion, has been accentuated with the passing of years and, at the same time, has been spiritualized and exalted.

Just as the Greeks, oppressed by natural reality, were able to create, with the help of myth, philosophy and plastic art, a superior reality [...] so Picasso has gone beyond the accidental and misleading reality of things in order to penetrate their idea, their essence. [...]

The pictorial, since it is an achieved [...] form and nowise nostalgic was [...] not [in agreement] with Picasso's essentially vertical manner. Since, however, he chose that form of art, he had need to go beyond himself in order to make his pictures plastic and architectural in character [...] In 1907 began that moving and hopeless struggle to reconcile the plastic idea with the "picture" [...] He was obliged to deform objects [as El Greco and Cézanne had done before him [...] Still unsatisfied, he renounced the arrested form, and decomposed objects,[4]

thus killing the picture but in so doing conceiving a new and a ruthlessly dehumanized style. There is, however, a vague sense of life soaring in space in the Picasso abstractions, and there is something of the Gothic cathedrals of the north in the upward thrust of their lines. "For the second time in the history of peoples," writes Uhde, "the Gothic ideal is realized in contact with Roman soil."[5]

And now the Gothic of Picasso is altered in Paris by the insistent Latinism of the real Parisians. It must be recognized that Picasso's most devout followers are invariably foreigners who have come to live in Paris not so much because they are French in sympathy, as because Paris has become the artistic capital of the modern world. But the style which has grown out of the meeting of Roman-Italian Cubists like Braque in constant association with a "Gothic" Cubist like Picasso is a new baroque, that composite which always seems to come when the curiosity of the questing Gothic temperament for a plastic equivalent to its mind encounters the rules of Greek symmetry and consistent order. The earliest phase of this baroque painting and sculpture is Signorelli and its grandest manifestation

---

4. [Ibid., 30–32; quotation emended.]
5. [Ibid., 33.]

is Michelangelo. It is El Greco, however, who seems to have the typical baroque mind. In a sort of ecstasy, his senses strained to suggest with plastic means what the soul of his chosen people sighed for. It was a great effort at impersonal identification with a force outside of himself. His painting became extravagantly stylized not because he himself was extravagantly eccentric or determined to cause a sensation but because he came to conceive of painting as an art of building forms in space, a science of projecting and receding planes, a movement of those lines which had emotional force and meaning in them, an enlargement of the unit of design, until every mark of the brush, every modulation of color, and every swirl of line repeated one insistent rhythm. Cézanne was to create an important epoch of art—which happens to be our own—with El Greco as the source of his inspiration. I have been told that this influence of El Greco on Cézanne has been exaggerated, since he had little opportunity really to come under this influence and may have known Greco's work indirectly. The fact remains that El Greco's *View of Toledo*[6] in the Havemeyer Collection anticipates the landscapes of Cézanne in a startling way which challenges a denial of a kinship of mind and method. Cézanne was a later, more poised and classic phase of baroque. In him there was desire for identification with the vast unity in nature and its incessant movement of related forms. This identification he established through a formula of color application which suggested both structure and movement as well as a consistent integration of color with form. A harmonizing, unifying principle, the architectural, dominates whatever is pictorial in Cézanne's art and causes it to anticipate an art of the future more concerned with a decorative order of design for *all* the people than with diversity of pictorial invention for the delectation of the few. A final phase of the baroque in this historical evolution of a single idea aspiring to be a style is Pablo Picasso. He aims to identify himself with metaphysics or mathematics or magic, like the searchers of his kind in the Middle Ages, or like the Arabs with their ideographic symbols

---

6. [c. 1599–1600, The Metropolitan Museum of Art, New York]

and arabesques. A new sensation in Twentieth Century Paris, he excited the rationalizing minds of French artists to a feverish activity on behalf of Style.

Whatever we think of Uhde's startling reversal of conception concerning the ancient Greeks and their mental attitude, there is certainly something Gothic, as the author points out, in Picasso. For Gothic art has been described as "persistently inquiring and disobedient to rules." Uhde's theory of the baroque as the style which follows the desire of a recrudescent Gothic feeling for a classic unity of structure and material is a suggestive one. However, what the reading of this book has done for me is to bring to my mind more clearly than ever before the recognition of a remarkable resemblance between the characters of El Greco and Picasso. Cézanne also seems involved in the story. Is he not the logical middle man between the other two? Of course, there is more fanaticism in El Greco and Picasso than in Cézanne, who was fanatical only in his earliest period. In all three there is a duality of temperament, a resolution to submerge the ego in the age, with a sort of passionate austerity, a noble concentration on the idea, the one idea with which, centuries apart, they all desired to identify themselves. The boy Picasso, like the young Cézanne, tried at first to express what he felt through overwrought and melodramatic subjects characteristic of what had inspired El Greco all his life. A more restrained emotion of intense but passive melancholy came next in Picasso's development. That was the later part of the blue period devoted to illustrations from the imagined lives of circus children, tired gymnasts, and tragic harlequins. Although the instrument of emotional expression is a line which Clive Bell describes as thin, anxious, and nervous, the design is often very beautiful and suggestive of the Greeks. Finally, in full reaction against romantic tendencies, classical memories, and his own technical facilities both as draftsman and painter, he divested himself of subjects altogether and made the abstract elements of formal pattern not only paramount but isolated and self-sufficient.

Perhaps I shall never fully understand the hieroglyphics of Cubism at its most abstract. What I feel is a decorative style in the making, like the chaos beginning to take shape before creation. An age of reconstructed mentality and of invented mechanism seems to be symbolized. If El Greco had lived in our day, he might have devised something similar. Certainly religion, such as it is now, would not have dominated him. Impressionism for him, as for Cézanne, would have been but a means to an end—as it was indeed in his own life when effects of light, cold, or incandescent were conceived and controlled for emotional expression. Cézanne, however, would not have approved altogether of his disciple, Picasso. At least, in his ripe maturity he was too sober a classicist to have tolerated fanaticism when it frankly threatened the sanctity of his museums and traditions and

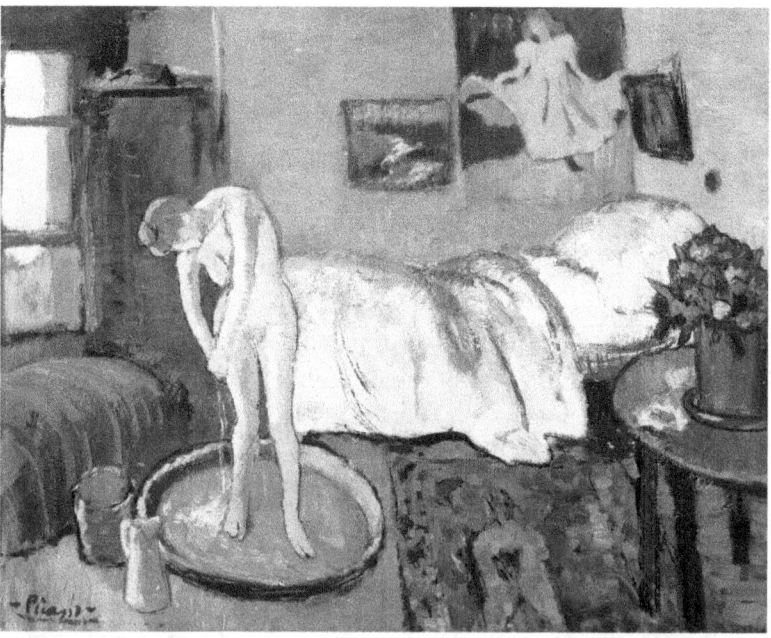

Pablo Picasso
The Blue Room, 1901
Oil on canvas
The Phillips Collection, Washington, D.C. Acquired in 1927
© 2022 Estate of Pablo Picasso / Artists Rights Society (ARS), New York

implied infidelity to his beloved Nature. Of the three baroque painters only Greco and Picasso are of the same Gothic family.

There was a mutual attraction in these two to a pervasive blue
tonality and to a range of a few colors distinctly Moorish in suggestion. The young Spaniard was brought up in the shadows of Moorish
buildings with their arabesques and colorful tiles. We would like to
know more about the boyhood of El Greco, but we vaguely recall
agonized altar paintings from his native Cretan churches which he
must have held in reverence. Uhde, intent on his startling Greek-
Gothic thesis, neglected a more important conjecture as to the
Oriental sources of Picasso's abstract intentions. Of our two modest examples of Picasso it is only necessary to say a few words. The
interior, entitled *Early Morning,*[7] wistfully and poignantly blue, with
a blue unlike any other in painting, with accents of clouded white,
greengold, wine-red, dates from the year after his arrival in Paris
from Barcelona. Already he was celebrated as a prodigy of dazzling
skill and arresting intellect. Ours is a succulent, sumptuous little
picture. Enjoying its strange, heady color we cannot resist a sharp
regret that he could not have worked for at least ten years in so rich
a vein. The design is rhythmical and in spite of the realism of the bed
and the early morning light the distortion and unreality of the figure are appropriate to a scene which is already more of a Hispano-
Moresque pattern than a picture.

Our other Picasso is a small but excellent creation of his period
of flat Cubism.[8] It is dated 1918. By that time he had moderated his
bleak austerity and was balancing restrained colors and varied textures to an abstract design in overlapping planes, edged and angular. There is an inevitableness and strange distinction about the
colors. The robin's-egg blue of a singular intensity is made more
sonorous by an accompaniment of oyster-gray, ivory-white, and

---

7. [Now titled *The Blue Room,* 1901, The Phillips Collection, Washington, D.C.,
acquired in 1927]

8. [*Abstraction, Biarritz,* 1918, The Phillips Collection, Washington, D.C., acquired in 1929]

tobacco-brown. The pure abstraction, without a trace of representation, without even fragments of remembered objects, can perhaps be compared to a bit of difficult modern music which vaguely stirs the senses and the mind with its unfamiliar scale, its strange intervals, its orientalism.

A COLLECTION STILL IN THE MAKING
(1930)

SINCE 1918, the experimental museum of modern art and its more or less remote sources which I am spending my life to form has been molded and corrected in full view of the public. In my book *A Collection in the Making,* I promised that all developments in the plan and purpose of the Phillips Memorial Gallery of Washington, D.C. would be reported from time to time for any who might be interested. It is unusual and indiscreet thus to take the public into one's confidence when one's project is still in a malleable state. What makes me pursue this policy notwithstanding its disadvantages and embarrassments is the conviction that without the public's appreciation of the problems and issues involved I cannot extend the benefits of a thought-provoking collection from the few to the many. Of course the work will go on regardless of the many since it is always on the faith and fervor of the few that any idealistic enterprise must be based. Though I welcome cooperation and am interested in people's opinions this does not mean that I am shifted from my course by every wind that blows. "Let all men count with you but none too much" is advice of the most practical value to a collector who intends to grow with his collection. This leaves me ready to listen and eager to learn yet reserving to myself the task of deciding all controversial questions. My wife is my constant associate and mentor, and she contributes to the gallery's counsels the point of view of a very sensitive creative artist. I have no other advisers. And I have no agents at all among the dealers. The capacity to decide for oneself is one's only safeguard against the contagions of fashion in art which are peculiarly prevalent today, and against the paralysis which afflicts the cautious collectors who only buy what is standardized and embalmed in tradition, with its permanent value more or

First published in *Formes,* no. 9 (November 1930), Reprinted in *The Artist Sees Differently.*

[247]

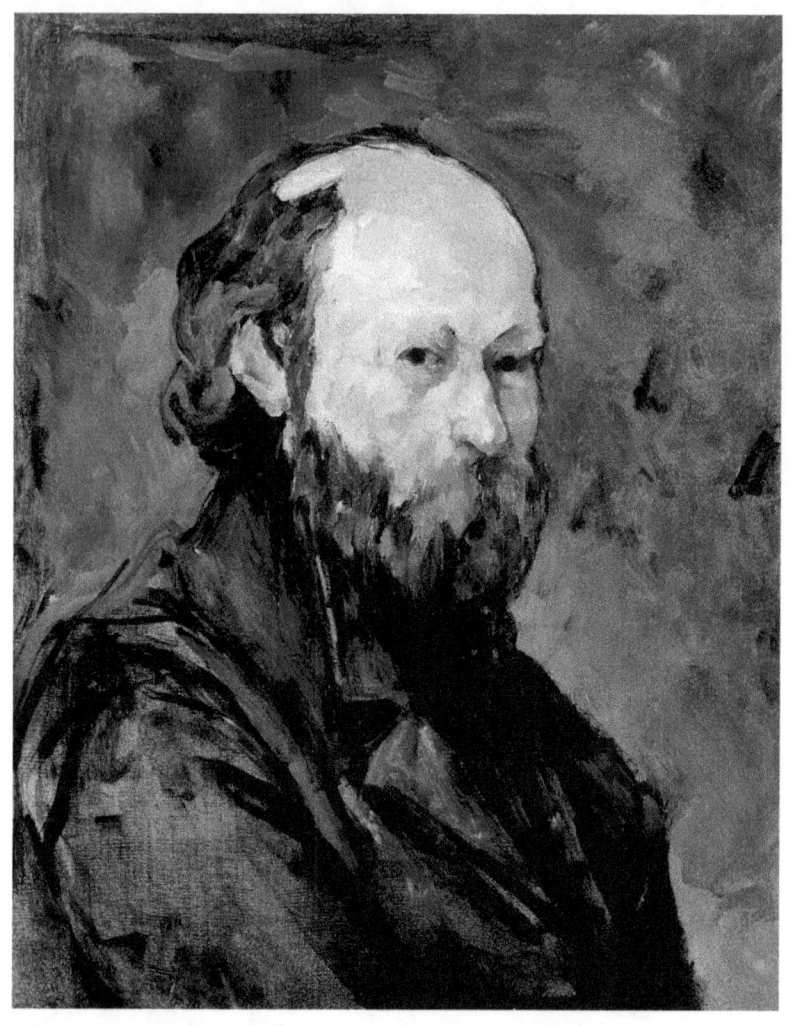

Paul Cézanne,
Self-Portrait, between 1878 and 1880
Oil on canvas
The Phillips Collection, Washington, D.C. Acquired in 1928

less guaranteed. Time does settle the problem of what is good in art and why it is good and I am not questioning the sound policy of the orthodox museums whose trustees with public fonds to spend cannot afford to make mistakes. But I am trying to emphasize the value of a service which the private collector can render unobtrusively not only to the living artist but to the cause of progressive art. And I am attempting to demonstrate the greater value of a public service of the same kind, but with its added educational function, which makes the experimental public or semi-public museum an actual necessity. Our enterprise and many others such as the Barnes Foundation, the Gallery of Living Art, the Museum of Modern Art, the Whitney Museum of American Art, John Cotton Dana's Newark Museum, the Chester Dale Collection in its work for the Museum of French Art, the Stieglitz experiment station, and, on the Pacific Coast, the Preston Harrison Collection,[1] all are carried on in the faith that the art of today is a force, a current charged with what is most alive in the age we live in, and therefore something to be stored and applied where it will do the most good as a source of dynamic creative energy. *My own special function is to find the independent artist and to stand sponsor for him against the herd mind whether it tyrannizes inside or outside of his own profession. I also pride myself on making a record of the many phases of artistic expression which are open to the modern painter.* The public must have a free and a fair contact with each artist's own particular qualities of mind and eye and heart and hand. There must be a renewed reverence for personality and a far-flung search for that precious boon to humanity—the creative imagination. Somehow the individual must survive the machine age. Let us all then cultivate catholicity of taste and deplore uniformity of technic and the rigid application of fixed ideas and rules even if we subscribe to them for our own use.

Having no trustees to consult I need not worry about making mistakes. I am free for adventures of the mind and many exciting voyages of discovery. Since the encouragement of living artists is

---

1. [The collection is now part of the Los Angeles County Museum.]

the most important function of art patronage I purchase freely and am ready to change my mind as often as I feel impelled to do so. If I understand my role as a new kind of museum director it is to buy, to exhibit and to interpret works of art not merely as isolated abjects but in their historical and aesthetic relationships. The importance of being of my own time seems to me so obvious that it hardly seems necessary to argue for the support of contemporary art, including current experiment out of which the standards of the future will be made. The greatest tragedy in the story of art from its beginnings to the present moment is the terrible neglect of the best artists during their brief stay on earth. The best artists would not be denied the recognition and the reward they so richly deserve if they would compromise with the taste of the uninstructed majority or else with the fads of the well-informed but fashion-following few. But compromise of either kind seems to them disgraceful. It is to enable them to remain brave and free and strong to resist the insidious temptations of commercialism without paying for their courage. and freedom at too grave a cost, that the true patron must stimulate and hearten them to be sincerely themselves with purchases of their experimental or unfashionable works and a serious study of their obscure or untimely intentions. It is not the fault of an artist that he has been born out of his due time. It is decidedly to his credit and a sign of his strength if he is true to himself regardless of the whirligig of taste and its reverses. Some of the best artists are behind "the times" while others are twenty years or more in advance of the majority opinion. If they :are attuned to the spirit of research quietly going on in the laboratories and observatories and libraries far from the market place then they are ahead of the herd although the actual trend of "the times" can best be studied through their barometric art. If they are, on the other hand, attuned to the spirit of antiquity or of that far more obsolete period than antiquity which preceded our own, then they too are "antiques" but they may be the finest and truest artists alive notwithstanding. The true artist needs a friend and the true patron of art has nothing better to give the world than the helping hand he extends to any lonely, lofty life made perilous because a free spirit cannot or will not see eye to eye with the crowd.

In 1918, when planning a memorial to my father and brother which would be a continued service to the country and the city they had served, it occurred to me that there was a need for a museum of stimulating and constantly changing exhibitions in which the best works of artists, especially painters, of many differing temperaments and talents and of many races, could be shown both separately and together, as evidences of what a universal privilege it is to have intense and intelligent visual life. All of us can acquire eyes wherewith to see the world as the artists see it, variously, selectively, intellectually or emotionally, in full possession of the latent capacity for seeing nature in pictures and pictures in nature. To look at one work of art hung by itself and cherished for itself is good. I planned that some day my museum building would have small rooms where, in ease and comfort and without distractions of conflicting interests, one might enjoy single works of art in special settings and favorable lights. Meanwhile, it was more important to show selected pictures or sculpture in the relations of the single exhibit to the Exhibition as a whole and then to trace the development of artistic ideas from their beginnings by bringing men of kindred minds and tastes together, no matter how far a part they might appear to be in the history and geography books and in the orthodox museums where items are arranged with chronological and national labels. It seemed to me of value also to prove the equally interesting claims of both Classicism and Romanticism and of both the pattern making and the representative instincts of men. Moreover, I was eager to demonstrate how good art of all kinds can be mixed—how a large collection is like a world, with the same attraction of opposites or invigorating contact of contending forces. The antagonistic elements in art as in humanity itself are not impossible to fuse.

Again and again I have stressed the unassuming simplicity and domestic comfort of the place where art is most truly at home. I have thought it worth while to revise the usual process for popularizing a picture gallery. Instead of marble halls with low standards and popular attractions to counteract the formal institutional architecture why not try the effect of rooms small or at least livable, with only good things on view whether people are ready for them or not. Ours is an informal institution functioning quietly and slowly, with considerable influence yet without any trace of pretentiousness. The educational ideal is never absent from our thoughts and plans for the Phillips Memorial Gallery and our Associate Director, C. Law Watkins, is already conducting conferences and informal talks in art appreciation for teachers of art in the schools of Washington and their classes, and day and night sessions in drawing and painting from the model in our studios and work-rooms.[2] Fundamentally, however, we wish the gallery to be a haven for those who enjoy getting out of themselves into the land of artists' dreams and their creative designs and their individualized observations. The artist sees with a difference from the man of affairs and in our gallery all that is required of visitors is that they must try to see with the eyes of the artist, even if such eyes are obviously and curiously different in their records from what the visitors have personally experienced or read about in books.

The Phillips Collection is based on a definite policy of supporting many methods of seeing and painting. The bane of impassioned preference and conviction among artists, critics and collectors is the burning issue of intolerance. The traditionalist likes a picture for the very reason that a modernist despises it, because it is an echo of the familiar past. Familiarity of aspect bores the champion of creative adventure but is the password to favor with the champion of a stan-

---

2. [The artist C. Law Watkins was a Yale classmate to Duncan Phillips, and in 1931 established the Phillips Gallery Art School on the fourth floor of the Phillips Memorial Gallery. In 1942, he became chair of the Department of Art at American University. After his death in 1945, the faculty in the Department of Art, the Phillips Gallery Arts School, and artist friends including Duncan Phillips, contributed gifts of art to establish the Watkins Memorial Collection as a tribute to their friend and mentor. These works serve as the foundation of the permanent collection at the American University Museum.]

dardized art. Why there should be this violent partisanship in regard to the artist's point of view is almost inexplicable. In life we are not so rabid in our demands that all men shall see and think exactly as we do, according to one set of ideas or another. I am not a propagandist for any one school but simply an advocate of independence for the artist from imposed dogma and. formula. I am hostile to the timorous academy which, in every nation and in every age, represses originality while it is yet a vital force struggling forward in the world, but finally standardizes whatever by-product of the original idea can be successfully manufactured and marketed. On the other hand, I am no less hostile to the faddists of the latest cult who denounce as plagiarism or senility everything that is not in the mode of the latest moment. I stand most sympathetically for the lonely artist in quest of beauty backed by no political influence and professional organization, independent of all cliques and movements. The policy of the Phillips Memorial Gallery is to choose the best representative painting as well as the best subjective designing and to do honor to both-interpreting each artist as a human being and affirming that if he has no personality to interpret then he must be a negligible follower of some school for drilling servile craftsmen in a dogma old or new. I open the door to all works of art which seem in any way true or beautiful, by whatever method they come, tested or tentative, traditional or experimental. In pursuit of this policy I am assembling a comparatively small collection of great masterpieces and carrying on all around it a research center where history can be illustrated in exhibition units and experimental paintings can be tested by being brought into the presence of established masterpieces of the past. I sometimes purchase and exhibit works so unfamiliar in style that they present the same difficulties as any language we have not yet learned. My interest in experiment is based on a belief that we should be as sympathetic to change and progress in art as in science. I stand for open-mindedness and tolerance of different points of view; for the cultivation of intelligent enjoyment of the intentions of artists and the varied *qualities* of their work, qualities which reveal them as especially gifted individuals well worth knowing and honoring. Art is part of the social purpose of the world and a gallery can be a meeting place of many minds, harmonized by a genuine respect for the spirit of art, which is none other than the spirit of pleasure in the exchange of different attitudes and sensibilities. By means of frequent transformations of the walls and challenging exhibitions in rooms bath large and small the visitor's curiosity is aroused and before his visit is at an end he has been called upon to make a not unpleasant effort. Without this frequent change and fascinating variety the domestic atmosphere might be sedative instead of stimulating. In such a place one can be instructed at the same time that one is being entertained and refreshed. On such terms of intimacy with artists it is possible to sympathize with their many-minded purposes and to revise one's antiquated notion that imitation is the goal of art and one's ancient fallacy that what is good for one is or should be good for all. The extension of the realm of beauty through explorations or discoveries constantly being made—is not this the most important sign of continuing life in art? The conservation of tradition is also important, but this implies continuity and change. The reverse is of course true. Advancing with the age we must never cease to draw upon the wealth and wisdom of the ages.

Looking back on the ten years of our corporate existence I have little to tell of increased wall space, only an old house inadequately equipped but finally turned over, still furnished, to the public for their enjoyment of pictures in a homelike setting. And I have nothing to report of the museum building which, some day, must be a permanent home for the collection. It has seemed the wisest course to construct for the future with paintings rather than with bricks or stones since it is impossible out of our limited family fonds to do bath at the same time. We dream of a school for critics and teachers functioning usefully around an art library and a well lighted storeroom. The actual paintings would be moved about in exhibition units—that is in groups possessed of collective significance, moved in whatever ways the Director and his teachers might require, from a gallery to a classroom and then back to the luminous storeroom there to be at all times available to students on sliding screens. For the present we must educate under difficulties. But already the old house is alive with that restless, eager life of the student who cannot rest from learning and who seeks not only to know but to do. For the present we can only help along with written and spoken interpretations of the paintings and of the particular ideas which have led to the choice of our changing exhibitions. The wonderful success of *Art and Understanding*[3] sustains me in the belief that there is need for and wide appreciation of a magazine which interprets the art of the present as it relates to the past and as it leads on into the future. I feel that such a periodical must be entirely disinterested and detached, that it must on the one hand moderate its trend to open-mindedness with a stern passion for sincerity, integrity and truth and on the other that it must temper its personal preferences with a tolerant appreciation for different points of view. It must, above all other considerations, relate art to life, referring it back to nature, and dedicating it resolutely to the making of an international mind and to those universal values which survive our changing boundaries, policies, fashions, and opinions. *Art and Understanding* must fill a unique place in the spiritual as well as in the cultural life of our country. The chief compensation we have for the profusely illustrated publications sold at or below cost is the improved standard of taste, the greater fitness to appreciate on the part of those visitors to our galleries who have prepared their minds by sympathetic reading. I speak of the changing taste and growing visual capacity of my visitors but this is of no greater consequence to the collection than what is happening all the while to myself as time and change mold current thought and opinion, including my own.

Every year, it seems that my taste is just beginning to attain to its maturity. Often I wonder what I will think of my decisions of today ten years from now. I can only live and think and act according to the degree of sound judgment and aesthetic sensitiveness given to me from day to day. In some museums, the mistakes are almost

---

3. [Only two issues of *Art and Understanding: A Phillips Publication* were published (in 1929 and 1930)].

irreparable. My collection is plastic and I am molding it all the time nearer to heart's desire. Sometimes excellent paintings must be sacrificed in exchange for others more urgently needed or more intimately wanted to complete or enrich Exhibition Units or to correct a serious error of omission. In our first catalogue there were many such shortcomings and I expressed our need for a fine marine in oil by Winslow Homer, an Ideal Head in perfect condition by George Fuller, a thoroughly American portrait or genre by Thomas W. Eakins, distinguished examples of Degas, Manet, Seurat, and Van Gogh, and a supremely fine portrait, figure composition, and still life by Cézanne. The Seurat is still absent. All the other wishes have been fulfilled. The quest, however, is never-ending. Our new acquisitions, fine as they are, only stimulate the desire for equally fine examples of other periods in the careers of such great masters.

At the time of the publication of our first catalogue, much of the best art of today was inadequately represented. American painting had been surveyed from Ryder, Twachtman, and Weir to Prendergast, Davies, and Luks, and a few favorite painters were to be seen comprehensively and at their best. I have now acquired for these exhibition units new inspirations in watercolor by that unique genius of the medium, John Marin, new reveries and rhapsodies in color-orchestration by that great mystic and decorator Augustus Vincent Tack, and new canvases of subtly colored and capricious brush drawing very intimate, lyrical and unforgettable, by Karl Knaths. All three of these strikingly dissimilar painters reveal the point of view of the ancient Chinese artists with their crisp and confident calligraphy, their bold conventions for design, their fine light and dark patterns and their elusive suggestions of things either seen or imagined. Additions have been made to our important Ryder and Davies units and new works acquired by many of our favorite American painters. Of the new Americans added to the collection, John D. Graham, Ernest Fiene, Stuart Davis, Morris Kantor, Harold Weston, Charles Burchfield, and Anne Goldthwaite are noteworthy. I feel that Weston is destined to be one of the finest artists of our time.

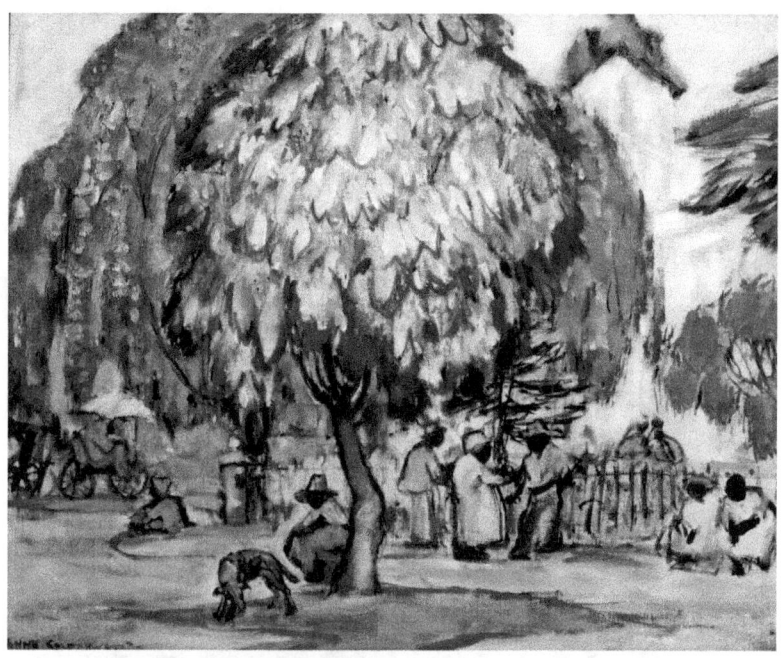

Anne Goldthwaite
Catalpa in Bloom, n.d.
Oil on canvas
The Phillips Collection, Washington, D.C. Acquired in 1930

As recently as 1925, the truly important contemporary art of Europe which centers and culminates in what is coming to be known as the School of Paris had been practically unexplored. We had, to be sure, made a fine beginning with Pierre Bonnard's *Early Spring* and *Woman and Dog*. His infinitely sensitive and subtle art of "crushed color," as Ralph Flint described it,[4] vibrating in exquisite modulations and tonic dissonances and composed in charming, capricious arrangements, has now been followed up with an ever increasing conviction of his preeminence as an incomparable poet of chroma tic song, a poet-painter who sees the world with constant surprise

_____

4. [Ralph Flint, "Current American Art Season," *Art and Understanding* 1, no. 2 (1930): 214.]

and delight, with a freshness of vision and a lyrical humor and joyousness inimitably his own. Bonnard is, in my opinion, the most
distinguished and original painter now living. He differs as much
from Degas and Renoir as Derain from Corot and Courbet. In sculpture there is a man no less outstanding. I refer to Despiau although
Maillol is a close second with his classic terracotta figurines. Despiau is in the Phillips Collection with his serene, splendid *Mme. Derain*—the original plaster of that masterpiece of portraiture and uni-

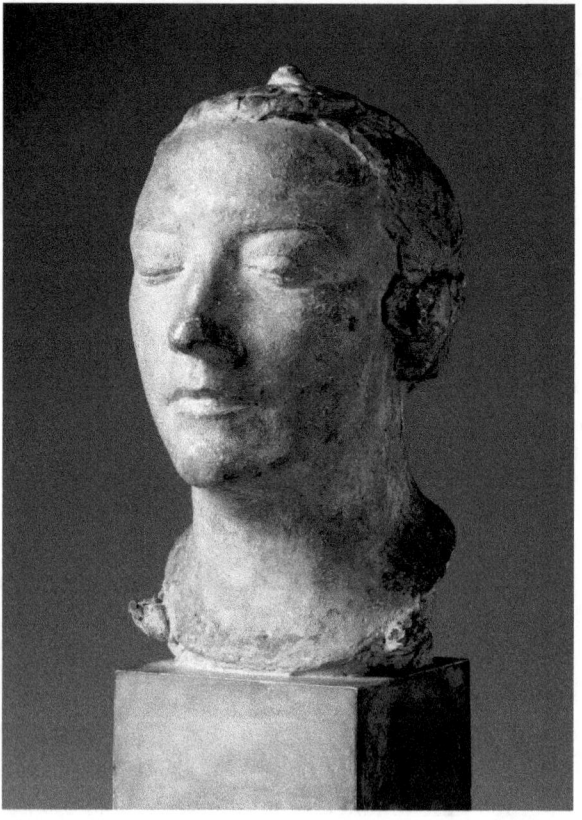

Charles Despiau,
Head of Madame Derain, 1922
Plaster
The Phillips Collection, Washington, D.C. Acquired in 1928

versal symbolism. Other progressive leaders acquired recently are Vuillard, Sickert, Maillol, Rouault, Matisse, Picasso, Derain, Braque, Segonzac, Friesz, Dufy, Marcoussis, Utrillo, Klee, Chirico, Lurçat, Per Krohg, Berman, and Fautrier. Our examples of Despiau, Bonnard, Vuillard, Derain, and Braque are especially important and represent these masters at precisely the periods in which they fulfilled themselves to the utmost. Braque, a man of exquisite tact and taste who has developed out of cubism a new decorative style and has had more influence on applied design than any other painter, is represented with five canvases which reveal this significant aspect of his art. Such masterpieces of Derain as our "Southern France" and "The Dancer" reveal his position in the direct line of the French classic tradition. Endowed with both vigor and sensitiveness and a flair for richly painted surfaces he is comparable to great masters of painting from the Renaissance to the Nineteenth Century. As in the case of Matisse his facility and popularity are distinct sources of danger in his path to further progress and yet Derain's *best* work of recent years is the best work he has ever done and good enough to establish his enduring fame.

It is the secret of success in collecting contemporary artists to wait for the time when a painter attains a balanced mastery of all his means and a mature ripeness of mind as well as method. I secured four paintings by Maurice Sterne which were painted at a time when his great gifts as a draftsman and sculptor were so much in demand that he was being drawn away from his brushes and pigments more or less against his will. What he painted during that time seems to have been done with a peculiarly enraptured zest and an enjoyment of color and brushwork which communicates to the beholder his love for the painter's art. A few years ago John Marin's water colors became more thrilling than ever and he rose to dizzy heights of inspired notation. Elemental forces were captured with ecstatic intuition and hurled on paper in a precarious, headlong manner which only his rare genius justified and explained. I had been slow to recognize and understand the earlier and easier Marin, but just at the right moment the mist that had concealed his mind from mine lifted suddenly and I was ready to acquire his swift and stirring improvisations. The latest work of Arthur G. Dove is as original and as American in conception as Marin's. It is permeated with a new Twentieth Century sensuousness, a robust joy, for instance, in the tactile character of objects which absorb light such as old weathered wood or rusty iron. Hardly less is he attracted to dramatic effects of radiations and reflections of light and to lustrous surfaces and textures. Dove has always been a powerful designer and the possessor of a palette of sombre, closely related tones, earthy or cosmic in suggestion. Superficially no two painters could be more unlike than the laconic Dove, who is concerned with the mere sight and touch of rugged, uncouth things for their own sake, and the romantic Tack, the material world well lost in celestial and spiritual meditations. And yet these two Independents are both intensely aware of the accidents of nature which can be developed, through their intervention, into an abstract art of ideas and essences.

I do not try to include all good contemporary artists in my comprehensive collecting. For all the tolerance and open-mindedness to which I aspire, I still have my strong likes and dislikes. Certain artists touch a responsive chord within me while others, more popular and famous perhaps, leave me cold. Regardless of whether or not my favorites happen to be favorites of other artists, critics and collectors, and regardless of whether or not they have present or prospective market value, yet they are men for me if I feel prompted to live with their works and to seek for more and yet more sparks and radiations from their spirits. It is not easy to keep one's poise and one's sincere personal viewpoint at a time when collecting has become a fad and certain types of work unfashionable. To me current valuations are of ephemeral interest only. They might be reversed within five years. Our children will live to see this happen even if we miss the instructive experience. Our children will have their own tastes and opinions which may or may not be good according to what we think today but which will probably be the result of the usual unfair reaction against the tastes and opinions of the preceding generation. Meanwhile we can only be true to ourselves and confident that if we have trained our sensibilities we cannot be far wrong, and that in defense of our sincerities we must be on our guard against much that we read and hear. Of one truth we may be certain. A good work of art cannot be permanently overlooked. It may be almost forgotten or completely out of favor for more than a century, but the time will come when full justice will be done to it at last, with arrears of sentimental adoration. It was ever thus and I need not recall the obscurity which after their deaths engulfed the names of El Greco, Rembrandt, Vermeer, Daumier, Guys, and countless lesser men who are now esteemed and imitated. There is too much of a tendency in these days of widespread public interest in art and of generous patronage of living artists to assume that the names we hear on all sides are the names to reckon with. Fortunately success is more of an indication of true artistic value today than it was in the Nineteenth Century when a painter's obscurity or prominence was often in reverse ratio to his real importance. Yet even at present I have little doubt that the artists who are destined to be considered the greatest of our time are now underrated and in some cases practically unknown. The men with the admiring crowds marching behind them, the officials, the critics, the collectors and the dealers organizing the crowd, these are the men against whose celebrity we may well be on our guard. They may be too much of their own time to be for all time and too much of their own tribe or town or nation to have universal appeal.

It is easy to make mistakes in the examples we buy even if we are sure that we are on the track of the artists who count with us personally. One of my methods is to have sent on approval quite a number of canvases by a painter who interests me in one way or another and then to hold several long and silent sessions of observation and reflection about these pictures while waiting for each to speak to advantage in its own way. Finally I know its special idea, intention and quality. It helps decision to shift paintings about from room to room, from one light to another, to see them all together and to test how socially adaptable they are for mixed exhibition. If they simply cannot mix that is a fact to be respectfully noted. I have said that all good art can be brought together and I repeat it with

renewed emphasis. Nevertheless a careful arrangement is necessary which provides separate wall spaces for those rare types who
seem to require segregation. Unit Exhibitions of these independents
should always be included in any schedule which aims to do full
justice to the best of every type of artist. Ours is still a many-minded
world and only the best of many different kinds of art can speak for
it adequately. Our civilization will lose all culture worthy of the name
if our age is allowed to become so standardized that its expression
in art is collective and not individual, with no deviations tolerated
by official or majority opinion from the dogmatic specifications of
academies whether Pre- or Post-Cézanne.

Of our greatest paintings little needs to be said here. When I first
purchased the *Dejeuner des Canotiers* by Renoir from the Durand-
Ruel private collection I realized that its universal fame would bring

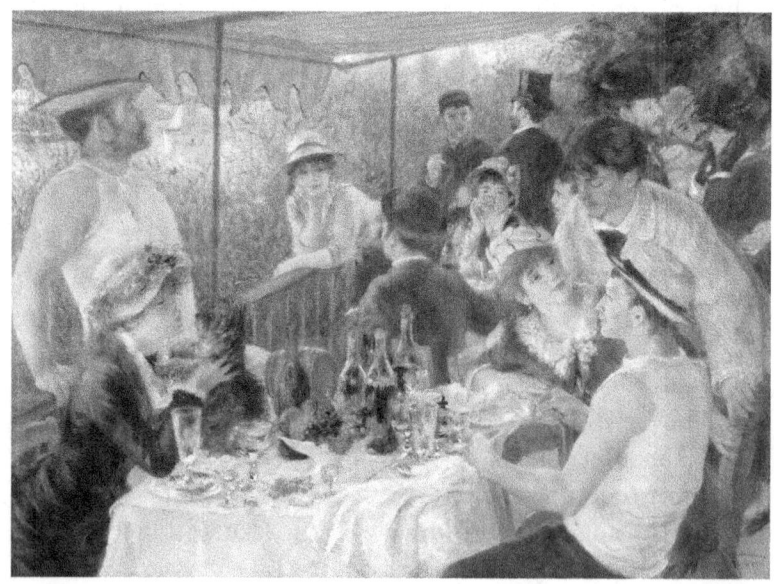

Pierre-Auguste Renoir
Luncheon of the Boating Party (*Dejeuner de Cantotiers*), between 1880–1881
Oil on canvas
The Phillips Collection, Washington, D.C. Acquired in 1923

pilgrims to pay homage from all over the civilized world. When they came I believed that they would find many other items less famous yet quite as fine. It is of course one of the landmarks of human achievement in painting, a culmination of the sumptuous representative and decorative art of the Sixteenth and Seventeenth Centuries, even though its date is as late as 1881. Titian and Rubens are the ancestors of Renoir in this glorious picture with its linear rhythm and its joyous and immense vitality. To the High Renaissance heritage of magisterial design and rich, glowing color the Impressionist gift of sun and air was added and the modern secrets for effects of evanescence and intimacy. Finally there is a prophecy of Renoir's own last period and its abstract low relief of luminous colors, its modeling in diffused light. After so ripe an achievement, change was necessary and Renoir himself became an experimentalist from that hour. The noble primitive of the new movement toward formal relations is Paul Cézanne who is represented in our Collection with two of his greatest works, the austere self-portrait chosen by Meier-Graefe as the frontispiece to his book on the master and called by him one of the two finest Cézanne portraits in existence and the lyrical and classic landscape of Mt. St. Victoire from the Reber Collection which is a particularly pure example of the architectonic achieved directly by the lightly laid and yet constructive action of color; not a touch added which does not function to great and ample purpose.

The Repentant Peter by El Greco, the Bowl of Plums by Chardin, the On the Stour by Constable, the Three Lawyers, Two Sculptors, and Bridge at Night by Daumier, the Paganini of Delacroix, the landscape, the portrait, and the classic figure of Corot, the Ballet Espagnol of Manet, the Rocks at Ornans of Courbet, the Moonlit Cove of Ryder, the Summer of Twachtman, the Public Garden at Arles by Van Gogh, the Notre Dame of Rousseau, The Palm and Open Window of Bonnard, The Dancer and Southern France of Derain, the Lemons and Napkin Ring and Abstraction of Braque—these are, I believe, creations which will live forever.

The greatest painting in the Collection is the Daumier master-piece, *L'Émeute* or, as I translate it, *The Uprising*. When this large can-vas was discovered not long ago in the old Paris quarter where the artist had lived, it was immediately hailed by Arsène Alexandre as "the most important and the most impressive of those we know or are ever likely to know of Daumier's."[5] While the Louvre was deliber-ating I cabled to have the picture shipped. It more than justified M. Alexandre's enthusiasm and my expectation. As Mather has written, "it is one of the world's greatest pictures. This is not *a* mob. It is *the* mob of all times. We think of Michel Angelo at the smoke-stained end of the Sistine Chapel"[6]—and he might have added of Rembrandt in his last, best, most passionate period. Here is Daumier the great-hearted humanitarian whose logical simplifications, anticipating those of our sophisticated modernists of today, were never made merely for the sake of a pattern but to focus the mind's eye on the salient contours, the expressive volumes and tones and masses, the universal, profound significance of a familiar incident.

The earliest work in the Collection is an Egyptian Limestone por-trait of a young man by a sculptor of about 1350 B.C., and the latest, chronologically, is a painting by a young girl just out of art school. It is with combinations of painting and sculpture, of works both ancient and modern, both foreign and American, of creative expres-sions both representative and abstract, that I teach the universal-ity of art as a unifying spirit and the continuity of human thought and aspiration.

---

5. ["An Unpublished Daumier," *The Burlington Magazine* 44, no. 252 (March 1924): 143; quotation emended.]

6. ["Painting from Dan to Beersheba," *The Arts* 2, no. 2 (February 1927): 78.]

MODERN ART, 1930

(1930)

CONTEMPORARY art is keeping up with contemporary science in arousing and holding public attention no less than in making brilliant advances into hitherto unexplored regions of the mind. It is so intensely and so exuberantly alive that it quickens the pulse and adds zest to the practice and the criticism of art during this formative period. A literature of interpretation has grown up around the new aesthetic ideas and the new plastic creations. Art, in its present state of growth and change, is a topic for everyone's more or less excited consideration and opinion. As I write I live again in memory all the thrills of the epoch-making season of 1929–30 in New York with its succession of important events. About 1,600 people each day, an average of over 3,000 on Saturdays, and of 35,000 in three weeks, have visited the Museum of Modern Art to see its loan exhibition of Painting in Paris. The widespread interest of this affair was not in spite of but precisely because of the contemporaneous character of all the paintings and the controversial character of most of them. It is clear that the public is fascinated by the contemporaneous and the controversial in art. The curiosity of the mob which packed the celebrated Armory Show of 1913 was an entirely different manifestation. Serious interest could easily be read on the faces of these visitors of 1930 and the general behavior of the crowd of last winter was surely respectful. There was little evidence of aggressive dislike and I observed no seeking for "sources of innocent merriment" as on former occasions of this kind. The exhibit was evidently regarded as a chance for serious study of the new art which is so rapidly crystallizing, which has passed from promise to achievement and about which so much has been written.

First published in *Art and Understanding* 1, no. 2 (March 1930). Reprinted in *The Artist Sees Differently*.

The fact is undeniable that the average visitor to a public view of so-called modern pictures in New York today is no stranger to the latest of aesthetic idioms. It can no longer be said that America does not see the best of the European modernism nor can it be claimed that we are spared the excessive demonstrations of old world radicalism. Consequently, the American public has become more or less habituated to the new language of design. Department store displays, magazine covers and advertising posters have been instrumental in changing our point of view. It appears that the American patron of art will soon require what he calls the 'modern note" and will actually feel compelled to disapprove of whatever does not conform to it. It is no longer necessary to teach the layman that art is not the craft of accurate imitation of nature. He knows that nature is the source and the storehouse for the artist's creations, but that a painter's powers of invention are poor indeed if he leaves the world on his canvas exactly as the mirror would reflect it. There is more need already for reminding our gallery visitors and even our connoisseurs that the acceptance of what is new in art today does not require the rejection of what was new only yesterday.

This period in art has a sentiment for itself very like the sentiment which youth has always cherished for its own youthfulness and with the same sarcastic scorn for the tastes and opinions of its elders. "Modernity is the battle cry of our generation." I quote this sentence from one of the many books on one of the many experimental decorators of the School of Paris. It would almost seem as if there had never been so self-conscious and self-satisfied a period as ours. Yet every age no doubt preens itself and attitudinizes, if only for the sake of keeping up appearances. What I regard as special to our own conceit about ultra modern art is a certain very youthful bravado which regards with intolerance any survivals of art as it was before these new ideas came into it. This attitude no doubt is taken over from the world of science, where new concepts so often eclipse and make uncouth the conclusions of the past. In a hymn by James Russell Lowell there is a stirring verse about the deliberate choice of *loneliness* a man must make to affirm the truth that is in him:

Then it is the brave man chooses, while the coward
    stands aside, [...]
And the multitude make virtue of the faith they
    had denied.[1]

It may not be long now before the multitude, in our largest centers of culture at least, will make virtue of their radicalism in art. Already the brave man's choice is to be true to himself even if it means to be unfashionable and neglected. Even today the self-styled modernists, contemporaneous to a fault, are not lonely at all in the choice they have made. They are in fact breathlessly followed and acclaimed. There is a precedent for their popularity. To what does our public passion for the latest mode correspond? Let us see. Those who would be known as modernists in art must account for and explain their following. Modernists of the past have never won fame and fortune. The great initiators and pioneers of art have stood alone, isolated and misunderstood except by the few who really counted and who made everything worthwhile. If schools were founded on their discoveries they knew nothing of it. El Greco was considered crazy. When Rembrandt broke away from professional portrait painting he was despised and repudiated and only recognized as a great master after his death. Chardin retired into his humble home and there he painted what pleased him regardless of the fashions set by the Court for a rococo which was quite alien to his taste. Constable and Turner were modernists whose inventions and innovations, which anticipated both the personal liberties of Romanticism and the nature studies of Impressionism, were condemned and ridiculed. If they received praise during their lives it was for their occasional compromises with public taste and their sincere loyalty to great traditions. Daumier was the greatest modernist of them all. Space does not permit my tribute to his pioneer courage. On the other hand many of the greatest painters have been powerful influences with the public of their time, have created a demand and immediately satisfied it,

---

1. ["The Present Crisis," in *The Poetical Works of James Russell Lowell* (Boston and New York: Houghton, Mifflin and Company, 1890), 68; quotation emended.]

have set fashions and have founded Schools. I need only mention Giotto, Bellini, Leonardo, Giorgione, Raphael, Watteau, Reynolds, and David. I need not bring up the less illustrious names, although I cannot resist mentioning among those who set fashions Gerome and Sargent. And today the fashion setting leaders are Matisse, Picasso, and Chirico. Their impetus started with Cézanne and Gauguin. Cézanne, however, was a real modernist who stood apart from and in advance of his time. It is Matisse and Picasso, following Gauguin, who are in step with it, as were Giotto, Giorgione, Raphael, Watteau, and the rest, supplying what the public has been made ready to demand. There are no doubt Cézannes of the future in our midst today. They are carrying on somewhere and somehow in obscurity or perhaps one admires them for the wrong reasons as was the case with Seurat. Let us beware lest those we call old-fashioned in subject or unconvincing in experiment should turn out to be the prophets of the future, the men of destiny.

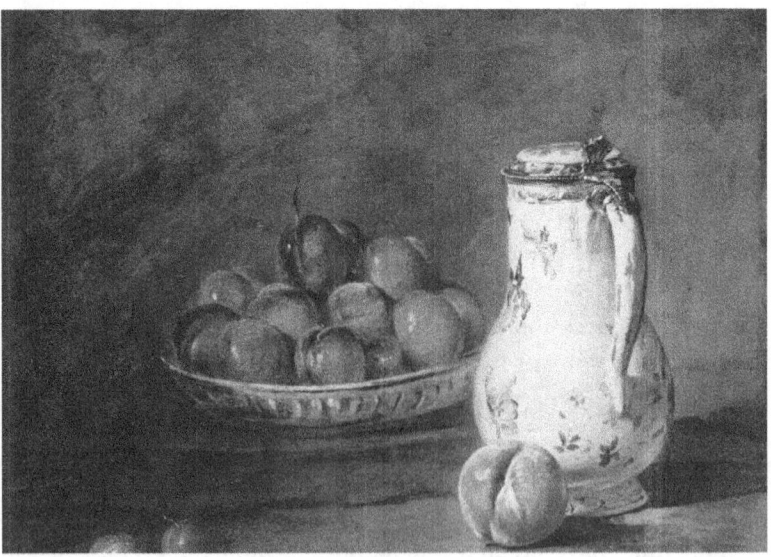

Jean-Baptiste-Simeon Chardin
A Bowl of Plums, c. 1728
Oil on canvas
The Phillips Collection, Washington, D.C. Acquired in 1920

The sudden reversal of taste in our period, the violent change of mode from Sargent to Picasso within fifteen years, is startling until we remember that there has been a steady stream of propaganda and publicity, the effects of which have been watched with keen intelligence until finally our deliciously shocked surmises and our subconscious expectations have been not only anticipated but produced at precisely the moment of our desire. At last we know what it is to be modern and what is to be our style for the first half of the Twentieth Century. Consciousness of a new style in art is like a child's consciousness of a new toy or a woman's awareness of a new gown or a man's of a new hat. Outfitted with a new mode in art, we find it difficult not to look upon those still satisfied with other styles as curiously old-fashioned. Art as it was before Matisse and Picasso is interesting only for the museum and its relics. The desire for a stimulating change in the atmosphere of one's home and of one's mind has finally been implanted in us and made to appear as a positive human need. And it *is* a need, as so many habits have a way of becoming. I, for one, am often restless for a change in art and positively hungry for some new sensations of color or of pattern. Frankly, it delights me to encourage experiment, and I derive more pleasure out of my experiment station than out of any other part of my work. The new interiors have cried out for a new kind of picture for the walls. A moderately stylized picture prepares the way and whets the appetite for a more radical one to keep it company. The new styles are grist for the conversational mill and this is by no means a trifling consideration. With those addicted to faddism art is more popular now than crossword puzzles were in their day. With those of us who pride ourselves on open-mindedness the incessant innovations in painting keep us actively entertaining new ideas and violently exercising our adaptabilities. With the artists who yearn to be in advance of their time there must be exasperation in the fact that their time and its public insists upon keeping up with them as they so desperately try to keep up with the resourcefully inventive Picasso. Modernism has become a "fait accompli." Only a short time ago I feared that the majority was being alienated by the

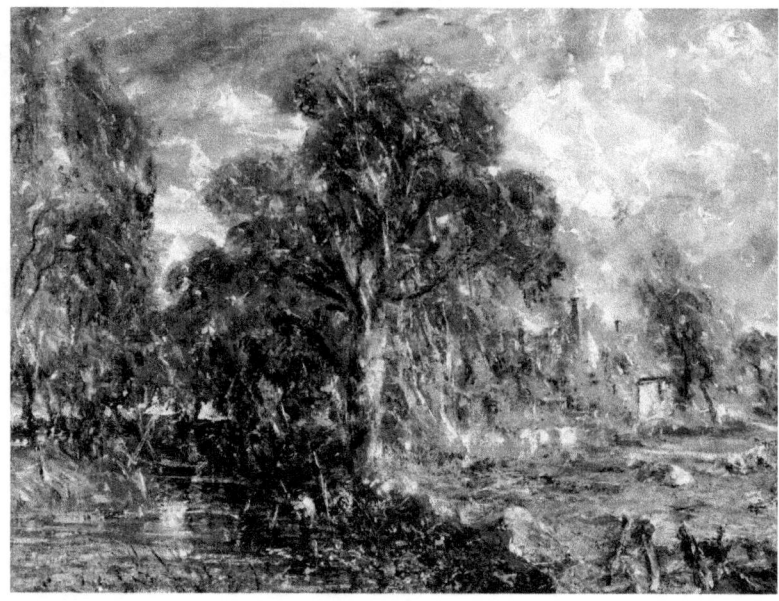

John Constable
On the River Stour, c. 1834–37
Oil on canvas
The Phillips Collection, Washington, D.C. Acquired in 1925

uncompromising abstractions and eccentric cerebrations of very prominent artists and I predicted that a highly sophisticated class of period-conscious patrons might easily monopolize and dominate progressive artists and widen and deepen the gulf between art and the general public. I had not reckoned with the fame and fascination of the much adored heroes of the movement. or had I reflected on the rapidity with which new ideas spread and grow when the soil has been prepared over a wide area. If the time is approaching when conservative people actually see for themselves that the new systems and theories of design correspond with the modern mind, its researches and discoveries, then it will simply be a matter of standardizing as decoration the best plastic patterns and of accepting as phenomena of genius the best pictorial supernaturalism.

Undeniably, Picasso and Chirico are logical equivalents in art for the age which has produced Freud, Einstein and Spengler. As everyone knows who has studied the history of art as an evolution, the leaders of the advance are always attuned to the spirit of investigation in their time. This is especially true of those modernists who, not too far ahead of their public, do not "stand and wait" like the prophets but who collect around them other bold spirits to put in circulation a new coinage of ideas. It was so with Manet and Monet. Matisse and Picasso are today the corresponding leaders attuned to their time. And I rejoice that we live in an age when the multitude seems to be actually advancing in step with these leaders who represent in art the most recent investigations and researches. When concepts change with startling suddenness we can, I suppose, expect creative art to change with corresponding speed. Artists of the type I am now talking about are barometers of what is going on in the world. An age of innovations and inventions, of shifting codes, of revised mentality and morality, is of course a period of tremendous incentive to artists and devotees of art who live where the current of progress flows swiftest and feel its unrest. ow it is clear that we cannot live in the world today and escape from mechanism, collectivism, standardization, specialization and investigation of anything and everything which remains relatively unknown. Artists are therefore confronted with the hidden states of mind, the borderlands of reason and intuition, the mysteries of consciousness and subconsciousness, the psychic powers of the few, the unplumbed resources of electricity and chemistry, in short the control of mind over matter. The progressive artist feels impelled to take the curse off a period which, in its scientific and collectivistic trend, is headed in the opposite direction from the artist's ancient course, namely personal expression. He must make a grandiose, impersonal style out of the arrangement of mechanical parts and their interdependence of function, their hardness of texture and their geometrical shapes. The authorities who support him must set a standard for collective taste and shepherd the usual flock of collective collectors. And so certain modes are being utilized and modified to specialties which the age seems to call for. The generalizing view has supplanted the particularizing. Synthesis has replaced analysis. Artists either work from nature towards geometry or starting from geometry return somewhat ponderously to nature. Just as modish art never quite becomes mathematics, so it never gets all the way back to humanity. Any art practiced on into our enlightened age which remains unaffectedly human and relating to life without any theorem or diagram, without any allegiance to abstraction or supernaturalism, is, I regret to say, shrugged at as old-fashioned.

The artist who is recognized as up-to-date wears one of three uniforms and King Pablo wears them all according to his whim. There is the neo-primitive mode, made popular by a real primitive, Henri Rousseau. It is only becoming to other real primitives and its adoption by the ultra sophisticates is falling out of favor. As for the "peintres de dimanches," the butcher, the baker, the candlestick maker, who sell their wares on the street corners, their funny little pictures simply reveal by contrast the genius of good old Rousseau, whose innate feeling for color and design and vivid reaction to life started the craze for childlike frankness and untrained naiveté. More imposing is the appearance of the modern artist who wears the stiff old garments of the formalist, abstractionist, or whatever else he may like to call himself, as he denies self and glorifies system. These artists are the aesthetes of today, and so stylish they are that they might suffer the fate of fashion plates and seem simply quaint to their own children.

Sometimes there is a great decorator, a man of true genius, who wears these garments as if he had been born to them. Such a man is Braque, a distinguished designer if ever there was one, whose every caprice of manner is courtly, who wears formal dress with the distinguished ease and the charming grace one likes to associate with aristocracy in sport clothes. One or two general principles of design, such as the all-over pattern and the construction of forms in space under architectural inspiration, are maintained and they succeed in making the formalists of our period more intelligently conscious of their function as artists than were the illustrators and the imitators of the Nineties and at the turn of the century. But whereas all artists have learned these truths they have not paraded in them and covered up with such correct garments their lack of personalities and ideas to go under the clothes. Less popular than the formalists, because less adaptable to applied art and interior decoration, are those who qualify to pass through the world causing everywhere a big thrill and a little shudder in the sinister role of supernaturalist. They make us aware of magic, but not in nature and not in ordinary human experience, only in abnormal psychology, in dislocated dream images and in various disorders of subconscious life. Metaphysical concepts are embodied pictorially. Soothsayers are once again needed. Both formalists and supernaturalists often produce inventions which beguile us for hours at a time and occasionally refer to our actual experiences in ways which startle us into sudden respect and a more sympathetic attention. For instance I have just acquired for my pictorial laboratory a dark and vivid canvas by Morris Kantor entitled *Union Square*. It depicts the agitated state of mind of one who lives in that crowded and confused section of New York. The street lamps, the lighted windows, and an equivalent for the racket and the roar of the outside world impinge upon the artist's seclusion and break through the walls of his studio until consciousness is all agog as in a dream and the relief of expression becomes a cubist problem with the parts to be put together again, as an architect builds rather than as a realist imitates. The result is beautiful in tone and pattern and not at all chaotic or disturbing in effect. Order has been brought out of the chaos of an all too familiar modern experience. The order tells about the chaos but presides over it and converts it into style. I have also been attracted lately by the lively pictures of Stuart Davis, who improvises with linear perspectives and color schemes and reveals a kinship to the improvising virtuoso, Picasso. That colossus bestrides both camps, inspiring imitators either to look up at his pose as a formalist of quite formidable power or to guess at his meaning as

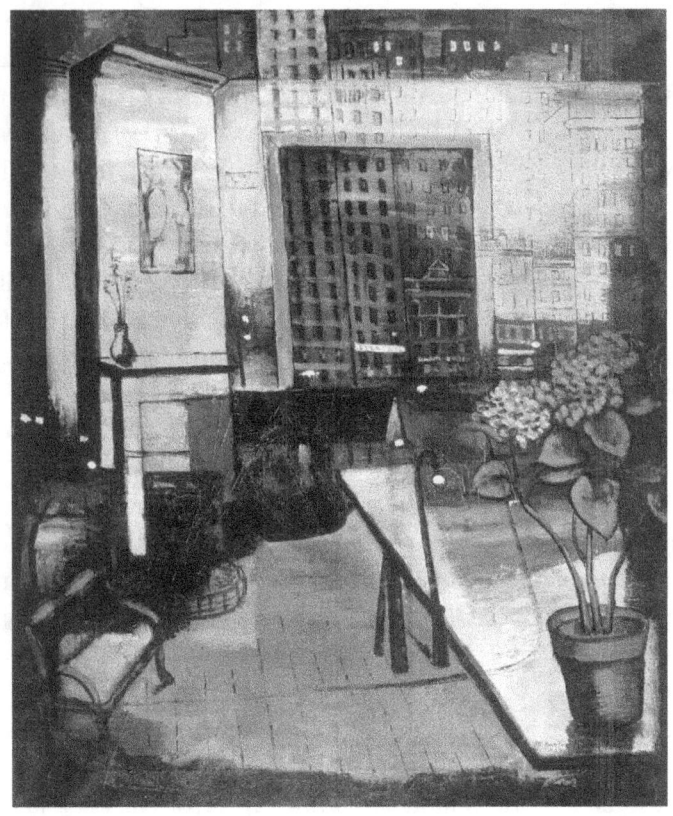

Morris Kantor
Union Square, 1928
Oil on canvas
The Phillips Collection, Washington, D.C. Acquired in 1930

a supernaturalist most strangely disturbing. Picasso is making history—breaking precedents every day. There is no doubt at all of his
genius. The only doubt is in regard to the results of his influence.

With such a glorious adventurer making front page publicity for
art in season and out of season, it is tempting to believe that our
age is suddenly of rather transcendent importance in its aesthetic
creations and that we who are busy in this world are important, too;
that if we pay rich tribute to the period we can share in its power
and glory. Our parents however belonged to a less enlightened

time. Any painter working in a style which is neither formalist nor
supernaturalist nor sensationally new is today as one buried alive.
Cézanne was useful for a while. Now he is, in the words of Leo Stein,
"a squeezed lemon." What matters it to us if Bonnard, like Cézanne,
belongs to the ages?* The New York, dealers, repeating propaganda
from Parisian dealers, pronounce that he is not of the hour. The prescribed uniforms of the faith are not of course required from artists
of the more or less remote past. If, however, a living painter is by
turn of mind or by habit of vision imbued with even the best qualities of the generation which preceded his own, then he is what we
revolted against. We can treat him with condescension only. If, living
on into our time, an artist is yet so oblivious to the spirit of our age
as to still be a sensitive lyricist, affected by light and atmospheric
colors, using these as instruments of emotional expression, then, for
the sake of progress, he must be denounced as vague, soft, over-
refined, a sensualist and a false prophet of escape from the hard
facts of modern life. No matter how original such great individualists as Bonnard and John Marin may be, how rare and inimitable
their vision, how subtle and sure their intuition and awareness of
nature, how incommunicable the secret of their touch, there is no
sympathy for such individualism and for such independence as they
display. John Marin blows through the world of modern art like a
strong bracing wind from the sea or the mountains but he requires
from the beholder an intuition like his own and an apprehension of
the elemental which transcends school and dogma. Such an artist as
Pierre Bonnard sees the world as no one ever saw it before, with a
magic which cannot be charted and which cannot even be felt if one
has no share at all in such rare endowment of vision, such genius
for inspired relations of color. And so I say that these masters and
other men such as Tack in his latest, most stirring color progressions
are not topical artists for the multitude. They are more difficult for

---

* Meier-Graefe, Élie Faure, Roger Fry, Clive Bell, Félix Fénéon, Leon Werth,
and many others have declared that Bonnard is one of the two or three finest
living artists. I am told that Matisse is of the same opinion.

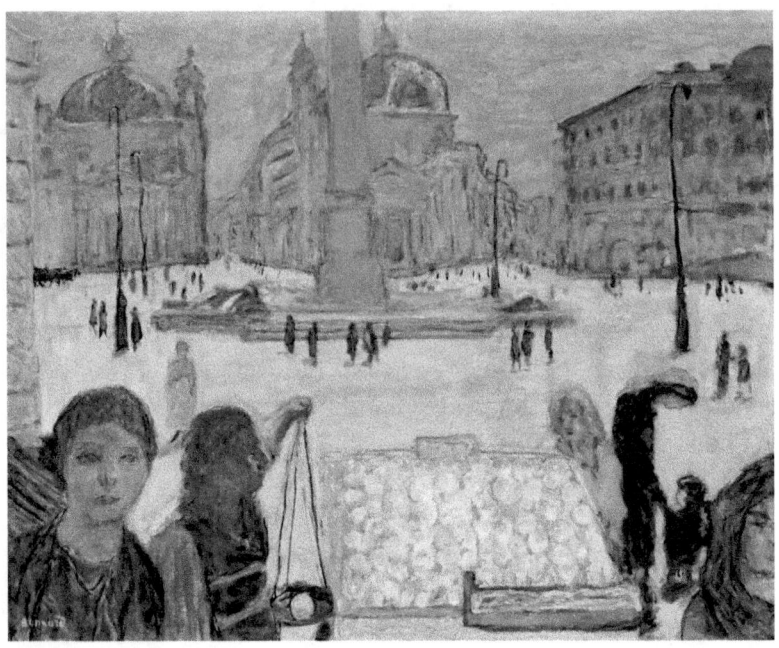

Pierre Bonnard
Piazza del Popolo, Rome, 1922
Oil on canvas
Private Collection; formerly in The Phillips Collection, Washington, D.C.
© 2022 Artists Rights Society (ARS), New York

the American connoisseur than the most cerebral Picasso or Léger. Why? Because they require sensibility for color, which is, as yet, undeveloped in this country, and because they are far in advance of their time. They are the genuine modernists who dare to be different from the mode of the moment, men who are altogether inimitable, and who, for that reason, will found no Schools and create no collective art. The future, however, may belong to them. The time element will surely come into painting and with it a renewed reverence for those painters who can move men to ecstasy and vision through their divine control of the emotional potentialities of light and color.

THE DECORATIVE PANELS OF
AUGUSTUS VINCENT TACK
(1930)

GREAT compositions in music need no literary interpretations. Program notes expressing the subjective reactions of an individual critic or commentator may or may not prepare the minds and the senses of a concert audience for the most alert and sensitive reception of the ordered and rhythmical sequence of creative sounds. Great compositions of color are no less independent of the written or spoken word. Just as the critic can never be sure that he has justly interpreted the creative artist so the artist himself can never communicate in words a symbolism which he has conceived as well as executed so self-sufficiently in color. Mystical thought, in a painter who is a painter and not a literary man, requires color for its expression. Whatever the painter himself can tell of his own symbolism, of the inspirational origin of his creative designing, and whatever any critic can read into the artist's abstractions through sympathetic reveries, may or may not prepare the mind and the senses of other b holders for the most alert and sensitive reception of the ordered and rhythmical sequence of color vibration

It is therefore with extreme reluctance that I write even a brief note on the new decorative panels which Augustus Vincent Tack has painted for the art library[1] of the Phillips Memorial Gallery. What he has told me of his conceptions for these great works I can and I should repeat as a matter of record. Yet such an art of color only reaches its plenitude of destined power when its ecstasies, profound meanings and spiritual revelations unfold from untold depths within us. As time goes on, through long sessions of observation and of thought

---

First published in *Art and Understanding* 1, no. 2 (March 1930).

1. [Now the Music Room of The Phillips Collection]

but without any aid whatever from those who dare to interpret such purely subjective experiences of the artist's soul, one may learn to approach to that intimate understanding of the artist's inspiration and his aspiration where one also catches glimpses of his ecstatic vision. For, as Carlyle expressed it, what the great mystic, whether poet, painter or musician, can do, is to "lead us to the edge of the Infinite to let us, for moments, gaze." For moments! But Carlyle had not reckoned with the greater degree of permanence, the more substantial embodiment of thought possible to color-music which leads us on and on into what Tack calls "the playgrounds of the imagination" and all those realms beyond human experience and beyond material and objective reality. The great artists of the Far East conceived of their pictorial and sculptural art as aids to meditation. Art

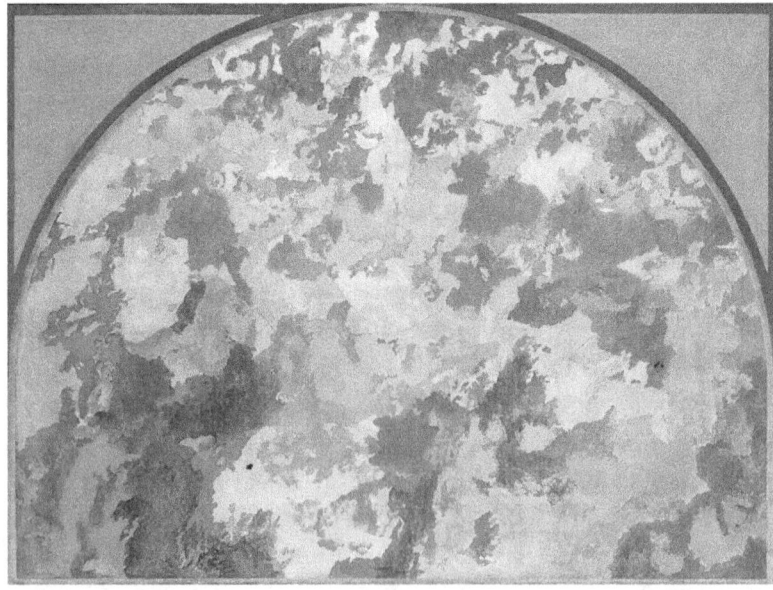

Augustus Vincent Tack
Ecstasy, 1929
Oil on canvas mounted on wallboard
The Phillips Collection, Washington, D.C. Acquired in 1930

and religion were closely related if not identical. The finite world of qualitative joys and of individual sensations was but a bright promise of the Infinite and Eternal for which our souls were preparing. Tack is a devout mystic who sees God in everything. He is inspired with the mysticism of an active Christianity rather than of a passive Buddhism and so his decorative imagination is dynamic, sensuous and joyous with the energy and the gaiety of those armored with the spiritual strength concerned with the here and now and not alone with the hereafter. He affirms his faith in Divine purpose through his grand patterns and it is as sincere a faith as ever inspired the Gothic builders.

The new decorations by Tack are comprehensive in their symbolism. Between the two mysteries of life's beginnings and its end surges the restless stream of human consciousness. Rhythm, Order and Balance are the active organic principles of Life and art. Ecstasy, Sorrow and Fortitude, these are the great emotional states of being. Exaltation of the Mind and Liberation of the Spirit—for these consummations life evolves.

The room in which such universal emotions and cosmic conceptions are to be suggested to those who come to meditate before them is to be barrel-vaulted with lunettes at each end. The vault is to be penetrated on each side with walls providing five decorative panels. At the four corners are elemental patterns conveying the idea of the outposts of Time, the borderlands of Eternity. Within these bounds of earthly experience Tack places, in his abundant and unprecedented language of subtly organized color and line, equivalents in design for the fullness of human life, its structural order, and its rich and subtle emotions. The lunette at one end is entitled Ecstasy. It conveys with surprising relations of thrilling color, azure, blue-violet, red-violet, red-orange, coral, yellow-green, and pearly whites, the radiant gladness of the heart for the great gift of life. In this decoration we feel the joy of time as it flees, the sense of Youth exultant, of Life triumphantly justifying itself in art and in all the other expressive outlets of the spirit. The exuberance of nature with its leaf edges and flower forms invites the artist to gallant adventures of discovery

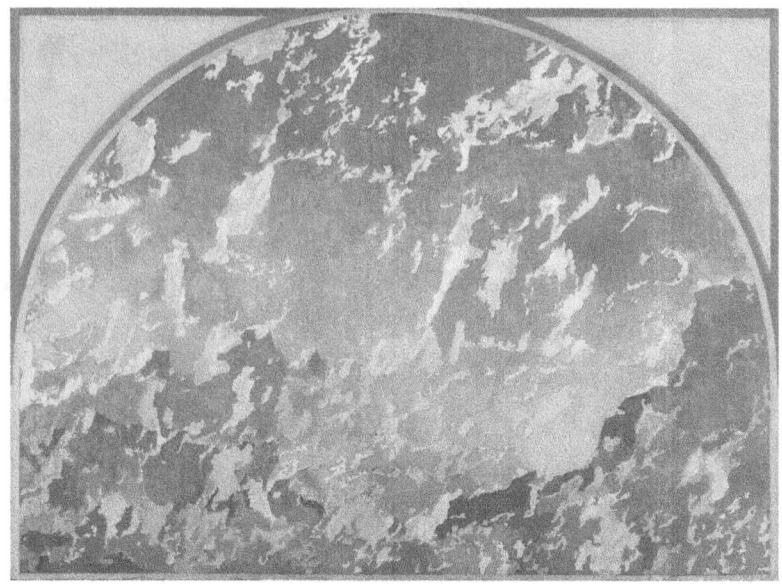

Augustus Vincent Tack
Liberation, 1929
Oil on canvas mounted on wallboard
The Phillips Collection, Washington, D.C. Acquired in 1930

and to endless experiments in adaptation. For art is nothing if not praise of life and intelligent use of nature for the soul s expression. The lunette at the opposite end conveys, with lapis lazuli, earth reds, red violets, sky blues and glorious cloudshine, the freedom of the spirit, the concept of Liberation. o matter what the exigencies of life—no matter how inexorable the complex, crowded world and its cruelties of circumstance, yet through idealism the human spirit soars and attains at last to that liberation from the earth and all that is limited in time which we dream of as immortality.

The technique of Tack's panels is a development through many experimental years. French Luminism, Twachtman's refinements upon it—"pointillisme" and its mosaics of color, Chinese landscape art of the great periods, and Odilon Redon, all these may have contributed to the unfolding of Tack's new art of orchestrated color, of linear boundaries and directions in an amplitude of space. When Dunoyer de Segonzac visited our Gallery and saw the paintings of Twachtman and Tack on the same wall, he immediately recognized the accord of spirit between them and asked me if they were not all the work of one man at different periods. He said that few American artists had impressed him so much, for this art seemed, for all its culture, to be completely original and self sufficient. One must pause, however, and linger for many an hour before the Tack color symphonies to appreciate the consummate craftsmanship and to penetrate into this world of pure spirit apprehended through subtle sensations. The sense of space is created entirely by light and dark values, for the planes are two dimensional and their edges are positive and clearly defined. The harmonies are deep and various. Encrustations and films of lighter tones drawn over solid and brilliant underpaintings enrich the surfaces to such an extent that ladders should be provided for those of us who take intense delight from beautiful textures of oil paint and rare color combinations closely observed.

—*w*—

THE ARTIST SEES DIFFERENTLY
(1931)

I

THIS introductory chapter might be called "Ideals of an Individualist" for that is precisely what I have in-tended to convey. The book which follows however deals chiefly with the art of painting and it is therefore with individualism in art that I am especially concerned. My book cannot be better introduced than as, in itself, an introduction. Primarily, it presents a report on a Collection of modern paintings which grows and changes and needs new commentary. Beyond that it pays a tribute of sincere devotion to an old-fashioned point of view and way of life which are distinctly out of favor today. Ours is an age which knows what it likes and what it wants and which does not particularly prize nor see how it can use individualism. Authoritarians for dogmas of every sort disapprove violently of each other and even more of the many presumptuous individuals who still see and think with a difference instead of collectively in terms of old or new thought, of old masters or new movements. Standards in art, based too often on commercial success and mere technical skill, are set up by academies of both the conservative and the rebel camps. Variations from these standards are" out of order." All-powerful is the mind of the majority or of that organized minority of fanatical reformers or shrewd, self-seeking opportunists which so often prevails over it. The mobilization of ready-made and second-hand opinions in groups and factions makes it unnecessary for anyone to waste time thinking or seeing for himself. A statistical use of fact and a mechanical use of formula are accepted as the appropriate means for an age of machines and of huge corporations. The artists are persuaded that they should use only the

---

First published in *The American Magazine of Art* 22, no. 2 (February 1931). Reprinted in *The Artist Sees Differently*.

ultra-modern categories, catch words and short cuts. And, whatever their procedure, they must be herded and classified in schools and movements about which we must declare ourselves as altogether for them or no less unreservedly against them. Artists may be resentful of organized governmental interference with their personal liberties and responsibilities. They may see plainly enough the connecting links between demagogues, dictators, dogmas, censors, sumptuary laws, class-consciousness and mass-mindedness. They may detest national, racial, and religious prejudice, suppressions and persecutions of liberals who insist upon the truth to make men free, prohibitions both by statute and by taboo and all other signs of crowd minds thinking the worst both about themselves and their neighbors. And yet they may fail to recognize that a collective art, as soon as it has become arrogant and intolerant of non-conformity, is part of the same distrust of the individual and of the same fanatical zeal for minding other people's business. They may properly appraise certain evils of our time; propaganda poisoning the springs of truth, bullying bluff and threat between outlaws and, I regret to say, between patriots of all nations, the as yet uncontrolled tariff wars and the unregenerate competitive building of armies and navies which breed war through prophesying it and assuming that it is inevitable. But the artists, they surely have done what they can through their universal language to interpret the world's scattered tribes to each other and to make a great symbol of the universal creative spirit? I wish I could feel that they have done their part. They may acquiesce in the belief that all prejudiced intolerance is a reversion to the pack. Yet do they realize, the artists, that these signs are to be found wherever a lack of self-respect in individuals has led to a soothing self-satisfaction when the same persons have merged themselves in groups? What of their own vainglorious academies and rival societies, their juries brandishing biased judgments and distributing medals and awards to the subservient, their craven proposals to tax foreign competitors to whom they feel hopelessly inferior, and their little cliques and factional fights not only of radicals and conservatives but within each side of that perpetual dispute? A generation or

two of individuals burdened with "inferiority complexes" can produce atrocities of intolerance inevitably inclining to rabid violence.
There are of course the extreme cases which deserve to be contemptuously consigned to oblivion—the unmitigated evils of organized
prejudice as disgraceful to America as our gangs of the underworld.
Tragic also in perversion of the sound purpose of preparedness is
the petty chauvinism of some of our patriotic societies. We can see
for ourselves how the disregard of the individual and consequently
his disrespect for himself and his submission with other sheep to the
shelter of the fold works out in business and social life. Regularity
in politics has its counterpart in mass education and the fixed standards set for college students, the learned professions and the arts.
Specialization breeds self-satisfaction with mere method or system.
Our democratic trust in and love for humanity in the mass and in the
abstract leads to the leveling of and indifference to individuals and
to ingloriously destroying their faith in themselves. Now art, with its
myriad marvels of diversity in talent and spirit should be the means
of raising the banner of individuation over a world grown insensitive
to the finer shades of feeling, a world of machines and of mechanized, or at least standardized men and women. Instead we find the
group mind operating in art as in everything else. The practitioners
of the new Schools are well pleased with their prominence and the
success of their striking simplifications of design corresponding to
the new labor-saving devices. But we can hardly take them on faith.
We must learn to discriminate between good and bad works of the
same kind, between abstractions which are personal and others
which are inhuman. At their best I take delight in their logic, their
devotion to style and their good taste, especially in creating effects
of rich color harmony with a very few unfamiliar and intermediate
tones. The popularity of such a subtle and such a personal colorist as
Braque proves that, as yet, all is well. At their worst I tire of the affectations of originality in the new idioms of art and the approximate
sameness of their imposed conventions, suggesting the rigid molds
into which art became fixed for interminable periods of ancient history when aesthetic consciousness was a collective discipline rather

than an individual inspiration. *Especially I resent the idea that the art of an age of machinery should be itself mechanical.* That is an obsession of modernistic pattern makers. In the works of Léger we are called upon to admire sharp edges, the flexible hardness of steel and the rigid surfaces of iron, the lustrous, soulless colors we apply to metal for our motor cars and buses. We are asked to feel the appalling impressiveness of the world of mechanism towards which we are tending. We may resent and avoid this sort of thing but we cannot be indifferent to it any more than we can be indifferent to the collective and mechanistic experiment on a vast scale now being conducted in Soviet Russia. The world itself is a laboratory in this transitional age and, if we look *through* modern art to whatever it signifies we may judge the trend of the times. It is fairly certain that we may expect more and more machines, more and more leisure and less and less capacity to enjoy or profit by it if art itself becomes automatic.

The traditionalists and all the backward looking devotees of discipline and impersonal decorum in art are now calling themselves humanists and although they suppose themselves embattled against modernism they have much in common with their doctrinaire rivals of the new dispensation. Fulminating in a futile way about modern plays, pictures and young people, these reactionaries find solace just resting their minds in the past or parading their protests against what they call the bad manners of modern art before some congenial club of like-minded old-timers. Although they have no sympathy for the new theories and do not in tend to make new adjustments to whatever is going on around them, the humanists of the museums have a family likeness to the dogmatists of the latest manifestos. The difference is that the modernistic critic condemns whatever is not, in his opinion, characteristic of the age or else an epochal rebellion against it—whereas the humanistic critic regards the present moment in art with disapproval and the future of art with fear and is embattled only for the past. But the dogmatists of bath camps would like to regulate art according to their own specifications. Beholding the period-consciousness and the complacency of our ultra-modern young artists and their sponsors, we may well determine never to be so adherent a part of the age, even though thrillingly immersed in it and proud and eager for its triumphs, as to be blind to its follies and its faults. *No matter how much we may admire the painters who seem to represent our period most vividly we must not be persuaded that we can do without less contemporaneous, more personal and variable expression.* The reflective, skeptical, sympathetic, open-minded observer has an immense advantage over the pledged person, pledged to see or to think in some collective way. Tolerance and the critical spirit have marked the periods of the finest culture and idealism and have contributed to the soundest mental health and happiness. Crowd tyranny determines the fate of nations, leads to the lowering of standards and the gradual extinction of distinguished individuals. To that extent it makes extremely doubtful the future of art and of almost everything worth while. Christianity was built around the individual and his spiritual needs. It has never been really tested because it has never been fully trusted. If we trained our children to see and to think for themselves as individuals they would not be such easy victims of war and other contagious fears and furies of the herd.

II

THE inevitable conclusion of any and all debates about art and aesthetics can be summed up by my title. The artist sees differently from the man of practical behavior and of normal or subnormal powers of observation and intuition. As Roger Fry pointed out in his great work *Vision and Design,*[1] the artist, on his way through the world, really takes time to look at it with rapture and wonder, to absorb its aspects to the utmost that he may use them for their own sake or as material for abstract pattern. The average man on the street or the farm, in the automobile or the office, is so intent on the next thing to do or to say that his preoccupation does not permit him to be the detached spectator of the phenomena of appearances or the detached specialist in subtleties of design. The

---

1. [New York: Brentano's, 1924.]

average man is an inarticulate type not an expressive individual, and his choice of a spokesman in art would be an interpreter, an outlet. The talk is usually about "beauty" from some preconceived idea of what that is. Naturally it cannot be recognized when it differs from the fixed, hereditary or popular image. In paleolithic days, the artist's mind was evidently attuned to every other mind and the only thing that set him apart from the mass of the tribe was not differentiated vision but special ability to work upon the emotions in one way or another, to gratify acquisitive or possessive instinct by imitation of appearances or to amuse excitement. Art with primitive peoples is a social function subordinate to the mind and the will of the majority. As men advance toward civilization it becomes more of a specialty, more of a solace for the few who value an abject which has no other purpose than to be seen with refinement: of observation and enjoyment, and perhaps, though not necessarily, as the artist saw it.

Artists see differently not only from other types of humanity but each from all the rest. To the extent that they often think and see with no considerable difference from the average person they are insignificant as artists. Art is nothing if it is not discriminating selection and passionate contemplation and therefore an important personal document. And art is not authentic unless it is also an expressive creation and consequently an intimate personal message. Art offers proof, if proof were needed, that human consciousness is complicated with myriad sensations of line, color and movement and impelled to aesthetic affirmations or denials of alternative theory or concept, and to aesthetic reactions of various degrees of sincerity and intensity. These reactions may lead either to representation of objects as such or to stylized decoration in which the objects have become units of design. In short, art proves the miracle of human personality and the unpredictable variations from type of the human species. It is my contention that ours is a world where too often such fascinating variations are deplored or discounted and the influence of the herd mind on the artist is still toward collective seeing habits and painting methods which level men with the force of a steam roller.

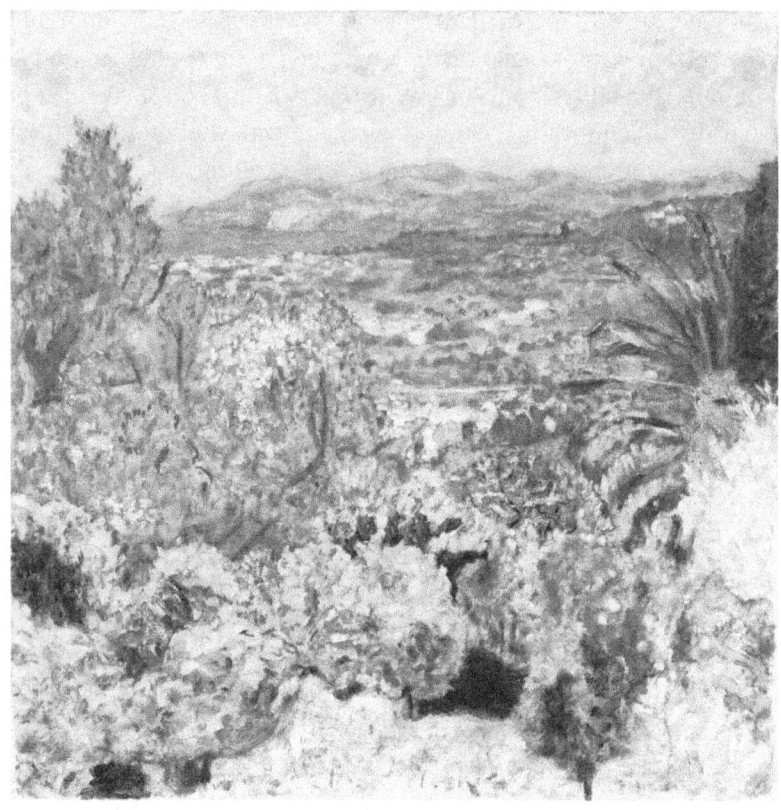

Pierre Bonnard
The Riviera, c. 1923
Oil on canvas
The Phillips Collection, Washington, D.C. Acquired in 1928
© 2022 Artists Rights Society (ARS), New York

From first to last, from prehistoric to ultra-modern realists and pattern makers, art has afforded to its followers a defense against the outer world and implied a faith in the artist's work as a shield as well as a symbol. From first to last the artists themselves have sought relief in creation and expression. By seeking identification with whatever moves them they are still winning compensatory joys, sublimated satisfactions, mystic bonds with unknown friends and

intimations of immortality. The resulting achievements of the symbolical impulse are usually great in proportion to the stimulus. All
men are potential artists if they have a creative urge and a selective,
an imaginative or an expressive faculty. Any one of these qualifica-
tions plus a little talent will provide the world with another artist,
in the rough. Many are called but few are chosen. These few are the
most sensitive and subtle of human beings and the most expressive
through their own medium and their own manner of using it. They
are chosen to speak for like-minded men and for those of us who are
interested in other ways of seeing than our own. Now no artist can
speak well save in his own language. The languages of art are as the
sands of the sea, beyond computation. New devices and designs are
constantly being contrived to communicate the ways in which each
artist differs in vision and in touch from every other. Nowadays art-
ist-ways often baffle our understanding until the new code has been
deciphered and we discover the abstract idea or the remote aesthetic
experience for which the curious work of art was the symbol. These
mysteries are worth solving for such comprehension admits the initiated into a world of wider horizons. One is made aware of dormant
delicacies of human consciousness. Dormant instincts for creative
expression are aroused. Amateur dabbling in the arts is an excellent
thing in that it helps appreciation of the artist's difficulties and his
aims. And I can testify that it is a great privilege to live with paintings of many different types, each species brought forth after its own
nature. The collector or the critic who exercises choice and passes
judgment is wise if on the one hand he avoids factional partisanship
and cultivates tolerance, while on the other hand he preserves his
own integrity of vision and of taste, cleaving to that. *Open-mindedness does not require from us neutrality nor even impartiality. The purpose of an open mind is to find one's own way about, avoiding preconceptions, prejudices and all other pitfalls.* It implies a preference for
one philosophy of life or one style of art over the rest after knowing
them all and it requires the selection of the best, that is, the best for
the individual artist and his problem. As Dr. Everett Dean Martin
has written, "When Aristotle sought to know the nature, or kind, of

any class of objects he looked for the most perfect representatives of that class. To know what kind of fruit the apple is, do not pick the stunted and defective specimens of the class, but the best, that which manifest the form most completely. So human nature is really manifest only in the best men."[2] He might have added that art also is manifest in the best artists which in my interpretation means not an average specimen of the kind we like best but the best of every kind, other tastes and opinions being as valid as our own. It is a mixed world and in the periods of its greatest vitality art has indicated the strange and fascinating mystery of conflicting purposes, contrasting temperaments and creative cross-currents, all fused somehow into an evolving cosmos of dynamic contacts and propulsions.

There are so many categories in art criticism that I am always interested in any attempts at simplification. Jan Gordon[3] divided artists into two classes. His first group, which he called Class A, is composed of artists driven by an inner urge, a spiritual force which compels them to find a way of expression corresponding to their great idea whatever it might be. El Greco and Blake, Rembrandt and Daumier, Cézanne and Van Gogh are outstanding examples. The other class, which Gordon calls of the B type, is by far the more ordinary for it contains most of the world's well trained and competent workers in the arts. Often they have amazing craftsmanship and in many cases original genius but the motive is lacking for emotional, humane and therefore moving expression. These B artists must struggle to find ideas sufficiently aglow to ignite an inner fire. With them the struggle is never how to say but what to say. Whereas the artist of the A type, conscious of a lack of executive skill commensurate with his great concept is always talking about technic because that is what bothers him, the Bs are, at their best, distrustful of their own technical abilities and eclectic versatilities and envious of a

---

2. [Everett Dean Martin, *Liberty* (New York: W.W. Norton, 1930), 188–89; quotation emended.]

3. [Jan Gordon, *Modern French Painters* (New York: Dodd, Mead and Company, 1923), 83ff.]

genuine innocence and ecstasy of mind and eye. Henri Matisse, for example, is a brilliant craftsman who sought his own salvation as an artist by trying to become again as a little child. It only taught him how to be a better artist and, in the course of his own re-education in what to eliminate and what to emphasize, he evolved a gay palette and a complex pattern which are as impersonal and coldly sophisticated as the academic realism from which he escaped. Curiously enough he tries to be gay and ends by being even colder than Picasso who tries so hard to be cerebral and impersonal and remains an acrobat—an actor—an Oriental or medieval alchemist. When Picasso forsakes the world of human beings and their emotions for pure abstraction, reverting to his Moorish ancestry and its preoccupation with proportions of colored shapes, one watches him in fascination to see what striking idea for a new fad in art will come out of this conjurer's head. The Bs are usually able to convince almost everyone except perhaps their own secret selves, that they are the greatest artists of their period. It was so with Van Dyke, with Boucher, with Ingres, with Fortuny, Sargent, and Rodin, and now with Matisse and Picasso. Virtuosity runs a course and knows its brie[hour of glory but the individuals who appeal most to us in the end are men of the A type whether they are the most accomplished and skillful craftsmen or not. They are the men who start from life as their inspiration and who work toward art as their means of expression, seeking ever for the finer essence of truth and of their own experience. Their works may be quite abstract yet they are full of feeling because their original source was in nature and in the heart of man. Of a different type are those intellectual and aesthetic craftsmen so much in evidence today who work from the abstract to the concrete, beginning with shapes as the units for a pattern or with a system for division of a space and ending with a picture more or less objective which is often so uninteresting that it would not hold us for a moment if we had not been told that it was produced by some devious process and that it represented profound cerebration. Picasso is a virtuoso, in fact a showman. He in vents highly artificial and sophisticated creations of absolute Form, presenting before our astonished eyes a "metamorphosis of things into symbols;" a transposition of the objective world into the metaphysical world. He is always seeking new ways for art to be a stirring experience and an experience distinct and different from any we have known in life. In the end he is capable of giving to a number of people a passion of enjoyment. Abstractions, cerebral or hyper-aesthetic, often cast a spell. Logical creations of forms in space which call to depths of unused rhythmical instincts within us, offering the added joy of recognizing the cosmic law of order working itself out in a congenial medium, such works of sheer sensibility or of reasoned intelligence are of course art for art' s sake. I confess that I am extremely susceptible to this kind of artistic fanaticism. It is, I believe, in a good cause and has its practical application to the making of new patterns for our pleasure and our use. Yet if I am not convinced that there was a real emotional experience of the artist which gave birth to his method then I am bound to suspect that it was only his method which gave birth to his subsequent emotional experience and ours. That seems to be simply another case of virtuosity and its thrills. The artists who, like a force of nature, are irresistible, are the unself-conscious individuals with something at least of their inner lives to tell, men of feeling who make their art expressive to the degree of intensity. Trial and error, loneliness and self-denial have made their expression poignant. In spite of their sufferings a love of life as it is or as it might be reveals their passion for reality or their capacity for dreams.

Nevertheless, in spite of my preferences and partialities, I hold that a profound respect for different opinions, tastes and temperaments than my own, with no insistence to impose on others my cherished ideas and impressions, would be in me a sign of the finest culture. If only I could rise to it! After all it is only that liberty which is demanded by the intelligence of mankind: John Galsworthy has argued for tolerance in his book *The Inn of Tranquillity:*

> [H]ow poor a business the partisan abuse of any kind of art
> in a world where each sort of mind has a full right to its own
> due expression. [...] He is but a poor philosopher who holds a

view so narrow as to exclude forms not to his personal taste.
[...] For what is Art but the perfect expression of self in contact with the world; and whether that self be of enlightening,
or of fairy-telling temperament, is of no moment whatsoever.
[...] Of all kinds of human energy, Art surely is the most free,
[...] and demands of us an essential tolerance of all its forms.[4]

It is in that faith that I hang and attempt to interpret exhibitions
of established paintings of the past mingled with paintings of the
unproved present and of experimental things by research workers of
today along with modern pictures still steeped in ancient tradition.
Academicians may be startled to find their canvases in close proximity to those by outsiders from the official ranks and to discover that
those outsiders are extremely intelligent craftsmen and not such
outlaws and barbarians after all. And the more radical progressives
may be more or less amazed to see that when hung side by side with
works of what they had been pleased to call respectable mediocrity
their own works seem less original than they had supposed, causing
no serious damage to the other no less legitimate point of view. The
challenge to thought in such a show is immediate and the clarifica-
tion of issues which had been confused by the special pleading of
rival factions is mutually beneficial to the observers and to those
impartially observed. As for the public in this age when quite a few
of art's sign posts point in such an opposite direction from what cautious people had been taught to travel, it is well for them to know that
there is so much daring, so much pioneering, not merely to pass the
time, but to orient oneself in the age and to discover for oneself that
although new roads have been opened for traffic the old roads are
still good. The difference, of course, is that the old roads lead back
persistently and for a long way into the past whereas the new roads
penetrate little by little into the undeveloped and unknown future.
Through mixed exhibitions I for my part learn, and hope in turn to
teach, the meanings of history, the evolution of ideas, the kinship of

---

4. [John Galsworthy, *The Inn of Tranquillity: Studies and Essays* (New York:
Charles Scribner's Sons, 1912), 276–77; quotation emended.]

men of old to men of today, the many-mindedness of every period in spite of the collective consciousness and the imposed conventions of some of them. Men of alien tongue and of no less alien technic can get together on a few fundamental principles such as selection, elimination of non-essentials, emphasis on the expressive part, inter-relation of the various parts to the whole. If, in an exhibition of opposites, the spectators will but open their minds to each work and to each human being back of it, they will come in time to the point of admitting that there can be unity wrought out of a bewildering variety and a fusion of apparently insoluble elements and a harmony coming at last out of discords and an order out of chaos simply through faith in the interlocking possibilities of the fragments. Then the puzzle will turn out to be a picture, the symbol of a world and of a social problem which must deal with individuals in precisely the same way, never demanding that they shall be all alike but forever fitting them into their own places until the goal is at last achieved and the unity and the harmony of art are recognized as the very goal of the soul's adventure.

—◁◈▷—

THE RENTAL PROBLEM
LETTER TO THE EDITOR
OF *THE AMERICAN MAGAZINE OF ART*
(1935)

SIR: I have read with genuine alarm the letters on the "Rental Issue"* by Mr. Francis H. Taylor, Director of the Worcester Museum, and by Miss Katherine Schmidt as Secretary for the American Society of Painters, Sculptors, and Gravers. That there could be a quarrel between artists and museums is cause enough for grave concern! I am on the side of the museums because I believe the artists have taken a stand detrimental to their own vital interests, of serious consequence not only to themselves but to art in the United States.

I wonder if the artists realize that if their works are rented by the museums, while they are being exhibited and offered for sale, they will have had to pass a jury, not of other artists, nor even of the museum staffs, but of trustees who will weigh the comparative rental values on a strictly business basis in order to give the public its money's worth. Who can doubt that the works which the director wishes to invite in spite of the rent will be subjected to cross-examination as to the drawing power, the popularity, or the guaranteed market value of each item? Whether the list will dwindle to a few names triple-starred with sales and surfeited with success, or

First published in *The American Magazine of Art* 28, no. 12 (December 1935): 734, 768–69 ("COMMENT AND CRITICISM"). [In the spring of 1935 the members of the Society of Painters, Sculptors, and Gravers adopted a resolution to establish a general policy of charging a rental fee of 1 percent per month of the price of any work of art to be exhibited with a $1,000 maximum and a $100 minimum for the first month and a ¼ percent weekly fee for the duration of the exhibition to create "economic security" for artists whose "other sources of livelihood have dried up." ("The Rental Issue," *The New York Times*, February 14, 1936).]

* In the *Arts Digest*, October 15, 1935, page 10.

include whatever might excite curiosity and increase attendance, will depend upon whether the institutions minister to a conservative community or to one which likes to be entertained by art as well as by the newspapers and the movies.

I am opposed to the jury system which is now so prevalent and which makes the rivalries and the politics of art so obvious in regard to the works included and excluded and to the prizes distributed by means of diplomatic skirmishes and compromises. I have favored an ever widening invitation list intended to cover the entire field without fear or favoritism, the undivided responsibility for selection of the specific works to be vested in one man, me director. But the change which would occur if rentals of contemporary creations were required would not only make juries of artists impossible but the director himself would become an anxious suppliant for what be needs. It would be the trustees who would see whether a picture was worth its rent.

Mr. Taylor's best points can be condensed as follows: "The legal and moral responsibility of a gallery with public funds to spend is to its public. Museums are incorporated to promote the arts rather than the artist. It must be acknowledged and remembered that the public is interested in other things besides contemporary American painting. It wants to be instructed as to the arts of the ages. The entire exhibition budget for a museum must not be spent for one kind of exhibition only. If the artists insist that they must not only sell their wares to museums but rent them, too, there will be nothing left for the other educational exhibitions which must constitute an important part of the museum's function. In the past, American museums of art have included living artists under the broadest interpretations of their powers."

Outside of New York with its dealers the museums have made it possible for the work of artists to be shown and sold and made known through the press in a way which has given an ever widening circle of artists an ever more expansive horizon of opportunity. Private patronage has followed where the museums have led. Works by unknown and struggling artists have been exhibited which certainly could not have been done if the museum directors had to justify rentals to their trustees. These business men would require that only works by the artists of established reputation could be rented.

To this last point Miss Schmidt replies that the successful men would of course charge more and therefore that they should be the ones omitted in favor of the artists in greater need, whose low prices would also make their works available at rental figures of inconsiderable amounts. Even if the museum trustees, during an emergency like the prolonged depression, should take a broader view of their obligations to art so as to give first and final consideration to the destitute artists, chiefly for humane reasons, and even if ,hey should be rewarded for this by reducing their costs in thus securing low priced pictures only, yet it would remain doubtful whether in more normal times they would permit their curators to rent works of art which, by their low market valuations, would appear to be of little worth. The historical fact that the greatest artists, since the rise of democracy, have had no commercial rating in their own day and have won little or no popular favor is never learned by those who believe that success is the sole criterion of skill and that success can only be measured in money. Since it is a matter of dollars and cents with museums according to Mr. Taylor and with artists, too, according to Miss Schmidt, let the artists be warned that if their demands are granted the standards of the street will prevail. The museums which have recently begun to exhibit generous cross-sections of American painting in all the zest of its significantly varied trends, aiming at least at the best of every kind of art for a many-minded world, would relinquish this fine program to fall back to the safer ground of giving the people what they like, what they have read about, what is either celebrated or safe or saleable. This would mean the omission of much that is important according to art's different scale of values. Whether this will be the result of the shortsighted policy of the artists' union in holding up their best friends, the museums, or whether the hold-up will fail, I am unable as yet to predict. In any case the artists have done themselves no good. Either they must suffer a severe setback in their perpetual and heroic struggle for existence

through the loss of the museums as their mainstay, or else, in forc-
ing their demands upon their friendly patrons, they appear in a less
favorable light than they have ever appeared before. It is possible
that the committee which committed the American Society of Painters, Sculptors, and Gravers to so rash a policy will be surprised at
the number of protests and resignations. Can real artists be union-
ized and herded? I wonder. In any case, the war between logical and
interdependent friends is ever the most cruel and unnecessary war
of all. From the standpoint of practical expediency no less than from
the loftier lookout of idealism, the painters, sculptors, and gravers
have been led astray. At a time like this who can deny that the artists
need the museums far more than the museums need the artists?

DUNCAN PHILLIPS

Director,
Phillips Memorial Gallery,
Washington, D.C.

THE LEADERSHIP OF GIORGIONE
(1936)

THERE have been at least four ways of writing illuminating commentary upon the thirty years of Venetian painting from 1495 to 1525 which include the old age of Giovanni Bellini, the entire career of his pupil Giorgione, and the first period of his other pupil Titian. As I compare the four versions which have been written concerning this delightful part of art history I am not surprised to discover that three dissimilar avenues of approach have led to one meeting of minds where the famous, unsigned, and undocumented landscape with figures in the Louvre, known there as the *Concert Champêtre,* is agreed upon as the outstanding picture of the period. Typical critics of three out of the four types assume that it was the work of Giorgione and so does the Museum catalogue. On the strength of their assumption the critics place him among the greatest artists of the ages. The "expert," however, whose iconoclasm I have chosen as typical of the fourth kind of criticism is beset with doubts which gather over his judgment while he broods in the dusty atmosphere of the archives. As we shall see, I might have chosen a wiser man of this same specialty who would have been glad to agree with the other critics. Louis Hourticq, however, disputes the attribution to Giorgione of what, in the world's eyes, has always been regarded as his greatest picture. The Louvre has stood firm in the faith although the challenging iconoclast is a Frenchman and a member of the Institute. But this able writer's purpose is to deflate what he calls "a Giorgione legend" based on what he thinks was Vasari's conception of a Venetian Leonardo who before be died had invented the emotional use of light and shadow. He knows from his research that Giorgio of Castelfranco died young,

First published in *The American Magazine of Art* 29, no. 5 (May 1936) and reprinted, in an expanded form, in Duncan Phillips, *The Leadership of Giorgione* (Washington, D.C.: The American Federation of Arts, 1937).

that he signed none of his works, and that he painted only four pictures which can be proved as his from old documents. These duly authenticated pictures are claimed by Hourticq to be so reticent in spirit and so different in drawing, in technic, and in substance from the great *Pastoral Concert* in the Louvre that it could not be the same hand. Before we consider his objections to the traditional attribution, let us note briefly the character of the other species of critic and the unanimity with which they stress the importance of Giorgione and of what has been considered his most characteristic creation.

The first approach is that which we know in its earliest Victorian phase through Walter Pater's beguiling essay on "The School of

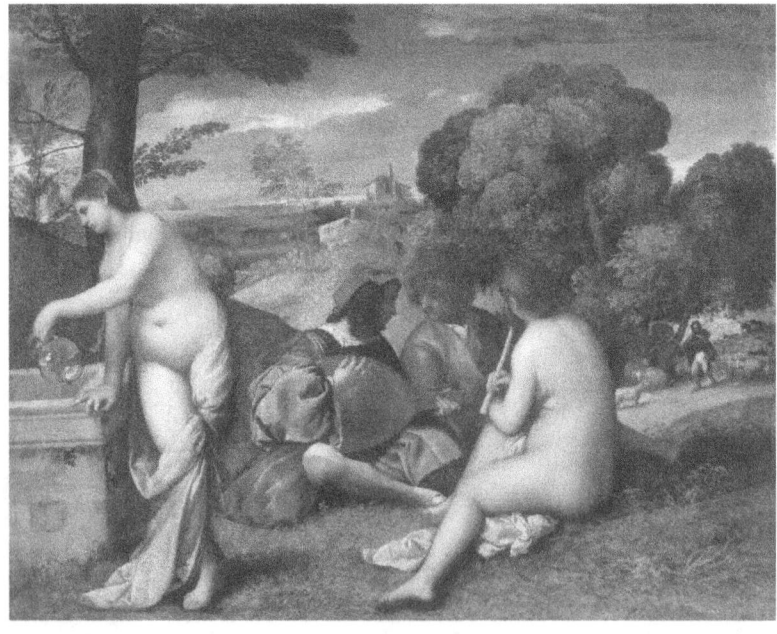

Titian (formerly attributed to Giorgione)
Pastoral Concert (Le Concert champêtre), 1500–1525
Oil on canvas
Musée du Louvre, Paris

Giorgione."[1] The way of Pater was the way of aesthetic contemplation as an inspiration to poetic prose. And yet the critical perception of historical values in this writer is as sound and convincing as if there had been no literary enchantment. Pater noted the beginnings of skeptical research on this subject but remained unperturbed in his confidence that the painter of the two "Concerts" of Florence and Paris was either Giorgione or else an *Anonimo* of precisely the same mentality and character. This man of genius, whatever his name, was the first painter who made nature's evanescent accidents in the visible world a source book of constant reference in the painter's self expression. As the observer of exquisite moments when lines, lights, and colors seem to be one with music, Giorgione required from Pater a tribute of cadenced subtleties of phrasing and of delicate felicities of suggestion. Into the scholar's style as he wrote there came a glamour similar to his theme. A sunset radiance would seen to have been woven into the texture of his words with the same gold thread Giorgio used for his urban and sylvan music makers, for his oak groves and his sheep pastures. A drowsy spell pervades the senses as we read. It is like the imagined sound of water at the well which the golden brown earth-woman pours from her crystal pitcher. A mood is captured like the painter's own nostalgia for the passing hour, his passion for the present moment, his sharp awareness of lights that fade, of Life that is too short a dream. Such transcription of lyric painting into lyric prose was, in itself, criticism of a special kind; imaginative interpretation in terms of sensibility.

The second way to the subject, a twentieth-century development from Pater, interprets the rhythms of history as revealed in the plastic arts, the alternations of synthesis and analysis, of collective functionalism under communal faith gradually replaced in the recurrent cycles by chat emancipated individualism, which, in the Renaissance, extended from the patrons of art to the artists themselves, not merely, tolerating but actually luxuriating in their varied, personal

---

1. [In Walter Pater, *The Renaissance: Studies in Art and Poetry* (New York: Macmillan, 1904), 135–61.]

reactions to environment and experience. The philosophical historian Elie Faure[2] has written of Giorgione and the young Titian that
they were the first to unite in their work all the elements that can
make painting a world of complete expression. Space was an outlet
for the eye and the mind. Color, light, and form were inseparable and
interrelated. Giorgione in his *Concert Champêtre* created "the first
modern symphony." Faure writes with an elaborate sentence structure and with erudite allusions but reduced to their simplest terms
his pages on our period amount to this: the Venetians were joyously
aware of their new freedom and converted their exhilaration into
ecstasy in such subjective pictures as the "Pastoral Concert" by Giorgione. Now both Pater and Faure are regarded as sentimentalists by
the student of painting from the strictly technical point of view, the
true critical analysis of the painter's processes and his problems,
the evaluation of what it means to be plastic on a flat surface. For
such teachers and disciplinarians as Albert C. Barnes there are few
greater periods of painting than the years 1500 to 1530 in Venice.
Giorgione led the way to the structural use of color combined with
light in an all-pervasive color atmosphere which unified the inner
organizations of line and mass. "Giorgione is the one man whose
richness of plastic values makes him a serious rival of Giotto for the
highest place in the hierarchy of art [...] [His color] functions in the
design to the greatest extent of which color is capable of functioning. In the 'Concert Champêtre' [...] the eye cannot rest anywhere
without finding the fullest satisfaction."[3] All this from a difficult and
exclusive connoisseur who has made himself morbidly deficient in
generosity and tolerance and who discounts charm in art, requiring what he calls "a legitimate foundation for poetry in painting"
and even for its enjoyment by the observer. The agreement as to the
greatness of Giorgione by the poet, the philosophical historian, and

---

2. [Elie Faure, *History of Art: Renaissance Art,* trans. Walter Pach (New York
and London: Harper & Brothers Publishers, 1923), 182–89.]

3. [Albert C. Barnes, *The Art of Painting* (New York: Harcourt, Brace and Company, 1925), 172–73; quotation emended.]

the anatomist of design takes it for granted that he and presumably he alone painted the unsigned *Pastoral Concert*. The fame of Giorgio as the painter of one of the world's greatest pictures would surely have been secure if he had only made a practice of signing his canvases and if, in the case of this masterpiece of his last year, be had not gone so far beyond the scope and power of his previous works that the skeptics of the fourth kind of art criticism have not merely questioned but actually denied that he painted it. The archivists are far from being in agreement on this problem. Any of us who know the few acknowledged facts and the special characteristics of mind and hand which reveal co us one or another of the two men involved in this problem, must look again at our beloved pastoral in order to separate what is Giorgione from what is Titian.[4] That they are both to be found on the surface of the picture is as dear to me as the more important Fact that Giorgione and Giorgione alone is there in substance and in spirit.

Several years before I read Louis Hourticq's book *La Jeunesse de Titien,*[5] in which he attributes the *Concert Champêtre,* to his hero, claiming that he began it as early as 1510 and painted on it from time to time until 1530, I had written to Bernhard Berenson asking him if Titian as Giorgione's artistic executor had not gone over the picture in places and at different dates. It was nice to think of Titian as keeping the pastoral near him as an inspiration and I saw his luminous color and his coruscating touch in the lute player whose golden-red garment seems to glow with the same warm glazes we find in the *Entombment*[6] of 1530. I recognized Titian again in the shepherd and his flock of the middle distance. They occur so often and always so pleasantly in his sub-Alpine backgrounds. Berenson replied as follows "When I saw the picture in full daylight, its superiority to anything Titian was doing at the time became at once mani-

---

4. [At the time of the writing of this essay, the painting was thought to be painted by Giorgione and retouched by Titian.]

5. [*La Jeunesse de Titien: Peinture et Poèsie* (Paris: Librairie Hachette, 1919].

6. [1559, Museo del Prado, Madrid]

fest." He urged me to set my mind at rest on whatever the younger master may have added. Even as modern restorations of surface can be recognized so we can detect and discount contemporary retouching by other hands than the creator's. Glazes can make a color scale cooler or warmer than at its origin. But if they leave the structure and design unchanged, we have the same balance and relativity of colors. The mental conception, the structure of design, the ensemble of color and form, these are the elements which reveal the creator's intention. The "Pastoral Concert" is the very essence of Giorgione's life-long intention and it is even more poignantly pervasive in its unique emotional quality than the nobly personal but still traditionally formal Madonna at Castelfranco[7] and the original and inventive but still somewhat primitive *Tempestuous Landscape with Soldier and Gypsy* in Venice.[8] According to Berenson, Giorgione conceived, designed, and executed the greater pact of the *Concert Champêtre* in 1510 just before his last illness. What Titian did to it in later years is interesting but unimportant. That he did something is probable. Fortunately it was not much. "There is," and now I quote Berenson exactly, "There is a touch of heavy rusticity in everything Titian painted up to 1530—always excepting the portraits."[9]

Even if we do not agree that Titian was countrified rather than idyllic in his own pastorals such as *The Three Ages*[10] of Bridgewater

---

7. [*Madonna and Child Between St. Francis and St. Nicasius*, c. 1503–4, Duomo of Castelfranco Veneto]

8. [*The Tempest*, c. 1508, Galleria dell'Accademia, Venice]

9. [Cf. Bernard Berenson, "De quelques copies d'après des originaux perdus de Giorgione," *Gazette des Beaux-Arts* 39 (October 1897): 274: "To those who have not studied the multiple aspects of Venetian art during the first ten or twenty years of the sixteenth century, this phase of Giorgione's genius has remained almost unknown; they have understood so little that...that the main works of Giorgione's great style have been, one after the other, disputed. The *Knight of Malta*, the *Pastoral Concert*, even—absurd as it may seem—the Dresden Venus, whose restitution to Giorgione by Morelli is one of the most memorable feats of modern criticism, have all been called into question."]

10. [*The Three Ages of Man*, c. 1512–14, Scottish National Gallery, Edinburgh. Bridgewater Collection Loan]

House in London, yet it is true that his mind was of a different sort, more obvious in its impressions, more normal, practical, and unimaginative. In this banal though charming allegory of Titian's which he painted about 1512 while less than wholeheartedly committed to Giorgione's arcadianism, there are babies and a very old man and the stump of a dead tree. These ace foils to the amorous dalliance of the bronzed shepherd boy and his little blonde sweetheart who looks up into his face with adoration and unreserved desires. As Mather has written, "nothing could be more explicit."[11] The landscape background of Titian's typical figure compositions is just that, a background, realistic like the people portrayed and inconsequential in any function it may have as an aid to the design or to the expression. In this it compares unfavorably not only with Giorgione's ripe *Pastoral Concert* but with his youthful *Tempesta*. No romance could be less romantic than Titian's *Three Ages* with its *tempus fugit* argument so obtrusively the motive of the picture. In his handsomely colored frescoes at Padua,[12] the scenery is marred by thin, weedy vegetation. The more suave idyll of the following year erroneously called *Sacred and Profane Love*[13] is especially pleasing in its distant glimpses of fauns and village spires, but these two vistas are independent of the figures of the foreground frieze. Titian reveals himself as a neo-Pagan realist, very much at his case in the material universe, and luxuriating in its visual and other physical pleasures. His mind is specific and eclectic, the mind of the average man of well educated intelligence. One feels the difference between his culture and Giorgione's in details such as the outline of a head. Compare the lovely profile of Giorgio's earth-woman at the well in the *Pastoral Concert,* her deep shadowed eyes, sensitive lips, and softly rounded contours, as plastic and generalized as a Greek coin, with what Titian derived from it for his "Venus at the Fountain of

---

11. [Frank Jewett Mather, Jr., *A History of Italian Painting* (London: Stanley Paul & Co., Ltd., 1923), 393.]
12. [1511, Scuola del Santo, Padua]
13. [1514, Galleria Borghese, Rome]

Love" as she leans towards her blonde and bland client with professional advice. The picture in Rome (Borghese Palace) is delightfully
refreshing with its Hellenic symmetries. But the face of the goddess
is only that of a sumptuous model showing one side of her obviously
classic features. The profile is sharply delineated with what seems to
me a second-hand inspiration.

Giorgione could be as epicurean as Titian. But in his celebration
of the pleasures of the senses he reveled in life from the vantage
point of distance, from the poet's and from the painter's point of
view. A blithe and contented detachment successfully avoids the disillusionment of worldliness. His preference for the role of spectator
and his zeal for the art of painting as an end in itself merged with a
fervent and a high-minded idealism.

That pastoral of his at the Louvre which marks an epoch and
which anticipates conscious romanticism and color construction in
modern painting, what else does it all mean? Only perhaps the music
we improvise at picnics, the fun Giorgio had with his lute out in the
fields, his friends in their latest fashions, the pipes of Pan and the
shepherd songs of a simpler age, the sun-browned flesh of country
girls close to the soil, their little classic heads, the great groves of
old trees in their late summer splendor, the last caressing gleams of
evening light, and far away the blue-shadowed mountains. That is
the extent of the subject and it is all quite dream-like and incongru-
ously assembled. The forthright mind of Titian might have made a
good story out of it. But the imagination of Giorgione converts its
sensuous and ambiguous imagery into a universal poem in praise of
peace and all the golden afternoons that ever were, when the heart
is light even as the shadows lengthen, when. in idleness and with no
vain regrets, loving time as it flies, drinking deep of the light while it
lingers, for yet another tranced moment we know the warmth of the
sun before it sinks and all the mellow generosity of the earth.

Hourticq has some small and some large reasons for thinking that
Titian painted this picture. There is a boy's face under curly hair in
a fresco at Padua very like the tousled blonde head of the shepherd

in our concert of the fields, the lad who blends his reeds with the lute of his well-dressed friend from the city. And there is a drawing in the Malcolm Collection at the British Museum,[14] possibly a study for a lost painting, where we are startled to find the seated girl of the Louvre pastoral, the very one who has her back to us and her right knee drawn up to prolong the diagonal line of her left leg and her flute. The pose is identical in the drawing and the compact, plump little model has the same small round head and sloping shoulders. A landscape background which Hourticq was prompt to seize upon for his argument contains Titian's jagged mountain called the Marma-role at Cadore, also some sheep like those which graze and sleep in the sunny meadow of the painting. We arc expected to infer from this that both drawing and painting are by Titian. It is clear to me that this drawing is a frank borrowing by Titian or Campagnola of a detail of Giorgione's masterpiece which was at the center of their thoughts.

Hourticq's dispute with the traditional and all but universal attri-bution of the *Pastoral Concert* to Giorgione depends chiefly upon conclusions which he draws from old manuscripts. Whatever we may think of the so called science of the experts and the reliance upon documents which are likely to be quite as fallible and biased as our own contemporary opinions, nevertheless the thesis of a man of learning based upon thorough research, is not to be taken lightly. Reinforced in our faith with the assurance that Berenson confirms Pater, Faure, and Barnes and therefore that all the critics of every category acclaim the new breadth, power, and intensity of the last period of Giorgione as we know it, not from the *fuoco Giorgionesco* of the early criticism, but from the visual evidence of the masterpiece in the Louvre, it is nevertheless important to hear Louis Hourticq when he refutes Vasari's mention of the fact that the last period was different from the others.

---

14. [1493–1576, British Museum, London]

His thesis is based upon the discovery (by Morelli)[15] of the early sixteenth-century chronicle of a collector and connoisseur by the name of Marcantonio Michiel who from 1525–1575 went to see Venetian private collections and listed the works by Venetian painters. From his records we can only identify with certainty four of the pictures which be definitely listed as "by Giorgione." Privately owned were the *Soldier and Gypsy* still in Venice, the *Three Philosophers* of Vienna,[16] and the *Sleeping Venus*[17] of Dresden. In addition to these three acknowledged authentications in his diaries of celebrated paintings he had seen, Michiel's citations include four other pictures which may or may not refer to less excellent works which we know. The most important of these references is the indirect mention by Michiel as a work by our leader of the now damaged *Christ and His Cross* in S. Rocco, Venice,[18] which makes that picture the fourth documented Giorgione. Two our of the four were recorded as having been finished by Giorgione's assistants Titian and Sebastiano. Hourticq jumps to the careless conclusion that having been left unfinished they must have been late works, examples of his last period. I am inclined to challenge this even in the case of the Venus, and I consider the opinion unsound and misleading in the case of the *Three Philosophers,* or the *Three Wise Men,* as I think it should be called, since it is surely one of the Biblical romances for which he created a demand. The Vienna picture might almost have been painted by Bellini himself as early as 1490. All that is progressive about it is the prominence of the landscape with the figures off at one side. And yet, from this obviously early work, probably dating back in its original execution to the turn of the century, Hourticq argues that since Giorgio painted that static, hieratic calm and those little stones of

---

15. [Giovanni Morelli, *Kunstkritische Studien über italienische Malerei: Die Galerien Borghese und Doria Panfili in Rom* (Leipzig: F.A. Brockhaus, 1890). See also Luke Uglow, "Giovanni Morelli and His Friend Giorgione: Connoisseurship, Science and Irony," *Journal of Art Historiography* 11 (December 2014).]

16. [c. 1505–1509, Kunsthistorisches Museum, Vienna]

17. [c. 1510, Gemäldegalerie Alte Meister, Dresden]

18. [*Christ Carrying the Cross,* 1505, Scuola Grande di San Rocco, Venice]

the foreground with all their evidence of a Quattrocentist mind and technic, leaving the task unfinished at his death, then that was the sort of work be must have been doing up to the end. He could never then have attained to a High-Renaissance breadth, could not even have started the *Sleeping Venus* which Michiel reported as having been merely "finished by Titian."

I am ready to concede that there is much of Titian left in the Venus at Dresden, even now that his cupid, mentioned by Michiel, has been removed. The visual evidence confirms the documents. I recognize that the village of high-roofed houses on a hill appears also in his *Christ and Magdalen*[19] in London, and the copied fragment of a *Cupid on a Balustrade*[20] in the Vienna Academy. And the rectangular mountain of the distance at the left with a low-lying building underneath, is the background for his Gypsy Madonna.[21] But two questions are in order. Were these motifs appropriated later because he felt that he had earned a proprietary right to them in the course of collaboration with Giorgione on the Venus? Or could the *Noli me Tangere* and the *Gypsy Madonna* have originated with Giorgione and been more or less completely repainted by Titian after 1510? The X-ray has proved just that in the case of the Madonna.

The pose of the Venus was copied precisely and line for line in his own Venus of the Uffizi.[22] But what a difference in the faces! I wish that the two countenances could be compared for a while in close proximity so that certain critics could learn the essential and fundamental differences of attitude and character between the two men. In contrast to Titian's open-eyed wanton, the portrait of a courtesan, Giorgio's goddess is an embodiment of an ideal In his first book, *La Jeunesse de Titien,* Hourticq accepted the face of the Dresden Venus and the rock behind her as the work of Giorgione. In

---

19. [*Noli me tangere*, c. 1514, The National Gallery, London]

20. [Studio of Titian, *Sleeping Woman in a Loggia with Cupid* (fragment), c. 1520, Akademie der Bildenden Künste, Vienna]

21. [c. 1510, Kunsthistorisches Museum, Vienna]

22. [*Venus of Urbino*, 1538, The Uffizi, Florence]

his later *Le Problème de Giorgione,*[23] he gives the delicately dreaming *Judith* in Russia[24] to Giorgio while attributing the Venus to Titian in every particular. Now the heads of the Judith and the Venus are so clearly by the same man at approximately the same date, that if Titian painted the *Venus,* then he must also have painted the *Judith.* But Hourricq forgot to put in this claim, and in acknowledging that the *Judith* is a Giorgione, he admitted the weakness of his own idea that the *Sleeping Venus* is a Titian. It is my belief that Titian finished the Dresden masterpiece in 1511. Giorgione had, long before, painted its essentials of linear expression and design—its rhythmical intervals of space and sleep. It is a work of about 1507, when he was in midstream and not at the very end of his short voyage.

The argument of Hourticq boils down to this: Assuming that the last period of Giorgione contained the *Three Wise Men* finished by a pupil, then it could not have also included the Louvre pastoral with its technical breadth and power and its emotional intensity. The *Adulteress before Christ* at Glasgow[25] is recognized as a work of the same time and in the same style as the pastoral in Paris. I agree. Its passionate color, linear movement and general air of excitement are the most striking antithesis we can possibly imagine to the rigidity and calm of the Bellinesque beginnings of Giorgio. The *Three Wise Men* and the *Adulteress before Christ* certainly could not have been painted by the same painter in the same period. But the unique mind of the poet-painter at different periods is I think to be found in both of them; the same subjective conceptions, in one case of dispassionate wisdom and in the other of passionate prejudice and sympathy. It is my belief that the *Three Wise Men* was an early work which Giorgione entrusted to Sebastiano, having lost interest in it himself, and that the *Pastoral Concert* and the *Adulteress* before Christ, are among the very latest works, the pastoral

23. [Paris: Librairie Hachette, 1930.]

24. [c. 1504, State Hermitage Museum, Saint Petersburg]

25. [*Christ and the Adulteress,* c. 1508–10, Kelvingrove Art Gallery and Museum, Glasgow]

essentially finished but the *Adulteress* merely begun in his studio in 1510 and executed in large part by Titian. Warm glazes of identical character, and dating, it would appear, as late as 1530, give to the two masterpieces a striking similarity. They are as clearly the work of Giorgione in his latest phase of development as the *Judith* and *Venus* are the expression of his middle years and the *Tempest* and *Castelfranco Madonna* of his earliest maturity. It is perfectly true that the three documented Giorgiones and the noble, never-questioned Madonna of his hometown all reveal a romanticist of fresh vision and invention and a keen observer of landscape under expressive conditions of light, but not a powerful realistic painter of nature and the human form. It is true that one could not, from these pictures, derive an impression of the revolutionary spirit who, in Ruskin's words, "went down to [Venice]—and became as a fiery heart to it,"[26] nor even of the "Venetian Leonardo" of the old tradition which Hourticq traces to Vasari. They do not give a clear indication that within a few years their maker would change into a painter of great power and intensity. And yet these early works, in their acute sensitiveness, their poignant expression of moods, their evocation of both storm and shine at Castelfranco, and their decorative patterns stir the emotions as even Titian's *Assumption* and his Bacchanals[27] fail to do. Atmospheric effects intensify the experiences of the little people in the pictures, apparently detached from each other in their secret thoughts and unaware of the world and its changing lights, yet all the while exquisitely sensitive to their surroundings. I am thinking particularly of the *Tempestuous Landscape with Soldier and Gypsy,* known in Venice as the *Tempesta.*

It is the most autographic of all Giorgio's autograph works and not only because it is undisputed and documented but because it

---

26. "The Two Boyhoods," in John Ruskin, *Modern Painters,* vol. 5 (London: George Allen, 1897), 315; quotation emended.].

27. [*The Worship of Venus,* 1516–18 and *The Bacchanal of the Andrians,* 1523–24, both in the Museo del Prado, Madrid; *Bacchus and Ariadne,* 1520–22, National Gallery, London; painted originally for the Alabaster Chamber of Alfonso I d'Este, Duke of Ferrara]

really prophesies everything that was coming afterwards, including the two Concerts of Paris and Florence. Mather has suggested that the *Tempesta* is a memory of an event. From what we know of the man, it is more probably an intimate emotional experience of which he was as usual only the imaginative interpreter. A summer storm with ominous thunder clouds reft with forked lightning advances upon a sultry, shadowy woodland where near a waterfall the meeting takes place. A young man stands on guard while a young mother nurses her baby. Their eyes are averted from each other and from the threatening sky. They are together and yet alone. The situation between them seems to be at a moment of crisis. The agitation of the weather is only a contributing factor to what happens at that hour. The inner life is revealed as far more intense than the life of passing circumstance, no matter how acute and dramatic. Even the strange illumination of the town and the sudden darkness down in the woods, the lightning flash in the blue-black sky and the ramparts of Castelfranco gleaming suddenly out of the murky air fail to distract the two young people from their unsolved problem. Romanticism is consciousness of the background. That storm with its corning rush of wind and rain is at the center of consciousness not only of the young man and the young mother but of all of us who are caught up by the emotions of the picture and who feel the significance of its triangular design with active storm in nature at the apex and passive storm in human beings at the base of the pyramid.

Giorgione set the scene and suggested therewith a dramatic situation in suspense. Or else he epitomized, with an ideal symbolic head or group of figures in a landscape, some lyrical state of mind. Then he stopped short of going further. Except in one or two late works, such as *The Adulteress before Christ,* which I think he planned with his dynamic associate Titian already chosen as the ultimate executant, his dramas did not take place. Nor did the mood explain itself with an analysis of the lyrical elements. What seemed to interest him most of all was the theme of spiritual loneliness in a world of human relations where people are intimate and interdependent

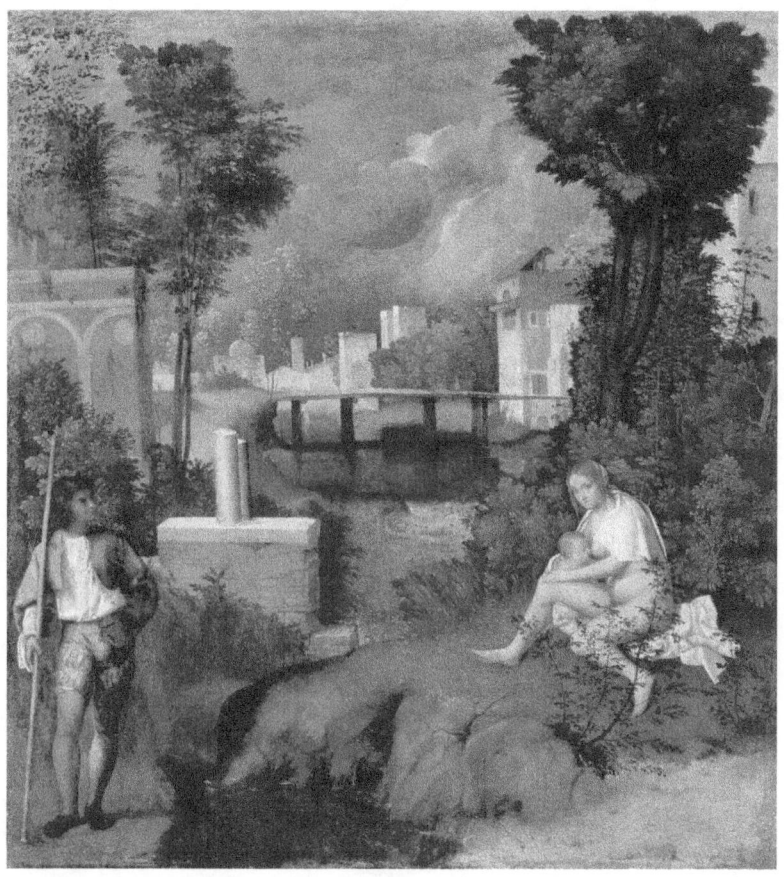

Giorgione
The Tempest. c. 1505
Oil on canvas
Galleria dell'Accademia, Venice

in spite of themselves. He did not grieve over the intellectual isolation which is the inevitable fate of all subjective artists. The age was
tolerant of his reveries and wanted pleasurable little pictures for the
home. Golden opportunities abounded for giving pleasure to others
and to himself with the soul-satisfying music of his symphonic color
compositions, integrated with, and the aesthetic equivalent for, his

[313]

meditations as an observer and his enchanted hours as a dreamer of dreams. Thus his hypersensitive lyricism, tinged ever so lightly with sadness, was cultivated under conditions so favorable to his freedom of introspection and invention that the result was an art of sheer joyousness, and of sensuous as well as spiritual well-being in a beautiful world. All his Life from the *Tempestuous Landscape with Soldier and Gypsy* to the *Pastoral Concert* and *The Concert* at the Pitti[28] he said virtually the same thing. He did not sign his canvases with his name but with his unique spirit and his unique genius for expressive design. No other artist can be mistaken for him if we come to understand the man and his special gifts. His closest associates followed his methods for a while and participated in his projects but without sharing the subtleties of his thought. He valued their intimacy and their aid and assisted them to develop their own artistic capacities of a different kind. Some critics like Hourticq have paid too little attention to Giorgio's consistent guidance of his own constantly evolving style. It was certain that he would change as he grew older, that a mellowness and a strengthening form would have to be found for a maturing and deepening substance. An ever-increasing receptivity to new methods of expression and to ripened reactions from experience led inevitably to his *Pastoral Concert* and its dream of physical sublimation and of peace at the glowing heart of nature.

---

28. [c. 1510, Palazzo Pitti, Florence]

THE DUALITY OF EILSHEMIUS
(1939)

EILSHEMIUS won his accolade at last! Museums have purchased his paintings, visiting foreign authorities on art have recognized him as the authentic genius of a uniquely American style, and now a big book* has been written about him which not only tells his story but settles his account with the world. It does not claim too much for him a some biographer are inclined to do for their heroes, but proposes for him a modest little room of his own among the immortal. All this constitutes earlier recognition and greater fame than ever came to innumerable artist of his caliber who died as they had lived, completely unknown.

The biography of Eilshemius which has just appeared is the work of a writer who has made his name in fiction. His first published story was triple starred in the 1938 collection of the Best Short Stories of that year. Since then, William Schack has been a contributor of prose and verse to various magazines and a freelance critic of the arts. His selection of Eilshemius as a subject for his biographical effort was a fortunate one since it gave him a chance to make a psychological novel out of a true story. It is the tale of a gifted man who was his own worst enemy: a man who had an abnormal craving for celebrity; who would not or could not wait for fame; whose career got off to a bad start because of an almost incredible blindness in the art world of the nineties; who, as his failures continued year after year, resorted to frenzied publicizing of his own talents and, finally, to pathological self-glorification. Thus he repelled the very people whose good opinion he needed. Thus "he forestalled by several decades the recognition that would have come inevitably

First published in the *Magazine of Art* 32 (December 1939).

  * William Schack, *And He Sat Among the Ashes: A Biography of Louis M. Eilshemius* (New York: American Artists Group, 1939).

[315]

to his unique and charming art in painting." Mr. Schack's book has compassionate candor and presents a complete record of the known facts and the private papers of the ill-fated genius he portrays. *And He Sat Among the Ashes* is precisely the work which was required as a source and reference book for all future research work on Eilshemius. Whatever the rank that is finally given to the artist, this volume should guarantee that there will be no further lack of knowledge and of interest in the man. It is to be hoped, of course, that in time the instinctive and inspirational art which was the essential part of him will be estimated on its own intrinsic merits without too much bias or prejudice, according to the personal reaction of future critics. Those of us who cherish his best, his early and middle years, but also the passionate reversions to childhood half hidden in the haunted gloom of his last and most afflicted period, have often wished that a big bonfire could be made, and without too much

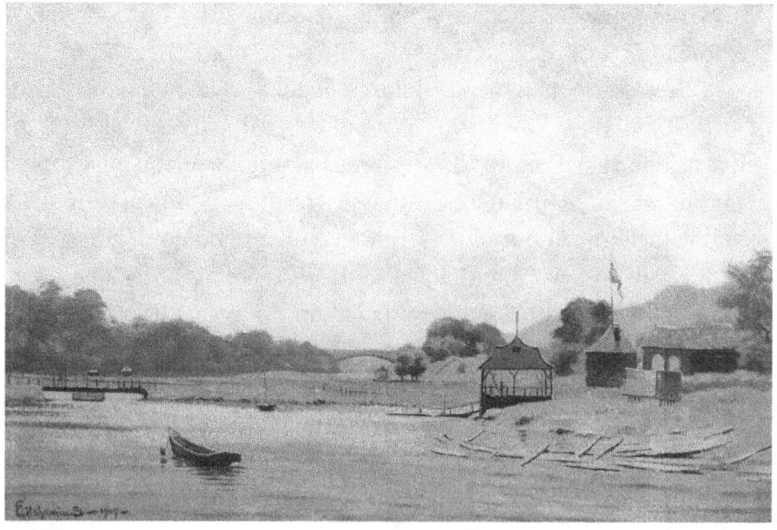

Louis Michel Eilshemius
Kingsbridge, 1909
Oil on paperboard
The Phillips Collection, Washington, D.C. Acquired in 1939

delay, of his cheapest and craziest things. I, for on, would throw the books of puerile verse into the blaze. And while this cleansing and consuming act was being carried out, his well-wishers for posterity would resolve to bear no more, tell no more, laugh no more about all the extravagant claim to supreme greatness. Those excesses of a wounded vanity were clearly symptomatic of a sick man who had yearned too constantly for fame and had been driven mad by total obscurity. As symptoms of the "delusions of grandeur" to which he escaped from his humiliating failures they have their value in the study. When be could no longer paint and while the world continued to look away or to sneer at him, those wild boastings and those fantastic titles conferred upon himself represented his flight into dreamland. All this needed sympathetic and scientific interpretation. Perhaps now that William Schack's narration has told everything, there can be an end to this for the rare enjoyment which his unique art and his naive spirit afford. It make Mr. Schack's tribute to Louis Eilshemius all the more impressive that he has suppressed nothing in his determination to reveal the whole truth. When. after close contact with the worst, the most mawkish lines he wrote, the most clumsy daubs he painted, when, in spite of all this, the critic ranks his man with Ryder, Homer, and Eakins, we can be sure that in the scales of Time his genius at his best will continue to outweigh his grotesque behavior calculated to attract attention. The book is timely. We must be reconciled to it in spite of its compilation of so much we would have preferred to have consigned to oblivion. The record is not irrelevant. It is significant. It carries with it an indictment of man's inhumanity to man. But there is also a warning to artists that they need to acquire an armor of humility and fortitude and that spiritual independence without which the creators of personal whimsy are at the mercy of the most cruel circumstance. If Mr. Schack's book is not only a psychological novel but also a clinical "case history" of progressive mental illness, this is as it had to be. It help us to understand certain contradictions and apparent inconsistencies. We come to know the conspicuous *duality* in both the life and art of Eilshemius.

Since his paintings were alway as spontaneous as birdsong and since all their felicities of observation, of transcription into a chosen scale of values, of dark accents excellently placed, of linear rhythms, and of improvised and descriptive brushstrokes were matters of the moment's inspiration, the critic has had less to say about the art of Eilshemius than about his life, his heredity, his environment, and his experience. It is far easier to write about the men of plan and purpose, the painters of intellect who change their style to accord with their latest taste, who develop progressively, accumulating wisdom and growing in power. Eilshemius possessed a very limited endowment, but apparently he had, even in boyhood, an unlimited ambition. He did not try to enrich his talents and to refine his sensibilities. Consequently, he deteriorated under the trials of discouragement. He had never really submitted to schooling and discipline, even in his promising youth when his wealthy father, the descendant of Dutch pastors, generously supplied him with the means to travel extensively and to study art in Dresden, New York, and Paris. The sheltered egocentric boy confidently dreamed of achieving immediate popularity and acclaim. Although he responded to the immediate influence of the painter Robert C. Minor, he rebelled in art school against the imposed pattern and was stubbornly an individualist, not so much in subject or in style as in unconscious quaintness, unself-critical versatility and inexpert nonconformity. The days before expressionism were intolerant of what were called mistakes in drawing, and they noted with disapproval the little evidences here and there that this man was *different.* They set it down as proof that he was an amateur and a conceited eccentric. Although wanting to stand well with the Academy, the young Eilshemius antagonized that august institution as much by his gauche self-assurance as by his originality and whimsical high spirits. The dualities of Eilshemius are to me the outstanding truth about him which Mr. Schack might have stressed with more explicit analysis. For instance, his paintings may be divided into two period of mature creation; if we can use the word mature for a personality which never really developed much beyond the unripe moods and the emotional values of adolescence. However, there is a marked difference between the picture of 1895 and 1910, when he traveled alone all over the world (returning frequently to paint his favorite American haunts, the Adirondacks, the Delaware Water Gap, the banks of the Hudson) and those done between that year and 1920 when he laid down his brushes in frustrated anger and exhausted imagination.

The lovely and lovable blonde landscapes of about 1905, with their pearly skies, their thinly and directly painted woodland dells or translucent open spaces, their dark and slender trees, and their tiny little people, usually ladies and children, who might have stepped out of some nursery periodical of "the age of innocence," remind us of our own childhood. We recognize the freshness of seeing and feeling which never come again with the same ecstasy as in the year when we were free to play and dream from morning till night. Judging from the photograph on page 7 of Mr. Schack's book, Louis was a winsome little boy when he was eleven. It must have been taken only a short time after the happy days when he romped with his brother Victor on the extensive lawn of their stately home at Laurel Hill Manor. There is a little painting in the Rockefeller Collection of the terraced gardens on different levels, and it is full of the tenderest nostalgic revery. Mr. Stephen Clark's *Croquet*[1] is another idyll of the same type, as is also the *Bridge for Fishing*[2] and the little canvas of children playing in the shallow water on the banks of the Hudson near Newburgh. Sometimes the work of this decade was unintentionally humorous as when he depicted in rich pigments a chorus girl in tights. I remember a little gem by the Eilshemius of the nineties. A Spanish cavalier serenades his señorita in the moonlight and reminds us curiously of the exotic sensation we experienced on first opening a fragrant box of Havana cigars. Sometimes, on a woodland path or in a city park I come upon little children out of an Eilshemius pastoral. That was a theme which recurred throughout his

----

1. [c. 1906, whereabouts unknown]

2. [*Adirondacks: Bridge for Fishing*, 1897, The Phillips Collection, Washington, D.C., acquired in 1933]

thirty years of painting. Mr. Schack makes an important point when be says, "There were hits and misses in his art rather than periods." Early and late the same subjects were chosen, and the same moods returned. The prevailing moods were two. There was the sunlit happy -hearted mood of rural romanticism in which he remembered good times out of doors in familiar places, and there was the mood of weird imaginings or of fantastic conceptions out of books—both variations of one state of mind. If anyone thinks that such subjects were the prerogative of the last tormented years, let him look at the *Don Quixote* of 1895 and *The Demon of the Rocks*[3] of 1901, painted the very year when he voyaged to the South Seas and laid up stores of memories which served him for the finest and most exhilarating work of his career: the *Queen's Family, Samoa*[4] of 1908. The sensational imageries were, of course, more unendurable in his period of decline, when they were subconscious and more or less pathological, than in the early period of literary and theatrical ventures. But the point was worth making that the man had his alternations of morning dew and blasting storm, his oscillations of playful spirit and bitter passion, so characteristic of the manic-depressive type.

"The latest paintings," writes Mr. Shack "are torn between two freedoms, the freedom of the artist at ease in his medium and the freedom of the mind no longer responsible to anyone but himself. The first freedom finds expression in a heightened lyrical vein and is the natural outgrowth of his early work." The *Malaga Beach* of 1915 is composed of subtly varied horizontals and diagonals with the dark silhouettes of sloping masts and sails designed across the harmoniously related tones of blue and tan in the sky, pools, and sand. It is the finesse of a seasoned artist of high talent, the consummation of the admirable patterns of 1908 when he painted the tranquil, luminous *Kingsbridge*,[5] the beautifully balanced and cal-

---

3. [Museum of Modern Art, New York]
4. [*The Queen's Family*, 1908, Parrish Art Museum, Water Mill, N.Y.]
5. [1909, The Phillips Collection, Washington, D.C., acquired in 1939]

ligraphic *Cabs for Hire,*[6] and the dramatic *Approaching Storm.*[7] Even finer perhaps than the beach scene is *The Haunted House*[8] of 1917 which Leo Stein considered the best picture in the American section of the Metropolitan Museum. But with the "second freedom" it became all too evident that the brooding, irresponsible mind had turned in upon itself and would occasionally vent its rage in sickly yellows and greens and in frantic figures symbolizing his despair. There is nothing wholly new, however, in this morbidity, only the degeneration of an old trend. And even the lurid painting entitled *Jealousy*[9] and *Found Drowned*[10] are the logical end result of a recurrent, ever darkening mood which first appeared in the *Don Quixote* of 1895. In 1915, *The Rejected Suitor*[11] combines qualities from each of the "two freedoms." It has a consistent and an apparently deliberate unit of design, reiterated in the ovals of the post-Civil-War chair backs and picture frames, in the young man's derby hat, and in the stern mother's bustle. This organized pattern not only saves the picture from unintentional comedy, but carries its inspiration into a somber tonal scale of olive green, grape blue, and amber. The picture is like an unchangeably perfect scene in a grim and dismal play by Ibsen. It is perhaps the memory of a deep personal hurt, of a rankling humiliation in that musty room, which might have had a determining influence in converting the once debonair Eilshemius into a thwarted, bitter, antisocial crank.

Curiously enough, it was a painting of that late period of disillusion and disgust, a nude entitled *Supplication*,[12] which was found and hailed with delight by the Cubist Marcel Duchamp in an exhibition of the Independents in 1917. This discovery led to Katherine S.

---

6. [1909, The Phillips Collection, Washington, D.C., acquired in 1933]

7. [1890, The Phillips Collection, Washington, D.C., acquired in 1937]

8. [c. 1917, The Metropolitan Museum of Art, New York]

9. [c. 1915, Philadelphia Museum of Art]

10. [*Tragedy of the Sea (Found Drowned)*, 1916, The Metropolitan Museum of Art, New York]

11. [1915, The Phillips Collection, Washington, D.C., acquired in 1932]

12. [*Rose-Marie Calling (Supplication)*, 1916, Collection of Michael Werner]

Dreier and two shows at her Société Anonyme, in 1920 and 1924, to Henry McBride and several hearty, generously appreciative articles acknowledging his previous mistake and ranking Eilshemius just below Ryder and above Fuller and Blakelock, to Valentine Dudensing, and a series of exhibitions in his popular gallery of fashionable French moderns. As Henry McBride truly observed as early as 1924, "expert opinion had to be freed of conventional seeing by many revolutions in taste before it could be expected to feel the genuine, living qualities" in unpremeditated painted poetry which its own generation had despised. The cumulative evidence of a great change culminated in the purchase of many pictures by museums and discriminating private collectors both in America and in Europe. Finally, the art historians accepted him as one of our best romantic artists. Shorty after that, the old painter was knocked down by an automobile and confined to his chair for the rest of his life. His rescue from oblivion might have occurred in time to give him some pleasure and to cure him of his now incurable habit of scolding the world if only he had sent to the Independents his lovable and skillful early landscape instead of his barroom nudes and melodramas!

The biographer's often repeated question in his book can be condensed to read, "What on earth was the matter with the Academy juries?" For many years they turned away from their halls of mediocrity those early lyrics of light and color and perfect atmospheric values which are worthy of comparison with George Inness and even with Corot, especially the early Corot. The Academicians had found something *different* and that is always a matter for grave suspicion. Perhaps they did not like the anticipation of modern shortcuts to expression in those simple and blonde, but mellow and sweetly old-fashioned pictures. There have been several explanations, none better than that of Henry McBride. Mr. Schack quotes it with only partial satisfaction: "The artists' ideas, feelings, and manners were hopelessly American at a time when American artists were struggling to be European. There was nothing fashionable in poor Mr. Eilshemius." His Venus was "faded, dingy and countrified" compared with the Venus of Paris. He had none of the virtuosity of Sargent and Chase, winners of instant success in their generation. His place was with the failures, with Ryder, Fuller and Blakelock, the seers, in their rare moments of exaltation. But Mr. Schack points out that although Blakelock was a tragic failure, the solitaries, Ryder and Newman, had a few devoted friends and patrons, and they were strong men and needed and expected only a little praise. Eilshemius had no sponsor at all, and he was helpless in the world and needed celebrity. His great expectations for himself and his total failure were crushing to a mind debilitated from the outset by self-deception. Sensitive people have told me that the signs of latent queerness even in the exquisite sunny landscape of the youthful Eilshemius. I have asked them what the signs might be and they speak of insistently dark accents in the midst of values more accurately observed. Or perhaps, they point out in the middle distance a child that is too diminutive in scale or a curious effect of amateurish drawing and uncouth conception in an otherwise expert and civilized painting. But no, they were only innocent and inconsistent, those early pictures. The were never even incipiently insane. Such impish conceits as the *Vaudeville Frolic*[13] were more whimsical than mad, and even the earlier *Demon of the Rocks*, which is quite delirious and horrific, is only a child's nightmare. In my opinion, the duality of the man was responsible for his many rebuffs by his profession. His baffling unexpectedness and irregularity were more than the academician could tolerate. His personal quality was too new and various and variable. He was either lazy or crazy or both, and this was not to be encouraged. It was not done at the National Academy of Design.

Long ago, Forbes Watson summed up the enigma and the essence of the Eilshemius fascination as follows: "The strange intangible spirit of the pictures arises from their combination of reality and the spirit life...His unconscious instinct prompts him when his painting

---

13. [*Vaudeville*, 1909, Philadelphia Museum of Art]

is good. When consciousness comes in, he is lost. He is a mystery. His achievement is as the gods please."[14]

Today he sits in a chair close to his bed with his back to the light. His legs have been crippled by his accident. He cannot go out on the street where only a block away from his door there are two exhibitions of his work in progress at the same time. His dual states of being continue to oscillate. If he has been incoherently abusive, he will soon be limp and gentle. There are quiet moments when he is not in ferment, "quiet hours too when he sits still, moving his head a little like a bird on a twig, for no reason at all but to show a sign of life. He has these quiet moments, not only when he is alone, but also when the visitors are familiar. Then he reminisces gently, even voices his resentments gently. He can smile a shadowy smile, brokenly echo his youthful chuckle. Behind the ghost one sees for an instant the high-spirited young man and one feels the tragic justice of his complaint, "Why didn't people come to see me when I was forty?" But now they do come, mostly dealers to buy his pictures *en bloc* with an eye for their rising values. He lack money now for his daily needs—now when he is famous—now when his works hang in carved frames on the walls of great museums! He was really rich once and traveled every where but that was when the world shunned him and his canvases collected dust in their disrepute. It is little wonder that William Schack thought of Job for his title. To be sure, the Book of Job had a happier ending. But that title for Eilshemius was not bad. "And he sat among the ashes."

In one of the latest painting by Eilshemius,[15] he symbolically depicted himself as adrift, all alone, in a fragile bark rushed along by the fierce current of wild, rapid water which swirl around and around an island under a witching moon. It is a symbol of all futility and frustration under the tantalus of beauty and romance. It tells of his endless effort to land on the island of desire. Today he should not

---

14. [Quoted in Schack, 263.]

15. [*The Dream*, 1917, The Phillips Collection, Washington, D.C., acquired in 1936]

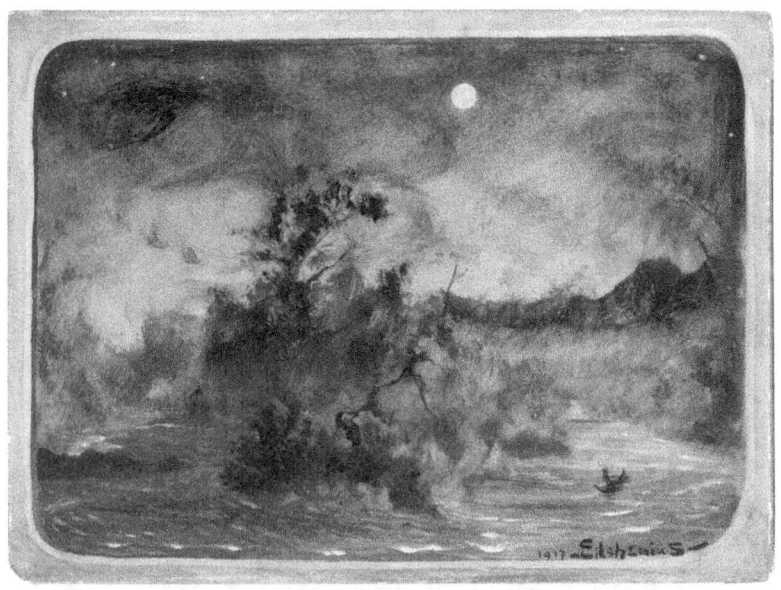

Louis Michel Eilshemius
The Dream, 1917
Oil on cardboard
The Phillips Collection, Washington, D.C. Acquired in 1936

feel that way about his life. For all his heartaches past and present he has painted enough good picture to make good with posterity. His fame came too late and his happiness never came at all, but let him take some comfort if he can in the thought that his pictures will give pleasures to generations yet unborn.

—⁓—

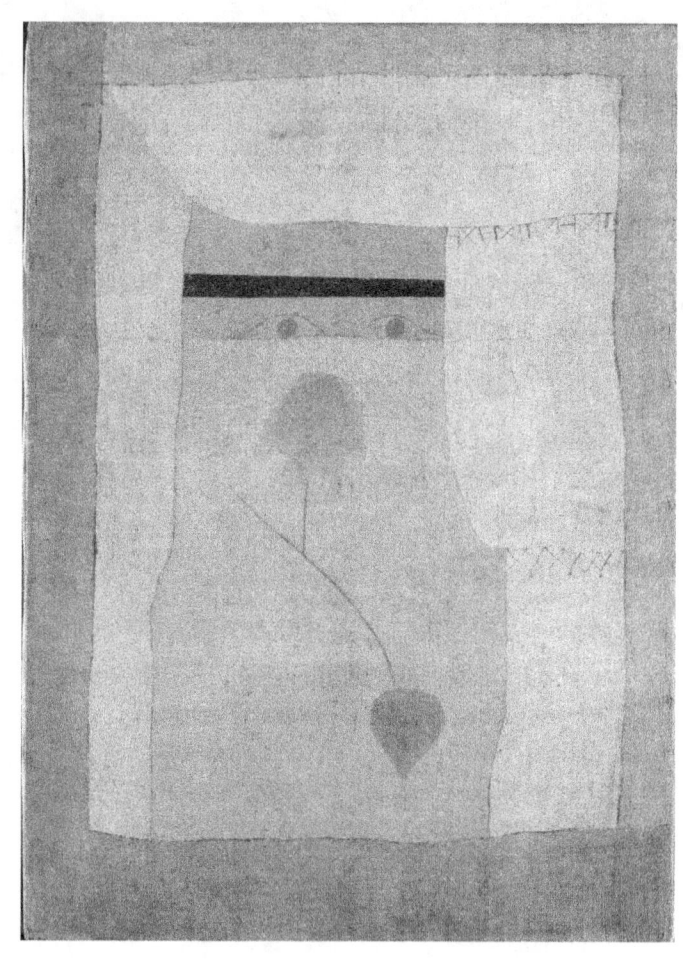

Paul Klee
Arab Song, 1932
Oil on burlap canvas
The Phillips Collection, Washington, D.C. Acquired in 1940
© 2022 Artists Rights Society (ARS), New York

PAUL KLEE

(1942)

PAUL KLEE was born in Switzerland in 1879. Both of his parents were cultured and musical. His mother was French. His father was a German-Swiss orchestra conductor. Paul studied in Germany because he loved German music and fairy tales. There he joined a group of searchers in the arts who called themselves the Blue Riders. They sought "to externalize the inner life". In 1920, the architect Walter Gropius called Klee to his famous and advanced art school, the "Bauhaus" to teach design.

From childhood he was a dreamer, a poet, and a brooding rebel. He refused the compulsion of the imposed pattern, the cultivation of intolerance and the worship of brutality. Always an alien in a nation poisoned by inhuman ideology he was exiled by Hitler and died in Italy, after taking what comfort he could from the inexhaustible resources of his own creative invention.

James J. Sweeney, in his Introduction to the new Oxford Press monograph on Klee, begins his essay with the inevitable sentence "Klee is a painter to be read as well as to be looked at."[1] In this he was of the Oriental tradition. The basic compositional character of Oriental and particularly Arabic art is its calligraphy, its ornamental line which may or may not be symbolical but which is always a movement-a continuity. Furthermore, like the arts of both the Near and Far East, the art of Paul Klee reflects not the world of nature but of man's imagination. To the child's make-believe Klee had more kinship than to the sophisticate's "let's suppose." Keeping fresh within himself the wonder and play instinct of the little child he matured it for a magic

---

First published as the Foreword to *Paul Klee: A Memorial Exhibition*, Phillips Memorial Gallery, Washington, D.C., 1942.

1. *Paul Klee*, edited by Karl Nierendorf, with an introduction by James Johnson Sweeney (New York: Oxford University Press, 1941).

alchemy, rich not only in textures but also in unobtrusive science and erudition. His technic had to do with ingenious relations of lines and colors and with the exploitation of the accidental characteristics of the surfaces on which he painted.

This virtuosity in craftsmanship was Klee's instrument for conveying suggestions of the stream of consciousness and for expressing a poignant awareness of the strangeness and sadness of life. Whimsy and a fine sense of nonsense relieved the all-pervasive melancholy of his mind and the irony of his comments on modern man"s confusions and pretensions. His art led his followers into a beguiling place—just around the corner yet impossible to find without his guidance. Startled as we are at first by the atmosphere of grotesque witchery in Klee's dreamland, we linger to enjoy the truly wonderful simplicities and the exquisite refinements of mind and hand.

No art could be more personal than the art of Klee. This private individualism, fervently on the side of the angels, was no doubt what seemed so dangerous to Hitler. And yet, paradoxical in every way— Klee could be and has often been mistaken for a detached dabbler in useless experiments—a self-sufficient obscurantist in an ivory tower. In Klee, the fine art of painting was not too proud to "bend to itself" the lesser art of weaving and the delights of antiquarianism and of connoisseurship. This he could do without loss of wonder and surprise and without missing the chance of "kissing joy as it flies." Thus he, too, could "live in eternity's sunrise" with Blake and the other mystics. For if Klee was in his element in a museum full of fragments of archaic design, he was even more happy and responsive in an aquarium watching the fish or in a colorful garden loving the birds.

THE AMERICAN PAINTINGS
OF THE PHILLIPS COLLECTION
(1944)

I believe fervently that art is international, a universal means of expression extending across boundaries and overcoming the barriers of trade, race, and language. There has never seemed to be a time when our Gallery was willing to devote all of its unfortunately limited space to either American or European paintings. We have always had loan exhibitions and we have always had rooms in which the pictures have been grouped according to instructive contrasts or affinities without specific references to national labels. We have felt that the distinctions in our painters both of the past and of the present, gain in significance by being mingled and compared with what is best in the painters of other lands.

It is a fact too little known that the bulk of our Collection consists of American paintings. Now and again it may be wise to review what we are assembling. But it is a special event, this exhibition. Our American paintings will hang on the walls of all our galleries and give some idea of the scope of our interests and the character of our choices, but we regret that not even all of our space will be sufficient. A few substitutions will be made during the exhibition. Certain pictures in the catalogue will have their "alternates." However, not even this expedient will enable us to show everything.

It should be noted that George Washington University is holding during the same period a large exhibition of our mystical decorations by Tack, that our Jacob Lawrence panels[1] are on a nation-wide circuit, that the Museum of Modern Art in New York has also borrowed what

---

First published as the Foreword to *The American Paintings of the Phillips Collection* (Phillips Memorial Gallery: Washington, D.C., 1944. Exhibition catalog).

1. [*The Migration Series,* between 1940 and 1941, 60 panels split between The Phillips Collection, Washington, D.C. (odd-numbered panels) and the Museum of Modern Art, New York (even-numbered panels), acquired in 1942.

[329]

is perhaps our best Ryder, the *Moonlit Cove*,[2] and that Prendergast's unique *Ponte della Paglia*.[3] Sloan's masterpiece *In the Wake of the Ferry*,[4] and Davies's famous picture *The Flood*[5] are touring the country in an exhibition of "The Eight" which reassembled the canvases submitted by the painters as a group to their first exhibition in New York.

I am not yet ready to draw a line of definite demarcation between the paintings which will constitute the Gallery's Permanent Collection of Americans and those which may some day be exchanged for other examples or given to other Institutions. We have what we call an "Encouragement Collection" for which we purchase freely and constantly. It consists for the most part either of promising beginnings or experiments which we endorse. No doubt this exhibition contains pictures now in those categories, which, in a not too-distant future, will no longer be questioned. Only time can tell which ones they are. Most of our American Old Masters, for example Whistler, Homer, Ryder, Eakins, and Twachtman, can be said to have passed the stage of being on trial, and this is true of at least a considerable number of our contemporaries. Although our minds, like our doors, are always open, yet we must keep on questioning our choices.

Incidentally, we derive great satisfaction from the work of the graduates of our own art school and the painters of our own city. If the Washington-Baltimore region is better represented than any other that is natural and as it should be, although we take no part in promoting group pressures and definitely do not admire an attitude among artists of self conscious regionalism.

American art is only attaining to its maturity in being as free and hospitable as America itself. This has become increasingly true since the start of the second world war in Europe. Celebrities of our Col-

---

2. [1880s, The Phillips Collection, Washington, D.C., acquired in 1924]

3. [c. 1898, reworked 1922, The Phillips Collection, Washington, D.C., acquired in 1922]

4. [*The Wake of the Ferry II*, 1907, The Phillips Collection, Washington, D.C., acquired in 1922]

5. [c. 1903, The Phillips Collection, Washington, D.C., acquired in 1924]

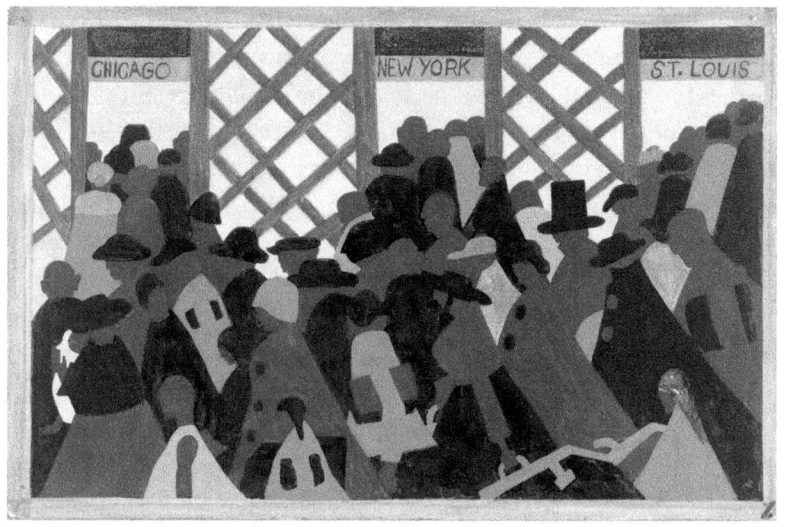

Jacob Lawrence
The Migration Series, Panel No. 1: During World War I There Was a Great Migration North by Southern African Americans, between 1940 and 1941
Casein tempera on hardboard
The Phillips Collection, Washington, D.C. Acquired in 1942
© 2022 The Jacob and Gwendolyn Knight Lawrence Foundation, Seattle/
Artists Rights Society (ARS), New York

lection (Eugene Berman, for instance) who had entered it a few years ago as Europeans have since become American citizens. Recently naturalized Americans from Russia, Hungary, Romania, and Spain are included in the present exhibition. Now more than ever before, American art means international art, and the studios of our Cosmopolis can help us in the necessary task of growing world-minds for our manifest destiny. In our country there is bound to be a fusion of various sensitivities, a unification of differences. We can afford to blur the clearcut edge of our creative colloquialisms for the compensating benefit of shedding some of our provincial self-satisfactions. Our art, like our national aim, can point the way to a new world of neighborly citizen states in which unity in variety and interdependence are taken for granted.

In this brief word of introduction there is no need to write even a condensed opinion on the state of American painting today. Nor is this the place for an outline history of the changes in our reactions to influences from older cultures. Suffice it to say that instead of the exaggerated humility as to our standing as artists which prevailed more or less from 1870 to 1930 (and especially perhaps in the 1920s when we were discovering the distinction of our brilliant French contemporaries) and instead of the widespread reaction in the Thirties, with its aggressive chauvinism which propagated the "American Scene," instead of these opposite extremes of adolescent nationalism in art, we are now assimilating worldwide aesthetic ideas regarding them as our heritage. All the world contributes to our spiritual and creative resources since all the world is contained in our Unites States. Realism, romanticism, classicism, impressionism, expressionism, and various phases of abstract constructivism—we have practitioners of all these points of departure and these ancient seeing habits.

In the Phillips Memorial Gallery, we propose to continue selecting what we consider good examples of the recurring manifestations of art's perennial many-mindedness. Although functional and organic design may seem to emphasized now as never before in accordance with the scientific and technological trend of our times, nevertheless as artists have seen and felt in the past so they will continue to see and to feel. Even if there could ever be a wholly collectivized and mechanized world, even in such an inconceivable society, Art, in its most essential social function, would endure as the expression of the Individual and of his kindred spirits.

—◦∿∿◦—

GEORGES BRAQUE
(1945)

GEORGES BRAQUE was born at Argenteuil near Paris in 1882. His boyhood was spent at Le Havre. There he found an art school which however had less influence on his career than the proximity of the sea and his memory of his first aesthetic experience in sharing the preoccupation of his parents and their environment while at work. They had a shop for art materials. His father was a house painter skilled in decorative lettering and in the imitation for commercial uses of the grain of wood and the vein of marble. This youthful interest had a formative influence upon the discovery and development of Braque's mature style similar to Renoir's early apprenticeship to porcelain and Rouault's to stained glass.

In the first years of the new century, Braque was an impressionist and a pointillist. In 1906, he had joined Matisse, Derain, Dufy and the other Fauves. This association, although for him a step in the wrong direction, linked him with pictorial innovators who were determined to stress functional uses of the elements of design. By 1909, Braque had tried his hand at seascapes, landscapes and figures, which revealed the study of Cézanne's mutually related planes and his famous sayings about the geometry in nature. Matisse noted at an exhibition that Braque's trees and ground forms were stated in cubes, a remark which led to the consciousness of a new ism, cubism. Braque and Picasso then proceeded to a disciplinary practice in diagramming planes. They dreamed of new symbols for the pictures of the new age. First there was the idea of extending Cézanne's "little sensation" into an abstract conception. Then came the rough-hewn many-faceted block, to mark on the picture plane all the dimensions of space—next the almost colorless edifice of modulated and rectilinear planes with a curve or two, or a letter or two, as foils—next an

---

Excerpted from an essay in *The Nation's Great Paintings: George Braque*, a pamphlet published by Twin Editions, New York, in 1945.

arrangement of cards tip-tilted and overlapping on a background no deeper than the surface of the canvas. Texture contrasts were gradually permitted as an enrichment of surface and a new innovation. Real fragments, actual odds and ends were inserted. Ultimately this "collage" would lead to a variety of painted surface effects.

In 1914, Braque was interrupted by the outbreak of the first world war just as he was arriving at the real starting point of his personal style. After being severely wounded and restored by surgery he returned to his easel and revealed at once the same creative purpose as before the war, but now clarified and with craftsmanship almost instantly at concert pitch.

From 1918 to 1930, Braque painted the outstanding decorations of his age. His influence on applied design spread from France around the world. He had evolved a curvilinear rhythm sometimes simple, more often complex. No longer restrained from rich sensuous painting he stylized bowls, and goblets, mandolins and guitars, fruits and flowers, and a few monumental nudes, and *décors de ballet.* It was the best style in Europe during that interval between the wars when

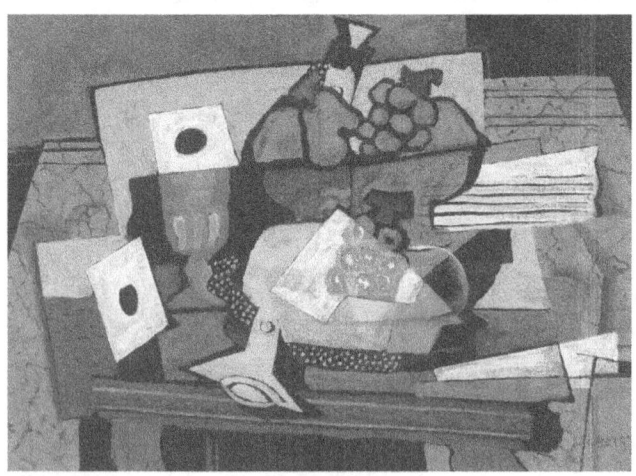

Georges Braque
Still Life with Grapes and Clarinet, 1927
Oil on canvas
The Phillips Collection, Washington, D.C. Acquired in 1929
© 2022 Artists Rights Society (ARS), New York / ADAGP, Paris

epicurism flourished for a little while and when cubism finally justified itself by producing works of art at once architectural and lyrical. There has seldom been more subtle color in painting and certainly never logic more charming.

The adjective lyrical is always needed to describe the artfully balanced and unquestionable relations of color and form in the best paintings of Georges Braque. There is poetry in their painterly appeal both to the senses and to the mind. By the time he had found his true course he had resolved to be content with limited means, believing as he did that "the limitation of a method secures its style while extension of methods in art leads to decadence." He trained himself for a life work as an artisan, a master craftsman in the great classic tradition of "nothing in excess." He would be both a builder and a stylist. He would make so sensitized and subtle a use of technical means that his art would be pure self-sufficient creation, a proof of what he called "the pictorial fact." It cannot be denied that, no matter how acceptable his aesthetic, the secret of the unique pleasure he was able to give was due less to doctrine and certainly less to formula than to his own distinguished sensibility. He belongs to the family of great French painters who mastered their instruments because they were born for them.

In the twelve years of his finest and most personal achievements, almost every picture Braque painted was a masterpiece of geometrical arabesque. Generally the angles of his earlier cubism had been subordinated to rhythmical curves and the severe limitations formerly imposed on his palette had been modified, not so much by addition of many new colors as by enrichment of the same ones with sanded, color saturated surfaces and with luminous pigments of the most surprising subtlety and harmony. There were canvases in which luxuriant shapes and tones gleamed in dappled light and shade. Yet even in this curvilinear period which was really a new Baroque, some of the finest works were consummations of the austere experimental diagrams of about 1912–14.

ARTHUR G. DOVE, 1880–1946

(1947)

THE significant fact in the uneventful and important life of the late Arthur G. Dove is that, after his 27th year, he renounced a career as a successful illustrator to paint in ways unprecedented among his fellow countrymen and different from anything that had been done or was later to be done in Europe or America. So profound was his conversion to non-objective lyricism as a new language for painting in which he hoped to express his inner self that he was spiritually ready to endure any hardship and make any sacrifice in order to paint as he pleased. Dove in 1908 was a discoverer, for his own need and as a pioneer for his country's progress, of a new freedom for imaginative design, He became a rebel against the preconception, still prevalent in American art schools and formidable, at the time, in his father's attitude, that realistic representation is the only excuse for any artist. Compelled to support with farming, etc., his own creative experiments, he resolved to live in rural solitude where living costs were low. The soil attracted him, seemed to call him home. The forms in nature could be his dictionary, The spirit which can emanate from material substance could be his goal.

While he sought for abstract equivalents to the character of his immediate environment and of the objects of his everyday experience, the trend of the abstractionists, both in Europe and in New York, was towards analysis and logic and the functioning of the pictorial elements as if they were mechanical parts. Systems were thriving. A decorative geometric style was in the making. For his own personal reasons, Dove had become a hermit, far from the changing fashions and fluctuating theories of the art world and its gregarious confusions. It soon was evident to him that he was destined to be an independent alchemist He would compose with the music of colored

---

First published in *The Magazine of Art* 40 (May 1947).

shape He had found a new direction. Ever so many Americans were following where he had led. The abstract was now a thoroughfare for fashionable traffic. But there was for him a less traveled trail—the way of caprice and fantasy contained in unliterary form and color. In the history of our period in painting he will be remembered as one of the few great individualists among the many contemporary painters of abstraction.

Arthur Dove had such a genuine love for the farm, its tools, its sheds, its animals, its soil, its seasons that one would naturally assume that he had been a country boy and the son of a farmer. That is only partly true. His father owned a farm near Geneva, N.Y., but he also owned a brickyard and city real estate. He was a conservative business man who expected his boy to get along, to make money. Since he had drawn pictures at the age of seven, he could earn a good income as an illustrator. Arthur went to Hobart College for two years and finished at Cornell, graduating in 1903. Illustrating for magazines seemed to him the best compromise between his taste and talents and his father's will to have him succeed. Success was easy. From 1903 to 1908 he contributed to *Collier's, McClure's, Judge,* the old *Life,* and the *Saturday Evening Post,* and was rated one of the best in a period when the illustrators were famous and prosperous. One of his closest friends was Alfred ("Alfie") Maurer, son of the Louis Maurer who drew race horses and fire horses for the Currier and Ives prints. Alfie had parental encouragement to become a professional painter and after studying with William M. Chase, won first prize in 1900 at the Carnegie Institute, Pittsburgh, with a good example of his teacher's admiration for Whistler. On a visit to Paris, young Maurer saw the work of Matisse and from that day he revolted against the twin tyrannies of tradition and of the too easily achieved success. So it was to be with Arthur G. Dove. He also went to Paris and saw the moderns. That was in 1907 when Matisse was at the beginning of his best period. Arthur B. Carles and Maurer were with Dove during that exciting time of discovery, self searching, and sudden conversion. Of the three, only Dove was able to detach himself promptly from the exciting European innovations. In 1910,

Alfred Stieglitz, looking about for young American painters who were unafraid of change and unstandardized in their nonconformity, assembled for exhibition a group which included along with Maurer and Carles and Dove, John Marin, Max Weber and Marsden Hartley. Two years later, in 1912, Dove had his first one-man show at the famous little experiment station entitled "291." His works were already abstract in character, and Arthur Dove's father was even more furiously disapproving of his son's apparent madness in giving up illustration for abstraction than Alfie Maurer's father had been when his prize-winner son turned deliberately into an obscure eccentric. But Alfred Stieglitz afforded a haven for the disinherited followers of the gleam. From 1912 to 1946 Dove had a yearly opportunity to show his work at Stieglitz's various galleries, successively at 291, the Intimate Gallery, and An American Place. The old impresario was a loyal and devoted admirer and a steadfast supporter of Arthur Dove to the very end.

The reason that Stieglitz persisted in his sponsorship of Dove in spite of the obstacles and discouragements he encountered in trying to make him appreciated end understood was precisely the fact that he found in him a rugged American quality of integrity and independence. Dove had something of his own to say and he was not only unafraid of change and wholly unstandardized, but courageous enough to be different from the other moderns and so personal as to discourage standardization. Not being a follower himself, he would disapprove of a following. Yet he could outlive the fashions if he remained consistent in his self-development and strong in the faith. My own discovery of Dove about 1922 was important in my evolution as a critic and collector. I had the writer's usual weakness for painters whose special qualities could be interpreted and even perhaps recreated in words. Fascinated from the first glimpse by Dove's unique vision in which the homemade simplicity of a countryman was combined with sophisticated subtlety and distinction, I then learned that l was being attracted to an artist because he was strictly yet sensuously visual, one who probably would resist all my efforts to interpret or even wholly to understand him. Perhaps he did not fully

understand his own inwardness but felt a compelling urge to interpret nature in terms of his more or less playful devices and technical inventions. One could not analyze him. He was no diagrammatic
designer. He was to whimsical that he would be embarrassing not
only to the literary critics but to the painters and teachers of painting who deal in theories and group movements, in demonstrating or
being demonstrated, in classifying or being classified. Dove in later
years talked about triads of color and "special conditions of light."
Some tones were light-reflecting and some were light-absorbent.
Mat surfaces could be rich and sensuous. There was the earthy,
the elemental, to be enjoyed in paint and yet somehow subtleties of
modulated color were fascinating and not to be thought inconsistent
with a passion for happenstance and the accidents of light, time, and
weather, All this was a painter's thinking—not that of a geometrician
or a showman.

Dove's whole life changed when in Paris he discovered that the
potentialities of abstract patterning would enable him to create painterly equivalents to the intrinsic character of objects—each visual perception a challenge to a lyrical metamorphosis, in which the essence
of nature's reality would be related to himself in a fantasy of color
shapes merging the external object with a personal, indefinite mood.
It may have been years later that this single-minded aim become
clear to the artist, but in 1908 when he returned from Paris he felt
free to start his experiments, his working from the object inward to
an expression of himself, a sensuous experience, instead of from
an imposed pattern or theory outward to a coded stylization of the
object, an intellectual exercise. It has been correctly said in criticism
of Dove that he never changed very much once his course was set and
his independence declared and his workshop duly isolated. That is
true but it was not his weakness. It was his strength. There was time
for insight in solitude and a great capacity for growth in the man as he
worked with his hands, assisted by his wit and guided by his inner eye,
inventing new configurations, experimenting with and perfecting the
reflecting or the mat surfaces and the unified or the contrasted textures. Of what he had seen in Paris, much was immediately discarded

as of no use for him. Matisse, for instance, disappears as an influence after that first picture of a lobster[1] which Stieglitz included in the group show of 1910. In his solo appearance of 1912, the best pictures were the pastels containing vaguely distinguishable objects in earthy shapes and all-over patterns. Already he had settled on a farm and resolved to make it his first research laboratory, remote from the city's varieties of attraction and distraction, really close to nature and the elements. His first two years of exhibiting had been for him a time of embattled controversy. Dove's work was shown in New York and Chicago and attracted more critical attention than it did in his later and greater years. He was seeking to explain what he was driving at and his talk was inclined to be more wordy than clarifying. He only began to make himself clear when, from 1912 to 1918, still in pastel, he referred humorously to cows and goats and farm implements, suggesting animal hides and rusty metals, ferns and leaves, and water tumbling over rocks. Then came the period of collage. It was while lie lived in a houseboat on Long Island. Braque and Picasso had shown the way with their arrangements of sandpaper and playing cards and newspaper clippings and strips of cloth or linoleum, "under the assumption," in the words of Jerome Mellquist, "that anything can be material to the painter." Such insistence upon the object clarified Dove's own pursuits.[2] What he wanted for himself was a painter of substance evocative of his rural or, for a while, of his waterfront existence. His raw materials would contain not only pigments and canvas and panels but sand, moss, weathered sails and wood, rusted iron, the animals of the pasture and the barn, the wild life of the fields and the air.

In the Museum of Modern Art one stops in pleased surprise before Dove's *Grandmother,*[3] a portrait achieved with a sample of her needle work, a page from her Bible, a flower and fern pressed within, and shingles from her old house.

---

1. [*The Lobster,* 1908, Amon Carter Museum of Art, Fort Worth, Texas]

2. [*The Emergence of an American Art* (New York: Charles Scribner's Sons, 1942), 365; quotation emended.]

3. [1925, Museum of Modern Art, New York]

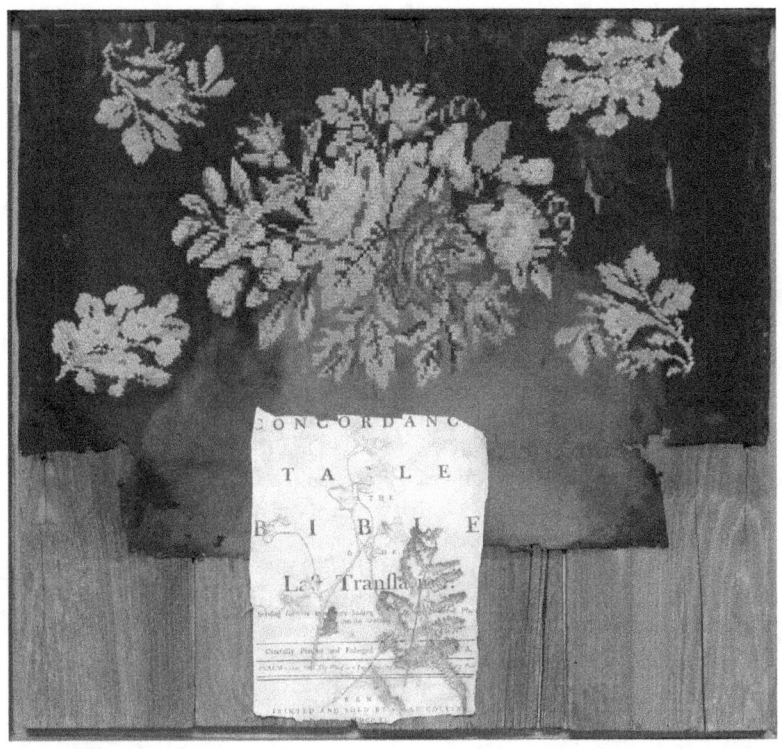

Arthur G. Dove
Grandmother, 1925
Shingles, needlepoint, page from Concordance, pressed flowers
and ferns mounted on cloth-covered wood
Museum of Modern Art, New York. Gift of Philip L. Goodwin (by exchange)
© The Estate of Arthur G. Dove, courtesy Terry Dintenfass, Inc.

In the collage *Nigger Go Fishin'*,[4] which was exhibited in the Contemporary American show at Jeu de Paume in Paris in 1938,[5] we think of Mark Twain rather than of Braque and Picasso. Against a background of trout pool, painted in tones of shadowed and dappled green, sand, blue and brown, among the objects arranged and enclosed behind glass in a box are sections of bamboo rod, a rot-

---

4. [Now titled *Goin Fishin'*, 1925, The Phillips Collection, Washington, D.C., acquired in 1937. Created in the summer of 1925, this assemblage is one of more than twenty-five collage works made of real objects, both manufactured and natural, that Dove created between 1924 and 1927 while living on a boat off Long Island near Huntington Harbor. *Goin' Fishin'* was the only work in this group given an offensive racist title. When first exhibited in 1926, Dove used the title *Fishin' Nigger*. Although the early titles for this object evolved, they always retained their racist language until Dove authorized a change before his death in 1946. Since 1947, a decade after it entered The Phillips Collection, the work has been known and exhibited as *Goin' Fishin'*. The original titles used until 1947 were understood at the time, as they are today, as openly racist and offensive language. Dove told critic Elizabeth McCausland in 1937 that the work was inspired by an African American fisherman he saw on a pier in Huntington Harbor. Critics in the 1920s and 1930s, all of whom were white, recognized this subject matter. Their commentary, however, focused on Dove's formal arrangement of everyday objects, often commenting on the work's inherent "Americanness" as compared to the contemporary collage experiments of European artists like Picasso and Braque. Well into the twenty-first century, scholars have continued to single out *Goin' Fishin'* for its inventiveness, while ignoring its racist origins. Only recently have scholars pulled back the curtain on the suppressed racist history of *Goin' Fishin'*. The Phillips Collection is committed to shining a light on those parts of its history and collection that raise questions about race and difference, as these questions are not only part of the past but are still very much with us today. It understands that museums have a responsibility to use works like *Goin' Fishin'* to spark a dialogue and inspire critical thinking.]

5. [*Trois siècles d'art aux États-Unis: peinture, sculpture, architecture, art populaire, photographie cinémâ*, Musée du Jeu de Paume, Paris, May–July 1938. The exhibition was assembled by the Museum of Modern Art, New York,comprised of approximately 300 paintings and watercolors, 40 sculptures, and 80 prints made by artists from all parts of the United States from 1609 through 1938, including John D. Rockefeller, Jr.'s Folk Art collection, and works by Allston, Bingham, Blakelock, Cassat, Chase, Copley, Davies, Eakins, Homer, Innes, Ryder, Sargent, Twachtman, and Whistler.

ted stump from an old tree, buttons for the black boy's eyes, and a glimpse of his blue denim overalls. The ingenious use of these things to bring out their contrasting textures and amusing theme has made the contrivance celebrated and admired even by those who have failed to appreciate Dove as a painter.

Perhaps the most unique achievements were the paintings in which metallic tones were incorporated and a light opposite invited to bring out radiations and reflections, In *Golden Storm,*[6] an opening of the sky gleams with thee dust of gold leaf applied to a rough block of wood. Cloud and earth forms in tones of coppery light overhang black waves which toss in agitation. Blue-green grasses bend in the blast. One thinks of Ryder's *Jonah*[7] and *Flying Dutchman.*[8] Another picture of an early date, also painted to be hung opposite a window, represents an expanse of ice thawing under a sun, the radiations of which are described vividly in the brush strokes. A favorite theme was *Willows in the Rain,* first done with actual twigs necked with gelatin against a sheet of glass, a collage bought by Georgia O'Keeffe.[9] She has always been one of Dove's most genuine admirers. Much later, in fact during his latest period, he painted rain once more, with columns of silver leaf which are dazzling opposite a window, darkling when the light is from the side. The silvery sheen or shadow dramatizes the movement of white and gray papers which turn and float and fall in a slanting rain. Brown branches traverse the crystal space.[10]

There was a time, from 1932–38, when Dove was so close to the soil on his father's farm and so happy in his physical toil and contemplative solitude that a primitive pantheism possessed him. There was worship of the sun and moon. He looked right into a glow of morning sunlight over the plowed furrows or else into the face of the full

---

6. [1925, The Phillips Collection, Washington, D.C., acquired in 1926]

7. [c. 1885–1895, Smithsonian American Art Museum, Washington, D.C.]

8. [completed by 1887, Smithsonian American Art Museum, Washington, D.C.]

9. [*Rain,* 1924, National Gallery of Art, Washington, D.C.]

10. [*Rain or Snow,* 1943, The Phillips Collection, Washington, D.C., acquired in 1943]

moon as it rose above the haunted hills. He was aware of the cycles of life and death in nature, of decaying tree trunks returning to the soil while the wind blows and new life begins. Like Thoreau by Walden Pond, Dove had become a poet in seclusion. The late Paul Rosenfeld, in the chapter on Dove, which is the best part of his best book, *Port of New York*, noted the painter's "wish to coincide with the objects before him, to catch their actual substance."[11] The artist was half serious and half smiling in such pictures as *Cows in Pasture*,[12] one of the masterpieces of the farm period, executed in tempera colors and a wax emulsion on a carefully prepared ground of talc and glue. The unobtrusive craftsmanship contributes to the expression of the title which, in this instance, is very important. The heavy sluggish shapes, the dull and mossy greens and browns, provide the mental picture of the animals at rest. Black and white and dun-colored, they are huddled in a pasture, their hind quarters settled comfortably into congenial turf. One head is seen. Silhouetted, a bull calf has a sleepy eye, and there is a bit of clover on his brain. The lazy contours suggest the slow and drowsy rumination. Cows, too, have their streams of consciousness. Painted in that same velvety surface are two Reminiscences, one of all-pervading Indians on a lake,[13] the other, also an Indian one, a memory of a day of wind blown trees and a kite riding the gale and a cloud shaped like the head of a moose.[14] Again and again one thinks of Indian patterns. It is not exactly a derivation. certainly not a conscious imitation, but it is a tribute to the decorative genius of the aboriginal Americans.

The upstate farming failed. For a while, Dove lived with his wife in a big room which had been a roller-skating rink at the top of a building

---

11. [*Port of New York: Essays on Fourteen American Moderns* (New York: Harcourt, Brace and Company, 1924), 172.]

12. [1935, The Phillips Collection, Washington, D.C., acquired in 1936]

13. [*Lake Afternoon*, 1935, The Phillips Collection, Washington, D.C., acquired in 1947]

14. [*Reminiscence*, 1937, The Phillips Collection, Washington, D.C., acquired in 1937]

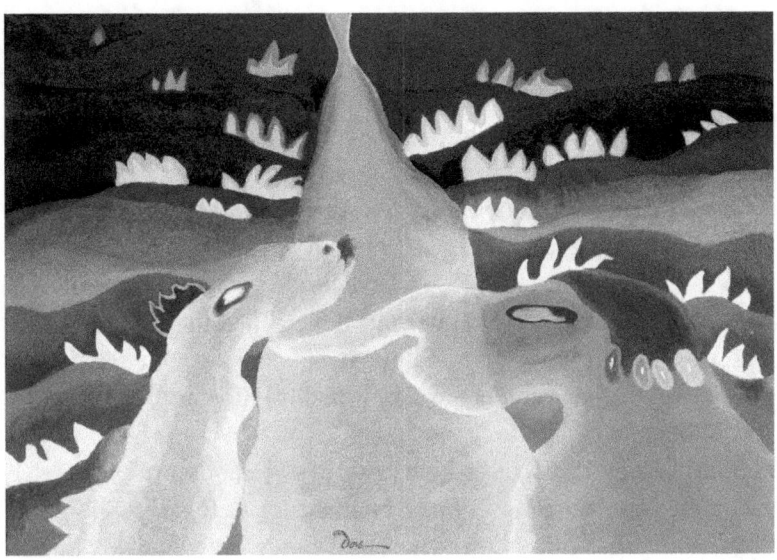

Arthur G. Dove
Lake Afternoon, 1935
Wax emulsion on canvas
The Phillips Collection, Washington, D.C. Acquired in 1947

his father owned in Geneva. There he painted the *Flour Mill,*[15] which is, I think, one of the great achievements of his career. The earlier, more actively linear calligraphy influenced perhaps by Kandinsky, in which Dove had emulated the syncopation of modern music, citing, in fact, Negro swing music, had been quite different. In *Flour Mill,* he made a Chinese character out of square, vibrant brush stroke a of yellow, blue, brown, and black, on a warm white. The modulations which are often so exquisite in Dove's mature canvases are, in this small upright masterpiece, scarcely discernible. And yet there is no lack of subtlety. For all their blazing intensity the colors have been far sought and subtly mixed. It is an inspired expression of color as light and of a very special "condition of light." The yellow is unbroken

---

15. [*Flour Mill II,* 1938, The Phillips Collection, Washington, D.C., acquired in 1938]

and yet it vibrates, flat and yet it has form. Dove had grown beyond
the explosive pyrotechnics of the Kandinsky of 1912 when that intellectual theorist had indulged in improvisation. Dove's arabesque has
not only a vital pulsation but majesty and that magic of light which
among all our contemporary painters is Dove's alone. The original
impression of a high noon of gleaming walls and chimneys under a
deep blue sky, the luminosity accented by swirls of smoke, has found
its perfect symbol in unrepresentative brush strokes inseparably and
inevitably shaped and colored. Dove has painted the exhilaration of
the sun at midday quite as vividly as it can be done with realism and
with the added emotion of surprise which reinforces and intensifies
the emotion of recognition.

John Dewey has written that "the [truly] spontaneous in art is
complete absorption in subject matter that is fresh."[16] Spontaneity in painting is not exclusively synonymous with a quickly improvised technique. There are many spontaneous technicians who have
nothing original in their vision nor anything of any consequence to
convey—only their virtuosity in display of their particular instrument
and its imitative or immediately evocative possibilities. There are also
great artists whose absorption in a fresh new world is so complete
that their mental and emotional response to immediate experience
can be lightly or roughly sketched, as in Dove's little watercolor notes,
but cannot be fully realized until the conception and emotion can be
"recollected in tranquility" and the sketch revised and the final form
painstakingly and lovingly rendered in subtle and beautiful surfaces;
until the inner eye's requirements have all been realized in more sensitized relations. The magnificent first versions of John Constable's
most famous landscapes, which are so much greater than the elabo-
rated and tightened replicas for the public exhibitions of the period,
were not sketches at all. No matter how quickly they were brushed,
we may be sure that their final execution was pondered for posterity. Only little children for whom all the world is new can paint as
the bird sings. Of course, there are the winged moments of the great

16. [*Art As Experience* (New York: Minton, Balch & Company, 1934), 70.]

expressionists, from Tintoretto to Constable to Van Gogh to Marin. But, again, to quote Dewey, "man…is not a bird. His most spontaneous outbursts, if expressive, are not…momentary."[17] Even optical impressionism is unconsciously conceptual and in pursuit of a reasoned purpose. Whether the tempo is slow or sped up depends upon the kind of expression desired. Arthur Dove was a conceptualist and a craftsman. He had a whimsical, intimately personal way of seeing and thinking about what he saw. The first ideas, a depiction of electricity for the air through a fanciful imagery of winter trees, their twigs wired to send out messages, or perhaps some butterfly wing inspiring a dream of delectable colors and lines; such food for his eye needed time for digestion and assimilation into his designs of color shapes. Dove had a freshness of vision always but only on rare occasions was he satisfied with technical spontaneity. More often, his resourceful, planned, and patiently manipulated craftsmanship was none the less integrated with his freshness of subject matter for being both deliberate and painstaking.

He had the self-reliant and adaptable character of the pioneer. When he had to support his painting and make it possible with the farm and the boats, when he went back once in a while to illustration, the time at his disposal for technical experimentation was limited. Later, when he became an invalid because of organic heart trouble—a condition which was to keep him inactive and confined to his room for many years, he did not permit this misfortune to end his career as a painter. It did not even interfere with his annual exhibitions at An American Place. What it did was to give him more time to develop the potentialities of his art and the range of his power in adapting technical execution to an even more profoundly personal conception. And so, during his later years at Centerport, Long Island, he painted his most sumptuously colorful arabesques, such exquisite decorative designs as *Green and Gold and Brown*[18] and *Pozzuoli Red*[19] as well as

17. [Ibid.]

18. [*Yellow, Blue-Green and Brown*, 1941, The Phillips Collection, Washington, D.C., acquired in 1941]

19. [1941, The Phillips Collection, Washington, D.C., acquired in 1941]

Rain or Snow to which I have referred, and the *Willows* in the collection of the Museum of Modern Art.[20] In his joyously executed compositions he was truly master of his fate and captain of his soul and conqueror or adversity and infirmity. He had been as full of sap and gusto in his earthiness and acceptance of all life as Walt Whitman, but he always had a sweetness and a droll whimsicality which old Walt would not have understood. Success came at last. He died at the moment when the return to favor of romanticism and the standardization of abstraction made his lone individualism in romantic patterning understandable. Had not art in his time tended to become too collective? And had not he remained an individualist even in the abstract field, which is the one most likely to be standardized and weighted with dull specifications? Dove was never dull and never stereotyped. He was a visionary and a nature poet like Ryder, but he was also a craftsman who loved a good job of painting for its own sake. In my notebook, I find a quotation which I attributed to Élie Faure, but not even Walter Pach who translated it can recall to what book it belongs. "When the professional artists transform Academies into associations of private interest surrounded by a servile multitude, Art can do nothing but take refuge in a few solitary hearts."

—⁓—

20. [1940, Museum of Modern Art, New York, Gift of Duncan Phillips]

MORRIS GRAVES

(1947)

MORRIS GRAVES was granted a Guggenheim Fellowship to study and paint in Japan. In his application he stated his desire "to communicate as an artist with Japanese artists, ascertaining the mutual progress of Orient and Occident in understanding the painter's power to revel world unity." He wrote of his hope of interpreting the degree and quality of unifying elements in the meeting of traditions commonly supposed to be so alien as to be forever separate. In endorsing his application I was eager to express my belief that Graves is not only one of the most original and inspired of our younger American artists but that he is one of the very few who offset the too prevalent expression that "Western painting is an adjunct of objective material existence." Better than any other American he could reveal to the Far East that we of the Western world also have our mystics who feel in contemplation of nature, the relation of man's life to the poetry, and the meaning of all life. Unfortunately, Graves never got to Japan. Stopped at Honolulu because the occupying authority would not grant him permission to enter the islands, he returned to the West Coast where he is now painting.

Graves was born in Fox Valley, Oregon, in 1910. His family had been home studying a claim there but after a year they were back in the hometown of Seattle. From the time Morris was seven until his second year in high school, he and his parents and the six other children lived at Richmond Beach, a neighboring town. The Pacific Ocean call to the boy to explore its distant wonders. As a cadet on American Male Line steamers sailing from Seattle, he made three trips to the Orient, receiving formative impressions in the Hawaiian Islands, Japan, and China. His schooling has been so often interrupted by his voyages that he was persuaded to finish high school

First published in the *Magazine of Art* 40, no. 8 (December 1947).

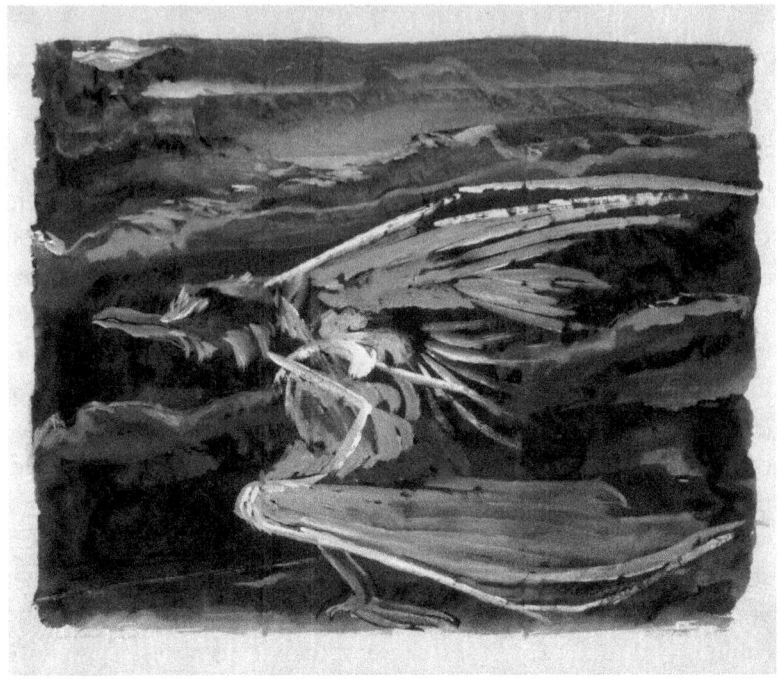

Morris Graves
Wounded Gull, 1943
Opaque watercolor on paper
The Phillips Collection, Washington, D.C. Acquired in 1945
© Morris Graves Foundation

at Beaumont, Texas, where he had stopped to visit an aunt on his way to Mexico. It is interesting to learn that he edited the school Annual and decorated it with bird motifs. It was in Texas that he had his first instruction in painting and showed promised both in oil and watercolor.

Returning to the Northwest he drew fir trees, birds, and animals. The beautiful *Moor Swan*[1] at the Seattle Museum dates from this early period, and a 1933 it won for him a one-hundred dollar

---

1. [1933, Seattle Art Museum]

prize and a studio shared with his sister and several artist friends. A Seattle group made up a fund which financed painting expeditions to picturesque parts of Oregon. His landscapes in oil were, I am told, heavy, moody, and dark. They were also experiments and wax encaustic over tempera.

Although exhibited in the West, Graves was unknown to Eastern critics until the exhibition at the Museum of Modern Art in New York in 1942, entitled *18 Artists from 9 States.* Of the eighteen, most of them like himself W.P.A. discoveries, Graves was the sensation of the show. By this time he had matured his style under the combined influences of Far Eastern Art in the Seattle Museum and the curiously vibrant technique of his West Coast friend Mark Tobey, who used a Chinese brush and tempera colors but then originality proving to Graves that such a style need not be even an Oriental reference. When success came to him in New York, his hope was confirmed that he could make brush drawings revealing his long study of the Orientals without being considered a mere imitator.

The war interrupted his projects. He was drafted, but ultimately released as a conscientious objector. The spiritual anguish stirred in him by this time of trial and soul-searching found an outlet in his Chalice and Purification series, and later in his "birds of the inner eye" and wounded gulls.

When we discovered Morris Graves at the Museum of Modern Art, and he became a national celebrity, it was the immediate impact of an original genius. It was announced that he had been to China and Japan and that he had studied Chinese and Japanese art most intensively at Seattle. Clearly, he derived from such Oriental sources. And yet, in spite of the widespread preconception that Western painting in the Eastern spirit and technique is no more authentic and acceptable than Chinese or Japanese painting in modern French, English,and American idioms, Graves encountered little emphasis upon and no disapproval of his obvious Far Eastern derivation. What was noted was the originality of his vision, the power and breadth of his drawing even on delicate paper, the inventive magic of his calligraphic expressions in details, and the revelation of an inner life for which a haunting and compassionate symbolic imagery had been conceived in the most subtle correspondence. These were indeed equivalents of a quintessential deism which could be as true of an American as of a Japanese. This nature study and the compassion too were universal rather than Oriental. And such reflection was long overdue.

Whether Graves triumphed in spite of his Orientalism or precisely because he broke down a barrier which should never have been inhibited Western artists—this may still be uncertain. The calligraphic expressions to which I have referred and an obscure fantasy in a few drawings to which only the subconscious mind might have help held the key, such deviations from the normal were of our period, in the movement known as Surrealism. Now Graves has written that he dislikes Surrealism and does not want to be identified with it. Nevertheless, he was included, during the years following his first New York acclaim, in exhibitions of practitioners of that school and also of neo-romanticists and abstractionists. This is indicative of a lingering prejudice against Eastern influence upon Western artists as well as of a lazy tendency to assign successful artists to fashionable categories.

In the summer of 1946, three of the finest works for shown in the American Exhibition at the Tate Gallery in London,[2] and he was one of the most admired of the living exhibitors. Again his Oriental brush drawings and composition were not as much noted as where his intimate symbolism and his inventive virtuosity. One British critic called him the American Paul Klee, and no one thought that was a strange thing to say, although Klee's mind was as different from that of Graves as the minds of the neo-romantics and surrealists with whom he had previously been herded. The secret of his success and of its stress on his personal expression of a complex inwardness instead of upon his acknowledged reference for ancient

2. [*American Painting: From the Eighteenth Century to the Present Day*, presented at The Tate Gallery in 1946, was the first international touring exhibition organized by the National Gallery of Art in Washington, D.C.]

Chinese aesthetics and philosophy, the added meaning of his being mentioned with Klee may be that both were recognized as among the first important artists to fuse the minds of Orient and Occident, putting into the melting pot only what profited them in each in order to convey their poignant commentary on the crucial period through which we are passing.

The time is here, says F.S.C. Northrup in *The Meeting of East and West*, "when we must learn how to combine Oriental and Occidental values with a breaking away from each tradition and a purpose to relate to compatible elements by enlarging the ideals of each to include those of the other so that they reinforce, sustain, and enrich each other."[3] That is exactly what Morris Graves has done and hopes to keep on doing. In Dr. Northrup's thesis, art has alternative functions: to get free play both to the aesthetic component of man's nature, which in the East is also the philosophical and religious part of him, and to the theoretic component—to his intellectual faculty, his conceptual explorations of time and space, his experimental physics and psychology, his encouragement of individuality, and his exhilaration in a dynamic universe in which mind is never passive. The aesthetic component in man's nature has no need of cerebration since "the great spirit of the universe" can be immediately sensed and self can't be lost in it, merged in "the all-embracing continuum" which is nature in its "aesthetic immediacy." Within this meditative calm there is great compassion for every living creature.

Art in the Far East delights in these qualitative evidences of variations within the great tradition, yet knows that they are as transitory as our sensations and introspections. What is far more important because it is for all time is that "all-embracing continuity" in which there is no distinction between subjective and objective since Deity is in everything.

---

3. [*The Meeting of East and West: An Inquiry Concerning World Understanding* (New York: Macmillan, 1946), 6.]

Now Morris Graves thinks of himself as a Western exemplar of the aesthetic component, spiritually realized only in the Far East, yet available to us of the West whenever we care to avail ourselves of any part of its peace. Graves has written: "Western painting has all too often diminished the potent presence of nature's forms, spiritually realized, by taking them out of their spatial context, in other words, out of the mind's environment, and re-stating them with inventive purpose. We need art to guide our journey from partial to full consciousness. I have attained to the conviction that it is my purpose through creative painting to convey to man that he has the ability for instantaneous as well as for his usual evolutionary knowledge of his cosmic significance. I seek for painting that miraculous union where the Seer and the Seen are one. The image language of creative art can reveal the illumination within the world soul—a language free from the barriers of natural tongues." All this and much more of the same sort of exalted deism pervades the mind of Morris Graves, and persuades him that he is more of an Oriental in his thought than he may actually be.

Let us see what appears to be the essence of his art. Surely, the introspective imagery of wildlife in the elements revealed the man himself in his art, and the images are concepts, and they are commentary. He would not be an artist who captivates the West today where it not for the almost subconscious intuitions and the personal complexities of an inner life symbolized, so far as I know, as it has never been before. Despite his genuine feeling of cosmic immersion and oneness with all life, his compassion and his symbolism are profoundly Occidental. It is his own West that has given him the freedom to explore the Eastern mind and to match his own mind with it and to discover that in him the East and the West are compatible. What's better ambassador of goodwill and understanding could we have sent to an Oriental country which we have just conquered in war and which is still under military occupation?

If Paul Klee invokes the spell of the East from the viewpoint of a cultivated, whimsical, witty, and melancholic Western painter and

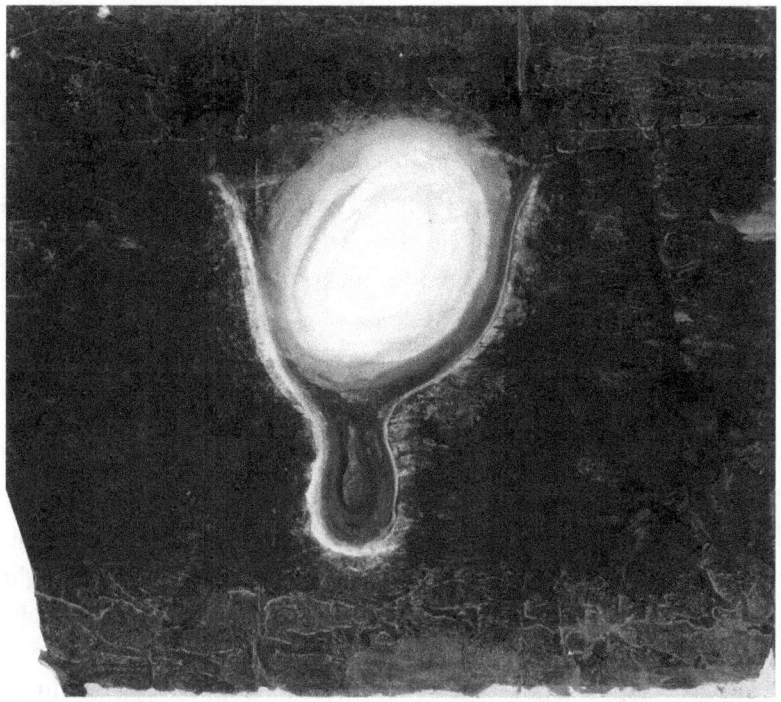

Morris Graves
Chalice, 1941
Opaque watercolor, chalk, and sumi ink on paper
The Phillips Collection, Washington, D.C. Acquired in 1942
© Morris Graves Foundation

philosopher, paying tribute from a great distance, Morris Graves feels a true kinship to the Taoists and Buddhists. Both artists deal in conceptions. The difference is not an kind, but in degree. In Klee, the theoretical component is far more compelling than the aesthetic; in Graves there is no theory at all and a great deal of work of cosmic awareness, yet he remains an intense individualist and more passionate and his protest than serene in his passive acceptance.

Although he combined quality of East and West and has a Western mind steeped in Eastern philosophy, he is most undeniably a citizen of that in a world of mysticism which, through the centuries, drawstring gather a universal brotherhood. If I understand him correctly, Graves is seeking by expanding his consciousness of a man's oneness with all that lives and dies, to symbolize the fate of a man through the fate of birds. He is moved by the wonderful strangeness of our universal consciousness at the edge of night, on the tides of infinity. He sees in human restlessness and spiritual searching a kinship to bird migrations. In the world at war he brooded on the perpetual battle in nature, on the struggle of beings meant to be free, destined to be the prey of the killer.

Graves knows birds—knows the characters among them. He is familiar with the sardonic owl, the moon-crazed crow, the mighty eagle, and the night spy, all-seeing eye and stealthy tread in the green wood's protective dimness. His heart has gone out to the scampering sanderlings on the beach, the fluttering young plovers in the shallows, the merry scoters shooting the rapids of the surf. He has felt vicariously the pangs of approaching death at the imagined sight of the old gull who with twisted plumage and shattered wings staggers on or sinks at last into his world of boundless sea and sky gone black. Perhaps in those later birds there is less of divine madness than in the earlier, cave-dwelling "little-known birds of the inner eye." Or the Blind Bird—could we ever forget him?—perched on a tumult of white lines diagramming perilous sounds. Such symbols are used to show birds as sharing human fears.

It was Mark Tobey who persuaded Graves to commit his visionary perceptions to thinnest tissue which could be made potent for the force of a mysticism touched with genius. One feels a solicitude for the survival of such precious, already crinkled papers. Yet it is as it had to be, for this phase of his work at least. And no I don't medium, and no other way, could the artist have expressed what he had to say about the brevity and insecurity of life.

He is seldom literary, not even in the supernatural blacks and whites of his *Chalice*.[4] What Graves has to tell is of what he has seen

---

4. [1941, The Phillips Collection, Washington, D.C., acquired in 1942.]

with the eyes of the mind. He's inspired drawing and design, his fine placements and measures in a space which is ever more spiritual and pictorial—these technical distinctions are worthy of comparison with great Chinese and Japanese nature of painting. In Japan he might have helped immeasurably in bridging the gap between Eastern and Western art and thought. He is our American mystic. As a poet painter he haunts our minds and senses like night sounds in a great stillness. He makes us more aware of our mystery and meaning. His art may be prophetic of a trend toward unity which, if it develops, will hasten man's destiny of spiritual evolution.

PIERRE BONNARD

(1949)

THE death in 1947 of Pierre Bonnard has at last established for him recognition as one of the greatest painters of the 20th Century. His indifference to publicity and his independence from the more conspicuous trends of his contemporaries had retarded his acceptance by a self-conscious period which, in spite of its many-mindedness, is nevertheless intolerant of the lone individual in its attraction to group movements and conformities to the latest fashions. Bonnard's free spirit has now been revealed as an inspiration to freedom from formula. It is no less clear that all through his life he had been pointing the way of liberation from all extra-pictorial irrelevance. He was in a very real sense a pure painter. Yet he was also a prophet of much that we call modern. In his zest for what appear to be accidents of composition and for seemingly casual and surprising color combinations he was an innovator who created plastic equivalents for intimate visual experiences and states of being. He created a vivid sense of reality in landscapes, still life and interiors far more like fantasy than like realism. The most painterly of painters, he is closer to that subjective stream of consciousness which has been increasingly the preoccupation of the modern poets than to the objective statements of his impressionist predecessors. Claude Monet's prismatic color as weather and light, a scientific instrument of precision, became for Bonnard an aesthetic instrument of personal expression to convey the spiritual climate and the inner radiance of his own often whimsical response to the joyous privilege of existing in the visual world.

Bonnard's life was uneventful and its start very much like that of other great masters. Born in 1867, the son of a government official, he studied law to please his father and it was not until after he

First published in the *Kenyon Review* 11 (Autumn 1949): 561–66.

had sold an advertising poster which Lautrec admired that he was permitted to enter the École des Beaux Arts. Later, at the Académie Julian, he met Denis, Vuillard, and Roussel. Attracted to Japanese prints in the little shops of Paris, he decided to adapt their lively patterns of line and their harmonious patches of color to depictions of Parisian boulevards, cafes and circuses. The low-toned street scenes and interiors which Bonnard and Vuillard painted in the 1890s were enlivened by a few bright notes of accented color. There was an inner resistance in both the young Intimists to the theories of Denis and Sérusier and to the exotic appeal of Gauguin. They persisted in looking around them, indoors and out. They limited their observations to their homes and families and to the neighborhoods they knew best in city and country. All his life Bonnard was to be consistent in one aim—to preserve, through many revisions and elaborations, the first mental image and the first ardent, spontaneously expressive urge. His was an art of immediate impressions and then of long and loving recollections and refinements which kept the freshness of the first conceptual sketch.

From 1912 to 1937 Bonnard divided his time between Vernon on the Seine and the Midi. In the later years, except for occasional visits to Paris, he lived in a little pink house at Le Cannet near Cagnes, where as John Rewald observed on a visit to the artist he could see every day from his door "orange, olive, and almond trees cascad[ing] in terraces to the Mediterranean."[1] After 1920 he was recognized as a *grand maître*. His mastery of his medium was acknowledged and reverenced but his retiring nature was respected, and he welcomed a protective seclusion from publicity and controversy. 1940 was a sad year, for it was then that his beloved France fell, his wife died, and also his dearest friend Vuillard. The photographs of him made at this time reveal his wistful bewilderment when interrupted from his painting. He retained his hold on life through his fervent absorption in the problems and the pleasures of his work in progress, the many

---

1. [*Pierre Bonnard* (New York: Museum of Modern Art, 1948. Exhibition catalog), 53; quotation emended.]

pictures carried on simultaneously, side by side, on a huge canvas tacked to the wall.

It is still said that Bonnard was the last great Impressionist and that Impressionism was the end of the preceding period against which, as is the way of the world, our period has been in revolt. Undeniably, Bonnard was a persistent nature painter, a painter of light that changes and of atmosphere that charms, long after the period when nature study in painting had been declared out of date. Even if we grant that Impressionism was the end of one epoch it was no less surely the beginning of another. The very revolt which it incited against its analytical study of nature was a stimulating influence and its affirmation of color as the basic and proper instrument of painting and its insistence that painting is an end in itself, with a life of its own independent of imposed subjects from books, this great reaction of the 19th Century liberated Bonnard for all sorts of dynamic 20th-Century explorations into the creative potentialities of color and light. Cézanne owed his microcosmos of color to the revolution of the Impressionists and became the link between this new scientific luminism and ageless classicism. He was a builder, with color as his building material. Bonnard is the supreme sensitivity, the music-maker of color. Each of his pictures is a personally chosen fragment of a world full of animation and loveliness. Each is a fastidious record of some immediate and intimate visual occurrence to which his eye, mind and hand had been at one time or another dedicated. Bonnard is the link between Impressionism and Expressionism. And that latest expressionist phase of the ever recurring romanticism of our universal human need is as significant a revelation of our times as Cubism and far closer to the fundamentally emotional core of art.

Equally valid although less easily appreciated in our period than the closed compositions and compact constructions of Cézanne are the expressions of wild opulent growth and continuing life *beyond* the frames which characterize many of the best landscapes of Bonnard. Early spring is a season the meaning of which can be communicated in no other way. In at least one painting of 1910 bearing that title, the poetry of the subject required from Bonnard's design a sensuous diffusion of interest and scattering of attention which is, I suppose, sheer anarchy to the strict classicist. There is in it certainly the disorganized vitality of what T. S. Soby has called "nature's wayward unpredictable pattern, its chronic state of unbalance." Yet such is spring and its compelling urge, its restless mood and its tug at the heart when change is everywhere and evanescence poignant. In this particular song of Bonnard's about the sun and the showers strange little children dart in and out among the flowering shrubs and the cloud shadows while the distance calls down a garden path through an old stone gate. Such spreading ecstasy is as rare if not as great a heritage as Cézanne's functional finality.

In the Interior entitled *The Checkered Tablecloth*,[2] something about the crushed colors and the varied textures reminds us of Chardin. Both artists were deeply fond of the intimacy of the bourgeois home and the little joys of every day. Both were delighted with the way the painter can seize upon the intrinsic charms of the simplest objects, noting with quiet rapture the reflections and refractions of light, the melodic patterning of colored shapes, the obbligato of muted harmonies in the surrounding areas. The differences of course are greater than the similarities. Chardin, even in the pantry and kitchen, was the classic builder in an architecture of aerial space. Bonnard was the whimsical fantasist, classic only in his early drawings for *Daphnis and Chloe*,[3] more often at his ease observing and creating pictures from remembered moments he had experienced in the innermost intimacy of his home or on the pavements of the Boulevard Clichy, or in the pastoral casualness of country lanes, or on terraced gardens overlooking the Mediterranean. His sensitivities were attuned to moods so sudden that they borrowed from the candid camera suggestions for the most arbitrary divisions of

---

2. c. 1925, Collection of Liza Phillips, on long-term loan to The Phillips Collection, Washington, D.C.

3. [In 1902, Ambroise Vollard commissioned Bonnard to create a series of lithographs for an illustrated edition of Longus's story *Daphnis and Chloe*.]

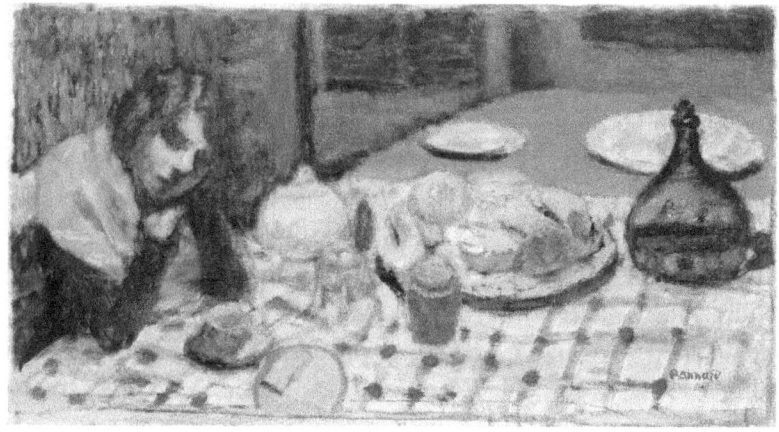

Pierre Bonnard
The Checkered Tablecloth, c. 1925
Oil on canvas
Collection of Liza Phillips, on long-term loan to The Phillips Collection
© 2022 Artists Rights Society (ARS), New York

and placements on the canvas. This passion for the instantaneous was derived from Degas who had a similar genius for compositional caprice. With Degas however the functional eye travel, even in the colorful late pastels, still depends on the drawing. In the land of Bonnard it is not the light but the color which leads the eye from one delightful place to another. The observer responsive to chromatic delectations and the painter in sensory and spiritual need of good painting can go for aesthetic nourishment, as well as for sheer enjoyment, from color to color as a bee from flower to flower.

In *The Checkered Tablecloth,* the two dissimilar reds are in a relationship close to dissonance yet more satisfying than challenging. They are consummated as a chord by notes of bright blue, pink and white, golden brown, lime green and darker blue. The picture has passages, for instance the seated woman's shaded eyes and the rich but muffled cloisonné tonalities of the background, which are like his works at the turn of the century. Those two reds, however, the one which approaches crimson and the shawl which is almost scarlet, are clearly from the resonant intensities of his culminating maturity of the 1920s. It is possible that the artist actually returned to an old canvas but more likely that in mid-career he combined qualities of his earlier and his later self.

Bonnard's art in essence continued to the end very much as it began. Yet his genius developed in his latest phase into an ecstatic Expressionism attaining during the twenty years 1927–1947 to an indisputable greatness. One of his last works was a unique masterpiece, unique for so blithe an artist, tinged as it is with a melancholy of introspection and compassionate tenderness. It portrays a wise, white circus horse, his long nose and neck a pyramidal shape, his searching eyes a symbol of the little more than animal that is still a little less than human. The background of burnt orange, red, blue and brown, reveals a sunlit stable truly sublimated by the artist's tribute. The final picture was a blossoming almond tree,[4] done in brushwork very like one of the Peach Trees from John Marin's orchards, and revealing a close kinship to Marin's inspired improvisations.

Never was sumptuousness more subtle and a painted surface more akin to great music than in Bonnard's latest landscapes and interiors. The sensuous juxtapositions and comminglements of color approach yet always avoid the perils of preciosity. The glamor pervades not only the great views of the Midi and not only his dining room with its fruits and flowers but his tiled bathroom and the little bather in the tub. As unafraid of glamor as of humor the artist deliberately subordinated figures to their light-enchanted environments, often seeing them as shadowy silhouettes against the pervading glow, amusing himself with the way his unposed people, his wife, his friends and neighbors, even his little dachshund, were idly or actively absorbed in their own private lives at an engrossing moment of time as it flies.

Bonnard was a shy, witty, and lovable man whose long life was full of little else than just painting to his heart's content. I have

---

4. [*Flowering Almond Tree*, 1946, Musée National d'Art Moderne, Paris]

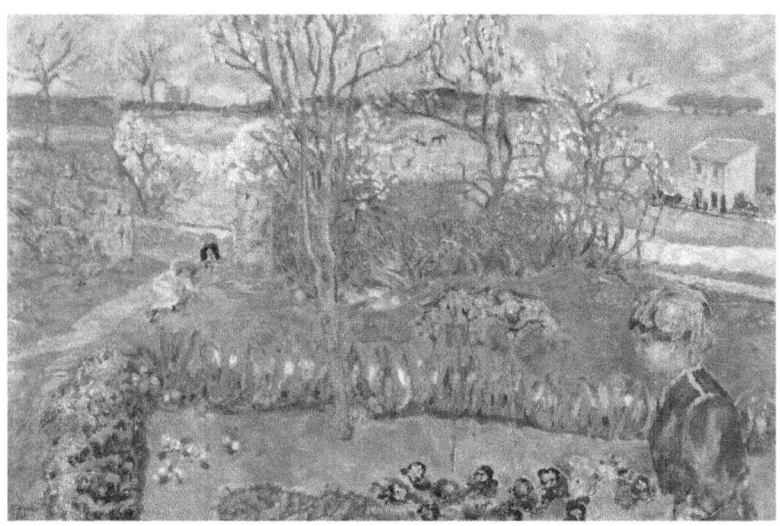

Pierre Bonnard
Early Spring, 1908
Oil on canvas
The Phillips Collection, Washington, D.C. Acquired in 1925
© 2022 Artists Rights Society (ARS), New York

stressed the fact that he had no time and no tolerance for theories and systems of design as substitutes for painting. He loved all that he painted and one does not love theories and systems. He lived for his art. I could never forget the eager awareness of his eyes restlessly gathering impressions. His art will live as long as people cherish the first perfect day in spring. Such art has a springtime of self-renewal in it and a heart-warming way of conveying, and always strictly in the painter's own language, the ever refreshing love of life.

LEE GATCH
(1949)

THE first painting I saw by Lee Gatch made on me an immediate impression of distinguished originality. Although it
was executed in the spirit of a sketch, the composition was structural
and subtle. The strong, almost crude colors were surprising and yet
exactly right for the subject. Marching down a wide, oyster-gray
road upon which their shadows fall, Highlanders approach diago-
nally across a long narrow canvas, their flags, their big white drums,
their kilted legs, and their bagpipes silhouetted against harvest field
in a stenography of sealing-wax red. In the middle distance an oval
mass of tall, smoky-blue trees recedes in a broken contour to the
square roof of a distant village almost blotted out under the rising
sun. We feel the rhythm of the march so insistently that we hardly
see the men in the imminence of their arrival, in the clangor and
shock of their fanfare which the colors symbolize. The painter has
brushed in the incident with the utmost confidence and economy
of means, knowing what to tell and what not to define. The writing
is by a big brush directed by an art of spontaneous eloquence. The
design is both expansive and compact. The flat, geometrical planes
of road, field, distant trees, and glowing sky seem to fit into their
places as if by magic and map out a taut pictorial space which is also
a true atmospheric space. In other words, the light and dark pattern
is in fine correspondence with the relative distances in the scene
described. The picture plane is brought down from the rosy gold
of the sky to the grayish white of the road and the more emphatic
whites of the flag and drum. The dark of the distant trees needs the
stark silhouette of the piper who leads the band. And the dull, dark
blue resolves the dissonance of orange and red.

Here was a discovery of an American expressionism summa-
rizing, in a swift synopsis of interlocking, pyramidal planes and

---

First published in the *Magazine of Art* 42, no. 8 (December 1949).

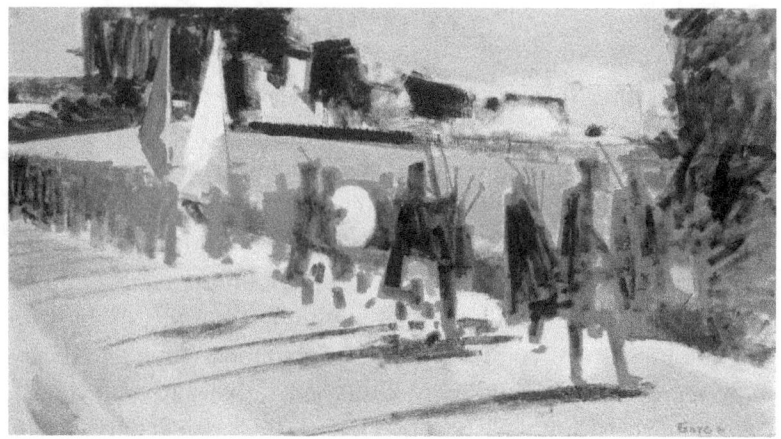

Lee Gatch
Highlanders, 1933
Oil on canvas
The Phillips Collection, Washington, D.C. Acquired in 1941
© 2022 Estate of Lee Gatch

dynamic, broken lines and colors something which we might never have had the luck to meet on such a suitable morning. Lee Gatch has confirmed the love of parades that is evident in this painting. As he says, "They organize themselves. One has simply to march with the men." This he has done with gusto, relating his rhythm to an inspired setting.

Lee Gatch, born in Baltimore in 1902, studied art at the Maryland Institute in that city. A scholarship to the American School at Fontainebleau transferred his training to France where later he became a pupil of André Lhote. In a letter telling of his progress in art, he wrote, "It was through sculpture that my eyes were opened. A little Negro head suddenly revealed to me its formal secrets. Studying in Paris, I was able to absorb and respect the cubic discipline and to use cubes and cylinders architecturally, never forgetting the transitions of that head—form sliding into form." Here, then, was the source in the marching *Highlanders*[1] of the planes fitting into their boundar-

---

1. [1933, The Phillips Collection, Washington, D.C., acquired in 1941]

ies and directions with the spontaneous balance of a brilliant sketch. What the "Académie Moderne" in Paris tries in vain to reduce to a formula, the primitive sculptor had intuitively extemporized.

Gatch became an expert in the technique of cubism, but he had already learned to trust more to his instinct and to move in his own way from analysis to synthesis, from architectural means to personal and decorative ends. The colored lithographs of Bonnard and Vuillard may also have charmed him. In at least one of his early paintings, *City at Evening,*[2] the dark and light contrast of flat planes and patches are as arbitrary as those *Art nouveau* prints of the nineties, but more intense and dramatic. The bridges of Paris and its tall houses gleam like old ivory at lamp-lighting time and carry down the afterglow from the turquoise river and sky, these lights balancing perfectly the bronze and black tones of the surrounding nightfall. All his experience in Paris, the "cubic discipline" especially, served Gatch well as a basis for the poetic expression of heightened consciousness and evocative suggestion which we find in the work of his maturity.

On his return to the United States, Lee Gatch determined to see in color and to design two-dimensionally. As his favorite shape for creative invention, he selected an exceptionally long overmantel, which required not only the rhythmic balance appropriate to a frieze but a degree of improvisation in treating the subject in such a way as to make the spatial intervals both functional and ornamental. What Picasso in 1918 had done to fill a vertical surface with flat semi-abstract patterns of tilted planes, using as his starting point a harlequin and a guitar, a sheet of music, a mask, and his three-cornered hat, Gatch was to do horizontally in a decorative cubic synthesis of his own. Instead of harlequins, he painted horses, some mounted and some blanketed, outside a stable of checkered light and shadow, with riders dressed for the hunt. Low rich tones of gray, tan, black, brown, and orange convey the light and dark pattern of the remembered moment. The shapes are cones and cylinders, but also long

---

2. [1933, The Phillips Collection, Washington, D.C., acquired in 1943]

coats and skirts and visored caps, the silhouette of a narrow feminine shoulder or of a lean horse's neck or leg, all contained within
the ample lines of a long low stable, its interior penetrated by shafts
of light, its vertical wall rising at one end to the diagonal and then
to the horizontal roof. The observation is sharpened and reduced
to a common denominator of geometrical fragments used as stenographic symbols of remembered tensions, of energies and skills held
back at the start of a zestful adventure.

Lee Gatch is a man of his own times. Of the arts of all the ages
which he studied in the Louvre, he remembers best the great expressionist painters who, like El Greco, intensified through distortion the
psychological character of their themes or who, like Daumier, gave to
contours and masses dramatic accentuation. His first exhibition in
New York was at J.B. Neumann's New Art Circle in 1927, and his second showing in 1932 was at the same gallery. where oils and watercolors by Paul Klee were usually to be seen. Perhaps Klee's counter-
point of wiry line and color fantasy, his mat and varied textures, and
his wit and wisdom and provocative obscurity encouraged Gatch to
break away from clean-cut stylistic mannerism and to seek his own
private iconography. Amid the confusion of sophisticated trends and
diversions, he has always steered his own course and remained true
to his resolve to be himself and to draw his subjects from his own
experience in his own country. Could he not try to be a representative painter while aspiring nonetheless to the self-sufficiency of
abstract art?

It is an American tradition for our open-minded poet-painters
to select from their studies only what they need for their self-lim-
ited, very personal, and specialized creations. Our greatest originals.
Albert P. Ryder, John Marin, and Arthur Dove, were so self-reliant
as to be almost self-sufficient. but there were others who, short of
eclecticism, were very curious about what was going on abroad and
eager to see what was in circulation which they could use and transform to their own purpose. Among these were Maurice Prendergast,
whose tapestried picnics are derived from (yet so unlike) Cézanne

and Seurat, and John Twachtman, who transformed Claude Monet's scientific demonstration of color as light into a rainbow palette to serve his own mysticism in his frozen brooks. His iridescent waterfalls, his cloud-bewildered hillsides and romantic canyons. Arthur B. Davies and, many years later, Charles Demuth were attracted to the decorative and lyrical possibilities of cubes as units of design: Davies superimposing prisms over his nymphs. Demuth fusing ruled lines with exquisite vignettes and washes.

To this American tradition Lee Gatch clearly belongs. He may never have seen the work of Jacques Villon but, like him, he has had the audacity to make a synthesis of the antithetical creeds of impressionism and cubism. Unlike Villon, however, who is as formal as Seurat, or at least as Roger de La Fresnaye, Gatch has always been essentially an expressionist, with a language of design closer to fantasy than to fact or formula. We recognize the Pennsylvania and New Jersey of his landscapes. but those barnyards and barn doors, those tangled farm gardens and state roads, those oil wells. those electric wires and towers and signs are symbols of an imagination which in its own very different way has been at times almost as exclusive as that of Paul Klee. Only one other contemporary American painter combines cubist and expressionist ideology—Karl Knaths: but in his fantasy, Knaths is more structural than Gatch and far more demonstrable and authoritative in his designs. Both men are imaginative composers in pictorial space who retain a lyrical feeling for atmospheric space. and both have kept their own sensibilities intact. Both are craftsmen who excel in mat textures over prepared grounds. and both are colorists who have enriched the American tradition for cultivating one's garden with carefully chosen seeds.

I have lingered over those charming early masterpieces by Gatch, *City at Evening, Fox Hunt,*[3] and *Highlanders,* chiefly because the artist later abandoned their emphatic patterns, their calligraphy or cubistic stylization, in search of more mystery and less immediate effectiveness. Gatch was not satisfied to remain a calligrapher nor a syn-

---

3. [1934, whereabouts unknown]

[369]

thetic cubist aiming at expressive decoration. *The Fox Hunt,* on the way to arabesque, led him to patterning his moods and to the attainment of plastic virtuosity and subtle orchestration. The essence of his originality in his next phase was to select for his theme only such moments or places as would have evaded even a description by Henry James. Gatch challenged his own powers of delicate suggestion and evocation by weaving a web of lovely texture between the mood he sought to render and the pleased but puzzled observer. In this period he could be compared to those contemporary poets who, disregarding their inability to dissociate words from the meanings they symbolize, seek in obscurity a sort of shelter. The sensuousness and suggestive wizardry of words without coherent meaning is undeniable, but such use of them is preciosity itself. It is, however, not fair to call Gatch "precious," since the language of colors and lines on a flat surface is not answerable to meaning at all and needs only to convey sensuously whatever imagination suggests. Gatch's painted poetry is soundly integrated in his color pattern, and he has never been more literary than whatever reference to his inner life is signified by an absent-minded, epicurean, and purely visual stream of consciousness. To introduce this difficult phase in the artist's own words, we quote again from his letter:

> By 1935 the angularity of my expression had softened through the insinuation of a new vision and a new desire for the sensuous arabesque existing in nature. I looked for special subjects: long dark hedges broken by a fan-like pattern of mellow orchard trees and a mesh of magenta briers working across the dark facade in a disheveled frieze. I packed long, narrow panels with small forms, making them vague as if out of focus or else just visible. In this way I could create areas simple and at the same time animated. I wished to see the color field scintillate and breathe with a sparkle like the unevenly dyed threads of a Navajo blanket. My best examples of this are *Yaddo Gardens*[4] and *Orientals at the Races.*[5] In the *Orientals* I used figures abstractly and in fragments.

---

4. [1935, whereabouts unknown]
5. [1939, The Phillips Collection, Washington, D.C., acquired in 1941]

One needs to peer into the embroidered enchantment of the latter to find the idea it contains. The faces of the exotic visitors are flat masks with slits for eyes. Robed in mysterious hieroglyphics, they overlook and are inscrutably detached from a visual and mental experience, which they absorb less in coordinated detail than as a beautiful and bewildering *composite* of their scattered observations, all vague, fragmentary, and fugitive. Race horses can be discovered, ridden by shadowy jockeys, galloping inside the rail, and beyond the track there are scattered hurdles. We see as they pass gleaming equine flanks and necks and. further away, yet still on the same picture plane, heads of horses with distended nostrils and excited ears. Everything, large and small. is merged, mellowed and enveloped in a golden haze of sun, dust and mystification.

In another panel of that period of composite imagery the arabesque is less sensuous and the mood more austere. The pale outlines and blonde tonality of the long mural entitled *Harvesters*[6] achieve an attenuation so remote that what we see could be a mirage induced by the heat over the wide area of treeless farmland. Telegraph poles and barns and mules and lean arms with pitchforks, and buckets of water are faintly discernible, but, in spite of the American scene, what is invoked is rather like a faded Egyptian fresco, even though this effect is only an accidental by-product of the artist's fantasy.

Gatch's recent paintings are increasingly landscapes of the mind from which figures have all but disappeared. The artist represents himself as looking in at a spectacle and, perhaps even more metaphorically. as looking back to an uncertain memory. Sometimes he is multiplied and can be identified with all the craning necks, prehistoric in their simplification, starkly silhouetted against the white heat at a fire. More frequently a sole spectator—just the back of his head and shoulders—appears at the center of a composition.

---

6. [1939, whereabouts unknown]

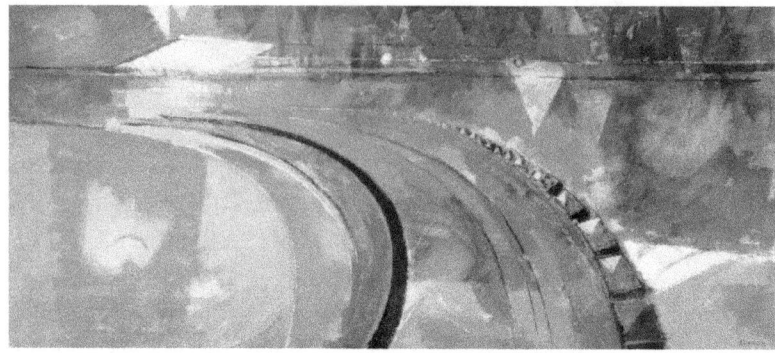

Lee Gatch
Industrial Night, 1948
Oil on canvas
The Phillips Collection, Washington, D.C. Acquired in 1949
© 2022 Estate of Lee Gatch

What we see beyond is the impression of the event—in one case a basketball game at a gymnasium, which becomes a primitive decoration celebrating the big ball for which the many outstretched fingers reach.

In the very latest of Gatch's paintings, there are no spectators—no figures at all. Yet the artist is still a passionately aware participant in the dramas of glamorous appearance. For now glamour has come back. Gatch is a romanticist; romance is the essence of whatever is signified in his new work. Overtones or afterthoughts are not permitted to interfere with our purely sensuous enjoyment of the colorful patterns. Any extraneous issues and opinions that intrude into his pictures are unintended commentary, becoming a spicy seasoning to enrich the visual flavor. It is enough for the painter to be exhilarated and to bask in revery or reminiscence. Driving with him over elliptical curves, along gleaming tracks, through an *Industrial Night*[7] of sapphire and gold, azure, and vermilion, we are asked to note by the way the crescent moon in the pale water, but more particularly to observe those curves in contrast to the vertical and pyramidal

---

7. [1948, The Phillips Collection, Washington, D.C., acquired in 1949]

lines of the oil wells on the dark shore and the diagonals of the draw-bridge to which all the curves lead. No thought about conditions of toil or natural resources or business, good or bad, can spoil our plea-sure in the painter's painterly vision. So it is with a dizzy *Carnival*[8] glimpsed from afar in fog. At a *Pleasure Garden*[9] there is a lighted screen ready for the film, a dance floor with a shaft of light awaiting the dancers, and little round tables on the edge of the limelight—but as yet neither performers nor diners. The artist makes no comment except to point out again the ovals, verticals, rectangles and diago-nals in a space sensation compounded of one dominant color and many variations on the theme; the light is the only important actor in the night's events.

The poet in Gatch is not without his moments of antipathy to this or that, his flashes of merriment and satirical wit. Yet he wants the observer to see with him pictorially and to be grave or gay with him according to his mood. He can be very serious, as in *Easter Morn-ing*[10] where crosses keep appearing in the path of the sun. And he can be unobtrusively funny, as with the halos and the horns he pro-vides for the big heads of his *Three Candidates for Election*[11] whose banners pass in political parade. The flaming, swaying movement of those oranges and reds bobbing up and down and coming ever nearer through the blue city night and its towering, faintly illumi-nated tan and violet walls symbolizes the confetti. the streamers and the bands—a fantastic extravaganza which is gloriously colorful.

> By the year 1940 [writes Gatch] I planned my canvases as single units of color—red, green or blue. My way towards abstraction was clear. With my translation of the subject through color the object became less of a solid, more one or another kind of color-movement through color-space, the idea existent only by suggestion. The moment for me to sacrifice the object occurs only when the subjective implications are strong and

---

8. [1952, Mildred Lane Kemper Art Museum, St. Louis]
9. [1945, whereabouts unknown]
10. [1943, whereabouts unknown]
11. [1948, The Phillips Collection, Washington, D.C., acquired in 1949]

valid. There is still much that I want to explore—imagine—recreate. For me art is the science of experience. My hopes for the future are to seek ever through reality for a finer mystical expression and a greater economy of means in reaching the essence of the idea.

Married to another fine artist, Elsie Driggs, and receiving at last the recognition he has long deserved, Lee Gatch seems to be rising rapidly to his peak as a painter. He now has the assurance and the talent to design with the clarity of a true mystic's inner eye.

THE PHILLIPS COLLECTION
AND RELATED THOUGHTS
(1954)

ON the dedication page of our Catalogue of the Phillips Collection[1] I stated what I believe to be a truth, that it is the Collection's diversity and its unity as a personal creation which gives to our Institution the special character that makes it something of a novelty among the public galleries of the world. Our emphasis is on the art of our own times with a few great masters of the earlier centuries as inspirational and source material. We are not unique. There are innumerable small collections of works by the same artists, of perhaps even greater consistency of distinction, which are occasionally exhibited for some charitable purpose. And there are innumerable public galleries of modern art, under courageous Directors and Trustees which are no less unlimited in their scope and generous in their patronage of living artists and in their recognition of progressive experiments in art. What is different in the Phillips Collection is that the diversity of styles, with a chosen standard for what I consider the best of each style, results not in eclecticism and not in partisan or news-conscious reporting but rather in an intimate unity of effect, an ambience or fusion, like that of a unifying light, corresponding to the private experience of many converging influences which go to the making of an artist's personal life, taste and creation. Artists and their pictures should feel at home in such an atmosphere. Many kinds of picture speak to and for many kinds of people through that single selection which appreciated them all, and reconciled their enjoyable differences through sym-

---

First published in a 1954 and originally presented as a radio talk entitled "The Pleasures of an Intimate Art Gallery," Washington, D.C., WCFM Radio, February 24, 1954.

1. [*The Phillips Collection: A Museum of Modern Art and Its Sources* (New York and London: Thames and Hudson, 1952).]

pathetic interpretation. Centuries and nationalities are mixed in our Gallery so that old and modern paintings can be brought together to be relevant and significant in some new context, some new contrast or analogy. So the visitor to our old house on a residential street, where the Collection is always on view, and frequently with a new look, discovers that he can enter the minds and experiences and expressive idiosyncrasies of others to the profitable enlargement of his taste and cultivation of his openmindedness. What I delight to collect, for the shared enjoyment of as many as possible, are the world's wonders of personality—not what can be put into a picture but what cannot be left out—that quintessence of self-captured in some expressive correspondence of aesthetic form —which gives us, in a gathering of pictures, the sense of meeting and getting to know the artists as people, of making new friends who had formerly been mere acquaintances. To that end we have Exhibition Units of a few favorite artists, their early and later work revealing their changes of direction, their evolving plan and purpose. Compared to the great museums with their historical sequences and their comprehensive review of different racial cultures and of contrasted periods of aesthetic eminence, seen in deep perspective, what we offer is the simple pleasure of becoming at close range so familiar with a Collection that is "ever in the Making" that we seem to be participating in the exciting thematic contacts of old and new, traditional and experimental.

Now, for more explicit comments, I will quote from my Introduction to our Catalogue. We were incorporated in 1918 as an educational institution. Incidentally, it seems that we were the earliest museum of modern art in the United States.

> Active in loan exhibitions, publications, an art school (now discontinued), many lectures and more concerts during the thirty-two years under my Directorship, we have maintained our character as a privately endowed and subsidized and as an intimately personal institution. The Collection has been the creation of two artists who love painting very much, my wife Marjorie Phillips and myself. It has been our wish to share

our treasures with all open-minded people. They are welcomed to feel at home with the pictures in an unpretentious
domestic setting which is at the same time physically restful and mentally stimulating. We enjoy many ways of seeing
and painting, none of which we claim to be the only right way.
Our catalogue reveals a catholicity of taste and a multiplic-
ity of interests. Yet we believe that there is a certain creative
unity in all the variety, such a unity as would be no less true of
other collections of comprehensive scope and personal taste
devoted to the delightful duty of supporting and interpreting
artists and relating them to each other in qualitative appreciations of their work. The Collection has grown and changed,
but all within the severely limited space of the same old 1897
Washington house where the idea for it was born. Such a setting is of course inappropriate to a "museum of modern art
and its sources" as our subtitle defines our character and it
would never have been acceptable for so many years if financial depressions and world wars had not been thwarting circumstances. Our inability to draw upon public funds is the
consequence of my will to maintain individuality of choice
and independence of policy. Ours is an unorthodox museum
with a way of its own in not segregating periods and nationalities, the better to show the universality of art and the continu-
ities of such ancient seeing habits as realism, expressionism,
and abstraction. It was necessary to decide whether to build
slowly and not buy or to buy freely and postpone building.
The second alternative was inevitable because of our wish to
exhibit and interpret a large and purposeful collection to the
public during our own lives. The decision has been made easier because our friends from all over the world have seemed
to like our many rearrangements and loan exhibitions in the
same old fondly familiar place.

Our subtitle, "A Museum of Modern Art and Its Sources,"
has never been accurately descriptive. We are not exclusively
modern. In fact, the first impression on entering is apt to be
decidedly un-modern. It may well be argued that according
to the usual meaning of the word we are not a museum at
all. Our sources are not the often remote or ancient origins
of current creations in the arts. They have not been within
our scope since they would require space for large sculpture

and for showcases. Nevertheless, the contemporary works in
our Collection far outnumber the works earlier than 1900.
Consequently we are a museum of contemporary art and so
also of modern art. Our sources of twentieth century painting
are great painters from the fifteenth century up to the portals
opening on today and tomorrow.

Our sources are also our modernists, in other words, our heroes
of evolutionary progress in art.

They include Giorgione—the inventor of romantic landscape as
an end in itself, of the easel picture intended for the home.

El Greco, the first impassioned expressionist—the first conscious
mannerist of the all-over pattern.

Chardin, who was, in a sense that painters understand, the first
modern painter—the first to accept and explore the complexity of
visual appearance and to make exquisite texture serve classic design.
Goya, who anticipated and inspired many of the most direct and
painterly portraits and commentaries of the nineteenth century.

Constable, the discoverer of naturalistic landscape and the freshness and nobility of nature.

Delacroix, of the concentric, impetuous rhythms and Ingres, the
virtuoso of line.

Daumier, whose sculptural simplifications of what he saw all
around him had universal truth and meaning.

Corot, who combined classic structure and grace with honest personal vision.

Courbet of the romantic realism.

Manet of the pictorial fact in flat full light.

Degas of the dedicated, incomparably skilled drawing and the
important innovations of design.

Renoir the great lover of life, for whom the visible world existed,
filled to the brim and overflowing with raptures for the painters; Renoir, who added the evanescence of Impressionism to the
Baroque rhythms of Rubens.

And Cézanne who used Impressionism to give nature's own colorful rhythms to the formal structure of Poussin. By discovering for-

mal elements of design in nature he has been claimed by abstract painters as their ancestor. He might have repudiated their claim.

Equally an influence is Van Gogh who, inventing new means, from a driving inner necessity, became the most inspired of the great expressionists.

And then our Americans: Ryder the visionary-and the poet painter of night skies and lonely voyagers; Homer at home with the ocean and the north woods, and Eakins the student of anatomy and human character.

Through these sources and many others—especially Seurat and Gauguin, who were the most direct influences—we come to our contemporaries.

In our century, we are especially proud of our examples of Bonnard, the enchanter, the ever young at heart; Matisse, the master of exotic arabesque; Rouault from the age of the Cathedrals; Braque, the twentieth-century Chardin.

Klee, the poet, sage and wit.

Marin, the calligrapher of the elements.

Dove and his completely original private symbols.

Kokoschka and his painterly exhilarations.

Knaths and his colorful yet severe sensitivities.

Of course we are not wholly without the restless prodigious Picasso and the severely mental Mondrian.

> I do not venture to anticipate posterity and the ultimate valuations of history. It is impossible to judge contemporary works of art without historical detachment. The Collector can only be true to himself. My choices have been frankly personal and pervaded by only two predominating interests—the proved recurrence of the mightier trends in art and the assembling of related and contrasted personalities of past and present. [...]
>
> In our unpretentious, disarmingly domestic and frankly undistinguished setting there are many obvious disadvantages and even dangers. But at least there is a sense of art lived with, worked with and loved. The audiences at our free concerts and lectures, and the throngs who attend our occasional loan exhibitions with their instructive labels and cat-

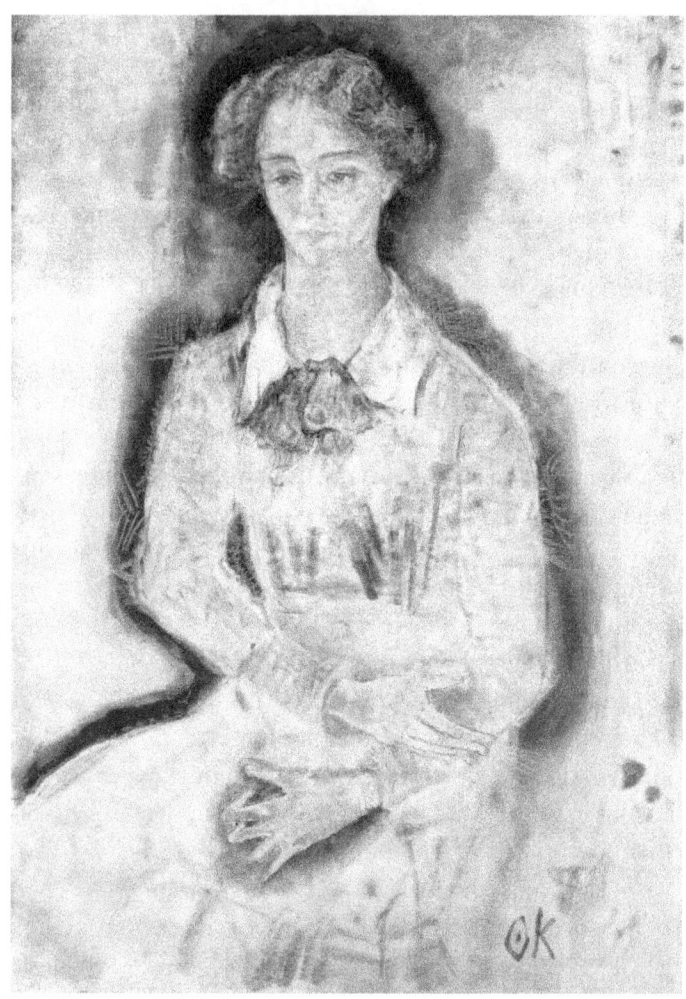

Oskar Kokoschka
Portrait of Lotte Franzos, 1909
Oil on canvas
The Phillips Collection, Washington, D.C. Acquired in 1941;
© 2022 Foundation Oskar Kokoschka/Artists Rights Society (ARS), New York/
ProLitteris, Zurich

alogues, are in marked contrast to the generally prevailing quiet of our galleries where there is an invitation to relax, to smoke, to think, and to enjoy. I believe I have used the word enjoy more than once in this preface and that is as it has to be, if I am to introduce this Collection made with enjoyment for the enjoyment of others. As we move into a future menaced by evil forces of tyranny and total war we must cling to our faith in art as the symbol of the creative life and as the stronghold of the free and aspiring individual.[2]

I will close with a selection from an editorial I wrote for the February 1953 issue of the *Magazine of Art* since it contains my philosophy as a nonpartisan collector and critic, and as an advocate of one trained mind and eye with undivided responsibility for the selection or the judgment of cross section exhibitions.

Aside from the issues, enmeshed in a mixed exhibition, my interest is primarily to detach and to salute the artistic personalities within the various stylistic trends. Comprehensive surveys, if chosen by one discriminating eye and mind, should be useful to reveal the fact that truly personal and nonconformist painters do keep seeing differently.

A critic can hardly be considered qualified to act as guide to the galleries unless, without any need to conceal his personal preferences, he can be tolerant and fair to other points of view than his own. If he can care more for personalities than for theories, he will approve if not actually relish the diversities which affirm our freedom from collectivism and our invigorating open-mindedness.

There cannot be one standard for all art. That is inconceivable, except under a dictatorship or the heavy hand of some dictatorial academy. In our free democracy there must be a separate standard for the best examples of each kind of painting or sculpture. That is an "acknowledged point of view," and its relativity is as natural to me as a collector and gallery director as the expression of a partisan standpoint is to the editor seeking to enliven his pages.

My dedicated detachment from partisanship does not imply neutrality. Eclecticism I deplore, because of its weak

---

2. [Ibid., vii–x.]

dilutions and its stale compounds. I am attracted to qualities of contemporary art precisely because they thrill me with
refreshing differences from any qualities I have cherished
before, and I admire the aesthetic interpretations of the age
we live in—even the symbols for the anarchy, the turmoil and
the inner tensions. Yet I am always trying to think beyond our
period consciousness to the older symbols in art of less dated
visual experience, wondering whether our geometric charts,
our automatic writing in ribbons and coils of color and our
nebulous apparitions are not too much of our own time to be
for all time.

The apparent taboo on lyrical realism, accepting it only if it
is "super" or "magical," is, I feel, an admission of jaded sensibilities, no longer capable of quiet response to subtle qualities
which never grow old, since they forever renew themselves in
the love of the artists for the visible world—for their medium
and for sheer creation. As artists saw and felt about nature
in the past, so they are still entitled to see and to feel. Nature
does not go out of date in our sensibilities! And we who love
the very texture of a well-painted surface cannot and will not
settle for color photography—nor confine our pleasure in
painting to what is for the moment fashionable.

The *continuity of tradition* is my most compelling interest in
forming and interpreting a collection of modern art and its
sources. The modern artist must be able to submit his work
to the test of being seen in the company of the nineteenth-
century Titans. The isolation of the "avant-garde" painter,
in the obscurity of his own choice, supported by the fellow
alchemists and the very small elite of enthusiasts for whose
admiration he paints, is only good for him if, with the proud
humility of a Cézanne, he regards his innovations and inventions as important evolutionary "work in progress", and his
therapy of escape from nature and the museums as not an
end in itself. I admire the argument of Morse Peckham's article in the November 1952 issue[3] wherein he develops inge-
niously the thesis that "no matter how much modern artists
feel that their break with the nineteenth century is complete,

---

3. [Morse Peckham, "The Triumoh of Romanticism," *Magazine of Art* 45, no. 7
(November 1952): 291–99.]

they represent not the denial of its romanticism but its tri-umph." I agree that if this aspect of our abstract expression is recognized by the artist and the public alike, there will be less estranging distance between them. While Arthur Dove was almost completely unknown, and painting, apart from the world, his delightful private symbolism, I who was helping to uphold him with yearly purchases, recognized in him not only the probable ancestor of a successful school of avant-garde painters but the heir of our romantic Ryder.

Herbert Read observed that "the artists of today, without great patrons to command them, must mold the taste of an approving public through the Critics." Now that the image has been all but obliterated by the symbol, the critic is apt to forget that there is a dualism in art which is still as true as it ever was-the image and the symbol—the outer and the inner world. Reconciliation of opposites is our unfinished busi-ness in the modern world, and unification through synthesis is the world's still-distant goal. All art is symbol, and yet all symbolism requires some imagery. The many-minded world needs to be expressed by artists of many minds, including those who remember nature. I prefer tolerant to partisan criticism, and I persist in relating to one or another of the ever-recurring and rival traditions of the past the evolu-tionary changes of our day. Even in this age of an enlarged electorate in art and a precarious market, I believe that progressive art will prosper. The insatiable curiosities of all men—which has ever been the strength of science—is spread-ing now to an understanding of the artists and their ever-widening horizons.[4]

---

4. [Duncan Phillips, "The Critic: Partisan or Referee?," *Magazine of Art* 46 (February 1953): 50, 88.; freely quoted.]

JOHN MARIN

(1955)

JOHN MARIN has passed into history. He now takes his place in the story of American painting with Whistler and Homer and Ryder. To each of them he had some affinity: to Whistler in his ability to vignette the pictorial essence of a moment of vision; to Homer in his passion for and knowledge of the sea off the coast of Maine and in his special mastery of watercolor as a medium; and to Ryder in his self-reliant invention and his integrity. Marin's telegraphic speed and fresh, exuberant expression may seem at art's opposite pole from Ryder's long-cherished dream and labored alchemy. Yet for me their basic kinship is very real. They were Yankees both and ancient mariners both, the lonely voyager over the perils of enameled pigments and untraveled, profoundly imaginative designs, and the bold adventurer of the moment's intuition who knew all the ways of the sea, who dared to be the intimate, the on-the-spot reporter of the flashing lights, the thrashing waves, the thrusts and tensions for which he knew the axis and the resolving balance. Marin had no equal as a wizard of equilibrium within a space construction of precariously active lines. His dynamism and his spontaneity are, we like to think, American qualities, yet surely no more so than the persistent inner vision of Ryder whose imagery was less of the adventuring eye and hand than of the withdrawn, contemplative mind. Ryder and Marin were nature poets whose complete absorption in their own intimate sources of inspiration resulted in works of art so different that their only underlying resemblances to each other were their single-minded independence and their regional American expression transcended by intimations of the universal.

_____

First published in *John Marin Memorial Exhibition* (Los Angeles: University of California Art Galleries, 1955. Exhibition catalog).

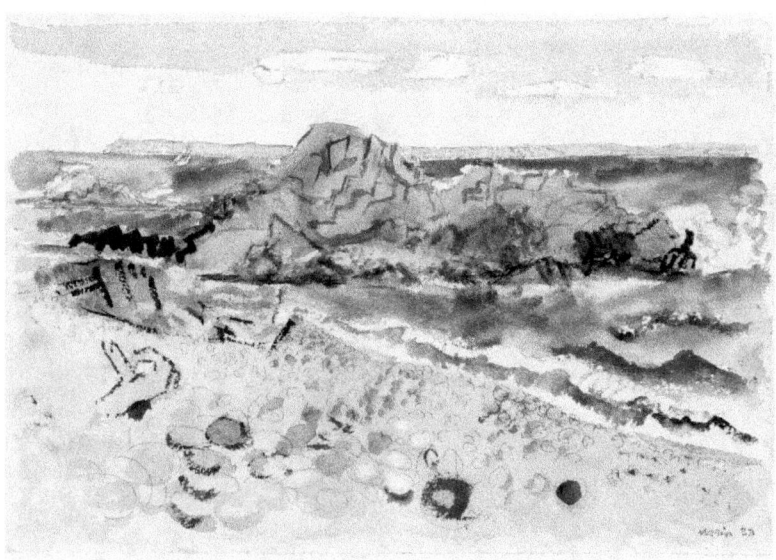

John Marin
Quoddy Head, Maine Coast, 1933
Watercolor, black chalk, and graphite pencil on paper
The Phillips Collection, Washington, D.C. Acquired in 1937
© 2022 Estate of John Marin/Artists Rights Society (ARS), New York

We are witnessing a period of art of private symbols and of sub-conscious calligraphy. It is really a survival of romanticism, whether the romance has to do with the exploration of space at the expense of the picture plane or the discovery of drama in design itself. This new manifestation of art for art's sake is called abstract expressionism and becomes fanatical when it is merely automatic writing by a more or less uncontrolled hand. It may be claimed that John Marin, especially in his latest canvases, when he opened up his compositions form their former enclosures, extending the rhythms and crosscurrents around and beyond the frames, anticipated such improvisations. just as the cubists could claim him because of his superimposed planes and the geometrical shapes which he used arbitrarily. Yet whatever he did was independent of all isms and his impetuosity

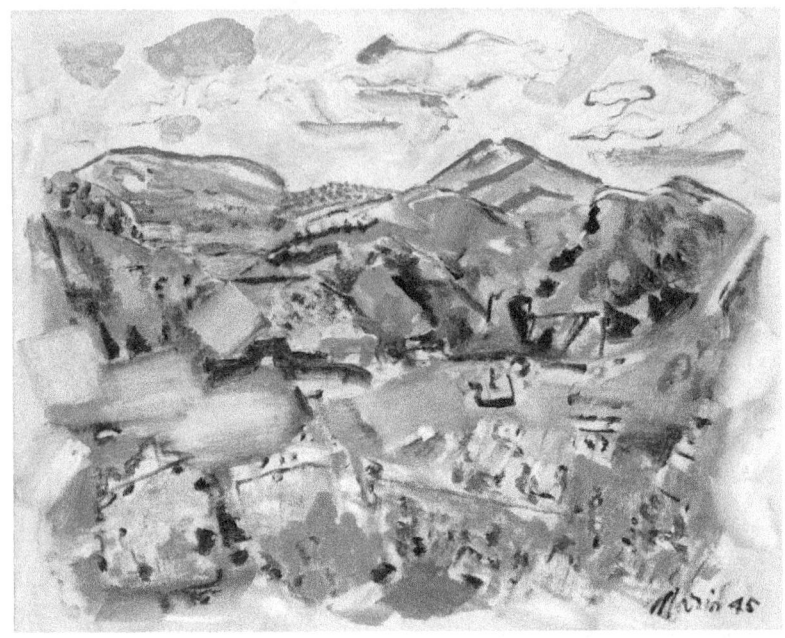

John Marin
Tunk Mountains, Autumn, Maine, 1945
Oil on canvas
The Phillips Collection, Washington, D.C. Acquired in 1946
© 2022 Estate of John Marin/Artists Rights Society (ARS), New York

was that of a poet-painter who used abbreviations and formal idioms either as means to convey his visual sensations or of extending
the painter's expressive freedoms. His genius for explosions of line
and color, especially in the Manhattan street scenes, was dedicated
to the theme of energy. Marin regarded himself as a lyrical realist,
which of course he was, although an expressionist rather than an
impressionist by temperament. His triangle for a pine or his zigzag
for a wave was crisply, almost colloquially descriptive, and the rectangles and the handsome hieroglyphics with which he ployed were
frankly decorative and never abstract or automatic. Mere illusion
was seldom, if ever, his aim even in the representative landscapes of

Maine, New Hampshire, and New Mexico. He wished to paint "after nature's example" and with an intensified economy of means appropriate to the tempo of his period. It is true that he aspired to the abstract condition of music, that he wished to make his art as structural and sequential as Bach. "That is the kind of music my piano likes to have played on," he remarked to MacKinley Helm when his visitor, who later became his biographer,[1] found him practicing his favorite composer in the glassed-in veranda of his cottage by the sea. "Did you note how the little tunes struck at each other? Balance and Force." Just as his piano liked that kind of music, so his paper had its own enjoyments. "You just put down a color that the paper will like." This reveals that Marin was not only an expressionist but a virtuoso in love with watercolor, his favorite instrument. Later, in such oils as the musically organized *Tunk Mountain in Autumn,*[2] he was equally solicitous for the special needs of the canvas and the colors. For a half-century of research and urgency he experimented on the frontiers of visual consciousness, and his ardors amounted to a joyous dynamic pantheism. Far from escaping from our tragic world into abstraction, he seemed to challenge fate with an ever brave and debonair philosophy of design.

---

1. [MacKinley Helm, *John Marin* (Boston: Pellegrini & Cudahy, 1948).]
2. [*Tunk Mountains, Autumn, Maine,* 1945, The Phillips Collection, Washington, D.C., acquired in 1946]

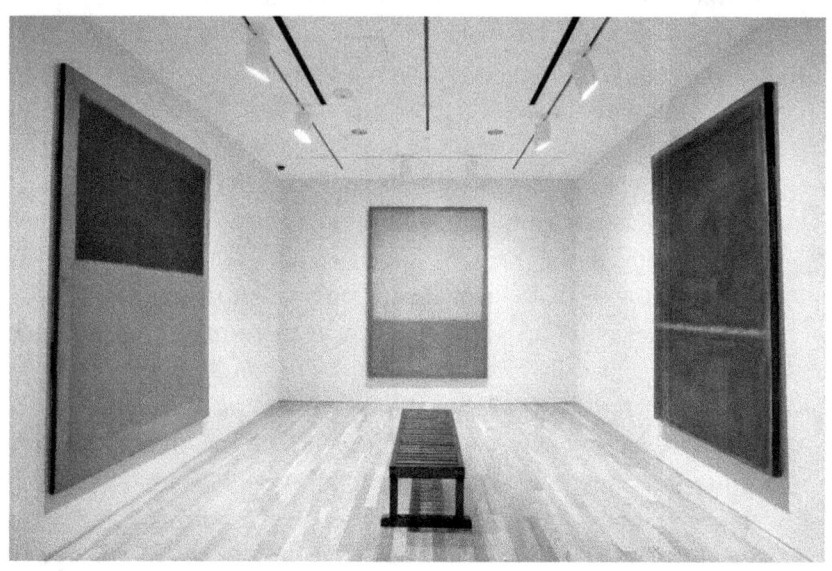

The Rothko Room, est. 1960
The Phillips Collection, Washington, D.C.,
From left to right: *Green and Tangerine on Red*, 1956, acquired in 1960;
Ochre and Red on Red, 1954, acquired in 1964; *Green and Maroon*, 1953,
acquired in 1957. Photo by Carl Bower, 2006
© 1998 Kate Rothko Prizel & Christopher Rothko/Artists Rights Society
(ARS), New York

MARK ROTHKO

(1964)

IN the soft-edged and rounded rectangles of Mark Rothko's mature style there is an enveloping magic which conveys to receptive observers a sense of being in the midst of greatness. It is the color of course. These canvases which have been called empty by the resistant skeptics and which certainly depict nothing at all are nevertheless a vibrant life-enhancing experience to those who make themselves ready for them. They cast a spell, lyric or tragic, which fills our existence while the moments linger. They not only pervade our consciousness but inspire contemplation. Our minds are challenged by the relativities; the relative measures of the two horizontal *presences,* one larger than the other, each acting on the other, and incomplete without the other, each mysteriously compounded of scumbled overtones yet all matte, saturated, rich layers soaked into richer depths. Rothko denies a desire to enchant. He only invites reflection. The weather his colors create can be ominous. Frequently, it is just vaguely troubled. There is never a conflict, not even a dissonance, rather a duality, some evanescent difference, some sudden awareness of the complexity of existence. Color atmosphere in painting is as old as Giovanni Bellini and his mountain backgrounds before sunrise or after sunset. We think also of late Turner and of late Bonnard. But in Rothko there is no pictorial reference at all to remembered experience. What we recall are not memories but old emotions disturbed or resolved—some sense of well-being suddenly shadowed by a cloud, yellow ochres strangely suffused with a drift of gray, prevailing over an ambience of rose, or the fire diminishing into a glow of embers, or the light outside when the night descends.

Unpublished manuscript.

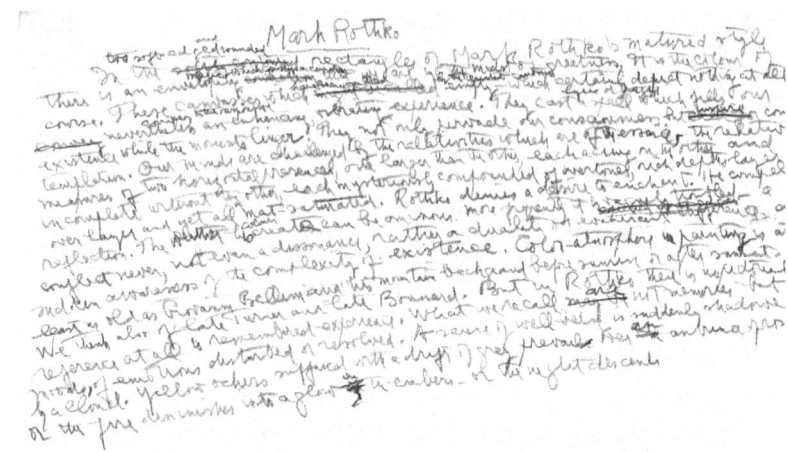

Handwritten manuscript, 1964
The Phillips Collection Archives, Washington, D.C.

INDEX OF ARTISTS

ILLUSTRATED ARTWORKS